DATE DUE

12-15-10			

Demco

The least you need to know about DOS

SECOND EDITION

Doug Lowe

Mike Murach & Associates
4697 West Jacquelyn Avenue, Fresno, California
(209) 275-3335

Production Team   Technical writer: Anne Prince
Editor: Judy Taylor

Graphics designer: Steve Ehlers

Other books for DOS users   *The Only DOS Book You'll Ever Need (Second Edition)* by Doug Lowe

The Least You Need to Know About Lotus 1-2-3 for DOS by Patrick Bultema

The Least You Need to Know About WordPerfect for DOS by Joel Murach

DOS, WordPerfect, and Lotus Essentials by Patrick Bultema and Joel Murach

©1993, Mike Murach & Associates, Inc.
All rights reserved.
Printed in the United States of America.

Cover art © 1993 Kate Solari Baker

10 9 8 7 6 5 4 3 2 1

ISBN: 0-911625-76-3

Library of Congress Cataloging-in-Publication Data

Lowe, Doug
  The least you need to know about DOS / Doug Lowe. --2nd ed.
    p. cm.
  Rev. ed. of: The least you need to know about DOS / Patrick
Bultema. c1991.
  ISBN 0-911625-76-3 : $20.00
  1. Operating systems (Computers) 2. PC-DOS (Computer file) 3. MS
-DOS (Computer file) I. Bultema, Patrick, 1959-   Least you need
to know about DOS. II. Title.
QA76.76.O63B854 1993
005.4'469--dc20   93-17025
                                                                  CIP

Contents

Preface		vii
Section 1	**An introduction to personal computers**	**1**
Chapter 1	Hardware concepts and terms for every PC user	3
Chapter 2	Software concepts and terms for every DOS user	17
Section 2	**A short course in DOS for every PC user**	**33**
Chapter 3	How to identify DOS drives, directories, files, and paths	35
Chapter 4	How to use DOS commands to start your application programs	45
Chapter 5	How to use eight more DOS commands	71
Chapter 6	How to set up the AUTOEXEC.BAT file so DOS gets started right	83
Section 3	**Other essential DOS skills**	**97**
Chapter 7	How to use batch files to start your programs	99
Chapter 8	How to manage the directories and files on a hard disk	107
Chapter 9	How to work with diskettes	139
Chapter 10	How to back up a hard disk using the Backup command	153
Chapter 11	How to back up a hard disk using Microsoft Backup (DOS 6.0)	171
Section 4	**How to use the DOS 5.0 or 6.0 shell**	**205**
Chapter 12	An introduction to the DOS shell	207
Chapter 13	How to use the DOS shell to create and use menus	225
Chapter 14	How to use the DOS shell to manage directories and files	237
Chapter 15	How to use the DOS shell to switch between programs quickly	259
Section 5	**Some additional perspective**	**267**
Chapter 16	Other DOS features that you ought to be aware of	269
Appendix	A quick summary of the commands presented in this book	285
Index		289

Preface

If you use a PC, you need to know something about DOS. Why? Because some PC functions *must* be done in DOS. Some functions can be done more efficiently in DOS than they can from an application program. And most PC problems have to be solved in DOS.

But that doesn't mean you have to be a DOS expert to use a PC. You just need a minimum set of DOS skills. For example, you need to know how to refer to DOS directories and files from your application programs; how to start your application programs from DOS or a shell, no matter who was using the PC last; how to manage your directories and files, so you can always find the file you're looking for; how to transfer data from one PC to another using diskettes; and how to back up the hard disk data on your PC. We call this book *The Least You Need to Know about DOS* because it will teach you that minimum set of skills as quickly and easily as possible.

When you finish this book, you'll be a competent, self-sufficient PC user. You'll know how to perform the essential DOS functions as efficiently as possible. You'll know when to use DOS and when to use your application programs for everyday PC functions. Most important, you'll understand how your system works so you'll be able to solve most of your problems by yourself. As a result, you'll rarely have to get help from the PC support group, the help desk, an 800 number, a colleague, a friend, or your spouse.

Who this book is for

Originally, we envisioned this book as a guide for readers who had little or no experience with PCs. But as we developed the first edition, I was continually getting calls for help from friends who were experienced PC users. To my surprise, most of their questions were answered in the first ten chapters of this book. In fact, if they'd all had copies of this book, I could have directed them to the chapters and illustrations that answered their questions.

That's when I realized that many experienced PC users don't have the skills presented in this book. That's why they need to ask for help so often. And that's one reason why they make only minor improvements in productivity when they switch from manual methods to PCs.

VIII Preface

With that in mind, I recommend this book for anyone who isn't comfortable with DOS. That includes people with little or no PC experience. But it also includes the tens of thousands of PC users who don't get the most from their PCs because they don't know as much about DOS as they ought to know.

In terms of hardware and software, this book is for anyone who uses DOS on a PC with a hard disk. When I refer to *DOS*, I mean any version from DOS 2.0 through DOS 6.0. When I refer to *PCs*, I mean any IBM PC, XT, AT, or PS/2, including IBM compatibles and clones. And when I say this book is for hard disk users, I mean that it focuses on hard disk PCs from page 1, so you won't have to switch your thinking from a diskette system halfway through.

What this book teaches

If you look at the table of contents, you'll see that this book is divided into five sections. The first three sections contain the ten chapters that teach the essential concepts, terms, and DOS skills all PC users must know. That's just 169 pages of information that you can read and master in a few hours. The last chapter in section 3, chapter 11, is also essential for DOS 6.0 users. It covers Microsoft Backup, the new DOS 6.0 backup utility that lets you back up your system far more easily than you can with the DOS Backup command.

In section 4, you can learn how to use the *shell program* that comes with DOS 5.0 and 6.0. If you have DOS 5.0 or 6.0 on your PC, you should definitely read the four chapters in this section because this shell can help you work more quickly and easily. If you have an earlier version of DOS, you can skip this section unless you want to learn more about shell programs and DOS 6.0.

In section 5, you can get some additional perspective on DOS. The one chapter in this section introduces you to advanced DOS commands and features and the DOS 6.0 utilities that are beyond the scope of this book. If you're interested in learning more about DOS, you should definitely read this chapter. Then, you can decide which features would help you most, and you can expand your DOS skills by learning to use those features.

How to use the illustrations

To help you learn more easily, this book is packed with illustrations. It has dozens of examples of DOS commands along with the DOS output from the commands. It also has dozens of screen images that show you how to use Microsoft Backup and the DOS shell. Illustrations like these make it easy for you to envision how a command or function works, so you can use this book for training even if you're not at your PC.

But the illustrations are more than just learning aids. They're also the best reference materials currently available. If, for example, you want to rename a directory, figure 8-19 shows you how to do it. If you want to copy files from a hard disk to a diskette, figure 9-6 shows you how to do it. And if you want to back up the files on your hard disk, figure 10-4 shows you how to do it. Normally, when you use one of the illustrations in this book for reference, you don't even have to read the related text because the illustration tells you everything you need to know to perform the function.

In the appendix, you'll find a quick summary of the commands presented in this book. But no reference summary at the back of any book is as thorough or as effective as the illustrations that are used throughout this book. That's why the summary in the appendix refers you to the figures used in the chapters.

What if you want to know more about DOS

This book assumes that your PC has been set up for you and that help is available to you for the technical functions that are rarely needed. As a result, this book doesn't teach you how to install DOS on your system. Or how to partition and format a hard disk. Or how to prevent and detect hard disk problems. Or how to improve the performance of your PC. For most PC users, those aren't essential skills.

But if your PC hasn't been set up for you or if you just want to know more about DOS, we offer an expanded version of this book called *The Only DOS Book You'll Ever Need*. We believe that it is the ideal book for people who provide support to less technical PC users. As a result, we recommend it for every corporate help desk, for every PC support person, and for the lead technical person in every user department. If you're interested in it, you can find complete information at the back of this book.

A note about this second edition

There are several ways in which this second edition of the *Least/DOS* differs from the first edition. First, it's been updated to include DOS 6.0. So whenever a command works differently in DOS 6.0 than it did in earlier versions of DOS, you'll find a notation of that. You'll also find coverage of new 6.0 commands that allow you to do essential functions more easily than you could before. And we've added the chapter on Microsoft Backup, the DOS 6.0 backup utility that's far more flexible than the DOS Backup command.

Second, in response to feedback from the first edition, we've divided two of the chapters into smaller chapters. In the first edition, chapters 4 and 5, which cover 12 basic DOS commands, were a single chapter. And chapters 6 and 7, on the AUTOEXEC.BAT file and batch files, were a single chapter. Many readers found it difficult to absorb so much information at once, though, especially when they were just beginning to learn about DOS. So by breaking these chapters down, we feel this book will be even easier to use for training than it was before.

Third, we've also improved the educational approach by adding learning objectives to every chapter and by expanding on the self-guided exercises at the end of each chapter in sections 2 and 3. The exercises, especially, are helpful because they give you step-by-step practice in using the commands and features presented in each chapter. By trying them out at your own PC, you'll better understand how the commands and features work. And you'll gain confidence in your own DOS knowledge and skills.

Conclusion

In the last ten years, more than 200 books have been written about DOS. But they haven't worked. If they had, the average PC user wouldn't still be struggling with DOS. Even today, the introductory DOS books are so superficial that they don't teach you what you need to know. And the "fat" DOS books are so impractical that they teach you more than you *want* to know, but less than you *need* to know.

That, of course, is why we developed this book. We developed it because we've watched too many smart people get frustrated by DOS and by books on DOS. We developed it because DOS just isn't that difficult. Above all, we developed it because we believe you can learn the essential DOS skills in just a few hours so you can use your PC without frustration forever after.

If you have any comments, questions, or criticisms, I would enjoy hearing from you. That's why there's a postage-paid comment form at the back of the book. I thank you for reading this book. And I sure hope it helps you work smarter, faster, and more independently. If it does, please drop me a note.

Mike Murach, Publisher
Fresno, California
April 1993

Section 1

An introduction to personal computers

Before you can use DOS effectively, you need to understand the concepts and terms that apply to the PC you're using. So the two chapters in this section provide you with the background you need. In chapter 1, you'll learn the hardware concepts and terms that every PC user should know. In chapter 2, you'll learn the software concepts and terms that every DOS user should know.

If you're already familiar with PC hardware, you can probably skip chapter 1. But you ought to at least skim the chapter to make sure you know the concepts and terms it presents. On the other hand, you should probably read chapter 2 even if you are familiar with PC software. This chapter presents some concepts that will make it easier for you to learn how to use DOS. It also presents some terms that will direct you to other chapters in this book.

Chapter 1

Hardware concepts and terms for every PC user

Do you know what kind of processor your PC has? Do you know the difference between internal memory and disk storage? Do you know the difference between double-density and high-density diskettes? Do you know why you usually lose your work when a power failure takes place while you're using an application program? Are you familiar with the terms listed in the first group at the end of this chapter?

If you've answered "yes" to all those questions, you can probably skip this chapter and go on to chapter 2. But if you've answered "no" to any of them, you should read this chapter. To use a PC effectively, you need to have a basic understanding of the equipment, or *hardware*, you're using. That's why this chapter presents the hardware concepts and terms that every PC user should know.

An introduction to PCs

In 1981, IBM introduced a microcomputer called the IBM *Personal Computer*, or *PC*. Today, the term *PC* can be used to refer to the original IBM PC, the IBM PC/XT (or just *XT*), the IBM PC/AT (or just *AT*), and the IBM *PS/2*. The term can also be used to refer to PCs that aren't made by IBM, like those made by Compaq, Tandy, and Dell. The PCs that aren't made by IBM are often called *clones* or *compatibles* because they work just like IBM PCs.

As I explained in the preface, this book is for people who use PCs. But it doesn't matter whether you have an XT, an AT, a PS/2, or an IBM compatible. Although one PC may be faster than another, DOS works the same on all of them.

The physical components of a PC

Figure 1-1 shows a typical PC. As you can see, it consists of five physical components: a printer, a monitor, a keyboard, a mouse, and a systems unit. In a laptop PC, the monitor, keyboard, and systems unit are combined into a single carrying case. But on most other systems, these units are separate and can be purchased separately. Because you're probably familiar with these five components already, I'll just describe them briefly.

4   Chapter 1

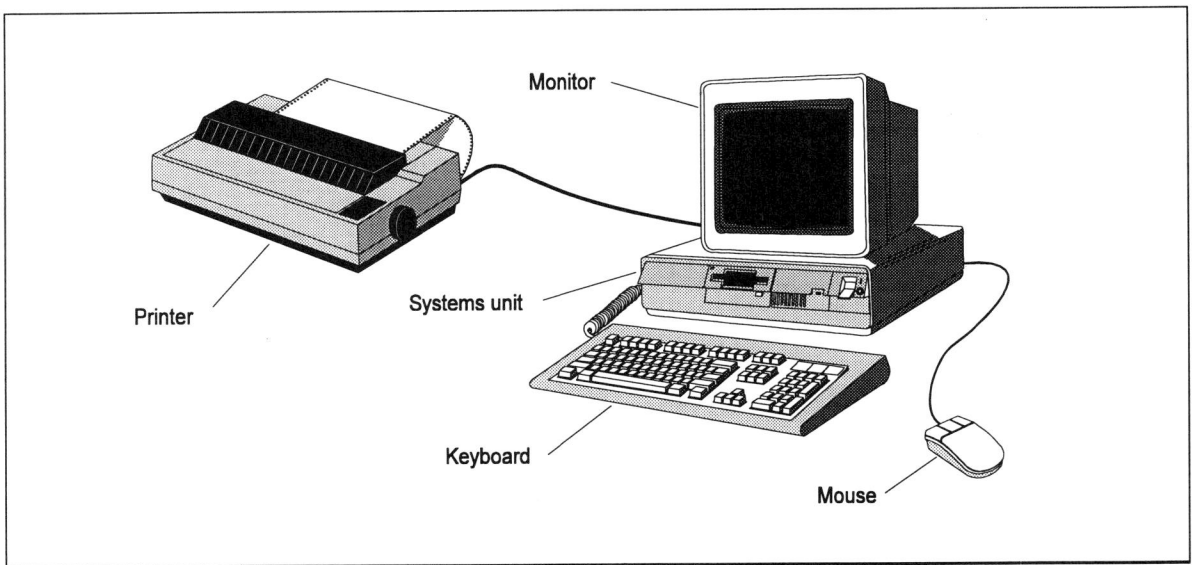

Figure 1-1   The physical components of a PC

The systems unit   The *systems unit* is the unit that the other physical components are connected to. This unit can also be referred to as the *electronics unit* or the *systems chassis*. As you will soon learn, this unit contains the processor that controls the operations of the PC. In contrast, the four other physical components are input and output devices.

The monitor   The *monitor* is an output device that can also be referred to as a *display*, a *screen*, or a *CRT* (which stands for *Cathode Ray Tube*). *Monochrome monitors* can display only one color, which is usually green or amber on a dark background, but *color monitors* can display a variety of colors. Today, most PCs are sold with a color monitor.

Like a television set, a monitor uses dot patterns to display characters and images. The more dots a monitor can display, the higher its *resolution* and the sharper its image. Not surprisingly, high-resolution monitors cost more than low-resolution monitors, just as color monitors cost more than monochrome monitors.

When a monitor is in operation, its images are controlled by an electronic *display adapter* within the systems unit. Today, monitors for PCs are available in six standard forms that are related to their display adapters as summarized in figure 1-2. The *Monochrome Display Adapter*, or *MDA*, is for the basic monochrome monitor. Because the original IBM version of the MDA could display only text, an MDA monitor couldn't display graphic images like a *Lotus 1-2-3* graph. However, a monochrome graphics display adapter called *Hercules* soon became so popular that

Adapter	Standard resolution
Monochrome Display Adapter (MDA)	720x348
Color Graphics Adapter (CGA)	640x200
Enhanced Graphics Adapter (EGA)	640x350
Video Graphics Array (VGA)	640x480
Super VGA (SVGA)	800x600
High-Resolution VGA (HRVGA)	1024x768

Figure 1-2   A summary of monitor characteristics

almost all monochrome monitors and display adapters now support it. The other five display adapters in figure 1-2 are for progressively better color graphics monitors: *CGA* stands for *Color Graphics Adapter*; *EGA* for *Enhanced Graphics Adapter*; *VGA* for *Video Graphics Array; SVGA* for *Super VGA*; and *HRVGA* for *High-Resolution VGA*. Most PCs sold today come with SVGA or better monitors and adapters.

The keyboard   The *keyboard* is the main input device of a PC. Although it resembles the keyboard of a typewriter, a PC keyboard has more keys, as you can see in figure 1-3. This figure shows the two most common types of PC keyboards: the 84-key and the 101-key keyboards. Although the 84-key keyboard was the original keyboard for the AT, the 101-key keyboard is now a standard component of all PS/2s and most other PCs.

If you study the keyboards in figure 1-3, you can see that they have several types of keys. First, the keyboards include a full set of typewriter keys. Second, they have a numeric pad on the right side of the keyboard in the same arrangement as the ten keys on a calculator. They also have either ten or twelve function keys, depending on the type of keyboard, numbered F1, F2, F3, and so on. And they have some special control keys such as the Escape key (Esc), the Control key (Ctrl), the Alternate key (Alt), the Page-up and Page-down keys, and so on.

The Arrow keys move the *cursor* on the screen of a monitor. The cursor is the underline or highlight that identifies a specific character or area of a screen. As a result, the Arrow keys are often called *cursor control keys*.

If you have an 84-key keyboard on your PC, you have to know how the Num-lock key works on it. Within the ten-key numeric pad of that keyboard, every

6 Chapter 1

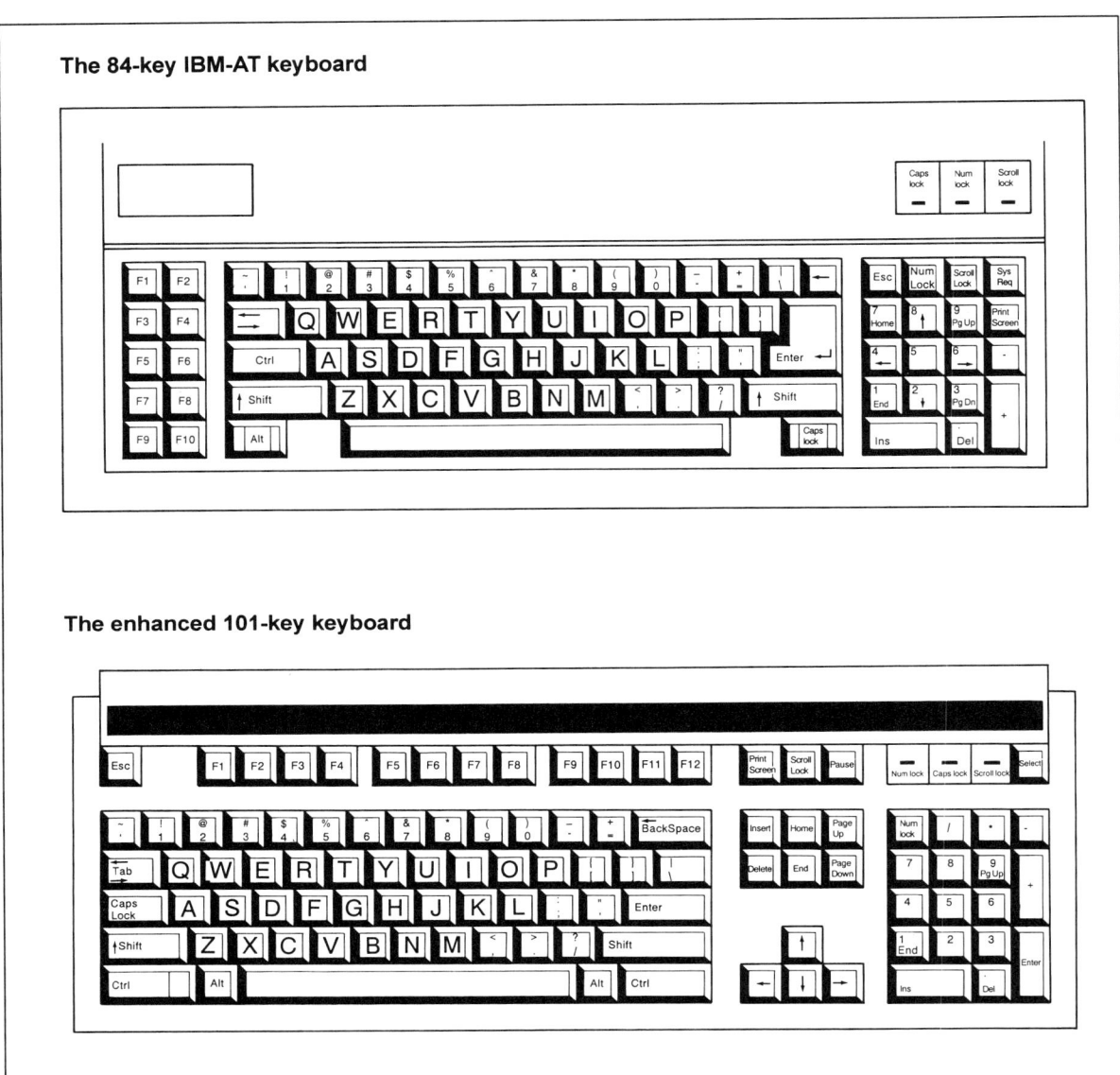

Figure 1-3 The two most common types of PC keyboards

key but the 5-key has a control function. For instance, the 7-key is also the Home key; the 8-key is also the Up arrow key; and the 9-key is also the Page-up (Pg-up) key. If the Num-lock light is on, each of the keys represents its decimal value or the decimal point. If the Num-lock light is off, each of the keys represents its control function. To turn the Num-lock light on or off, you press the Num-lock key.

Because this doubling up of keyboard meanings can cause some entry errors, most people prefer the 101-key keyboard shown in figure 1-3. Here, the control functions of the ten-key pad are duplicated on control keys that are located between the typewriter keys and the numeric pad. Then, if you keep the Num-lock light lit, you can use the control pad for control functions and the numeric pad for numeric entries.

The mouse   A *mouse* is a small hand-held input device that has two or three buttons on it. If you've ever used a mouse or seen one used, you know that it's just a pointing device. When you move the mouse across a table top (or across a *mouse pad* on the table top), a pointer on the monitor moves in the same direction. This pointer on the monitor is called the *mouse cursor*.

With a little practice, you can easily and quickly move the mouse cursor anywhere on the screen. Then, you can *click* or *double-click* the buttons on top of the mouse to perform various actions. If you *click-and-drag* a mouse, you can highlight portions of the screen.

Exactly how you use a mouse, or whether you can use a mouse at all, depends on the programs you're using. For instance, the early releases of DOS didn't provide for the use of a mouse. More recent releases do let you use a mouse for certain functions, though. So in this book, I'll show you how to perform those functions using either a mouse or the keyboard.

The printer   The *printer* is an output device. Although many different kinds of printers have been developed, the most widely used printers are dot-matrix printers and laser printers.

A *dot-matrix printer* works by striking small pins against an inked ribbon. The resulting dots form characters or graphic images on the paper. Today, most dot-matrix printers are either 9-pin or 24-pin printers. As you might expect, 24-pin printers print with better quality than 9-pin printers. But both can print text in two different modes: *draft mode* and *letter quality mode*. Not surprisingly, the draft mode is faster, but the letter quality mode is easier to read. For instance, my 24-pin printer prints at 216 cps (characters per second) in draft mode and 72 cps in letter quality mode. As a result, I sometimes print a document in draft mode first, then use letter quality mode for the final copy that other people will see.

Most dot-matrix printers can print text characters in more than one size and more than one typeface, or *font*. They can print type styles such as italics and boldface. They can print graphics such as charts and diagrams. And they can handle cut forms as well as continuous forms. In general, the more you pay for a dot-matrix printer, the faster it prints and the more features it comes with.

In contrast to dot-matrix printers, *laser printers* work on the same principle as photocopiers. These printers are not only faster than dot-matrix printers, but they're also quieter (since no pins are striking the paper) and they print with better quality. Most laser printers print at 300 dpi (dots per inch), but 600-dpi printers are also available. Naturally, the print quality, or resolution, of a laser printer depends on the number of dots per inch, and high-resolution printers are more expensive than low-resolution printers.

At one time, dot-matrix printers were far less expensive than laser printers, and far more common. But as laser printer prices have dropped, the quality and speed they provide have made them more and more popular. In fact, nowadays most people at least consider purchasing a laser printer instead of a dot-matrix printer when they buy a PC. And many businesses are making laser printers available to employees in every department.

The primary components of the systems unit

If you've ever opened up the systems unit of a PC, you know that it is full of electronic components. These components are attached to electronic cards that are inserted into the unit. Although you don't have to understand how any of these components work, you should have a conceptual idea of what the primary components are and what they do.

Figure 1-4 is a conceptual drawing of the components of a typical PC. Within the systems unit, you can see four primary components: the diskette drive or drives, the hard disk, internal memory, and the processor.

The diskette drive or drives A *diskette* is the actual recording medium on which data is stored, and the *diskette drive* is the device that writes data on the diskette and reads data from the diskette. Diskettes are also called *floppy disks*, but I'll refer to them as diskettes throughout this book. To read data from a diskette or write data on a diskette, you insert the diskette into the slot on a diskette drive and close the drive's latch (if it has a latch).

Figure 1-5 illustrates the sizes of the diskettes that can be used with PCs. Originally, all PCs, XTs, and ATs used 5-1/4 inch diskettes, and all PS/2s used the newer 3-1/2 inch diskettes. Today, however, most PCs come with 3-1/2 inch diskette drives, and many come with both a 5-1/4 and a 3-1/2 inch drive.

The amount of data you can store on a diskette depends on its size and on whether it's a *double-density* diskette, a *high-density* diskette, or, in the case of 3-1/2 inch diskettes, an *extended-density* diskette. Each type has a different storage capacity that is measured in *bytes* of data. For practical purposes, you can think of one byte of data as one character of data, and you can think of a character as a letter, a digit (0-9), or a special character such as #, %, or &. Thus, ten bytes of diskette storage are required to store the word *impossible*; four bytes are required to store the number *4188*; and two bytes are required to store *$9*.

Hardware concepts and terms for every PC user   9

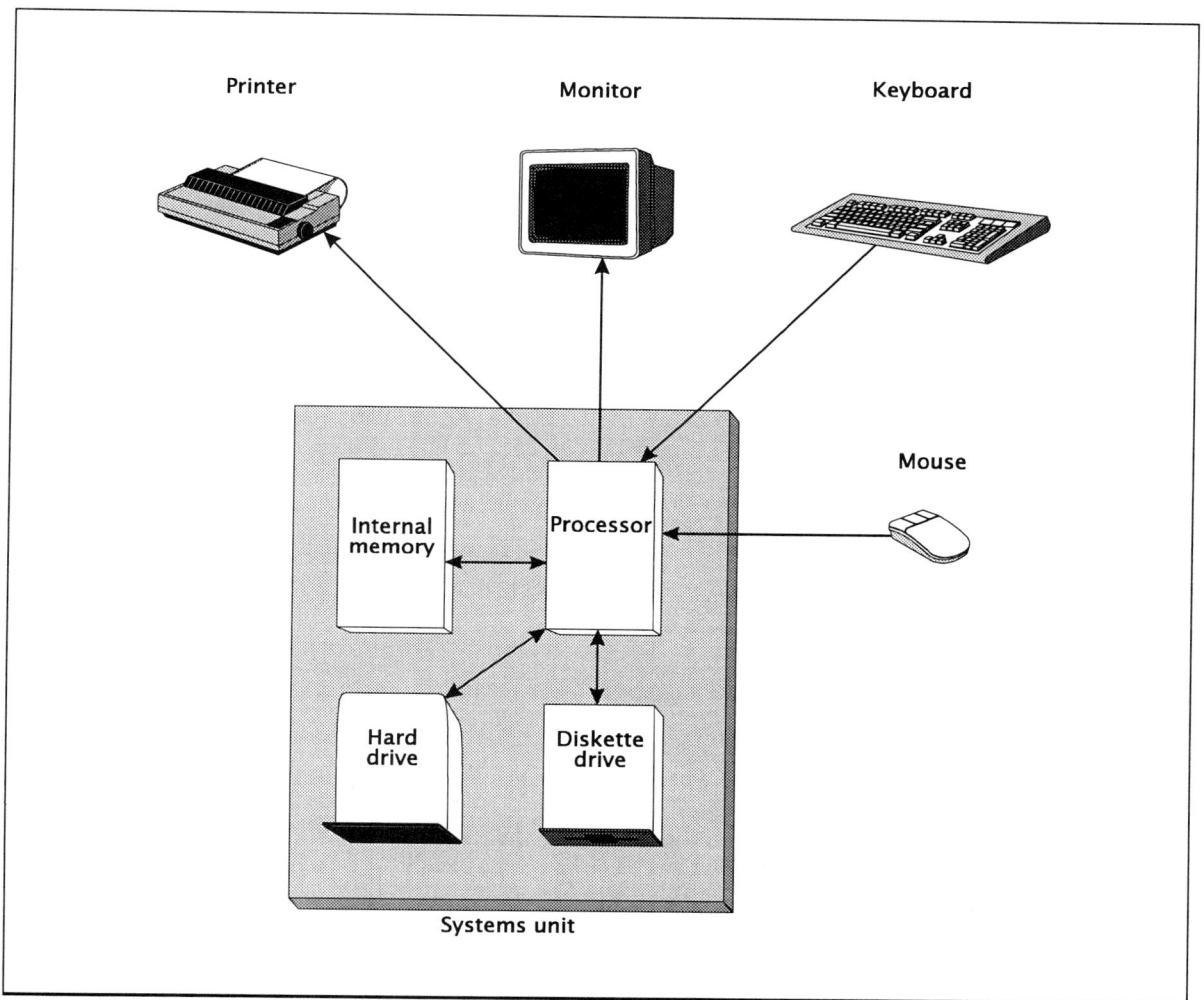

Figure 1-4   The internal components of the systems unit

For 5-1/4 inch double-density diskettes, the storage capacity is 360,000 bytes, or 360KB (where *K* stands for 1,000, *B* stands for bytes, and *KB* stands for *kilobyte*, which is approximately 1,000 bytes). In contrast, high-density diskettes allow for 1,200KB, or 1.2MB (where *M* stands for 1,000,000, *B* stands for byte, and *MB* stands for *megabyte*, which is approximately one million bytes). For 3-1/2 inch diskettes, double-density capacity is 720KB, high-density capacity is 1.44MB, and extended-density capacity is 2.88MB.

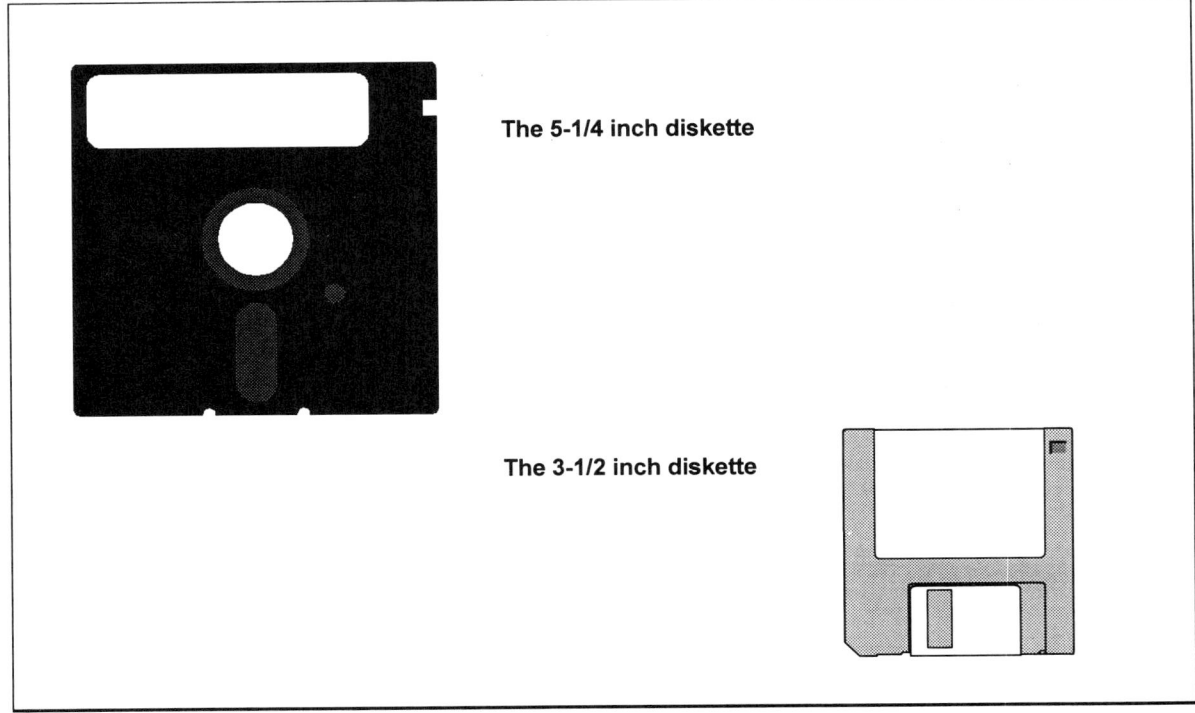

Figure 1-5 The two diskette sizes

Figure 1-6 summarizes the diskette sizes and capacities. Because the labelling for diskettes is often confusing, this figure also lists the common labelling designations for each type of diskette.

When you use a diskette to transfer data from one PC to another, you must make sure that you're using a diskette that is the right size and capacity for the system you're transferring the data to. For example, a 5-1/4 inch drive on an AT can read and write either double- or high-density diskettes. However, on older PCs like the XT, a 5-1/4 inch diskette drive can usually read and write only double-density diskettes. As a result, you must use double-density diskettes to transfer data between an XT and an AT.

The hard disk In contrast to diskettes, a *hard disk* is installed inside the systems unit, and the recording medium and the drive are sealed together in a single unit. As a result, a hard disk can't be removed from the PC the way a diskette can. That's why hard disks are sometimes called *fixed disks*. In this book, though, I'll use the term *hard disk*.

Size	Capacity	Common labelling notation
5-1/4"	360KB	5-1/4" Double-Sided Double-Density 5-1/4" DSDD
5-1/4"	1.2MB	5-1/4" Double-Sided High-Density 5-1/4" DSHD
3-1/2"	720KB	3-1/2" Double-Sided Double-Density 3-1/2" 2DD 3-1/2" 1.0M formatted capacity
3-1/2"	1.44MB	3-1/2" Double-Sided High-Density 3-1/2" 2HD 3-1/2" 2.0M formatted capacity
3-1/2"	2.88MB	3-1/2" Double-Sided Extended-Density 3-1/2" 2ED 3-1/2" 4.0M formatted capacity

Figure 1-6   A summary of diskette characteristics

Today, most hard disks have capacities of 40MB or more, and you can buy hard disks with capacities of 1,000MB or more. To put that into perspective, consider that one megabyte of disk storage can hold about 500 pages of word processing text. So an 80MB hard disk can hold 40,000 pages of text, while a 1.2MB diskette can hold only about 600 pages. To look at it another way, an 80MB disk can store the equivalent of about 66 diskettes that have a capacity of 1.2MB.

Because you can store so much data on a hard disk, you have to manage a hard disk more carefully than you manage diskettes. In particular, you have to use directories to organize the data on a hard disk. And you have to back up the data on a hard disk so you won't lose it in the event of a hardware or software problem. As you read this book, you'll learn the skills that will help you get the most from your hard disk.

Since your PC has a hard disk, you probably won't use diskettes much because all of your programs will be stored on the hard disk. However, you still need at least one diskette drive on your PC. You'll use it to back up the data on your hard disk to diskettes, to install new programs from diskettes to your hard disk, and to transfer data from one PC to another.

Internal memory   Before your PC can operate on the data that is stored on a diskette or a hard disk, the data must be read into the *internal memory* of the systems unit. This memory can also be called *internal storage* or *RAM* (for *Random Access Memory*), but I'll refer to it as internal memory throughout this book.

Like diskette or hard disk storage, the capacity of internal memory is measured in kilobytes or megabytes. Although the original PCs were typically sold with less than 1MB of internal memory, PCs today are usually sold with 2MB or 4MB of internal memory. And the most powerful PCs are sold with 8MB, 16MB, or even 32MB of internal memory.

Because a program must be stored in internal memory before it can be used, each program requires a specific amount of internal memory. For instance, *WordPerfect* 5.1 requires a PC with at least 384KB of internal memory, and *Lotus 1-2-3* release 3.4 requires 1MB of internal memory. However, because the PC was originally designed for a maximum of 640KB, only a few programs require more than 640KB of memory.

This first 640KB of internal memory can be referred to as *conventional memory*. If your PC doesn't have a full 640KB of conventional memory (the first PCs had only 128KB) and you want to use a program that requires more memory than your PC has, you can add more conventional memory to it. On most PCs, you can do that by buying memory chips that you plug into the *motherboard*, the main electronic circuit board of your systems unit. On some older PCs, you must buy a *memory expansion card* that you plug into an *expansion slot* within the systems unit. In either case, you have to open the system unit's case before you can add the memory.

In addition to conventional memory, most computers today can support extra memory called *extended memory*. However, programs must be specially designed to work with extended memory. As a result, some programs, such as *Lotus 1-2-3*, can use extended memory, while others, such as *WordPerfect*, cannot. So before you purchase extended memory for your computer, make sure the programs you use can support it.

When you're using a PC, your current work is stored in internal memory. However, the data in internal memory is erased when the power for the PC is turned off, either deliberately or due to a power failure. That's why you must store your work to diskette or hard disk storage before you turn your PC off. Otherwise, your work is lost. In contrast to internal memory, diskettes and hard disks retain the data that has been stored on them whether the power is on or not.

The processor If you look back to figure 1-4, you can see that all of the components I've described so far are connected to the *processor*. When a program is in operation, the processor controls all of the other components of the PC by executing the instructions of the program. Other terms for a processor are *microprocessor*, *central processing unit*, and *CPU*, but I'll use the term *processor* throughout this book.

In a PC, the entire processor is contained in a single *microprocessor chip*. Most of these chips are manufactured by Intel and have names like the 8088, the 80286, the 80386, and the 80486, as summarized in figure 1-7. As you can see, the shortened versions of the chip names are the 286, the 386SX, the 386, the 486SX, and so on. (A few other manufacturers have recently begun manufacturing processor chips that are

Hardware concepts and terms for every PC user

Processor names	Abbreviated names	Clock speeds
8088	None	4.77 - 10Mhz
80286	286	6 - 20Mhz
80386SX	386SX	16 - 20Mhz
80386DX	386	16 - 33Mhz
80486SX	486SX	25 - 33Mhz
80486DX	486	25 - 50Mhz
80486DX2	486DX2	50 - 66Mhz

Figure 1-7 A summary of PC processors

compatible with the Intel chips. But DOS and your application programs work the same, whether your PC uses a genuine Intel chip or a compatible.)

Because the processor controls all of the operations of a PC, the speed of the processor can have an important effect on how fast a program runs on your PC. One measure of processor speed is *clock speed*. In general, the faster the clock speed, the faster the computer operates. The clock speed of the original IBM PC was 4.77 million cycles per second, or 4.77Mhz (*Mhz* stands for *Megahertz*). Today, as you can see in figure 1-7, some processors have clock speeds in the 25 to 66Mhz range.

You should realize, though, that clock speed isn't the only factor that influences your processor's speed. Which processor chip your system is based on often makes an even bigger difference than the clock speed of the processor. For example, the 286 is inherently faster than the 8088. Thus, a 286 running at a clock speed of 8Mhz is about five times as fast as an 8088 running at 8Mhz. Similarly, a 386 running at 20Mhz is about three times as fast as a 286 running at 20Mhz. And a 486 is about half again as fast as a 386 running at the same speed.

Besides performance, you should know that different processors provide different technical features. Some programs are designed to take advantage of some of the features of a specific processor, and some even require a specific processor. Release 3.1 of *Lotus 1-2-3*, for example, requires that you have at least a 286 processor so it can use some of the special features that are provided by the more advanced processors. In contrast, release 2.3 of *Lotus 1-2-3* works with all processors from the 8088 on.

Some perspective on hardware

Throughout this chapter, I've tried to simplify the concepts and keep the number of new terms to a minimum. In general, I've tried to present only those PC concepts you need to know in order to use your software effectively. And I've tried to present only those terms that you're most likely to encounter in manuals and in magazine articles.

Nevertheless, this chapter presents more than you need to know about hardware if all you want to do is use your PC effectively. As a result, you shouldn't feel that you need to know all of the terms in this chapter before you continue. That's why I've divided them into two groups. If you're familiar with the terms in the first group that follows, you're ready to go on to the next chapter.

Terms you should be familiar with before you continue

hardware	printer
personal computer	dot-matrix printer
PC	laser printer
XT	diskette
AT	diskette drive
PS/2	double-density
compatible	high-density
systems unit	extended-density
monitor	byte
monochrome monitor	kilobyte (KB)
color monitor	megabyte (MB)
keyboard	hard disk
cursor	internal memory
cursor control keys	conventional memory
mouse	processor
mouse cursor	microprocessor chip

Objectives

1. List the primary physical components of a PC.
2. List the primary components of a systems unit.
3. Explain why you should save your work before you turn the PC off.

Other terms presented in this chapter

clone
electronics unit
systems chassis
display
screen
CRT
Cathode Ray Tube
resolution
display adapter
Monochrome Display Adapter
MDA
CGA
Color Graphics Adapter
EGA
Enhanced Graphics Adapter
VGA
Video Graphics Array
SVGA
Super VGA
HRVGA
High-Resolution VGA

mouse pad
click
double-click
click-and-drag
draft mode
letter quality mode
font
floppy disk
fixed disk
internal storage
RAM
Random Access Memory
motherboard
memory expansion card
expansion slot
extended memory
microprocessor
central processing unit
CPU
clock speed
Megahertz (Mhz)

Chapter 2

Software concepts and terms for every DOS user

Do you know the difference between an application program and an operating system program? Do you know what the primary functions of DOS are? Do you know what happens when you use the DOS command processor to start an application program? Do you know what version of DOS you're using?

Unless you can answer an unqualified "yes" to those questions, you should read this chapter before you go on to the next one. To use a PC effectively, you must have a basic understanding of PC *software*. The term *software* refers to the *programs* that direct the operations of the PC hardware. When you complete this chapter, you'll have the software background you need for learning how to use DOS.

The two types of programs every PC requires

In broad terms, PC software can be divided into two types: application programs and operating system programs. To do work on your PC, you need both types of programs. In case you're not already familiar with both types, here's some information about each.

Application programs   An *application program* is a program you use to do your work. It lets you *apply* your PC to the jobs that you want to do on a PC. For instance, *WordPerfect* is an application program that lets you apply your PC to jobs like writing letters, memos, and reports. And *Lotus 1-2-3* is an application program that lets you apply your PC to the job of creating spreadsheets.

Figure 2-1 lists three of the most popular types of application programs: word processing, spreadsheet, and database programs. This figure also lists some of the most popular programs of each type. If you've used a PC at all, you've probably used one or more of these programs.

When you use a *word processing program*, you prepare *documents* like letters, memos, or reports. When you use a *spreadsheet program*, you prepare *spreadsheets* like budgets or profit projections. And when you use a *database program*, you create and maintain a *database* to store information, like an employee, customer, or vendor

Program type	Examples	Operates upon
Word processing	*WordPerfect* *Microsoft Word*	Documents
Spreadsheet	*Lotus 1-2-3* *Quattro Pro*	Spreadsheets
Database	*dBase IV* *Paradox* *Q&A*	Records within a database

Figure 2-1 Three of the most popular types of application programs

database. Once you establish a database, you can extract information from it in the form of reports and other documents.

Word processing, spreadsheet, and database programs are considered to be *general-purpose programs* because you can use them for so many different jobs. But many other kinds of general-purpose programs are also available. For instance, *presentation graphics programs* let you create charts, diagrams, and other graphic presentations. *Desktop publishing programs* let you create documents with published quality. And *drawing programs* let you create professional-quality illustrations.

In contrast to general-purpose programs, some programs are designed for special, narrowly-defined purposes. For example, you can buy a program that will help you manage rental properties, a program that will help you manage accounts receivable for a retail business, and a program that will analyze the quality of your writing. In fact, so many application programs are available today, it's difficult to categorize them.

Operating system programs   An *operating system* is a program that lets your application programs run on your PC. For instance, an operating system lets you load an application program into internal memory so you can use it. An operating system also provides functions that let your application programs read a file from a disk drive, print on a printer, and so on.

The concept of an operating system is elusive because much of what the operating system does goes on without your knowing about it. When you save your work on a hard disk, for example, it is the operating system, not the application program, that actually writes the data on the disk. In other words, your application program communicates with the operating system without your knowing about it. Without the operating system, your application program wouldn't work.

Operating system	Current version	Characteristics	Special requirements
DOS	6.0	640K memory limit	None

Windows	3.1	4,096MB memory limit
		Multi-tasking capabilities
		Graphical User Interface
		Runs DOS or *Windows* programs
			80286 processor
			    (80386 recommended)
			1MB internal memory
			    (4MB recommended)
			8MB disk space

OS/2	2.0	4,096MB memory limit Multi-tasking capabilities Graphical User Interface Runs DOS, *Windows*, or OS/2 programs	80386 processor 4MB internal memory (8MB recommended) 15MB disk space

Figure 2-2 The three operating systems for PCs

Figure 2-2 presents the three main operating systems you can use on a single-user PC today: DOS, Microsoft *Windows*, and OS/2. *DOS* (pronounced *doss*) is short for *Disk Operating System.* It's the most widely used operating system, and you'll learn about it in detail in this book.

Windows gets its name from the fact that it provides a *graphical user interface* (or *GUI*, pronounced *gooey*) built around the idea of dividing your screen into one or more rectangular areas called "windows." Each window can contain a different application program, and you can use the mouse to move or resize a window to arrange the information on your screen just the way you want it. One of the most compelling reasons for using *Windows* is that it lets you run more than one application program at a time. Another benefit of *Windows* is that it doesn't suffer from the 640KB memory limit of DOS. Under *Windows*, your application programs can access as much internal memory as is available on your PC. Most PCs sold today come with both DOS and *Windows* already installed.

OS/2, which is short for *Operating System/2*, was designed to eventually replace DOS as a more powerful and more reliable operating system. Like Microsoft *Windows*, OS/2 uses a graphical user interface with resizable windows in which you can run your application programs; it lets you run more than one program at once; and it doesn't limit your application programs to 640KB of internal memory. Although most experts agree that OS/2 is a technically superior operating system, DOS and *Windows* continue to dominate because of the huge number of PCs already using DOS and the perception that OS/2 is more difficult to install and maintain than DOS or *Windows*.

When you purchase an application program for your PC, make sure you get a version that's compatible with the operating system you're using. All of the operating systems listed in figure 2-2 can run DOS application programs. But if you're using *Windows*, you're better off purchasing *Windows* versions of your application programs. That way, your applications can take full advantage of *Windows'* advanced features. If you're running OS/2 version 2.0, you can run DOS or *Windows* applications, or you can purchase OS/2 versions of your applications (if you can find them; few software vendors have produced OS/2 versions of their programs).

As I mentioned, DOS is by far the most widely used operating system on PCs today, and that won't change for a while. It doesn't look as if OS/2 will overtake DOS, although *Windows* is becoming more popular all the time. If you're using *Windows*, this book will be useful, but you'll want to read an introductory *Windows* book as well (I recommend *The Least You Need to Know about Windows* by Steve Eckols).

When DOS is sold by Microsoft Corporation, the company that created it, it's called *MS-DOS*; when it's sold by IBM Corporation, it's called *PC-DOS*; and some PC manufacturers provide their own modified versions of DOS. Fortunately, all of the manufacturers' versions work essentially the same way, so I'll use the term *DOS* in this book to apply to all of them.

What DOS provides

When you turn on a hard disk PC, it starts by loading a portion of DOS into internal memory. This portion of DOS occupies a portion of internal memory, usually from 40 to 70KB in size, as shown in the schematic drawing in figure 2-3. Because this portion of DOS remains in internal memory until you turn off your PC, DOS functions are available to you and your application programs whenever your PC is running.

In general terms, DOS provides three types of functions: command processing, DOS services, and DOS commands. You need to have a basic understanding of all three of these functions to use your PC effectively.

Command processing The DOS *command processor* is loaded into internal memory when you start your PC. When the command processor is in control of the system, it displays a *command prompt* like the one shown in figure 2-4. Generally, this command prompt is displayed when your PC finishes its start-up procedure.

When the command prompt is displayed, the command processor is waiting for you to enter a command. For instance, you normally enter the letters *wp* to start *WordPerfect* and the numbers *123* to start *Lotus 1-2-3*. You can also start DOS commands from the command prompt, as you will learn in a moment.

Figure 2-5 illustrates how DOS uses the command processor to switch from one application program to another. When you start your PC, the DOS command processor is loaded into the internal memory of your system along with some other parts of DOS. As I mentioned earlier, this portion of DOS resides in internal memory

Software concepts and terms for every DOS user **21**

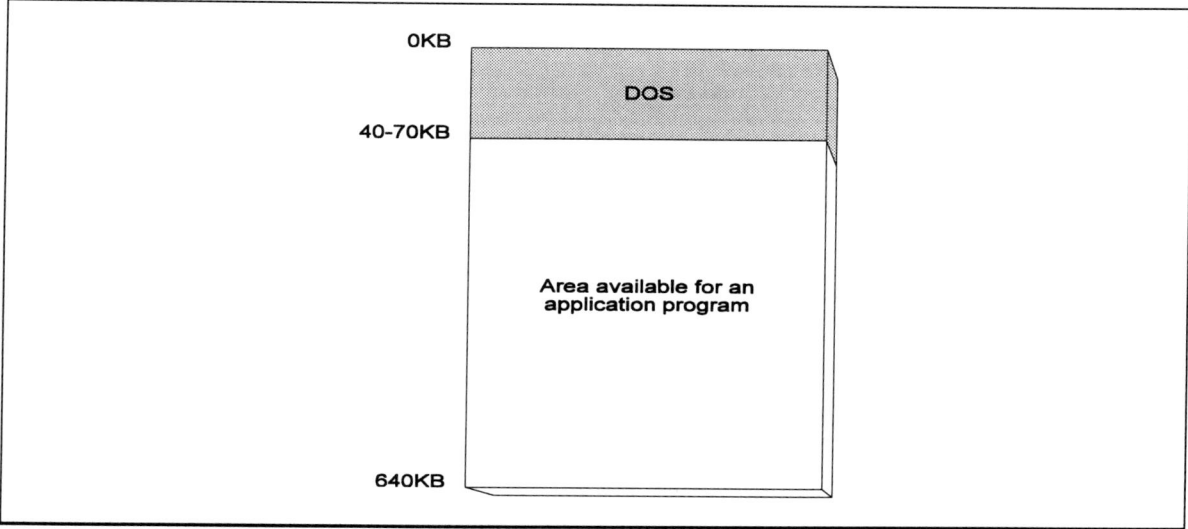

Figure 2-3 The contents of internal memory after DOS has been loaded into it

Figure 2-4 A typical DOS command prompt

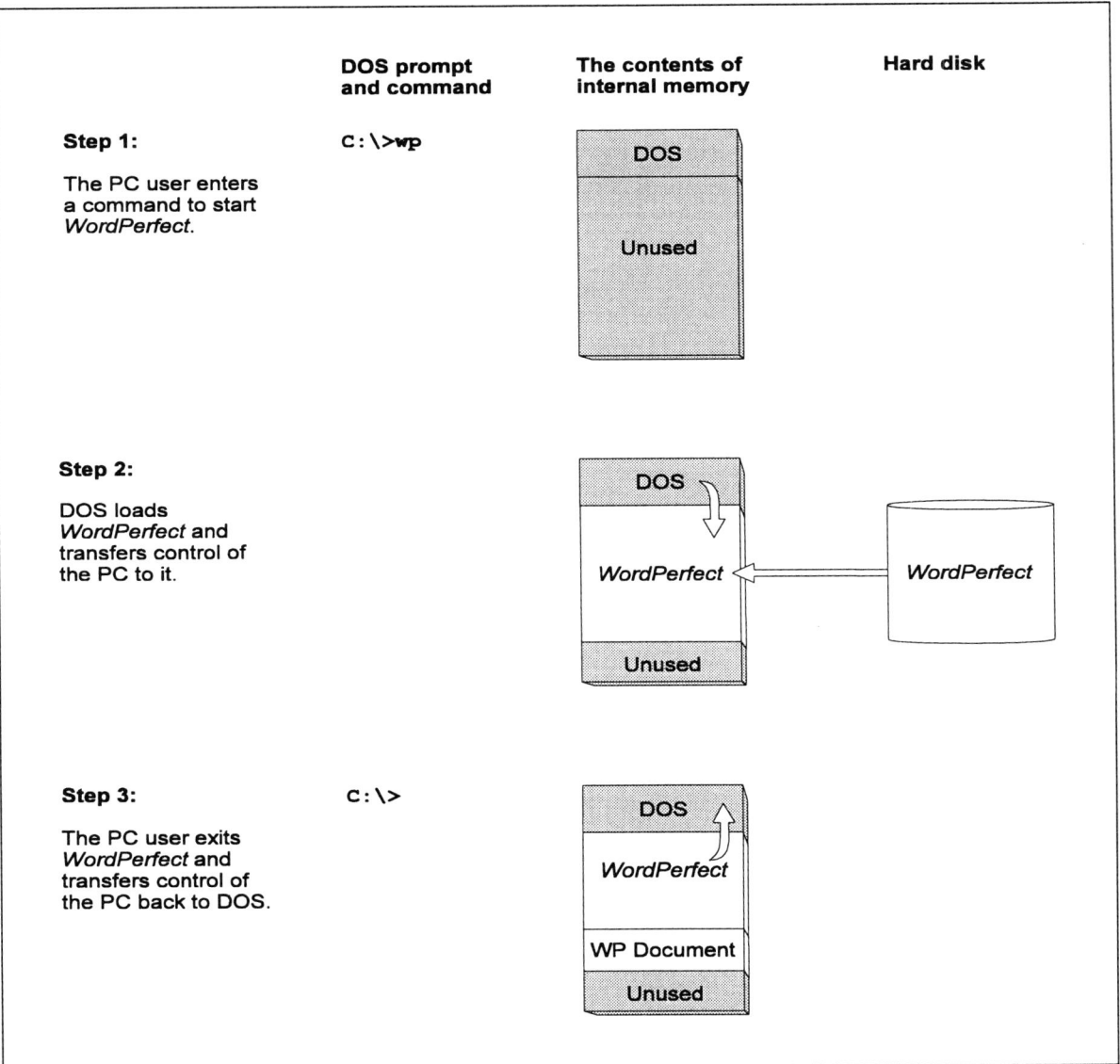

Figure 2-5 How DOS goes from one application program to the next (part 1 of 2)

Software concepts and terms for every DOS user   **23**

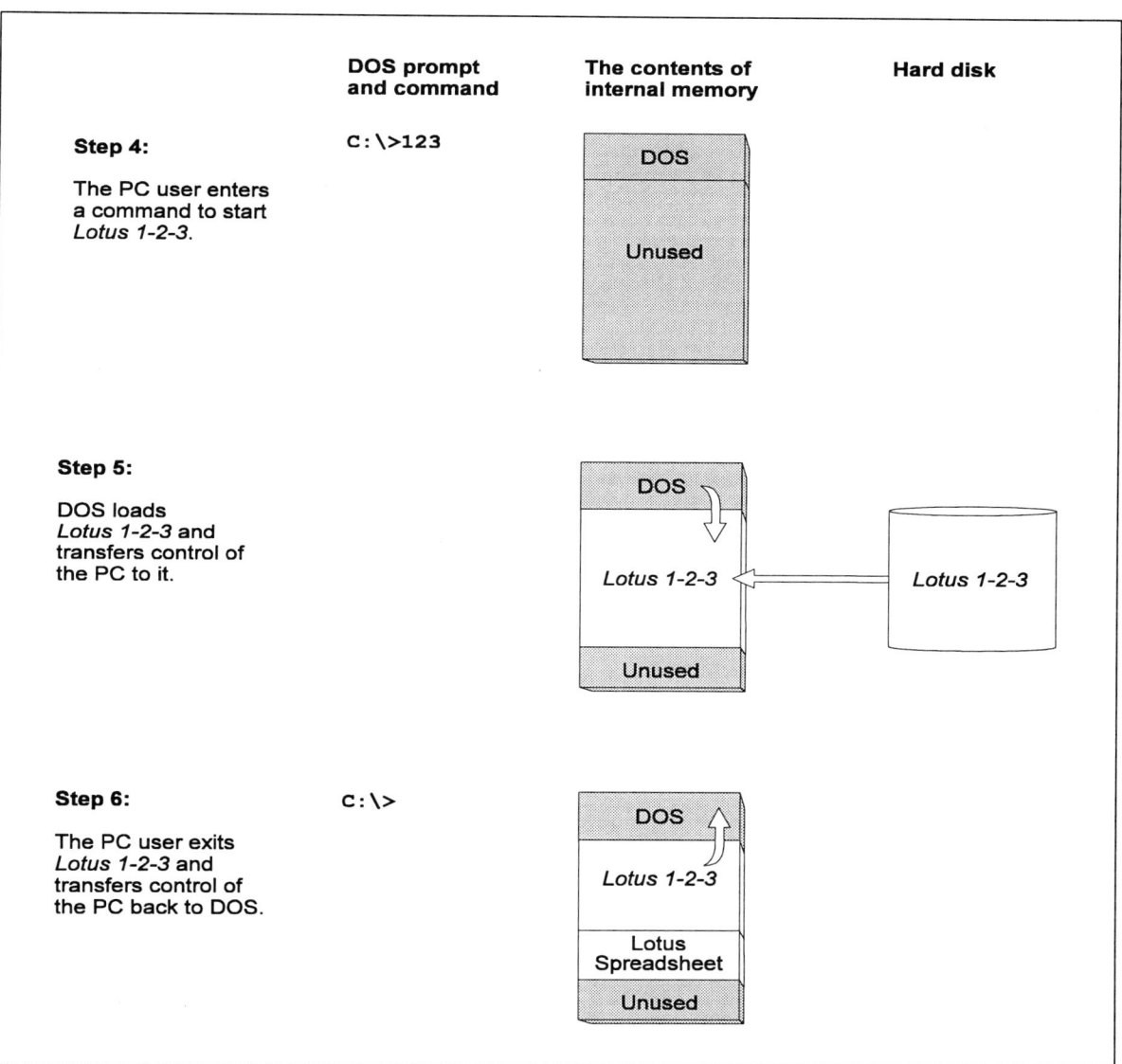

Figure 2-5   How DOS goes from one application program to the next (part 2 of 2)

whenever the PC is in operation. This is indicated by the contents of internal memory in step 1 of the figure.

When you enter *wp* at the command prompt, the command processor loads *WordPerfect* from the hard disk into internal memory, as shown in step 2. This is called *loading a program*. Then, the command processor passes control of the PC to the first instruction of the *WordPerfect* program. When you instruct *WordPerfect* to retrieve a document, it copies the document file from the disk into internal memory. This is called *loading a file*. When you finish your word processing activities and exit the *WordPerfect* program, control is passed back to the command processor, as shown in step 3. Then, the memory used by *WordPerfect* and the document is released, and the command processor waits for another command from the PC user.

When you enter *123* at the command prompt as shown in step 4 of figure 2-5, the command processor loads *Lotus 1-2-3* into internal memory as shown in step 5. Then, the command processor passes control to the first instruction of the application program. When you finish your spreadsheet work and exit the *Lotus 1-2-3* program, control is passed back to the command processor as shown in step 6. Then, the command processor waits for your next command. In this way, the command processor lets you switch from one program to the next.

This figure also shows why it's crucial to save the file you've been working on to disk before you exit from an application program. If you look back at step 4, you'll see that, once you've exited from a program, DOS treats the internal memory used by the program as though it were unused. So if you don't save the file you've been working on before you exit, your work will be lost.

DOS services When an application program is running, DOS provides *DOS services* to the program. Some of the most important of these services are called *input/output services*, or *I/O services*. These services make it possible for the application program to receive input from the input devices of the PC and to give output through the output devices of the PC.

To illustrate, figure 2-6 shows how DOS provides I/O services when an application program wants to retrieve data from a hard disk. Here, you can see that an application program doesn't access disk data directly. Instead, it requests DOS to do the work for it. In step 1, the application program asks DOS to retrieve data from the disk. In step 2, DOS directs the disk device to read the requested data. In step 3, the disk device reads the data and sends it back to DOS. Finally, in step 4, DOS returns the requested data to the application program.

Actually, this process is much more complicated than figure 2-6 indicates. For example, DOS must be able to retrieve data from any type of disk drive, whether it's a 5-1/4 inch or 3-1/2 inch diskette drive, a 30MB hard disk, or a 300MB hard disk. In addition, DOS must be able to handle a variety of error conditions that might be encountered. For example, what if the data can't be found? Or what if a hardware failure occurs? By taking care of these kinds of details, DOS insures that all application programs handle disk access in a consistent manner.

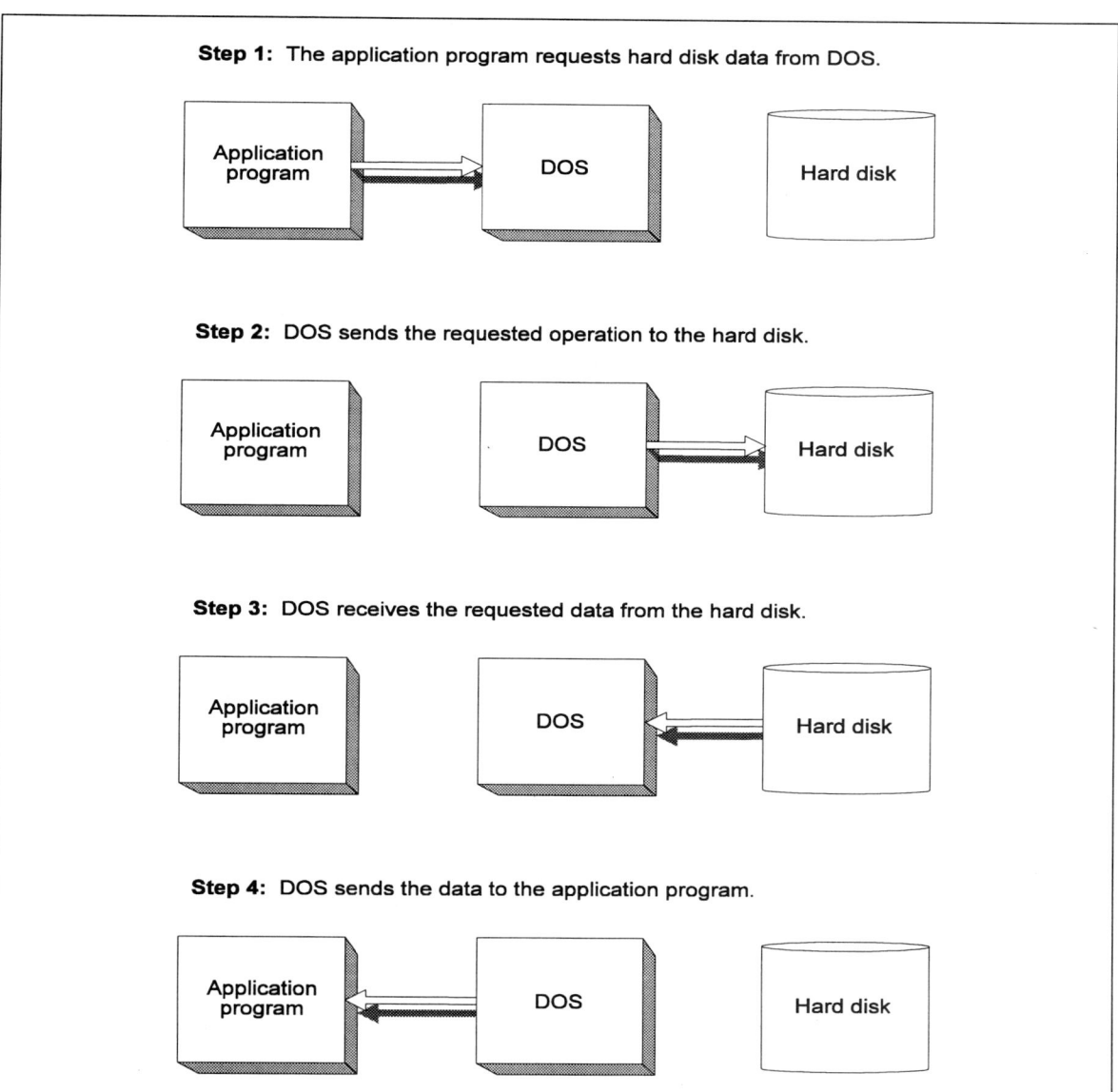

Figure 2-6 How DOS provides an input service to an application program

As part of its services, DOS also manages all of the files that are stored on a hard disk or diskette. In DOS terms, each document, spreadsheet, database, or program on a hard disk or diskette is called a *file*. So although you might think of a file as a document file, a spreadsheet file, a database file, or a program file, DOS makes no distinction between them. It manages all of the files in the same way.

To keep track of the files, DOS requires that they be organized into *directories*. Then, in the directory entry for each file, DOS records the file name, the disk location, the file size in bytes, the date the file was last changed, and the time the file was last changed. As a result, an application program doesn't have to know these details when it requests an input or output operation for a disk file. Instead, the application program has to supply just the name of the file and the name of the directory that contains the file. In the next chapter, you'll learn how to refer to the files and directories you use on a DOS system.

Because you only use DOS services through your application programs, you don't have to be concerned about them. Most of the time, in fact, you won't even be aware that the services have been provided for you. When something goes wrong with a service request, though, you sometimes get a message directly from DOS. Then, it's obvious that the DOS services are in use.

DOS commands In addition to the DOS services that you use indirectly through an application program, DOS provides commands that you can use directly from the command prompt. Most of these commands let you manage the files and directories on a disk. But some provide other types of functions.

Figure 2-7 presents twelve typical *DOS commands*, organized by type. The first group, for example, provides functions you can use to manage the files on a disk. These commands let you delete, rename, or copy one or more files. The other commands provide functions for managing directories, backing up the files on a hard disk, and so on.

In sections 2 and 3 of this book, you'll learn how to use these and other DOS commands. You'll also learn when and how to use them for maximum efficiency.

How DOS has evolved

Over the years, DOS has changed substantially, as summarized in figure 2-8. Here, you can see that each new version of DOS is given a *version number* like 2.0 or 3.3. In general, a change in the first digit of a version number means a major revision of the program; a change in the digits to the right of the decimal point means a minor revision. This is true for application programs as well as for DOS. If you want to find out what version of DOS you have on your system, just type VER at the command prompt and press the Enter key.

As you can see in figure 2-8, the original version of DOS was a modest operating system that was designed for diskette systems. Later versions provided for hardware developments like hard disks, 1.2MB diskette drives, 3-1/2 inch diskette

Command type	Command	Function
File management	DEL	Deletes one or more files from disk storage.
	REN	Renames one or more files in disk storage.
	COPY	Copies one or more files from one disk location to another.
Directory management	MD	Makes a new directory.
	RD	Removes an empty directory.
Backup	BACKUP	Copies the files and directories on a hard disk to a series of diskettes.
	RESTORE	Copies the backup files and directories on a series of diskettes to a hard disk.
Date and time	DATE	Requests the current date and sets the internal clock using this information.
	TIME	Requests the current time and sets the internal clock using this information.
Error checking and recovery	CHKDSK	Checks a disk for errors and attempts to correct the errors.
Information display	VER	Displays the version of DOS in use.
	DIR	Displays the files and directories on a disk drive.

Figure 2-7   Twelve typical DOS commands

drives, and hard disks larger than 32MB. They also provided new commands, capabilities, and features.

With version 4.0, Microsoft began to include a program called the *DOS shell* with DOS. This program makes it easier for you to perform routine DOS functions like copying files and managing your directories. When you use the DOS shell, you can set up your system so a screen like one of the ones in figure 2-9 is displayed whenever you start your PC. Then, you can use the functions of the DOS shell to manage files and directories and to start your application programs without entering the commands at the command prompt.

Frankly, the DOS shell that Microsoft included with version 4.0 had too many limitations to be of much use, but fortunately Microsoft thoroughly revamped the shell for version 5.0. The shell that comes with DOS 6.0 is nearly identical to the DOS 5.0 shell, so section 4 of this book teaches them together. If you're currently

Version	Major improvements
1.0	
2.0	Support for hard disks Directories
3.0	Support for 1.2MB diskette drives
3.1	Support for networks
3.2	Support for 3-1/2 inch diskette drives
3.3	Multiple logical drives on a hard disk New commands
4.0	Support for hard disk drives of more than 32MB Extended memory support DOS shell
5.0	Less conventional memory required Improved use of extended memory Task switching Full-screen editor New DOS shell and other utility programs
6.0	New utility programs, including high-speed backup, anti-virus, and disk defragmentation utilities Improved configuration options Disk compression to double disk space Support for portable computers

Figure 2-8 The evolution of DOS

using an earlier version of DOS, you may decide to upgrade to DOS 6.0 after you see how the shell works.

Although the DOS 5.0/6.0 shell makes it easier for you to use DOS, you still have to know how DOS commands work. So you should read sections 2 and 3 of this book before you read section 4. To make the most efficient use of DOS, you'll often use DOS commands entered at the command prompt for some functions, even though you have the DOS shell.

Software concepts and terms for every DOS user **29**

The first screen of the DOS 4.0 shell

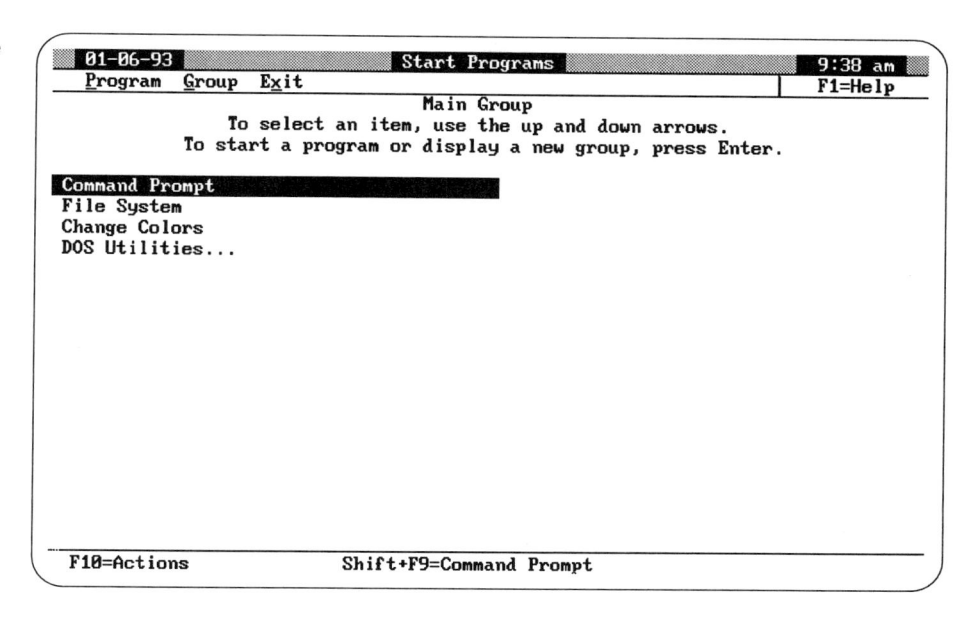

```
 01-06-93                 Start Programs                    9:38 am
 Program  Group  Exit                                       F1=Help
                            Main Group
             To select an item, use the up and down arrows.
            To start a program or display a new group, press Enter.

 Command Prompt
 File System
 Change Colors
 DOS Utilities...




 F10=Actions          Shift+F9=Command Prompt
```

The first screen of the DOS 5.0/6.0 shell

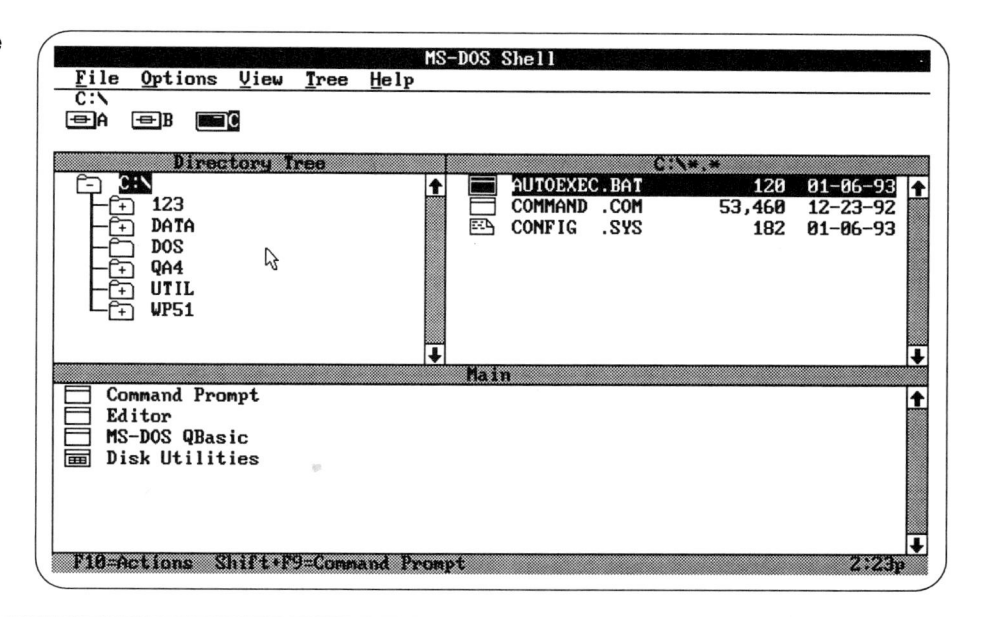

```
                              MS-DOS Shell
 File  Options  View  Tree  Help
 C:\
  [=]A   [=]B   [=]C

 ┌──────── Directory Tree ────────┐ ┌──────── C:\*.* ────────┐
 │  📁 C:\                        │ │ AUTOEXEC.BAT  120  01-06-93 │
 │    ├─ 123                      │ │ COMMAND .COM  53,460 12-23-92│
 │    ├─ DATA                     │ │ CONFIG  .SYS  182  01-06-93 │
 │    ├─ DOS                      │ │                             │
 │    ├─ QA4                      │ │                             │
 │    ├─ UTIL                     │ │                             │
 │    └─ WP51                     │ │                             │
 └────────────────────────────────┘ └─────────────────────────────┘
 ┌──────────────────────── Main ────────────────────────┐
 │  Command Prompt                                       │
 │  Editor                                               │
 │  MS-DOS QBasic                                        │
 │  Disk Utilities                                       │
 └───────────────────────────────────────────────────────┘
 F10=Actions  Shift+F9=Command Prompt                2:23p
```

Figure 2-9   The opening screens of the DOS 4.0 and DOS 5.0/6.0 shells

With DOS 6.0, Microsoft also added a number of *utility programs* (or just *utilities*). Utility programs make DOS more versatile and easier to use by providing functions that the DOS commands don't provide or by providing ways to do DOS functions more quickly and easily than you can with the DOS commands. Many of the DOS 6.0 utilities are similar to utility programs that other companies have developed in the past and sold separately from DOS. For example, if you have an earlier version of DOS, you may have a backup utility on your system that provides for quick and easy backups. Or you may have a shell program other than the DOS shell that lets you do DOS functions without knowing much about DOS commands. Of the utilities that have been added in DOS 6.0, there are two that I want you to be aware of. One is DoubleSpace, a facility that effectively doubles the capacity of your hard disk by compressing the data that's stored on it. The other is the backup utility, Microsoft Backup, which I'll teach you to use in detail in chapter 11.

Although you can use this book with any version of DOS that's 2.0 or later, you're probably using a version of DOS that's 3.0 or later. If you're using a version of DOS that's earlier than 3.0, you probably should upgrade to DOS 6.0 as soon as you can. Nevertheless, I'll let you know whenever I present a DOS feature that requires a version more recent than 2.0.

Some perspective on software

The evolution of PC software since 1981 has been impressive. During that time, we've gone from small application programs that performed a limited number of functions to large programs that perform more functions than the average user knows what to do with. We've gone from programs that worked only in text mode on monochrome monitors to programs that use both text and graphic modes on color monitors. And we've gone from programs that printed text in only one font to programs that can print complex graphics as well as text in many fonts.

Although application programs have gotten easier to use, DOS hasn't. As a result, most PC users still have a difficult time using DOS effectively, just as they did back in the early 1980s. In fact, most PC users seem to avoid DOS whenever they can. They have to learn how to use DOS to start their application programs, of course, but that's all many of them want to know about DOS.

Unfortunately, you need to know more than that if you want to get the maximum benefit from your PC. If you don't know how to use DOS, you won't be able to manage your files and directories as effectively as you should, so they'll eventually get out of control. You won't back up your files as efficiently or as frequently as you should, so you won't be protected from a hard disk disaster. If someone changes the way your PC is set up, you may not even be able to start your application programs. And whenever something goes wrong, you'll be at the mercy of someone who does know DOS.

That's why the next two sections in this book will teach you the DOS skills all PC users should have. In section 2, you'll learn the DOS skills you need for working with your application programs. In section 3, you'll learn additional skills that will save you time and trouble each day. Once you've mastered these skills, you'll be able to use your PC effectively.

Terms

software
program
application program
word processing program
document
spreadsheet program
spreadsheet
database program
database
general-purpose program
presentation graphics program
desktop publishing program
drawing program
operating system
DOS
Disk Operating System
Windows
graphical user interface (GUI)

OS/2
Operating System/2
MS-DOS
PC-DOS
command processor
command prompt
loading a program
loading a file
DOS service
input/output service
I/O service
file
directory
DOS command
version number
DOS shell
utility program
utility

Objectives

1. Describe the primary difference between an application program and an operating system program.
2. In general terms, explain how command processing works on a DOS system.
3. In general terms, explain how a DOS I/O service for a disk device works when an application program is in operation.
4. Explain the significance of the digits before and after the decimal point in the version number for a software product.

Section 2

A short course in DOS for every PC user

When you use an application program on a PC, you need to know something about DOS. At the least, you need to know how to identify DOS drives, directories, and files so you can save and retrieve your work files. But you should also know how to start your application programs from the command prompt. And if you have to enter the same set of commands each day after you turn your PC on, you should know how to start up your PC so it executes those commands automatically. These are the skills you'll learn in this section.

When you finish this section, your PC and its software will be less mysterious to you. You'll understand how to use directories and files as you save and retrieve your work files. You'll know how to use 12 DOS commands. And you'll always be able to start your application programs, no matter who used the PC last or for what purpose.

Chapter 3

How to identify DOS drives, directories, files, and paths

Although most application programs today try to shield you from the intricacies of DOS, all of them use DOS specifications for files. As a result, you should know how to refer to DOS disk drives, directories, and files, whether or not you ever use DOS itself. In this chapter, you'll learn how to refer to any file on a DOS system by specifying its drive, directory, and file name.

To start, you'll learn how to give a complete file specification for any file on a DOS system. Then, you'll learn what the default drive and current directory are and how they affect your file specifications. Last, you'll learn how to use DOS file specifications within your application programs.

How to specify the drive, path, and file name for any DOS file

Whenever you use an application program or DOS to access a file, you have to specify what file you want to access and where the file is located. You supply this information using a *file specification*. A complete file specification consists of three parts: a drive, a path, and a file name. Figure 3-1 shows complete specifications for a file on a diskette and for a file on a hard disk. Now, I'll explain what each part of a file specification is.

The drive   DOS identifies a PC's hard disk drive and diskette drives by letters. For instance, the first diskette drive on every system is always drive A, and the second diskette drive, if there is one, is always drive B.

The hard disk, or at least the first portion of it, is always identified as drive C, even on a single-diskette system where there isn't a drive B. However, one hard disk can be divided into more than one drive, as shown in figure 3-2. Then, the first drive is drive C; the second is drive D; and so on.

In PC and DOS literature, these drives are often referred to as *logical drives* to distinguish them from the hard disk, or physical disk drive. Thus, one physical drive

```
Example 1:  A typical drive, path, and file name for a document file on a diskette

           Path
   Disk   |
   drive  |   File name
     |    |      |
     B:\MONTHSUM.DOC
                  |
               Extension

Example 2:  A typical drive, path, and file name for a spreadsheet file on a hard disk

              Path
   Disk     |
   drive    |      File name
     |   ___|___      |
     C:\123\MMA\PROFORMA.WK1
         |    |         |
     Directory Subdirectory Extension
```

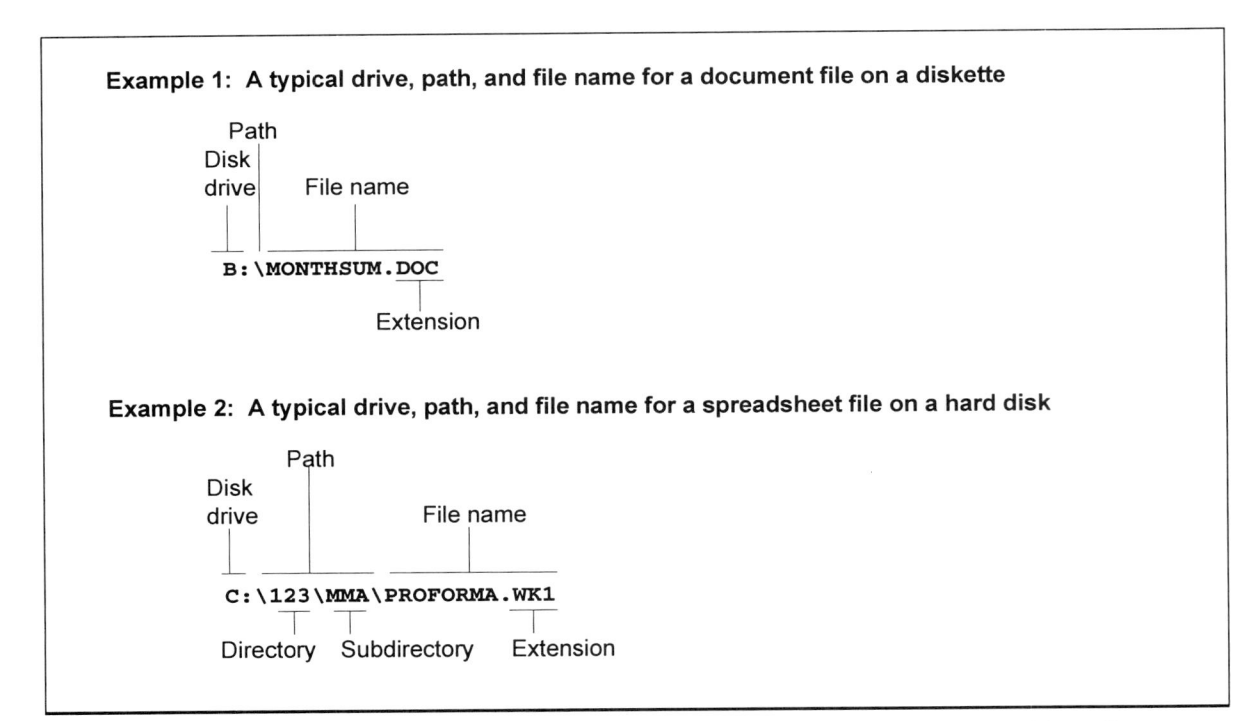

Figure 3-1 Typical drives, paths, and file names for word processing and spreadsheet files

is divided into two or more logical drives. From a practical point of view, however, you can think of each logical drive as a physical drive. As a result, I won't distinguish between the two in the remainder of this book. I'll simply refer to disk drives by letter, as in "the C drive" or "the D drive."

This division of a hard disk into more than one drive originally started because DOS was unable to accommodate hard disks that had capacities larger than 32MB. As a result, a 120MB hard disk had to be divided into four 30MB drives. DOS 3.3 was the first version of DOS to provide for this division directly. Before DOS 3.3, you had to use non-standard software to divide a drive larger than 32MB into smaller, usable drives. Today, DOS 4.0 through 6.0 can treat an entire 120MB disk as the C drive, and it's uncommon to find a large hard disk broken down into more than two drives.

In this book, I assume that your hard disk has already been set up for you. At the least, then, you know that your PC has a C drive. In the next chapter, I'll show you how to find out whether your PC has other drives, and I'll show you how to find out the capacity of each drive in chapter 5.

To specify the disk drive in a file specification, you always give the drive letter followed by a colon. In figure 3-1, you can see that example 1 specifies the B drive, which is the second diskette drive of a PC. Example 2 specifies the C drive.

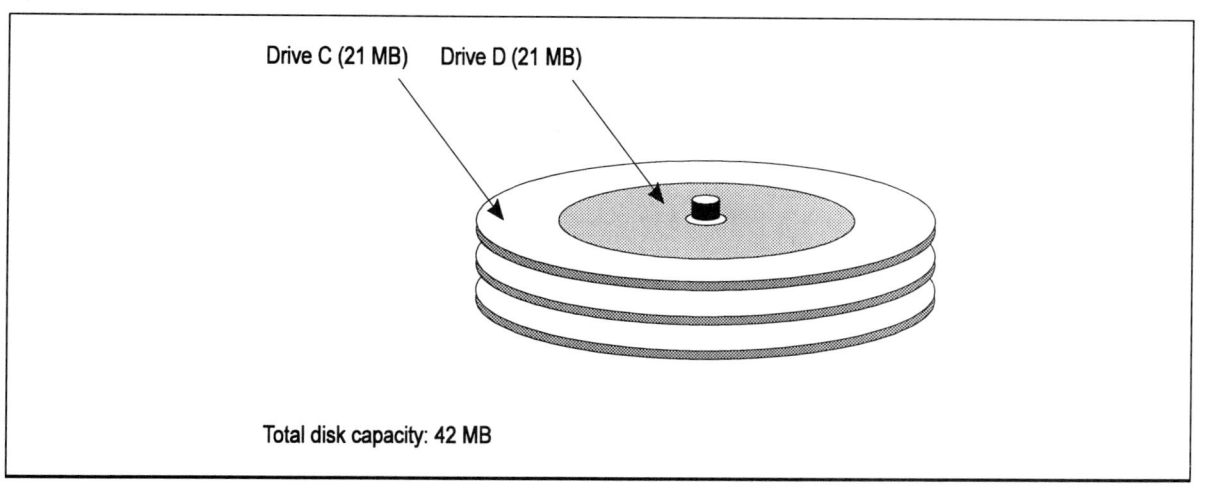

How to identify DOS drives, directories, files, and paths **37**

Drive C (21 MB)   Drive D (21 MB)

Total disk capacity: 42 MB

Figure 3-2   Two drives on one hard disk

The path   In chapter 2, I mentioned that DOS has you organize or group files into *directories*. The 1,368 files on my system, for example, are organized into 39 different directories. These directories are just a special type of file that DOS uses to keep track of the names and locations of the files that are stored on a disk. On a DOS system, every file must be stored in a directory.

Figure 3-3 illustrates a typical directory structure for a hard disk. For each hard disk or diskette, the top-level directory is always called the *root directory*. In this figure, the root directory contains references to five other directories named DOS, UTIL, WP51, 123, and QA. These directories contain the files for DOS, for some utility programs, for *WordPerfect*, for *Lotus 1-2-3*, and for *Q&A*.

Because one directory can contain entries for other directories, the subordinate directories can be referred to as *subdirectories*. In figure 3-3, for instance, the WP51 directory has two subdirectories named MMA and PROJ1, and the 123 directory has two subdirectories named MMA and DOUG. These subdirectories are just like any other directory; they're just subordinate to a higher-level directory. As a result, subdirectories can also be referred to as directories.

The *path* of a file specification identifies the directory for the file. More specifically, the path tells DOS how to get from the root directory to the directory that contains the entry for the file you want. In the directory structure in figure 3-3, the shaded path goes from the root directory to the WP51 directory to the PROJ1 directory.

Below the directory structure in figure 3-3, you can see the specifications for the paths of the eleven directories shown in the structure. The first backslash (\ ) represents the root directory. The level-1 directories are identified by the backslash

38 Chapter 3

The directory structure

```
Root directory ─┬─ DOS
                ├─ UTIL
                ├─ WP51 ──┬─ MMA
                │         └─ PROJ1
                ├─ 123  ──┬─ MMA
                │         └─ DOUG
                └─ QA   ─── MMA
```

The paths for the eleven directories in the structure

```
\
\DOS
\UTIL
\WP51
\WP51\MMA
\WP51\PROJ1
\123
\123\MMA
\123\DOUG
\QA
\QA\MMA
```

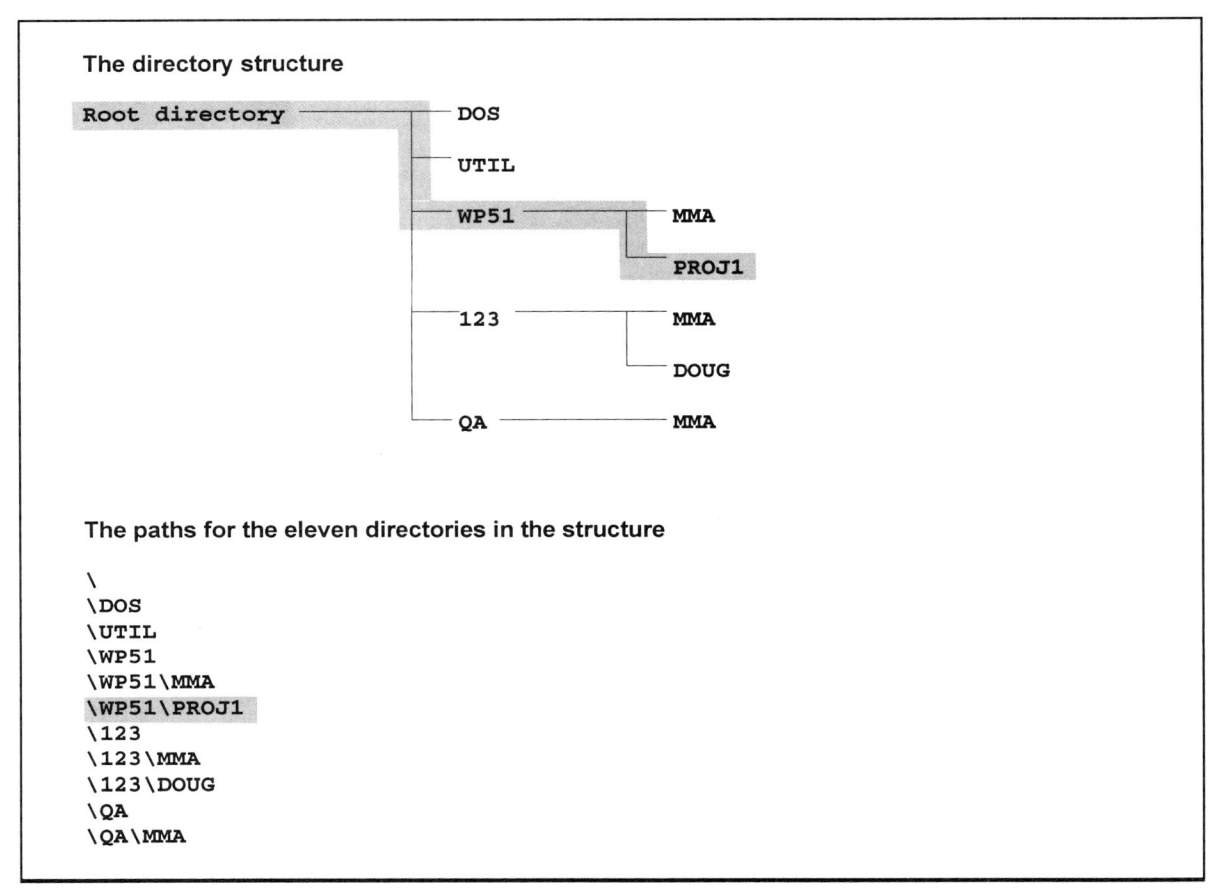

Figure 3-3   The paths for the directories of a hard disk

followed by the directory name, as in \DOS, \UTIL, \WP51, \123, and \QA. And the level-2 directories, or subdirectories, are identified by the backslash, the level-1 directory name, another backslash, and the level-2 directory name, as in \WP51\MMA and \WP51\PROJ1.

Note in figure 3-3 that \PROJ1 isn't a valid path. To be valid, it must be preceded by its directory as in this path: \WP51\PROJ1. Note also that the same subdirectory name can be used within more than one directory. Thus, an MMA directory is subordinate to the WP51 directory, the 123 directory, and the QA directory. For DOS to tell these three directories apart, they must be referred to as \WP51\MMA, \123\MMA, and \QA\MMA.

If you refer back to figure 3-1, you can see that the path in the first example is just the root directory. The path in the second example, however, is the MMA subdirectory within the 123 directory within the root directory.

The file name Whenever you save a new file on a hard disk or a diskette, whether you use DOS or an application program, you need to be able to create a valid *file name* for it. If you refer back to figure 3-1, you can see that a file name can be separated into two parts by a period. The part that comes before the period is required. I'll refer to this as the *name* portion of the file name. The part after the period is optional and is called the *extension*.

Figure 3-4 gives the rules for forming valid file names. If you use just letters and numbers in your names, you don't have to worry about the special characters listed in rule 3. Then, you just have to make sure that the name before the period is from one to eight characters and that the extension is from one to three characters. However, you may find that you can benefit from using characters like the hyphen (-) in file names. So don't completely rule out these other characters. Note also in rule 4 that DOS doesn't care whether you use uppercase or lowercase letters when you specify a file name. Both are treated the same. As you can see in the last two examples of valid file names, you can omit the period if you don't specify an extension.

Although extensions are optional, many programs use them. For instance, *Lotus 1-2-3* uses WK1 or WK3 as the extension for the spreadsheet files you create, and *Microsoft Word* uses DOC as the extension for the document files you create. When you use these programs, though, you don't have to include the extension when you create a file name because the application program adds it automatically.

How the default drive and current directory affect a file specification

Whenever your PC is running, one and only one drive is the DOS *default drive*. In fact, DOS displays the default drive as part of its command prompt. Similarly, one directory is identified as the *current directory* for each drive. When you use DOS, you don't have to specify the drive and path in a file specification if the file is in the current directory on the default drive.

Some application programs work that way too. They assume that the DOS default drive and current directory are intended whenever the drive and path are omitted from a file specification. That can simplify your file specifications considerably because it often means that you only have to specify the file name. *WordPerfect* 5.0, for example, looks for a file in the current directory on the default drive whenever the drive and path are omitted from a file specification.

In contrast, some application programs have their own default drives and directories. When you use one of these programs to save or access files, the DOS default drive and current directory don't matter. Instead, the program looks for a file in its own default directory on its own default drive. For example, *Lotus 1-2-3* and *Q&A* are programs that keep track of their own default directories and drives. Then,

The rules for forming file names

1. The name must consist of from one to eight characters.

2. The extension is optional. If you have one, it must be from one to three characters, and it must be separated from the name by a period as in this example:

    `MONTHSUM.JAN`

3. You can use any character in the name or the extension except for the space and any of these characters:

    `. , < > ? / : ; " ' [ ] | \ + = *`

4. You can use either lowercase or uppercase letters in the name or the extension of a file name, but they are treated the same. As a result, the two names that follow are the same:

    `MONTHSUM.JAN`   and   `monthsum.jan`

Valid file names

```
JAN93.WK1
letter.doc
5-16-92.doc
FEB93RPT
ltr10-21
```

Invalid file names

`JANUARY93.WK1`	(The name is more than 8 characters.)
`JAN:93.WK1`	(The colon is an invalid character.)
`JAN93.TEXT`	(The extension is more than 3 characters.)

Figure 3-4   The rules for forming file names

when the file you want is in the program's default directory on the default drive, you can omit the drive and path from the file specification.

You should also realize that the current directory can affect how DOS interprets the path you use in a file specification. If you begin the path with a backslash, the directory path begins with the root directory. In this case, the current directory has no effect on the path. However, if you do not begin the path with a backslash, the path

```
A1: '1992 Sales Analysis                                              FILES
Enter name of file to save: C:\123\MMA\*.wk1
1QSLS.WK1        2QSLS.WK1        3QSLS.WK1        4QSLS.WK1        92-SLS.WK1
    A           B          C           D          E          F          G          H
1   1992 Sales Analysis
2
3   PRODUCT     JAN        FEB         MAR        APR        MAY        JUN        JUL
4   =================================================================================
5   Product 1   92520      74016       90669.5    120276     118425.6   93445.2    75165.6
6   Product 2   130050     104040      127449     169065     166464     131350.2   101439
7
8
```

Figure 3-5 The drive and directory information that *Lotus 1-2-3* displays when you save or retrieve a file

begins at the current directory rather than the root directory. In that case, you can omit the current directory from the path.

To illustrate, suppose you want to access a file named JAN93.WK1 in the 123\MMA directory. If you use a complete path, like this:

\123\MMA\JAN93.WK1

the path will access the file no matter which directory is current. However, if the 123 directory is current, you can start the path like this:

MMA\JAN93.WK1

Because the first backslash is omitted, DOS looks for the MMA subdirectory in the current directory (123) rather than in the root directory.

Although omitting the current directory information from the path can sometimes save you a few keystrokes, it can also create problems. For example, suppose you believe the 123 directory is current, but in reality the current directory is WKDOCS. Then, when you save a file using the path MMA\JAN93.WK1, the JAN93.WK1 file will be saved in the WKDOCS\MMA directory, not in 123\MMA. As a result, you should give the complete directory path whenever you aren't certain what the current directory is.

How to use file specifications in application programs

Once you understand DOS file specifications, you shouldn't have any trouble using them in your application programs. With some programs, the complete file specifications appear on the screen so you can see the drive and path for each file you save or retrieve. Figure 3-5, for example, shows the screen *Lotus 1-2-3* displays when you save or retrieve a file. As you can see in the second line of the screen, *Lotus* displays the complete drive and path it uses for the file. Then, if the drive and directory are set to the ones you want to use, all you have to do is enter a file name to

---

The prompt for the Save command

    Document to be saved:

The prompt for the Retrieve command

    Document to be retrieved:

Figure 3-6   The *WordPerfect* prompts for the Save and Retrieve commands

retrieve or save a file. If the drive and directory aren't the ones you want, you can set them the way you want them before you retrieve or save a file.

Other programs, however, don't always display complete specifications. When you use the Save or Retrieve commands in *WordPerfect*, for example, you get the prompts shown in figure 3-6. But these prompts don't tell you what the drive and path are. Then, if you enter just the file name for a Save command, that file will be saved in the current directory on the default drive. But if the default drive and directory are not the ones you think they are, you won't know where your file is getting stored.

To avoid problems, you should make sure you know what the defaults are whenever you give an incomplete file specification. If you don't know, you should give the complete specification, which includes the drive and path. Then, the file will always be stored on the drive and directory given by the complete file specification, no matter what the default drive and directory are.

How to use the * wildcard in the file specification for an application program

If you look closely at the file specification in the second line of figure 3-5, you'll see that it contains an asterisk:

    C:\123\MMA*.WK1

This * is one of the two types of *wildcards* that DOS provides. It is called the * *wildcard* (asterisk wildcard), and it represents one or more characters of any kind. As a result, this *Lotus* command displays all the files that have an extension of WK1. Since only spreadsheets have this extension, this command displays all the spreadsheets in the directory, but not any other kinds of files.

Some common forms of file names that contain wildcards are illustrated in figure 3-7. As you can see, *.* refers to files with any name before the period and any extension; *.WK1 refers to files with an extension of WK1; *.DOC refers to files with an extension of DOC; and *. refers to files that don't have an extension. Many application programs use simple wildcard specifications like these.

In chapter 8, you'll learn how to use wildcards in DOS commands. There, you'll learn how to use the * wildcard in more complex forms, and you'll learn how to use

Wildcard example	Meaning
`*.*`	All files (any name, any extension)
`*.WK1`	All files with an extension of WK1
`*.DOC`	All files with an extension of DOC
`*.`	All files without any extension

Figure 3-7 Some common forms of file specifications that contain * wildcards

the ? wildcard. In the meantime, you don't have to use * wildcards at all. You just have to understand what they mean in the specifications displayed by your programs.

If you do change a wildcard specification that is displayed by an application program, you should realize that the function that is going to be performed will be changed accordingly. For example, if you use *WordPerfect's* List command to display the files in a directory, *WordPerfect* gives you a prompt like this that shows the default directory:

```
Dir C:\WP51\PROJ1\*.*
```

If you change the *.* specification to *.DOC and then press the Enter key, *WordPerfect* will list only the files that have an extension of DOC, not all the files in the directory. Sometimes, it makes sense to change a specification in this way so the application program does its function on just those files you specify.

Some perspective on DOS drives, paths, and file names

In the next chapter, you'll see how drives, paths, and file names are used in DOS commands. You'll also realize that a typical DOS system has to keep track of hundreds of files stored in a dozen or more directories. Because directories and files can easily get out of control when you use several application programs, chapter 8 will show you how to manage the directories and files on your system.

Terms

file specification
logical drive
directory
root directory
subdirectory
path

file name
extension
default drive
current directory
wildcard
* wildcard

Chapter 3

Objectives

1. Given the drive, directory, subdirectory, and name for a file, give a complete specification for the file.
2. Given the default drive and current directory for a file and given a complete file specification for the file, give the shortest file specification that will identify the file.

Exercises

1. Give the complete file specification for a file named MMASLS with the extension WK1 that's stored in the WK1 directory on drive D.
2. Give the complete file specification for a file named MMASLS with the extension WK1 that's stored in the MMA directory, which is subordinate to the 123 directory on drive C.
3. Give the complete file specification for a file named REPORT1 (no extension) that's stored in the \DOC\MIKE directory on drive D.
4. Give the complete file specification for a file named REPORT1.DOC that's stored in the directory named MIKE, which is subordinate to the WP51 directory on drive C.
5. The current directory is \WP51 and the current drive is C. What's the shortest file specification that you can use for accessing a file with this specification: C:\WP51\MMA\MONRPT.DOC?
6. The current directory is \WP51 and the current drive is C. What's the shortest file specification that you can use for accessing a file with this specification: C:\123\MMA\MONSLS.WK1?
7. The current directory is \WP51\MMA and the current drive is C. What's the shortest file specification that you can use for accessing a file with this specification: C:\123\MMA\MONSLS.WK1?

Chapter 4

How to use DOS commands to start your application programs

In this chapter, you'll learn how to use DOS commands to start your application programs from the command prompt. You need to know how to do this even if your PC has a shell or a menu that makes it easy for you to start your application programs. Once you understand how to start programs from the command prompt, you will be more in control of your PC.

This chapter starts by showing you how to enter a DOS command. Then, you'll learn how to use four DOS commands to start your application programs. When you complete this chapter, you'll have a better understanding of how DOS works and why you need to know how to use it.

As you read this chapter, you can try the DOS commands on your own PC right after you read about them. Or you can read the entire chapter first and then try the DOS commands using the figures as guidelines. If you would like more direction as you experiment with the commands, you can do the guided exercises at the end of the chapter. As you experiment on your own PC, you'll see how your system varies from the system used for the examples in this book.

What DOS does when you start your PC

DOS is stored on the hard disk of your PC. So to start your system, all you have to do is turn on the monitor and the systems unit. If all of the components of your PC are connected to a surge protector or some other single power source, all you have to do is throw the switch on that unit.

Before you turn the systems unit on, though, you must make sure that you don't have a diskette in drive A and that the door of drive A is open. If drive A contains a diskette, your PC looks for DOS on the diskette instead of the hard disk. Then, if the diskette doesn't have DOS on it, your PC will display an error message. At that time, you can take the diskette out of drive A and restart your systems unit.

When you start your PC, it automatically performs two functions. First, it checks itself to make sure it's working properly. This is called the *self-test*, or *POST (Power-On-Self-Test)*, routine. If anything goes wrong during this test, the PC displays an error message. On most PCs, the self-test takes just a few seconds. On some, though, it takes much longer. During this time, your monitor may look as though nothing is happening. But since you can't do any work on your PC until the self-test is over, you just have to wait.

Second, the PC loads DOS from the C drive of the hard disk. This is called *booting the system*, which comes from the expression "pulling yourself up by your own bootstraps." During this process, DOS loads itself into internal memory and prepares itself to execute your application programs.

The DOS command prompt   As DOS initializes itself, it may display several messages on the monitor. It may also ask you to enter the date and time. Eventually, though, DOS should display either the *command prompt* or a DOS shell. If the DOS shell appears, press the F3 key to exit from the shell and get to the prompt. If some program other than the DOS shell appears, exit from it and get to the prompt. You have to be at the DOS prompt before you can try out the commands presented in this chapter.

In its standard form, the prompt looks like this:

    C>

This prompt displays just the default drive. However, some PCs are set up so the prompt displays the current directory along with the default drive in this form:

    C:\123\MMA>

No matter what the prompt looks like, though, it means that the DOS command processor is waiting for your command.

How to enter and correct a DOS command

To enter a DOS command, you type in the command at the command prompt and press the Enter key. That's all there is to it. On some keyboards, the Enter key is called the Return key. And on other keyboards, the Enter key is marked only with this symbol: (↵). Throughout this book, though, I'll refer to this key as the Enter key, no matter how it's marked on your keyboard.

Although you always have to press the Enter key to enter a command, I won't indicate that in the examples in this book. Instead, I'll just assume you know that you have to press the Enter key after each command. I'll also assume you know that the command always comes right after the (>) symbol in the command prompt. As a result, to enter the command in this example:

    C>dir a:

you type *dir a:* and press the Enter key.

```
                    ┌──────── The keyword, or command name, tells DOS which command you want to use.
                    │  ┌───── The parameters tell DOS which files or directories you want the command to process.
                    │  │  ┌── The switches let you control various aspects of a command's processing.
                    │  │  │
                   dir c: /w
```

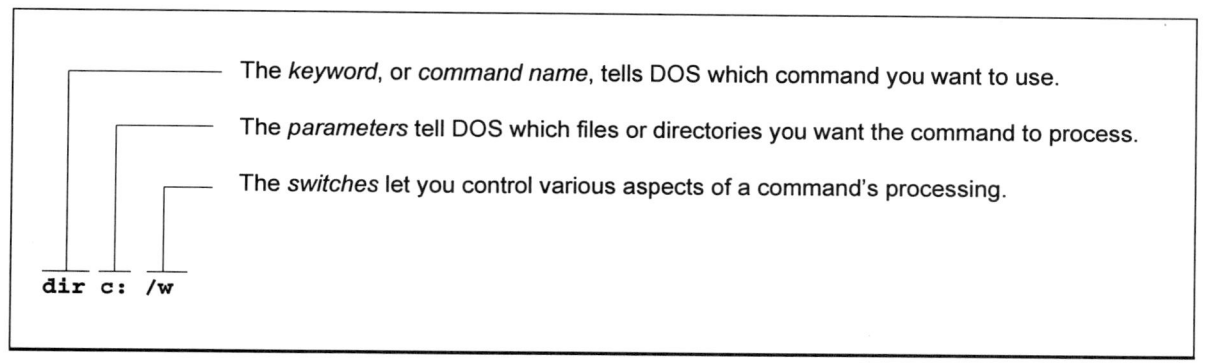

Figure 4-1 The basic format of a DOS command

With few exceptions, DOS doesn't care whether you use uppercase or lowercase letters in commands. So whenever possible, I'll use lowercase letters for them. This will help you tell the commands from the DOS prompts and messages, which are displayed in uppercase letters.

The basic format of a DOS command Figure 4-1 gives the basic format for any DOS command. As you can see, a command can consist of three parts. The first part is the *keyword*. Since it identifies the command, it can also be called the *command name*. The second part consists of one or more *parameters*; they tell DOS what drives, directories, or files the command should work on. The third part consists of one or more *switches*; they tell DOS which variations of the command you want.

As you will see in a moment, some command formats consist of a keyword only; some consist of a keyword and parameters; and some consist of a keyword, parameters, and switches. You'll also see that the parameters and switches are often optional. In figure 4-1, for example, the Directory command contains a keyword (dir), one parameter (c:), and one switch (/w). But Directory commands can also be used without parameters and without switches.

When you enter a command at the command prompt, you must separate the parts of a command so DOS can tell what they are. Normally, you do this by typing in one or more spaces between the parts. So if a command consists of the keyword, a parameter, and a switch, you normally enter it like this:

```
C>dir \dos /w
```

Here, the keyword is *dir*; the parameter is *\dos*; and the switch is */w*.

For the examples in this book, the parts of a command are always separated by one or more spaces. You should realize, though, that DOS also recognizes the backslash and the slash as separators. As a result, DOS interprets this command:

```
dir\dos/w
```

Keystrokes	Function
F3	Retypes all of the characters from the last command you entered.
Ctrl+Pause or Ctrl+C	Interrupts the execution of the command and cancels it.

Figure 4-2 Keystrokes that help you correct, repeat, or cancel a command

as though it were written as:

```
dir \dos /w
```

Nevertheless, it's usually best to separate the parts of a command with spaces. That way, the commands are easier to read, and you can be sure that DOS is going to interpret them the way you mean them.

If you're a little confused at this point by the use of both slashes and backslashes in a command, you're not alone. The use of both leads to typing errors even for experienced DOS users. You use the backslash in parameters and the regular slash in switches. You don't always need a backslash in a parameter, though. And not all switches start with a slash, although most of them do. Yes, this can be confusing.

How to correct, repeat, or cancel a command   If you make a mistake entering a command, but you notice it before you press the Enter key, you can just backspace and correct it. If you press the Enter key before you realize you made a mistake, DOS will display an error message that indicates something is wrong with your command. One way to correct it is to enter the entire command again in its corrected form.

However, you can also use the Function key shown in figure 4-2 to help you correct a command. If a command is lengthy, using the F3 key is usually more efficient than entering the entire command again. If, for example, you press the F3 key after you get an error message from DOS, all of the characters from the last command that you entered appear at the new prompt. Then, you can backspace and make the required corrections. You can also use this key if you want to repeat the execution of a command.

Figure 4-2 also shows the keystroke combinations you can use if you want to cancel a command. First, you can cancel a command by holding down the Ctrl key while you press the Pause, or Break, key. Second, if your keyboard doesn't have a Pause key, you can cancel the command by holding down the Ctrl key while you press the letter *c*.

Name	Format	Function
Prompt	`PROMPT $p$g`	Changes the format of the command prompt so it shows the default drive and current directory.
Change drive	`Drive-spec`	Changes the default drive to the drive specified.
Directory	`DIR [file-spec] [/P] [/W]`	Displays a directory listing for the specified files. The switches let you control how the command displays the listing.
Change directory	`CD [directory]`	Changes the current directory. If the parameter is omitted, this command displays the path of the current directory.

Figure 4-3 Four DOS commands that will help you start your programs

How to use four DOS commands that can help you start your application programs

Figure 4-3 gives the formats and functions for four DOS commands. Using just these commands, you'll be able to start all your application programs from the command prompt. Although you won't use the Prompt command much, it will help you use the other three commands. And you'll use the other three commands frequently.

In the formats in figure 4-3, I've used uppercase letters for the keyword and switches for each command, and I've used lowercase letters for the parameters. If the parameters or switches are optional, I've enclosed them in brackets [ ]. I've also used the abbreviation *spec* for the word *specification*. This is the notation that's used in most DOS manuals, and it's the one that's used throughout this book.

To use the commands in figure 4-3, you start by entering the keyword. Next, if the command requires parameters or switches, you enter them, making sure that you use one or more spaces to separate the parts of the command. Then, when you've got the command the way you want it, you press the Enter key so DOS will execute it.

When you enter a command, I recommend that you use lowercase letters for all its parts. Because DOS treats uppercase and lowercase letters as equals, this won't affect your commands in any way. But it will make it easier for you to enter commands.

The Prompt command When the command prompt is in its standard form (C>), it tells you what the default drive is, but it doesn't tell you what the current directory is. To change the form of the prompt so it does tell you what the current directory is, you use the Prompt command with the parameter shown in figure 4-3: pg.

```
C>prompt $p$g

C:\>a:

A:\>b:

B:\>d:

D:\>e:
Invalid drive specification

D:\>
```

Figure 4-4 The Prompt command and four examples of the Change-drive command

The use of this command is illustrated in the first line of figure 4-4 (I've shaded the commands in this figure so you can see the command prompts more easily). After the Prompt command is executed, the prompt is changed to show that the current directory for the C drive is the root directory (C:\>). Then, if the current directory is changed to the DOS directory, the prompt will look like this:

`C:\DOS>`

This enhanced form of the prompt stays in effect until you turn your PC off.

Most likely, your PC is already set up to display the current drive and directory in the command prompt. If so, you shouldn't ever have to use the Prompt command. But if your PC isn't set up this way, you should always use the Prompt command to set your prompt to the enhanced form when you start a DOS session. Then, in chapter 6, you can learn how to set up your PC so it starts the way you want it to. After that, you won't have to use the Prompt command any more.

The Change-drive command To use the Change-drive command, you just type the letter of the drive that you want as the default drive followed by a colon. When you press the Enter key, DOS changes the default drive and displays the new default drive in the command prompt. To illustrate, the first three Change-drive commands in figure 4-4 change the drive from C to A, from A to B, and from B to D.

To find out how many drives your hard disk is divided into, you can issue the Change-drive command to change from the C drive to the D drive. If DOS doesn't display a message that tells you there is no D drive, you can continue with the E, F, and G drives until you get a message that says there's no such drive. In figure 4-4, the last Change-drive command tries to change the default drive to the E drive, but DOS displays an error message that says that the drive doesn't exist. As a result, you know that the C and D drives are the only valid drives for the hard disk.

```
C:\>dir

 Volume in drive C is HD42

 Volume Serial Number is 1983-5D30
 Directory of C:\


DOS              <DIR>        08-05-92   2:55p
COMMAND    COM         53022  10-26-92   6:00a
CONFIG     SYS           135  12-03-92  11:41a
QA4              <DIR>        12-03-92   1:06p
AUTOEXEC   BAT            91  12-04-92   1:19p
WP51             <DIR>        12-03-92  12:34p
123              <DIR>        12-03-92   1:22p
UTIL             <DIR>        12-03-92   2:04p
DATA             <DIR>        12-03-92   2:08p
        9 File(s)         53277 bytes
                       24786944 bytes free

C:\>
```

Figure 4-5   The operation of the Directory command for the root directory on the C drive

If you're using DOS 6.0 and DoubleSpace has been installed, you'll also have an additional drive letter that's assigned to the DoubleSpace *host volume*. This host volume is used by DoubleSpace to enable data compression, so you shouldn't use it to store files. In most cases, the host volume is assigned drive letter H.

The Directory command   The Directory command displays a directory listing of the directory or file you specify in the file specification parameter. If you enter the command without a file specification, DOS displays a listing of the current directory on the default drive. As a result, the Directory command in figure 4-5 displays the root directory for the C drive. This directory listing consists of five entries for each file. From left to right, they are the name of the file, the file extension, the size of the file in bytes, the date the file was last changed, and the time the file was last changed.

Note that this directory listing doesn't include the period that separates the name portion of the file name from the extension. Instead, it lists the name portion in the first column of the listing and the extension in the second column. So the root directory that's listed in figure 4-5 contains three files named

    COMMAND.COM
    CONFIG.SYS
    AUTOEXEC.BAT

To read a directory listing properly, you must mentally convert the file names in the listing to this form.

Incidentally, the three files that are listed in figure 4-5 affect the operation of your PC, so you shouldn't delete them. The COMMAND.COM file contains the DOS command processor and other DOS commands that are stored in internal memory, so it's critical to the operation of your system. Similarly, the CONFIG.SYS file contains information about your system that is required for it to function properly. And the AUTOEXEC.BAT file tells your system what commands to execute as part of its start-up procedure. The CONFIG.SYS and AUTOEXEC.BAT files must be stored in the root directory of the C drive (if you don't find an AUTOEXEC.BAT file there, I'll show you how to create one in chapter 6). And the COMMAND.COM file is usually stored in the root directory, too.

The directory listing in figure 4-5 also includes six directories as indicated by <DIR> in the column that gives the file size. Although a directory name can have an extension, most don't. Remember, though, a directory is just a special type of file that contains entries for other files.

If you look at the format for the Directory command in figure 4-6, you can see two of the switches that are available for it. The independent operation of these switches is illustrated in figure 4-6, but you can use both of these switches in a single Directory command. In figure 4-6, I've highlighted the commands to distinguish them from the command output. As you can see, the /W switch causes DOS to display a directory in a wide format with only the name and extension for each file. And the /P switch causes DOS to pause when the screen is filled. Then, when you press any key on the keyboard, the Directory command displays the next screen full of entries and pauses again. If you don't use this switch for a directory that fills more than one screen, the directory entries scroll by so fast you can't read them, and the scrolling continues until the last screen of entries is displayed.

If you look again at the directory displays in figure 4-6, you can see that they start with entries for two directories (in DOS 5.0 and later versions, the entries for directories are bracketed when the /W switch is used). The first directory is designated by a single period (.), and the second directory is designated by two periods (..). You'll always see these entries for a directory that isn't the root directory because DOS uses them to keep track of where it is in the directory structure. The single period represents an entry for the current directory, and the double period represents an entry for the parent directory.

The *parent directory* is the directory that immediately precedes the current directory in its path. In figure 4-6, the parent directory for the WP51 directory is the root directory on drive C. I mention this because you'll sometimes see the dots and the term *parent directory* when you're using an application program.

The Change-directory command   The Change-directory command lets you change the current directory, as illustrated in figure 4-7. Here, you can see the results of each command by noticing how the DOS command prompt changes (I've shaded the commands so the changes are more apparent). The first command changes the

How to use DOS commands to start your application programs 53

The format of the Directory command

```
DIR [file-spec] [/P] [/W]
```

The /W switch displays the directory listing in a wide format

```
C:\>dir \wp51 /w

 Volume in drive C is HD42
 Volume Serial Number is 1983-5D30
 Directory of  C:\WP51

[.]             [..]            INSTALL.EXE     STANDARD.CRS    WP.LRS
CONVERT.EXE     GRAPHCNV.EXE    GRAB.COM        MACROCNV.EXE    WPINFO.EXE
CURSOR.COM      FIXBIOS.COM     SPELL.EXE       CHARACTR.DOC    WP51-386.PIF
WP51-286.PIF    WP-PIF.DVP      NWPSETUP.EXE    WPHELP.FIL      ALTRNAT.WPK
MACROS.WPK      ENHANCED.WPK    SHORTCUT.WPK    EQUATION.WPK    LABELS.WPM
CODES.WPM       REVEALBX.WPM    REVEALCO.WPM    REVEALTX.WPM    FOOTEND.WPM
ENDFOOT.WPM     INLINE.WPM      LIBRARY.STY     WP.EXE          PRINTER.TST
WP.FIL          KEYS.MRS        WP.MRS          WPSMALL.DRS     STANDARD.IRS
STANDARD.PRS    STANDARD.VRS    WP.QRS          WP{WP}US.LEX    WP{WP}.SPW
WP{WP}US.HYC    WP{WP}US.THS    EGA512.FRS      EGAITAL.FRS     EGASMC.FRS
EGAUND.FRS      HRF12.FRS       HRF6.FRS        VGAUND.FRS      VGASMC.FRS
VGAITAL.FRS     VGA512.FRS      8514A.VRS       ATI.VRS         GENIUS.VRS
INCOLOR.VRS     PARADISE.VRS    VIDEO7.VRS      WP.DRS          WPDM1.ALL
WPHP1.ALL       WP51.INS        WP{WP}US.LCN    EPFX1050.PRS    WP{WP}.SET
EPLQ850.PRS     HPLASEII.PRS
       72 file(s)     3463870 bytes
                     24778752 bytes free
```

The /P switch pauses the directory listing after it fills the screen

```
C:\>dir \wp51 /p

 Volume in drive C is HD42
 Volume Serial Number is 1983-5D30
 Directory of C:\WP51

.              <DIR>       12-03-92   12:34p
..             <DIR>       12-03-92   12:34p
INSTALL   EXE     55808   02-07-90   12:00p
STANDARD  CRS      2555   02-07-90   12:00p
WP        LRS     18971   02-07-90   12:00p
CONVERT   EXE    109049   02-07-90   12:00p
GRAPHCNV  EXE    111104   02-07-90   12:00p
GRAB      COM     16450   02-07-90   12:00p
MACROCNV  EXE     26063   02-07-90   12:00p
WPINFO    EXE      8704   02-07-90   12:00p
CURSOR    COM      1452   02-07-90   12:00p
FIXBIOS   COM        50   02-07-90   12:00p
SPELL     EXE     55808   02-07-90   12:00p
CHARACTR  DOC     43029   02-07-90   12:00p
WP51-386  PIF       369   02-07-90   12:00p
WP51-286  PIF       369   02-07-90   12:00p
WP-PIF    DVP       416   02-07-90   12:00p
NWPSETUP  EXE     28672   02-07-90   12:00p
WPHELP    FIL    188832   02-07-90   12:00p
Press any key to continue . . .
```

Figure 4-6   How the /W and /P switches of the Directory command affect the screen display

Chapter 4

The format of the Change-directory command

```
CD [directory]
```

Examples

```
C:\>cd \dos

C:\DOS>cd \

C:\>cd \dos

C:\DOS>cd \wp51

C:\WP51>cd mma

C:\WP51\MMA>cd \123\mma

C:\123\MMA>
```

Figure 4-7 The operation of the Change-directory command

current directory from the root directory to the DOS directory, so the command prompt changes from C:\> to C:\DOS>. The second command changes the current directory back to the root directory. And so on.

When you start the parameter of a Change-directory command with a backslash, DOS assumes that your specification starts with the root directory. When you start the parameter without a backslash, DOS assumes that the parameter is a subdirectory contained within the current directory, as illustrated by the fifth command in figure 4-7. Here, this command:

```
cd mma
```

changes the current directory from C:\WP51 to C:\WP51\MMA.

How to start an application program from the DOS command prompt

With the four commands I've just presented, you should be able to start any application program from the command prompt if you know what directory the program is in and what the name of the program is. There are two methods for doing this. The first one works for all versions of DOS; the second one works for all versions starting with version 3.0.

Method 1: Set the default drive and current directory to the program directory before issuing the command name
When you talk about a word processing or spreadsheet program, it sounds like you're talking about a single program file. However, if you use the Directory command to display the files in the directory for an application program, you'll see that a typical application program consists of many files. For instance, if you look back at figure 4-6, you'll see that my directory for *WordPerfect* 5.1 contains 72 files. Many of these files contain supporting data that *WordPerfect* uses, like tables, dictionaries, and thesauruses. But eleven of the files are *command files*. Command files always have file names with an extension of COM or EXE, and DOS can execute them as commands.

To start an application program, you need to know the name of the command file that's designed to start the program. Then, you enter this name *without* the COM or EXE extension to start the program. For instance, the name of the starting command file for *WordPerfect* is WP.EXE, so WP is the command name that starts the program. The name of the starting command file for *Lotus 1-2-3* is 123.EXE, so 123 is the command name that starts the program. Although a program may consist of more than one command file, only one of the files is designed to start the program.

If you don't know the name of the command file that starts the program, you can look in its program manual to get the correct name. Otherwise, you can use the Directory command to list the files in the directory. If you look for files with COM and EXE extensions, you can usually figure out which file is the one that is designed to start the program. To help you in your search, you can use wildcard file specifications in the Directory command, like this:

```
dir *.exe
dir *.com
```

Then, the Directory command will list only the files with the extension you specify.

Before you execute the starting command file, though, you need to change the current directory to the one that contains the program's files. This is illustrated in figure 4-8, which shows you how to start three different programs: *WordPerfect*, *Lotus 1-2-3*, and *Q&A*. In all three examples, the first command is a Change-directory command that sets the current directory to the one that contains the program. The second command is the command name that starts the program. You can start programs in other ways, but this procedure is the only one that works on all systems for all programs.

Of course, these examples assume that all program directories are on the C drive. If they aren't, you have to use a three-step procedure for starting a program from the command prompt. First, use the Change-drive command to change the default drive to the one that contains the program directory you want. Second, use the Change-directory command to change the current directory to the program directory. Third, enter the name of the command file that starts the program.

Method 2: Enter the program's path along with the command name (DOS 3.0 or later)
If you're using a version of DOS that's 3.0 or later, you can

Example 1:	Starting *WordPerfect* 5.1 from the WP51 directory with the command name WP
	`C:\>cd \wp51` `C:\WP51>wp`
Example 2:	Starting *Lotus 1-2-3* from the 123 directory with the command name 123
	`C:\WP51>cd \123` `C:\123>123`
Example 3:	Starting *Q&A* from the QA4 directory with the command name QA
	`C:\123>cd \qa4` `C:\QA4>qa`

Figure 4-8 How to start an application program when you know its directory and name

code a program's path along with its command name. If, for example, *WordPerfect* is in the WP51 directory on the C drive, you can start it with this command:

`c:\wp51\wp`

This command tells DOS to look in the WP51 directory on the C drive for a command file named WP.COM or WP.EXE.

If the command name and the directory name are the same, the command you enter looks a bit peculiar. If, for example, the command named WORD is stored in a directory named WORD, the command to execute the program looks like this:

`c:\word\word`

This just tells DOS to execute the command file named WORD that is stored in the WORD directory on the C drive.

Before you try to start a program this way, you should realize that it won't work with all application programs. For instance, some releases of *Lotus 1-2-3* require that the current directory be set to the program directory before the program is run. That way, the program can find the files it requires for operation. As a result, you have to use the method in figure 4-8 for starting programs like these.

How to start a program when you don't know its directory

If you're working on someone else's PC or you're trying to start a program that you use infrequently, you may not remember the name of the directory it's in. Usually, though, you'll be able to start the program by using the commands you've learned in this chapter.

How to use DOS commands to start your application programs   **57**

```
Example 1:    C:\>promp $p$g
              Bad command or file name

Example 2:    C:\>dir wp.exe
              Volume in drive C is HD42
              Volume Serial Number is 1983-5D30
              Directory of C:\

              File not found

Example 3:    C:\>dir /d
              Invalid switch -   d

Example 4:    C:\>a:
              Not ready reading drive A
              Abort, Retry, Fail? f
              Current drive is no longer valid>c:

              C:\>
```

Figure 4-9   The most common DOS error messages as they appear on your screen

To find the directory for a program, you can start by using the Directory command to display the root directory on the C drive. Often, this directory will contain the program directories for the system, and you'll be able to figure out which directory contains the program you're trying to start. If the root directory on the C drive doesn't contain the directory you're looking for, you can display the root directories of the other drives. One of these directories ought to contain the directory you're looking for.

Once you know the drive and path of the program directory, you can start the program in three steps or less. First, use the Change-drive command to set the default drive to the one that contains the program directory. Second, use the Change-directory command to set the current directory to the program directory. Third, enter the name of the command file that is designed to start the program.

How to handle the most common DOS error messages

If you've been trying the commands on your own system as you've read this chapter, you've probably encountered one or more *DOS error messages*. Some of the ones you'll see most often are shown in figure 4-9.

As you can see in the first example, if you spell the keyword of a command wrong, DOS will tell you that you've used a "bad command or file name." However, DOS also displays this message when it can't find the command file you tried to execute. If, for example, you haven't changed the current directory to the program directory before you issue the command for starting an application program, you'll usually get this error message.

The second example shows you the message you get if DOS can't find the file you've specified within a command: "File not found." Here, DOS looks for a file named WP.EXE in the current directory, but none exists. That may be because the file's been deleted somehow. But sometimes you get this message because you've entered the file name wrong. And sometimes you get it because you didn't give a complete file specification and the file isn't in the current directory of the default drive. Then, to correct the problem, all you have to do is give a complete specification.

If you use a parameter or switch that isn't valid for a command, DOS displays this message: "Invalid parameter" or "Invalid switch," as shown in the third example. If you're using DOS 4.0 or later, the message tells you which parameter or switch is invalid; for earlier versions of DOS, you have to check the format of the command to find out what's wrong. Then, to correct the problem, you just reissue the command in its proper form. Often, you get this message when you accidentally use a slash (/) instead of a backslash (\) within a path specification.

The last message in figure 4-9 is this:

Not ready reading drive A
Abort, Retry, Fail?

You get this message when you specify diskette drive A, but that drive doesn't contain a diskette or the door for that drive isn't closed. Often, you get this message because you forgot to put the diskette in drive A before you issued a command that requires the drive. Then, to correct the problem, you put the diskette in the drive, close the door, and enter the letter *r* for Retry.

If you get that error message because you specified drive A by accident, you just enter the letter *f* for Fail. Then, DOS may display this error message as shown in figure 4-9:

Current drive is no longer valid>

This means that DOS no longer knows what its default drive should be. To correct this problem, you just enter a drive specification like C: to reset the default drive.

Although DOS has many other error messages, these are the most common ones. If DOS displays a message you're not familiar with, you can usually figure out what's wrong by carefully inspecting the command you entered. Otherwise, you can look in the back of your DOS manual for a summary of all of the DOS error messages. This summary should tell you how to respond to each message.

Format	Example	DOS 5.0 function	DOS 6.0 function
`HELP`	`C:\>help`	Displays a brief summary of the function of each DOS command.	Goes into the full-screen Help feature; displays a list of DOS 6.0 commands so you can choose the one you want to know about.
`HELP command-name`	`C:\>help dir`	Displays the syntax for the named command with a brief explanation of each syntax element.	Goes into the full-screen Help feature and displays Help information for the named command.
`Command-name /?`	`C:\>dir /?`	Displays the syntax for the named command with a brief explanation of each syntax element.	Displays brief Help information for the command at the command prompt (like the Help information given by the DOS 5.0 Help feature).

Figure 4-10 Three ways to use the DOS 5.0 and DOS 6.0 Help features

How to use the DOS 5.0 and 6.0 Help features

Unlike earlier versions of DOS, versions 5.0 and 6.0 both provide *Help features* that you can use to get information about the format and switches of a command. When you use these features, the information is displayed on the screen, so you don't have to look it up anywhere else.

Figure 4-10 summarizes the three ways that you can get Help information for a command in either DOS 5.0 or DOS 6.0. As you can tell from this figure, the two versions of the Help feature are very different. So I'll present them one at a time. You only have to read about the feature that's available on your PC.

The DOS 5.0 Help feature   The Help information provided by DOS 5.0 is limited. If you enter just the command name, *help*, DOS 5.0 displays a brief summary of the function of each DOS command. If you enter the word *help* followed by another command name, DOS 5.0 displays the Help information for that command. This includes the command format and a one- or two-line explanation of each element in the format. And if you enter the name of the command that you want information for followed by /?, you get the same Help information that you get when you enter *help* followed by the command name.

The DOS 5.0 Help feature may save you from looking up commands in the DOS reference manual when you're already familiar with the command and you just need

60   Chapter 4

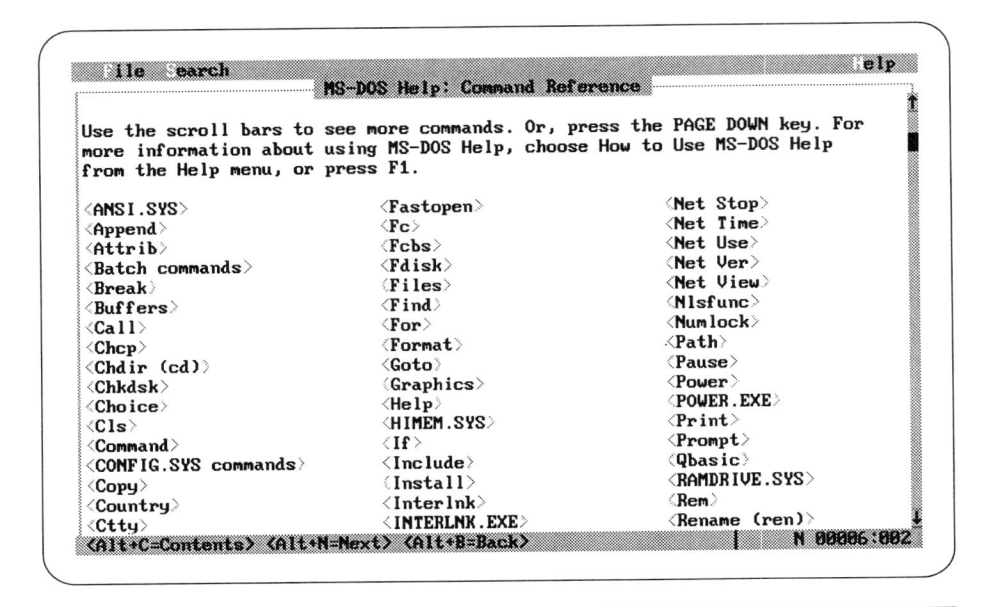

```
┌─────────────────────────────────────────────────────────────────────┐
│ File  Search                                                   Help │
│ ┌─────────────────── MS-DOS Help: Command Reference ──────────────┐ │
│ │ Use the scroll bars to see more commands. Or, press the PAGE DOWN key. For │
│ │ more information about using MS-DOS Help, choose How to Use MS-DOS Help    │
│ │ from the Help menu, or press F1.                                           │
│ │                                                                            │
│ │ <ANSI.SYS>              <Fastopen>              <Net Stop>                 │
│ │ <Append>                <Fc>                    <Net Time>                 │
│ │ <Attrib>                <Fcbs>                  <Net Use>                  │
│ │ <Batch commands>        <Fdisk>                 <Net Ver>                  │
│ │ <Break>                 <Files>                 <Net View>                 │
│ │ <Buffers>               <Find>                  <Nlsfunc>                  │
│ │ <Call>                  <For>                   <Numlock>                  │
│ │ <Chcp>                  <Format>                <Path>                     │
│ │ <Chdir (cd)>            <Goto>                  <Pause>                    │
│ │ <Chkdsk>                <Graphics>              <Power>                    │
│ │ <Choice>                <Help>                  <POWER.EXE>                │
│ │ <Cls>                   <HIMEM.SYS>             <Print>                    │
│ │ <Command>               <If>                    <Prompt>                   │
│ │ <CONFIG.SYS commands>   <Include>               <Qbasic>                   │
│ │ <Copy>                  <Install>               <RAMDRIVE.SYS>             │
│ │ <Country>               <Interlnk>              <Rem>                      │
│ │ <Ctty>                  <INTERLNK.EXE>          <Rename (ren)>             │
│ │ <Alt+C=Contents> <Alt+N=Next> <Alt+B=Back>           N 00006:002           │
│ └────────────────────────────────────────────────────────────────┘ │
└─────────────────────────────────────────────────────────────────────┘
```

Figure 4-11   The opening screen of DOS 6.0's full-screen Help feature, MS-DOS Help

to be reminded of its syntax. But if you need more detailed information about what the command does, you'll probably have to use the reference manual.

The DOS 6.0 Help feature   In contrast to the DOS 5.0 Help feature, the DOS 6.0 Help feature provides a complete, easy-to-use command reference. So complete, in fact, that DOS 6.0 doesn't come with a printed command reference. So unless you use only a few simple DOS commands that you have memorized, I think you'll use this Help feature often.

To access Help information in DOS 6.0, you can use the same three formats that you use in DOS 5.0, as shown in figure 4-10. But only the third format, a command name followed by /?, works the same as in DOS 5.0. It displays the command syntax and a brief explanation of each syntax element. In contrast, the other two formats take you into DOS 6.0's full-screen Help feature, called MS-DOS Help.

If you enter the command name, *help*, by itself, DOS 6.0 displays a screen like the one in figure 4-11. As you can see, this is a table of contents for all the DOS 6.0 commands. To move the cursor around within this table of contents, you use the cursor control keys, the Page-up and Page-down keys, and the Tab key. For example, if you want to see what additional commands there are, you can use the Down arrow key or the Page-down key to display another screenful of entries. To move from one entry to another, you can use the Tab key to move the cursor forward one entry, and the Shift+Tab key combination to move back to the previous entry.

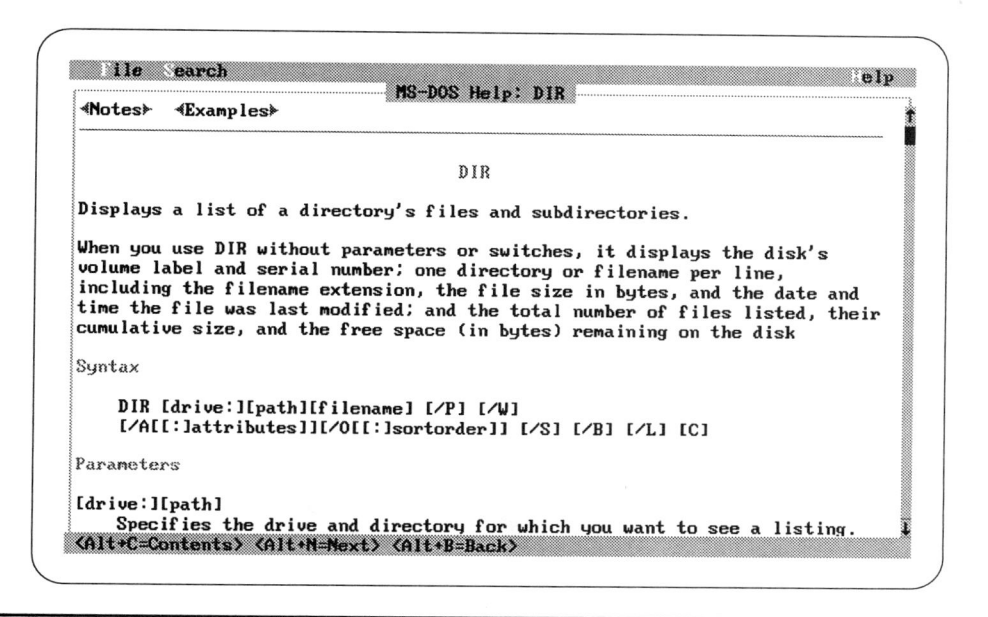

```
┌─────────────────────────────────────────────────────────────┐
│ ▓File ▓Search                                         ▓elp │
│                      MS-DOS Help: DIR                       │
│  ◄Notes► ◄Examples►                                        ↑│
│                                                            ▓│
│                           DIR                               │
│  Displays a list of a directory's files and subdirectories. │
│                                                             │
│  When you use DIR without parameters or switches, it displays the disk's│
│  volume label and serial number; one directory or filename per line,│
│  including the filename extension, the file size in bytes, and the date and│
│  time the file was last modified; and the total number of files listed, their│
│  cumulative size, and the free space (in bytes) remaining on the disk│
│                                                             │
│  Syntax                                                     │
│                                                             │
│     DIR [drive:][path][filename] [/P] [/W]                  │
│     [/A[[:]attributes]][/O[[:]sortorder]] [/S] [/B] [/L] [C]│
│                                                             │
│  Parameters                                                 │
│                                                             │
│  [drive:][path]                                             │
│     Specifies the drive and directory for which you want to see a listing.↓│
│  <Alt+C=Contents> <Alt+N=Next> <Alt+B=Back>                 │
└─────────────────────────────────────────────────────────────┘
```

Figure 4-12   The first screen of syntax information for the Directory command

To get Help information on a specific command, you move the cursor to the command name and press the Enter key. Then, DOS 6.0 displays extensive information on the syntax of the command. For example, figure 4-12 shows the first syntax screen for the Directory command. Again, you can use the Arrow keys and the Page-up and Page-down keys to scroll through this information and find out what you need to know. You can also move the cursor to the "Notes" or "Examples" options that appear near the top of the screen. Then, when you press the Enter key, MS-DOS Help displays additional information on how to use the command.

At any point, if you want to go back to the table of contents, you can press the Alt+C key combination. If you want to move back through the screens you've already looked at, one at a time, you can press the Alt+B key combination. And if you want to know more about how MS-DOS Help works, you can press the F1 key.

At the top of the screens in figures 4-11 and 4-12, you can see that MS-DOS Help provides you with three *menus*: File, Search, and Help. These menus allow you to do certain tasks within MS-DOS Help. Figure 4-13, for example, shows the options on the File menu. Here, the Print option allows you to get a printed copy of Help information; and the Exit option lets you exit MS-DOS Help and return to the command prompt.

To select a menu option, you press the Alt key to activate the menu system. Then, you can continue in one of two ways. You can move the cursor to the menu you

62   Chapter 4

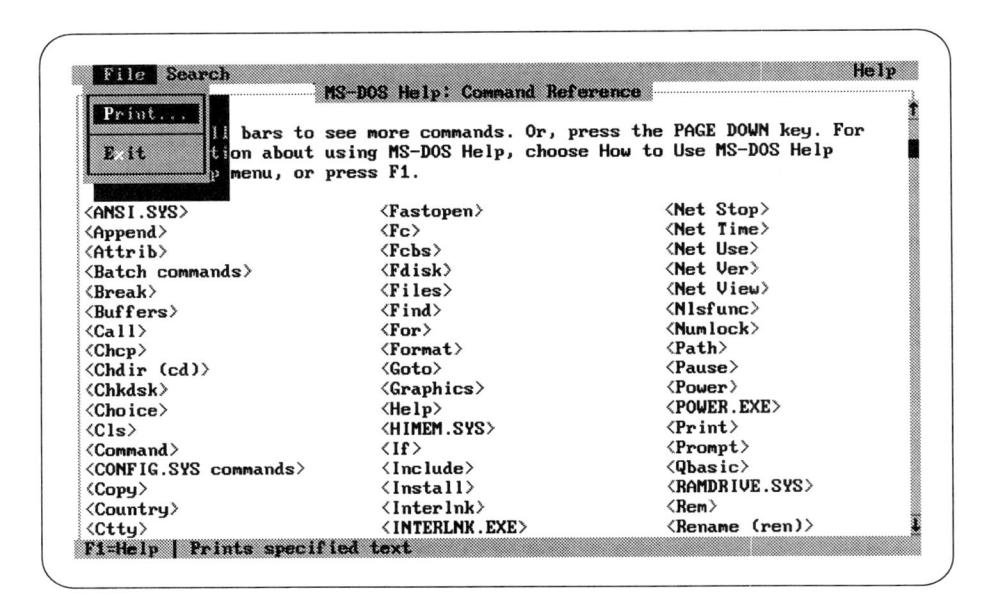

```
┌─────────────────────────────────────────────────────────────────────┐
│  File  Search                                                  Help │
│  ┌──────────┐───── MS-DOS Help: Command Reference ─────────────     │
│  │ Print... │                                                       │
│  │          │  bars to see more commands. Or, press the PAGE DOWN key. For
│  │ Exit     │  on about using MS-DOS Help, choose How to Use MS-DOS Help
│  │          │  menu, or press F1.
│  └──────────┘
│    <ANSI.SYS>              <Fastopen>              <Net Stop>
│    <Append>                <Fc>                    <Net Time>
│    <Attrib>                <Fcbs>                  <Net Use>
│    <Batch commands>        <Fdisk>                 <Net Ver>
│    <Break>                 <Files>                 <Net View>
│    <Buffers>               <Find>                  <Nlsfunc>
│    <Call>                  <For>                   <Numlock>
│    <Chcp>                  <Format>                <Path>
│    <Chdir (cd)>            <Goto>                  <Pause>
│    <Chkdsk>                <Graphics>              <Power>
│    <Choice>                <Help>                  <POWER.EXE>
│    <Cls>                   <HIMEM.SYS>             <Print>
│    <Command>               <If>                    <Prompt>
│    <CONFIG.SYS commands>   <Include>               <Qbasic>
│    <Copy>                  <Install>               <RAMDRIVE.SYS>
│    <Country>               <Interlnk>              <Rem>
│    <Ctty>                  <INTERLNK.EXE>          <Rename (ren)>
│  F1=Help | Prints specified text
└─────────────────────────────────────────────────────────────────────┘
```

Figure 4-13   The File menu of MS-DOS Help

want, press the Enter key to open the menu, move the cursor to the menu command you want, and press the Enter key to start the command. Or, you can press the letter that's highlighted in the menu name to open the menu, and then press the letter that's highlighted in the menu command to start the command.

The second Help command format in figure 4-10 also activates MS-DOS Help. But instead of taking you to the table of contents, it takes you directly to the first syntax screen for the command you specify. For example, if you enter this command at the command prompt:

    help dir

DOS 6.0 will take you to the screen shown in figure 4-12. At this point, you can move through MS-DOS Help just as if you had entered at the table of contents screen.

If you have a mouse attached to your PC, you can use it instead of the keyboard to move through MS-DOS Help and to execute menu commands. But because you won't need the mouse for anything else for a while, I'm not going to show you how to use it right now; I want you to be able to focus on DOS commands for the time being. Later on, when you learn how to use the DOS 6.0 Backup utility and shell in chapters 11 and 12, I'll explain all the details of using a mouse. (If you already know how to use a mouse, you'll be able to use it for MS-DOS Help without any problems.)

How to shut down your PC

In general, you shouldn't turn your PC off when you're using an application program. If you do, you'll lose the work that is stored in internal memory. Instead, you should save your work and exit properly from the application program. Then, when DOS displays the command prompt, you can turn off your PC. It's also a good idea to remove diskettes from the diskette drives before you turn your system off, but that isn't essential.

How to restart your PC without turning it off and on

Occasionally, you may need to restart your PC because you've gotten hung up by a software or hardware problem. To do that, you can shut down your PC as described above and then turn it on again. Or you can press this key combination: Ctrl+Alt+Delete. This means to press the Delete key while holding down both the Ctrl and Alt keys. This boots DOS, but doesn't force the PC to go through its self-test again.

If you enter this key combination when you're in the middle of an application program, be aware that you'll probably lose all the work you've done since the last time you saved the document to the hard disk or to a diskette. As a result, you should think of the Ctrl+Alt+Delete key combination as a panic switch. Use it only when your PC has gone haywire because of a software or hardware problem. (In chapter 6, I'll show you a specific instance in which this key combination comes in handy.)

Some perspective on DOS

The hardest part about learning to use DOS is getting started. Before you can do much of anything, you need to know how to enter a command, what the command formats are, and how to handle DOS error messages.

But now that you've seen how four of the DOS commands work, you should have a better idea of why you need to learn DOS. First, if your PC doesn't have a shell that you use for starting your programs, you have to start your application programs from the command prompt. Second, even if your PC does have a shell, you need to be able to start programs from the command prompt when you add new programs to your system.

Perhaps the most important reason for learning DOS, though, is that it helps you understand your system. As much as the software developers would like you to believe that you can use an application program without any knowledge of DOS, that just isn't true. If you want to have more control over your PC, you need to know more about DOS.

64 Chapter 4

Terms

self-test
POST (Power-On-Self-Test)
booting the system
command prompt
keyword
command name
parameter

switch
host volume
parent directory
command file
DOS error message
Help feature
menu

Objectives

1. Given the directory name and the command name for a program, start the program from the command prompt.

2. Given a drive and directory, use a DOS command to display a list of the files in the directory.

Exercises

These exercises are designed to step you through the commands and procedures presented in this chapter. The practice you get from these exercises will form the foundation for using the other DOS commands and procedures presented in the rest of this book. So take your time doing these exercises, and work carefully. What you learn here will start you on your way to becoming a competent and assured DOS user.

1. When you start your PC, it will display the command prompt, the first screen of a shell program, a menu program, or perhaps an application program. You need to be at the command prompt to start these exercises, so exit from whatever appears on the screen until the command prompt is displayed. To exit from the DOS shell, for example, you can press the F3 key. If you can't figure out how to get to the DOS command prompt, ask for help.

2. When the command prompt is displayed, look it over closely. It should look like one of these prompts:

    `C>` or `C:\>`

    If your prompt looks like the second one, you can skip to the next exercise. But if it looks like the first one, you can improve the prompt so that it includes the current directory. To do this, you issue a Prompt command like the first command in figure 4-4. So do this now by typing this command at the command prompt:

    `prompt $p$g`

    Then, press the Enter key. After the command is executed, the command prompt should look like the second one above. This prompt includes the backslash, which means that the current directory is the root directory on the C drive. (By the way, if your prompt looked like the second prompt above when you started your PC, the Prompt command won't change your prompt's appearance.)

3. To see what other hard drives are on your PC, enter a Change-drive command to change from the C drive to the D drive. To do that, type

    `d:`

    at the command prompt and press the Enter key. If your PC doesn't have a D drive, you will get this error message:

    `Invalid drive specification`
    `C:\>`

    This means that your PC has one hard drive, the C drive. However, if you have a D drive, the prompt will be changed to indicate that the D drive is the current drive. Then, see if your PC has other hard drives by issuing the Change-drive command again. This time, check for drive E by typing

    `e:`

    at the command prompt and pressing the Enter key.
    Now, continue issuing the Change-drive command for successive letters until you get the "Invalid drive specification" message. How many hard drives does your PC have?
    Before you go on to the next exercise, make sure that the current drive is drive C. If the current drive isn't the C drive, change back to it by typing

    `c:`

    and pressing the Enter key.

4. Now that you know how many hard drives your PC has, the next step is to use the Directory command to find out what directories are on those drives. In the following exercises, I'll use just the C drive. If, however, you have other hard drives on your PC, you should find out what directories they contain.
    To display the directory listing for the root directory of the C drive, type the Directory command at the command prompt:

    `dir`

    and press the Enter key. If the listing for this directory fills more than one screen, the listing will scroll off the screen too fast to read. To prevent the display from scrolling this way, you can issue the Directory command again, but this time with the /P switch so the display will pause after each screen. To do that, type

    `dir /p`

    at the command prompt and press the Enter key. When you want to display the next screen, press any key.
    As the directory listing for the root directory of the C drive is displayed on each screen, look for the directories that are subordinate to the root directory. These are indicated by

    `<DIR>`

after the name. If you look at figure 4-5, for example, you can see that six directories are listed. Here the six directories are: DOS for the operating system; QA4, for *Q&A* release 4.0; WP51 for *WordPerfect* release 5.1; 123 for *Lotus 1-2-3*, UTIL for various utility programs; and DATA for data files like word processing documents and spreadsheets.

Take a look at the listing displayed on your PC, and find two directories that contain application programs. (If you don't have two application programs on your PC, pick any other directory.) Then, write down the names of those directories. You'll need them later. If you can't figure out which directories contain application programs, ask someone to help you.

Another way to display the results of the Directory command is in wide format with the /W switch. Now, issue the Directory command with the /W switch by typing

    dir /w

and pressing the Enter key.

While the listing is displayed, look at the entries for the CONFIG.SYS and AUTOEXEC.BAT files and for the COMMAND.COM file if it's there. Remember, these files are critical to the operation of your PC, so you should be careful never to delete them by accident. (If you don't have an AUTOEXEC.BAT file, chapter 6 will show you how to create one for your system.)

5. Since most PCs are set up with a DOS directory that contains the files that DOS needs to operate, use the Change-directory command to change from the root directory to the DOS directory. If, for example, the DOS directory on your PC is named DOS, you type

    cd \dos

after the command prompt and press the Enter key. Note that the command above uses a backslash, not a regular slash. After the command is executed, the command prompt should look like this:

    C:\DOS>

to indicate that the current directory is now the DOS directory on the C drive.

Next, use the Change-directory command to change to one of the directories you noted in exercise 4. Then, use the Change-directory command to change to the other directory you noted. Last, type this Change-directory command to change back to the root directory on the C drive:

    cd \

6. Use the Change-directory command to change to the directory that contains the DOS files again. Next, use the Directory command with the /P switch to display the current directory. To do that, type

    dir /p

after the command prompt and press the Enter key. When the first screen is full, the command pauses. Then, to see the next screen of the listing, press any key.

As you review the screens, note that many of the files in this directory have extensions of COM or EXE. These files contain DOS commands. For instance, the PRINT.COM file contains the Print command that you'll learn how to use in the next chapter. Finally, complete the command by pressing any key until the listing is complete and you're at the command prompt.

7. To practice repeating and cancelling a DOS command, press the F3 key to display the last command you entered at the prompt. Then, press the Enter key to run the command. When DOS pauses after the first screen is full, cancel the command by pressing the Ctrl+C key combination (hold down the Ctrl key while you press the letter *c*) or by pressing the Ctrl+Pause (Break) key combination (if your PC has a Pause key).

8. Without changing the current directory (C:\DOS>), use the Directory command with both the /P and /W switches to display a directory listing for one of the directories you noted in exercise 4. If, for example, you're changing to the *WordPerfect* 5.1 directory, you type this command:

    `dir \wp51 /p /w`

    The backslash indicates that the WP51 subdirectory is subordinate to the root directory. The switches cause the directory listing to display in the wide format, and, if necessary, pause the display when a screen is full. As you review the listing, note that a few of the files have COM or EXE extensions. If the program is *WordPerfect*, one of these files is named WP.EXE, which is the starting command file for the program.

9. Without changing the current directory, use the Directory command with or without switches to display the directory for the other directory you noted in exercise 4. Notice again that a few of the files have COM or EXE extensions. If the program is *Lotus 1-2-3*, the file named 123.EXE is the command file that starts the spreadsheet program.

10. Now, you're ready to start one of your application programs from the command prompt using the procedure shown in figure 4-8. First, change the current directory to the appropriate program directory. Then, type the command name that starts that program and press the Enter key. This causes DOS to execute the starting command file in the current directory, thus starting your program. Next, exit from your application program and return to the DOS prompt.

11. If you're using DOS 3.0 or later, use this Change-directory command to change the current directory to the root directory

    `cd \`

and press the Enter key. Then, try to start your application program using the second method for starting a program that's described in this chapter. To do that, enter the path for the program's directory along with its command name. If, for example, you're using *WordPerfect*, and your *WordPerfect* directory is \WP51 on the C drive, you enter this command

```
c:\wp51\wp
```

and press the Enter key. (If drive C is already the current drive, you can omit the c: in the command.)

Did your program start using this method? If not, your program requires that the current directory be set to the program's directory whenever the program is in operation. If your program did start, exit from it to return to DOS.

12. (For DOS 5.0 users) To see how the DOS 5.0 help feature works, type the word *help* at the DOS command prompt. You'll see a list of the DOS commands and their functions in alphabetical order. Notice the instruction at the top of the screen: it tells you how to get more information about a command by entering the Help command followed by the command name. For now, scroll through the list a screen at a time by pressing any key. At the last screen, you can return to the command prompt by pressing any key again.

    Next, use the Help feature to get more information on the Directory command. You can do this at the DOS prompt by typing

    ```
    help dir
    ```

    and pressing the Enter key. As you can see, the Directory command has several switches other than the /P and /W switches. (In chapter 8, you'll learn about the /O and /S switches.)

    The other command format you can use at the DOS prompt to get information about a specific command is the command name followed by /?. So try the Directory command again, but this time use this format. If you like, try the other commands you know and see what the Help feature tells you about them.

13. (For DOS 6.0 users) To see what the DOS 6.0 Help feature offers, access it from the DOS prompt by typing the word *help* and pressing the Enter key. This will take you to the first screen of MS-DOS Help, which is a table of contents. To move between the contents screens, press the Page-down key repeatedly, until you get to the last screen. Then, press the Page-up key repeatedly to return to the first screen. To move between items on the screen, you use the Arrow keys, the Tab key, and the Shift+Tab key combination. Take a moment to experiment with these keys until you understand how they work. Now, before you go on, return to the first contents screen.

    To get information on a specific command, you move the cursor to the command and press the Enter key. To see the Help information for the Prompt command, for example, move the cursor to <Prompt> and press the Enter key. This will take you to the first syntax screen for the Prompt command. Use the

Arrow keys and the Page-up and Page-down keys to scroll back and forth through this information. To get additional information about this command, move the cursor to "Notes" near the top of the screen and press the Enter key. Scroll through the information. Then, move the cursor to "Examples" near the top of the screen and press the Enter key; scroll through this information. Then, press the Alt+C key combination to return to the table of contents.

Move the cursor to <DIR> and press the Enter key. Then, press the Alt key to activate the menu bar at the top of the screen. The File and Search menus give you access to other Help functions. I'll show you how to use the File menu; then you can explore the Search menu on your own.

When you activate the menus, the cursor will be on the File menu. Press the letter *f* to see the options on this menu. To access one of these options, you can press the highlighted letter in the option, or you can move the cursor to the option and press the Enter key. To get information on an option, move the cursor to it and press the F1 key. To cancel an option or menu choice, press the Esc key. Now, move the cursor to the Print option and press the F1 key. This gives you information on the Print option. Then, press the Esc key to return to the File menu, and press *x* or move the cursor to the Exit option and press the Enter key. This will take you back to the command prompt.

At the command prompt, type *prompt /?*. You can see the difference between the information that's displayed using this Help format and the information that MS-DOS Help gives you.

Chapter 5

How to use eight more DOS commands

In the last chapter, you learned how to use four DOS commands that can help you get your application programs started. Many PC users get by with just those commands. In fact, if the start-up procedure on your PC includes the Prompt command, you only need three of the four commands presented in the last chapter.

In this chapter, however, I'm going to present eight more commands. Although you won't need them all the time, you should know how to use them because they let you perform functions that you usually can't do from an application program. Before you learn how to use these commands, though, you should understand the differences between the two types of commands that DOS provides.

The two types of DOS commands

When you use DOS, you should realize that there are two types of commands: internal commands and external commands. Although DOS is always able to find and execute its internal commands, you sometimes need to tell DOS where to find its external commands.

Internal commands   As I explained in chapter 2, part of DOS stays in the internal memory of your systems unit whenever your PC is turned on. This portion of DOS includes the command processor, and it also includes many of the DOS commands.

The commands that DOS keeps in internal memory are known as *internal commands*. Because they are always in internal memory, DOS always knows where to find them. To use one of these commands, all you ever have to do is enter the command name at the command prompt. The four commands presented in the last chapter are all internal commands.

External commands   If a command isn't kept in internal memory, it's called an *external command*. Each of these commands is stored in a disk file called a *command file*. On a DOS system, the names of command files always have an extension of COM or EXE.

72 Chapter 5

In the last chapter, you learned about the command files that are used to start application programs. These are usually stored in program directories. In contrast, command files for DOS functions are usually stored in the DOS directory on one of the drives of your PC. On some older systems, however, you'll find the DOS command files in the root directory of the C drive. (If you're using a system that's set up like this, you should consider updating to a new version of DOS.)

Before DOS can execute an external command, it must find the command file for the command and load the command into internal memory. You use the Path command, which is presented in this chapter, to tell DOS where these files are kept.

Eight more commands

Figure 5-1 summarizes the eight commands that you'll learn how to use in this chapter. Of these, only the Check-disk and the Print commands are external commands. The other six commands are internal commands.

The Clear-screen command The Clear-screen command clears the screen of any messages and puts the command prompt at the top of the screen. It has no parameters or switches. You can use this command to clear the screen before you issue a command that displays information.

The Version command Figure 5-2 shows how to use the Version command. As you can see, this command displays a message that tells what version of DOS you're using. Since some application programs require specific versions of DOS, this command can tell you whether you have the right version of DOS for the program you're trying to use.

The Date and Time commands Figure 5-3 shows you how to use the Date and Time commands. Here, I've highlighted the commands as well as the date and time entries made by the PC user. If you don't want to make any changes to the date or time that's displayed, just press the Enter key when DOS asks you for a new value, and you'll return to the command prompt.

If your PC displays these commands as part of your start-up procedure, you probably know how to use them already. But you should realize that you can issue them from the DOS prompt whenever you need to check or correct the date or time. For example, twice a year you'll need to set the clock when the time changes to standard time and back again to daylight savings time.

The versions of DOS before 4.0 use a 24-hour clock. As a result, 4:09 p.m. must be entered into the system as 16:09. Beginning with DOS 4.0, however, this changed. Although you can still enter the time in 24-hour form, you can also enter 4:09 p.m. as 4:09pm or 4:09p, as shown in figure 5-3.

The Path command Figure 5-4 shows you how to use the Path command to display or establish a list of directories that DOS searches for external command files.

Name	Format	Function
Clear screen	`CLS`	Clears the monitor screen.
Version	`VER`	Displays a message that tells what version of DOS is installed.
Date	`DATE`	Lets you inspect and change the current date.
Time	`TIME`	Lets you inspect and change the current time.
Path	`PATH=directory-list`	Tells DOS which directories to search for command files when external commands are issued. If the directory list is omitted, this command displays the directory list from the last Path command.
Check disk	`CHKDSK [drive]`	Displays messages about the disk drive that's specified and about the PC's internal memory.
Type	`TYPE file-spec`	Displays the contents of a text file.
Print	`PRINT file-spec`	Prints the contents of a text file.

Figure 5-1 Eight DOS commands that can help you use your system

```
C:\>ver

MS-DOS Version 6.00
```

Figure 5-2 The operation of the Version command

```
C:\>date
Current date is Tue 12-10-1992
Enter new date (mm-dd-yy): 12-1-92

C:\>time
Current time is 4:06:56.37p
Enter new time: 4:09p
```

Figure 5-3 The operation of the Date and Time commands

Whenever you enter an external command, DOS looks for the command file first in the current directory. If it doesn't find the command file there, it searches the directories given by the Path command in the order in which they were listed.

If you enter a Path command at the prompt without a directory list, DOS tells you what the current path list is. This is illustrated by the first example in figure 5-4. Here, DOS displays the directory list that was established by the last Path command. This list includes two directories on the C drive: the DOS directory and the UTIL directory. On most systems, the current list will include the directory that contains the DOS files, but the directory name isn't always DOS.

Most systems are set up so they automatically issue an appropriate Path command when the system is booted. If your system isn't set up this way, you can issue a Path command that includes the DOS directory in the directory list. This is illustrated by the second example in figure 5-4. Here, the first Path command doesn't include a directory list, so DOS displays the current list, which consists of the UTIL and WP51 directories. Then, the second Path command includes a directory list that consists of the DOS, UTIL, and WP51 directories. The third Path command in this example doesn't have a directory list, so DOS displays the new directory list. This shows that the second Path command worked correctly.

When you want to add a directory to the current directory list, you should do it as shown in the second example to make sure that the list includes all of the required directories. If you establish the DOS directory with a command like this

`path=c:\dos`

the DOS directory will be the only one in the list. In other words, DOS doesn't add the directories given in the Path command to the current directory list. Instead, it replaces the current directory list with the list given in the Path command.

In the next chapter, you'll learn how to issue a Path command as part of your PC's start-up procedure. Once you set that up, you won't have to issue Path commands from the command prompt. As a result, you'll rarely use this command.

The Check-disk command   Figure 5-5 shows you how to use the Check-disk command to display information about a specific disk. Here again, I've highlighted the commands to separate them from the data that's displayed by DOS. Note that the first Check-disk command doesn't specify a disk drive, so it operates on the default drive, which is drive C. In contrast, the second command specifies drive B, a diskette drive.

As you can see, the Check-disk command shows the total number of bytes of storage available on each disk; how that storage is used; and how much storage is available for new files. When you need to know whether a hard disk or diskette has enough space for a program or data file, you can use this command to find out.

The Check-disk command breaks the disk storage down to show how many bytes of storage are used for *hidden files* (files that DOS doesn't want you to access), how many for directories, and how many for user files. This command also shows how many bytes are in *bad sectors*. These are units of disk space that are damaged, so they

The format of the Path command

```
PATH=directory-list
```

Example 1:   A Path command that displays the current directory list.

```
C:\>path
PATH=C:\DOS;C:\UTIL
```

Example 2:   Three Path commands that show how to add the DOS directory to the current directory list. The first one displays the current directory list, the second one establishes a new list that includes the DOS directory, and the third one displays the new directory list.

```
C:\>path
PATH=C:\UTIL;C:\WP51

C:\>path=c:\dos;c:\util;c:\wp51

C:\>path
PATH=C:\DOS;C:\UTIL;C:\WP51
```

Figure 5-4   The operation of the Path command

can't store data reliably. Since DOS knows about these bad sectors and doesn't use them, they're nothing to worry about. In fact, most disks have some bad sectors.

In DOS 4.0 and later versions, this command also displays information about the *allocation units* on the disk. An allocation unit is the smallest unit of storage that's used for a file. Even if a file contains only one byte of data, it uses a whole allocation unit. So there have to be enough allocation units available for a file, as well as enough disk space, or the file won't fit on the disk. As you can see in figure 5-5, the size of an allocation unit differs depending on the disk.

The last two lines of information for each drive tell how many bytes of conventional internal memory your system has and how many bytes aren't being used. In figure 5-5, these lines tell you that the PC has 655,360 bytes (640KB), and that 584,512 are free. If you subtract the second number from the first, you can see that 70,848 bytes of memory are used by DOS.

Besides displaying the information shown in figure 5-5, the Check-disk command looks for various types of disk errors. If it finds any, it displays messages about these errors along with the other information. If you get one of these error messages, you often need to get technical help. But if you want to learn how to handle some of the most common error conditions on your own, you can refer to our advanced DOS book, *The Only DOS Book You'll Ever Need*.

Chapter 5

The format of the Check-disk command

```
CHKDSK [drive]
```

Example 1

```
C:\>chkdsk

Volume HD42         created 08-05-1992 2:49p
Volume Serial Number is 1983-5D30

 44363776 bytes total disk space
    79872 bytes in 2 hidden files
    40960 bytes in 15 directories
 19443712 bytes in 569 user files
    20480 bytes in bad sectors
 24778752 bytes available on disk

     2048 bytes in each allocation unit
    21662 total allocation units on disk
    12099 available allocation units on disk

   655360 total bytes memory
   584512 bytes free
```

Example 2

```
C:\>chkdsk b:

   362496 bytes total disk space
   155648 bytes in 10 user files
   206848 bytes available on disk

     1024 bytes in each allocation unit
      354 total allocation units on disk
      202 available allocation units on disk

   655360 total bytes memory
   584512 bytes free

C:\>
```

Figure 5-5   The operation of the Check-disk command

The Check-disk command is the first external command that I've presented in this chapter. As a result, DOS may not be able to find its command file when you issue the command. If it can't, DOS will display this message:

```
Bad command or file name
```

If that happens, you can use the Change-directory command to change the current directory to the one that contains the DOS files. Or you can use the Path command to add the DOS directory to the current directory list. Then, you can issue the Check-disk command again.

The Type and Print commands   The Type command lets you display the contents of a file; the Print command lets you print the contents of a file. However, these commands work only on *text files*. These files contain only characters that are in a standard code called *ASCII*. As a result, you can't use these commands to display or print the contents of the data files used by your application programs, such as word processing, spreadsheet, or database files.

Figure 5-6 shows how I used these commands to display and print the contents of a DOS text file named CONFIG.SYS. Here again, I've highlighted the commands to help you separate them from the DOS output. Since the commands don't specify a drive or directory for the CONFIG.SYS file, DOS looked for it in the current directory (the root directory) on the default drive (the C drive). As you can see, this file contains seven lines of text.

Since the Print command is another external command, you may have to change the current directory to the one that contains the DOS files. Or you can use a Path command to add the DOS directory to the current directory list. Also, the Print command displays a message like the one in figure 5-6 that asks you to name the list device. If your system has been set up properly, all you have to do is press the Enter key when this message appears.

You can use the Type and Print commands to display or print the contents of the README files that come with software products. These are text files that usually contain corrections and changes to the manuals that come with the products. Because the files are often lengthy, it's usually better to print them than to display them. But if you want to read a file while it's displayed, you can control the scrolling of the text by using the Pause key.

Some perspective on DOS

In this chapter and the last one, you've seen how twelve of the DOS commands work. As you try these commands on your own PC, you'll gain a better feel for what DOS does and how it helps you control your system. You'll also realize that you can now do some jobs that you couldn't do without the DOS commands. For instance, you can set the date and time of your system, you can check the available capacity of your disk drives, and you can use the Path command to tell DOS where to look for commands so DOS and your application programs work right.

The formats of the Type and Print commands

    TYPE file-spec

    PRINT file-spec

The display of the Type and Print commands

```
C:\>type config.sys
DEVICE=C:\DOS\SETVER.EXE
FILES=30
BUFFERS=30
DEVICE=C:\DOS\HIMEM.SYS
STACKS=9,256
SHELL=C:\DOS\COMMAND.COM C:\DOS\   /p
DOS=HIGH

C:\>print config.sys
Name of list device [PRN]:
Resident part of PRINT installed

   C:\CONFIG.SYS is currently being printed

C:\>
```

The printed output of the Print command

```
DEVICE=C:\DOS\SETVER.EXE
FILES=30
BUFFERS=30
DEVICE=C:\DOS\HIMEM.SYS
STACKS=9,256
SHELL=C:\DOS\COMMAND.COM C:\DOS\   /p
DOS=HIGH
```

Figure 5-6   The operation of the Type and Print commands

In the next chapter, you'll learn how to use the AUTOEXEC.BAT file to control the start-up procedure on your system. That chapter will clear up some of the mysteries of how your PC gets started and why it operates the way it does.

Terms

internal command
external command
command file
hidden file

bad sector
allocation unit
text file
ASCII

Objectives

1. Use a DOS command to find out what version of DOS your PC is using.
2. Use DOS commands to check the system date and time and to correct them if they're inaccurate.
3. Use a DOS command to find out what directories are in the current path.
4. Use a DOS command to find out how much storage is available on any of the disk drives on your system.
5. Use a DOS command to display or print any text file on your PC.
6. Use the proper combination of commands to start any external command, even if the DOS directory isn't in the list established by the Path command.

Exercises

1. Use this Version command to find out what version of DOS you're using on your PC:

   `ver`

   Then, use this Clear-screen command to clear the monitor screen:

   `cls`

2. Use the Date and Time commands to find out whether the date and time are set correctly for your system. If they aren't, correct them. If you experiment with the entries for the date and the time, you can see how DOS interprets your entries by running the command again to display the new value.

3. Use this Path command without a directory list to see whether your system has a current directory list:

   `path`

   If it does, check to see whether the DOS directory is included in the list, but don't change the list. If the directory is in the list, you will be able to run the external commands without changing the current directory to the DOS directory.

4. Use the Directory command with the /W switch to display the directory listing for the DOS directory. Then, look for files named CHKDSK.COM and PRINT.COM if you're using DOS 4.0 or an earlier version, or CHKDSK.EXE and PRINT.EXE if you're using DOS 5.0 or later. These are the command files for the two external commands that are presented in this chapter.

5. Use a Check-disk command like the one that follows to find out the capacities of the drives on your PC's hard disk:

    `chkdsk c:`

    Remember that this command is an external command. To execute it, the DOS directory must either be in the current directory list as shown by the Path command, or the current directory must be set to the DOS directory.

    After you execute the command for drive C, do it for any other drives on your hard disk. Study the output to find out how many bytes are available for new files on each disk drive.

    Then, use the Check-disk command to find out the capacity of a diskette in the A drive and the B drive (if you have a B drive). Remember that the diskette drives on some PCs can handle both double-density and high-density diskettes. Then, the capacity depends on the diskette, not the drive. Make sure that the diskette that you use has been formatted because the command won't work if it isn't (you'll learn how to format a diskette in chapter 9).

6. Make sure that the current directory is the root directory on the C drive. Then, use this Type command to display the CONFIG.SYS file in the root directory of the C drive:

    `type config.sys`

    Next, use the Type command to display the COMMAND.COM file in the root directory of the C drive. Since this isn't a text file, the command will display illegible output.

    Last, use the Type command to display the AUTOEXEC.BAT file in the root directory of the C drive. As you'll learn in the next chapter, this file contains the DOS commands that are executed when you start your PC. This file should contain both a Prompt command and a Path command. If it doesn't, you should edit the file to include these commands. And if you don't have an AUTOEXEC.BAT file, you should create one. You can find out how to edit your existing AUTOEXEC.BAT file or how to create one in chapter 6.

7. Use the Print command to print the contents of the CONFIG.SYS file in the root directory of the C drive. When this command displays a message about the name of the list device like the message in figure 5-6, just press the Enter key.

8. Use the Change-drive and Change-directory commands to change to the drive and directory that contains the program files for one of your application programs, such as the program directory for your word processing or spreadsheet program. Then, use the Directory command with the /P and /W switches to display the directory listing. In this listing, look for README files. If you find one or more, write down their complete names including extensions and use the Type command to display one of them. If the file scrolls off the screen, press the Pause key to stop the scrolling and press the key again to restart the scrolling (if

the scrolling doesn't restart, try pressing the Enter or the Esc key). To cancel the command, use the Ctrl+Pause (Break) key combination or the Ctrl+C key combination.

Note: If you don't find a README file for one of your application programs, you might find one for DOS in your DOS directory. Also, you may want to use the Print command to print out any README files you find since these files usually have corrections and additions to the information that's in the program's manual.

Chapter 6

How to set up the AUTOEXEC.BAT file so DOS gets started right

When you start your PC, DOS looks for two files in the root directory of the C drive. The first, CONFIG.SYS, contains special configuration commands that tell DOS how to initialize itself. The second, AUTOEXEC.BAT, contains one or more DOS commands that are always executed when you start your PC. If DOS can't find an AUTOEXEC.BAT file in the root directory of drive C, it executes the Date and Time commands.

The AUTOEXEC.BAT file is simply a list of DOS commands, as shown in the sample in figure 6-1. Because it can contain any commands, it can have a significant effect on the way your system starts up and works. At the least, it will save you from having to enter the same set of commands at the DOS prompt each time you start your PC.

In this chapter, you'll learn which commands you should consider including in your AUTOEXEC.BAT file and why. Then, you'll learn three methods for creating or changing the file. Last, you'll learn how to test your file without turning the PC off and on.

Before you start, however, you should realize that the AUTOEXEC.BAT file is a *batch file*. A batch file is a file that contains one or more DOS commands. The file names for all batch files have BAT as the extension so DOS can distinguish them from other types of files. The only difference between the AUTOEXEC batch file and other batch files is that the AUTOEXEC file is automatically executed when the system is started. Consequently, much of what you learn in this chapter applies to any batch file.

Commands to use in your AUTOEXEC.BAT file

Although the AUTOEXEC.BAT file in figure 6-1 is a simple one, the commands it contains are typical of those you'll want to include in your own AUTOEXEC.BAT. The Echo command isn't crucial for getting your PC started up smoothly, but it is

```
echo off
prompt $p$g
path=c:\dos;c:\util
cls
```

Figure 6-1 A simple AUTOEXEC.BAT file

useful, so I'll show you how it works in this section. In contrast, the Prompt and Path commands are critical in getting your PC set up right, so you should always include them in your AUTOEXEC.BAT. And you'll also want to include other commands, such as the Clear-screen command, that you normally enter each time you turn on your PC.

How to use the Echo command in a batch file Figure 6-2 presents the Echo command, a command designed specifically for batch files. You can use it to specify whether or not you want batch file commands displayed as they are executed. You can also use it to display messages.

In the batch file in figure 6-1, OFF is specified, so the commands in the file aren't displayed (or "echoed") as they are executed. However, if the commands in the batch file generate any messages, these messages are displayed. Since ON is the default condition, you need to use an Echo-on command only if an Echo-off command has been issued previously.

If the parameter is anything other than ON or OFF, the Echo command treats it as a message you want displayed on the monitor. The message is displayed whether or not the current Echo status is "on" or "off." This is illustrated by the third and fourth examples in figure 6-2, and I'll show you how this works in an AUTOEXEC.BAT file later in this chapter.

Why you should include the Prompt and Path commands in your AUTOEXEC.BAT file In general, the AUTOEXEC.BAT file should include at least two commands following the Echo-off command. One should be a Prompt command like the second command in figure 6-1. As you learned in chapter 4, this command tells DOS to display the default drive and current directory in the command prompt.

The other command that should be included in the AUTOEXEC.BAT file is a Path command. As you learned in chapter 5, this command establishes the list of directories that DOS searches whenever it receives an external command that isn't in the current directory. In figure 6-1, the Path command tells DOS to search two directories on the C drive in this order: first DOS, then UTIL.

At the least, the Path command in the AUTOEXEC.BAT file should include the DOS directory. Then, DOS will always know where to find its external commands. In

---

Format

```
ECHO [ON] [OFF] [message]
```

Function

If the parameter is ON, this command tells DOS to display all batch file commands as they are executed. If the parameter is OFF, this command tells DOS not to display the batch file commands as they are executed. The OFF parameter stays in effect until the next Echo command is executed. If there's a Message parameter, the message is displayed. If no parameters are used, DOS displays a message that tells whether the Echo status is on or off.

Examples

```
echo on

echo off

echo Please record your PC time at the computer center
echo after each session.
```

Figure 6-2 The Echo command for use in batch files

addition, the Path command should include the directory that contains the other batch files for your system. On many systems, these files are in the UTIL directory or the BAT directory.

Beyond this, you may want to include one or more of the directories that contain application programs, but that depends on the requirements of your programs. Often, you don't gain anything by putting the directory of an application program in the directory list because the current directory has to be set to the program directory anyway before you can start the program. Then, since DOS always starts its search for a command in the current directory, it never gets to the directory list.

Since DOS doesn't use the Path command when it's looking for data files, you shouldn't include data directories in your Path command. Similarly, you shouldn't include the root directory of the C drive in your Path command unless it contains command or batch files that aren't executed automatically as part of the start-up procedure.

You shouldn't include diskette drives in your Path command either. If you do, DOS will search them when it can't find a command in the directories that precede the diskette directories in the search path. Then, if you don't have a diskette in the drive that's specified, DOS will display an error message indicating that the drive isn't ready. That just slows you down.

An AUTOEXEC.BAT file that displays a message

```
echo off
prompt $p$g
path=c:\dos;c:\util
cls
echo Please record your PC time at the computer center when
echo you're done. We're trying to keep track of the usage of
echo each system this month.
echo Thanks for your cooperation.
```

An AUTOEXEC.BAT file that starts *Lotus 1-2-3*

```
echo off
prompt $p$g
path=c:\dos;c:\util
cd \123
123
```

An AUTOEXEC.BAT file that starts the DOS 5.0/6.0 shell

```
echo off
prompt $p$g
path=c:\dos;c:\util
dosshell
```

Figure 6-3 Expanded versions of AUTOEXEC.BAT files

Other commands to consider for your AUTOEXEC.BAT file Beyond the Path and Prompt commands, your AUTOEXEC.BAT file should contain whatever commands are appropriate for your system. For example, if you enter the same series of commands each time you start your PC, you should put those commands in this file. And some hardware components require that special commands be put in this file.

To illustrate expanded versions of AUTOEXEC.BAT files, figure 6-3 presents three more. The first file ends with several Echo commands that display a message for the PC user who starts the system. The second file ends with two commands that start an application program (*Lotus 1-2-3*). This is useful if you regularly use just one program. Then, you don't have to start the program from the command prompt each time you use the PC. The third file ends with a Dosshell command that starts the DOS 5.0/6.0 shell. If you don't end the AUTOEXEC.BAT file with this command, DOS 5.0 or 6.0 will start with the command prompt just like earlier versions of DOS.

Three ways to create or change an AUTOEXEC.BAT file

Now that you've seen how the AUTOEXEC.BAT file works, you can decide whether or not your own AUTOEXEC.BAT file is adequate for your system. To begin, use the Directory command to check the root directory of the C drive to find out whether your PC has an AUTOEXEC.BAT file. If it doesn't, you definitely should create one. If it does, you can use the Type or Print command to look at the contents of the file. Then, if the file doesn't contain the proper Prompt and Path commands, you should take the time to change it. (Before you make any changes, though, be sure to use a Print command to get a printout of the existing file so you have a backup copy in case the changes don't work.)

Because the AUTOEXEC.BAT file is just a text file, you can use several different methods to create or change it. If you have a full-screen *text editor* on your PC like the one that comes with DOS 5.0 or 6.0, the easiest way to work with a text file is to use that editor. If you have a word processing program like *WordPerfect* that makes it easy to work with text files, you can use that for creating and changing the AUTOEXEC.BAT file. And if neither of these methods works for you, you can use the Edlin program that comes with all versions of DOS except DOS 6.0. (If you upgrade to DOS 6.0 from an earlier version of DOS, Edlin will still be in your DOS directory. But if you purchased your computer with DOS 6.0 already installed, Edlin won't be available.)

These methods are now presented in the sequence I've just given, but remember that you only need to know how to use one of them. So if you have DOS 5.0 or 6.0, you may want to read only about the first method. On the other hand, if you're using an earlier version of DOS, you can read about the other two methods and then decide which one to use.

How to use the DOS 5.0/6.0 Edit command to create or change a batch file

Both DOS 5.0 and 6.0 provide a command called Edit that makes it easy for you to create and change text files. To start the Edit command, you type *edit* followed by the name of the file you want to edit, as in this example:

```
C:\>edit autoexec.bat
```

Then, the Edit command invokes a full-screen text editor as shown in figure 6-4. If the file name you specified is for an existing file, as in figure 6-4, the file is displayed and you make the necessary changes to it. On the other hand, if the file name you specified is for a new file, the main area of the screen will be blank. Then, to create the file, you just add commands to it. In either case, when you're done with the file, you save it to the hard disk.

Like a word processing program, Edit lets you use the arrow keys to move the cursor where you want it, and any text you type will be added at the cursor location. In addition, you can use the Delete or Backspace keys to delete characters. And you can use the Insert key to change from Insert to Typeover mode or vice versa. (In Typeover mode, the characters you enter replace the characters at the cursor; in Insert mode, the characters you enter are inserted at the cursor.)

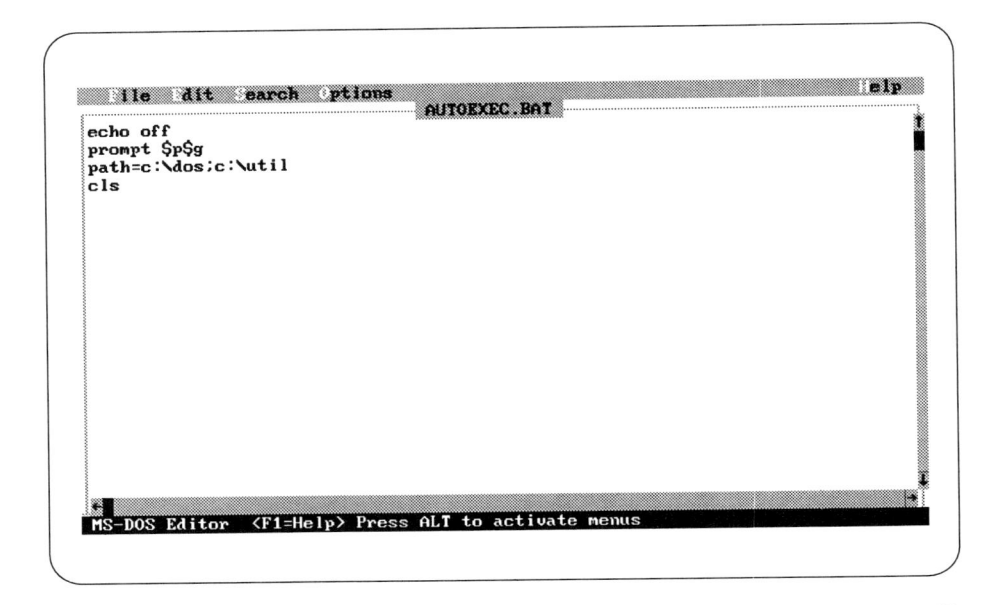

Figure 6-4 An AUTOEXEC.BAT file displayed by the DOS 5.0/6.0 Edit command

You can also highlight the text you want to copy, move, or delete. To do that, you move the cursor to the beginning of the text. Then, you hold down the Shift key as you use the arrow keys to highlight the text you want to edit.

Edit also provides menus that make it easy to select the commands that you need to edit a file. Figure 6-5, for example, shows the commands on the Edit menu. Here, the Cut command temporarily deletes the highlighted text; the Copy command copies the highlighted text; the Paste command inserts text that you deleted or copied using the Cut or Copy command; and the Clear command permanently deletes the highlighted text.

To select one of these commands, you press the Alt key to activate the menu system. Then, you can use one of two techniques. You can use the Left and Right arrow keys to move to the menu you want, press the Enter key to open the menu, use the Down arrow key to move to the command option you want, and press the Enter key again to start the command. Or you can press the key for the letter that's highlighted in the menu name to open the menu, and then press the key for the letter that's highlighted in the command to start the command.

After you have created or edited a file, you save it using one of the commands on the File menu shown in figure 6-6. Here, the New command clears the screen so you can create a new file. The Open command loads an existing file from disk storage so you can edit it. The Save command saves the file using the current file name. The Save-as command lets you specify the file name you want to use to save the file. The

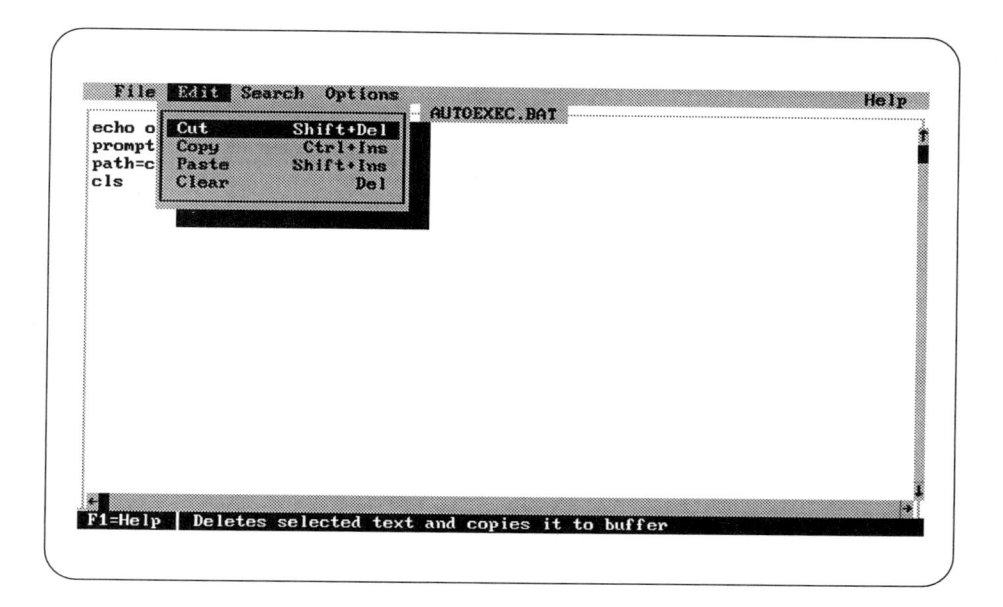

How to set up the AUTOEXEC.BAT file so DOS gets started right   **89**

Figure 6-5   The Edit menu of the DOS 5.0/6.0 Edit command

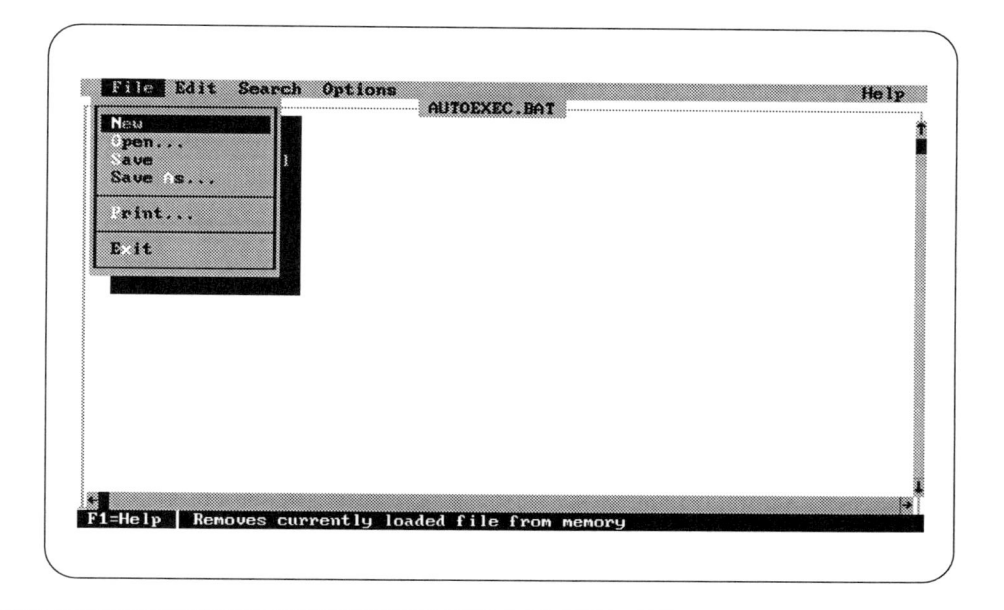

Figure 6-6   The File menu of the DOS 5.0/6.0 Edit command

Print command prints the file. And the Exit command stops the editor and returns you to the command prompt.

Although this is just a brief introduction to the Edit command, that's all you need to know for editing small files. If you work with this program for a few minutes, you'll see that it's quite easy to use. So if you have DOS 5.0 or 6.0, you'll probably want to use this program for creating and changing your AUTOEXEC.BAT file. (By the way, if you know how to use a mouse, you can use it instead of the keyboard to activate menu options or highlight text. But you don't have to worry about the mouse for now. I'll show you how to use it when you need it more extensively in chapters 11 and 12.)

How to use a word processing program to create or change a batch file   If you don't have DOS 5.0 or 6.0, you can use the text feature of your word processing program to create and change batch files. In this case, you must make sure that you retrieve an existing batch file as a text file, not as a word processing file. Also, after you create a new batch file or change an existing one, you must make sure you save the file as a text file, not as a word processing file.

When you use *WordPerfect*, for example, you use the Text-in feature to retrieve a batch file. Then, you use the regular word processing commands to change the file. When you're done, you use the Text-out feature to save the file as a DOS text file. Not all word processing programs make it that easy to work with text files, though, so this isn't always practical with other programs.

How to use Edlin to create or change a batch file   Before DOS 5.0, the only text editor supplied with DOS was Edlin. But unlike the DOS 5.0/6.0 Edit command, Edlin lets you edit only one line at a time. This makes Edlin awkward to use. In addition, the Edlin commands are likely to be confusing at first. So if you have another method you can use for editing batch files, you'll probably want to skip this information on Edlin.

Figure 6-7 presents some of Edlin's most useful commands. As you can see, the formats of these commands use line numbers and single letters to invoke functions. In figure 6-8, you can see how these commands are used to edit an AUTOEXEC.BAT file. Here, all of the entries made by the PC user are shaded.

The file specification that's entered with the Edlin command indicates the file you want to edit or create. If this file doesn't exist, Edlin assumes you're creating a new file. If the file does exist, Edlin displays the following message:

    End of input file

Then, on the next line, it displays an asterisk (*) that indicates it's waiting for a command.

In figure 6-8, the first command is the letter L. (I entered the commands in uppercase letters in this example so you can distinguish between the letter L and the number 1. You can use lowercase letters when you're working on your own, though.)

Edlin commands

Command	Format	Function
Insert	`(line-number)I`	Inserts one or more lines before the line number indicated.
Edit	`line-number`	Edits the line indicated by the line number.
Delete	`(line-number or numbers)D`	Deletes the line or lines indicated by the line numbers.
List	`L`	Lists the current version of the file.
End	`E`	Ends the editing session and saves the file.
Quit	`Q`	Quits the editing session without saving the file.

Keystrokes for the Insert command

Keys	Function
Ctrl+Pause or Ctrl+C	Ends the Insert command.

Figure 6-7 A summary of the most useful commands and keystrokes for Edlin

This List command tells Edlin to list the current version of the file. As you can see, the file consists of four commands.

The second command in figure 6-8 is the line number 1. Because no command code is given with the line number, this tells Edlin that you want to edit line 1. In this case, the Echo-off command is changed to an Echo-on command so the commands in the batch file will be displayed as they are executed. When you edit a line, Edlin displays the current version of the line and prompts you to enter a new line to replace it.

The third command in figure 6-8 (4D) tells Edlin to delete the fourth line in the file. Then, the fourth command (L) tells Edlin to list the current version of the file. Now, the file has only three lines because one has been deleted.

The fifth command in figure 6-8 (4I) tells Edlin that lines are going to be inserted into the file before the fourth line. Since the file has only three lines, the lines are inserted after the last line in the file. Because you can insert one or more lines with this command, you need to tell Edlin when you're through. To do this, you hold down

```
C:\DOS>edlin c:\autoexec.bat
End of input file

*L
            1:*echo off
            2: prompt $p$g
            3: path=c:\dos;c:\util
            4: cls
*1
            1:*echo off
            1:*echo on
*4D
*L
            1: echo on
            2: prompt $p$g
            3: path=c:\dos;c:\util
*4I
            4:*cd \wp51
            5:*wp
            6:*^C
*L
            1: echo on
            2: prompt $p$g
            3: path=c:\dos;c:\util
            4: cd \wp51
            5: wp
*E

C:\DOS>
```

Figure 6-8   How to use Edlin to modify a batch file

the Ctrl key and press the Pause (Break) key or the letter *c*. Note that this is the same keystroke combination you use to cancel a command that's being executed by DOS. When this combination is used within Edlin, it appears as ^C, and it ends the Insert command.

The sixth command in figure 6-8 is the List command again; it lists the changed version of the file. Since the file is now in the form that the user wants, the next command is the End command. The keystroke for this command is the letter *e*. This command ends Edlin and saves the edited file. As a result, the command prompt appears on the monitor. If you want to end Edlin without saving the edited file, you enter the letter *q* for the Quit command.

Although Edlin is a bit confusing when you first start to use it, you can get used to it after a short time. That's particularly true if you limit yourself to the commands and keystrokes shown in figure 6-7. Although Edlin provides several other commands and several other keystrokes and keystroke combinations, they just make Edlin that much harder to use.

When you use Edlin to edit an existing file, it automatically creates a backup file for you. If, for example, you're editing the AUTOEXEC.BAT file, Edlin saves the original version of the file under the name AUTOEXEC.BAK. Then, if the new version of the file doesn't work right, you still have the original version to work with. To reinstate the original as the AUTOEXEC.BAT file, you can use this Copy command:

```
copy c:\autoexec.bak c:\autoexec.bat
```

The use of this command is explained in chapter 8.

If you're using Edlin to create a new batch file, you get this message after you enter the command and file name at the command prompt:

```
New file
```

Then, you use the Insert command to insert the commands you want in the batch file. After you enter the last command, you turn off the Insert command using the Ctrl+C or Ctrl+Pause (Break) key combination. Next, you save the file and return to the prompt by entering the letter *e*.

How to test an AUTOEXEC.BAT file

When you finish creating or changing an AUTOEXEC.BAT file, you should test it to make sure it works right. One way to do that is to turn the PC off and turn it back on again. Then, the PC performs its self-test and boots DOS. As part of the booting process, the commands in the AUTOEXEC.BAT file are executed.

A more efficient way to restart DOS is to use the key combination I introduced in chapter 4: Ctrl+Alt+Delete. This boots DOS, but doesn't force the PC to go through its self-test again.

Some perspective on the AUTOEXEC.BAT file

Once you have your AUTOEXEC.BAT file set up properly, you shouldn't have to change it unless you change some of the hardware components of your system or add a program to your system that requires a special command. If, for example, you add a mouse to your PC, you may have to add a command to the AUTOEXEC.BAT file. Similarly, you may need to update your Path command when you install a new application program. Many installation programs make the required AUTOEXEC.BAT changes for you, however. So you may not need to make the changes yourself.

Besides the commands you've learned here, DOS provides additional commands that are often placed in the AUTOEXEC.BAT file. For example, DOS 6.0 comes with a command called Smartdrv that can be included in your AUTOEXEC.BAT file to speed up disk operations. So don't be surprised if you find several commands besides Prompt and Path in your AUTOEXEC.BAT file.

Terms

batch file
text editor

Objectives

1. In general terms, list the directories that should be included in the Path command in the AUTOEXEC.BAT file.

2. List three types of commands or programs you can use to create or change any batch file, including the AUTOEXEC.BAT file.

3. Check whether you have an AUTOEXEC.BAT file on your PC. If not, create an appropriate one using one of the commands or programs that's available to you.

4. If you already have an AUTOEXEC.BAT file on your PC, make changes to it as needed using one of the commands or programs that's available to you.

Exercises

1. Use the Directory command to look at the root directory on the C drive and see if you already have an AUTOEXEC.BAT file. If you do, use the Print command to print a copy of the file:

    ```
    print c:\autoexec.bat
    ```

2. (For DOS 5.0 or 6.0 users) If your AUTOEXEC.BAT file doesn't include a Dosshell command, use the Edit command to modify the file so it will start the DOS shell. To begin, enter this command:

    ```
    edit c:\autoexec.bat
    ```

    This will start the full-screen editor, and the commands in your AUTOEXEC.BAT file will be displayed on the screen.

    Experiment with using the arrow keys to move the cursor around the screen. Then, move the cursor to the end of the file, and add this command:

    ```
    dosshell
    ```

    To save the file, press the Alt key to activate the menu system. Now press the Enter key or the letter *f* to open the File menu, and press the letter *s* to execute the Save command. Then, activate the menu system again, open the File menu, and press the letter *x* to execute the Exit command. This returns you to the DOS prompt.

    To test your change, use the Ctrl+Alt+Delete key combination to restart your PC. When the Dosshell command you added is executed, the DOS shell will appear on your screen. To exit from the DOS shell, you can use the Exit command of the File menu, just as you did in Edit. Or you can press the F3 key.

    If you don't want to keep the Dosshell command in your AUTOEXEC.BAT file, enter the Edit command for the file again. Then, move the cursor to the Dosshell command and use the Delete key to delete the command. Check the file contents against the printout you made in exercise 1 and make sure the file is in its original form. Then, save the file and exit from Edit using the commands on the File menu just as you did earlier in this exercise.

3. (If you're using a version of DOS before DOS 5.0) Use Edlin to add a Date command to your AUTOEXEC.BAT file. To begin, enter this command:

   edlin c:\autoexec.bat

   Edlin will display the "End of input file" message, followed on the next line by an asterisk that shows it's waiting for a command.

   At the asterisk, enter the letter L. This will display the AUTOEXEC.BAT file. Now, enter the following:

   1I

   This tells Edlin you want to insert a new line before line 1. Then, enter the Date command:

   date

   and press the Enter key. Use the Ctrl+C or Ctrl+Pause (Break) key combination to end the Insert command. Then, enter L to list the file again and notice how the Date command has been added. Now, enter E to end the Edlin session and save the AUTOEXEC.BAT file.

   To test your change, use the Ctrl+Alt+Delete key combination to restart your PC. When the Date command you added is executed, DOS will display the date and wait for you to enter a new date; just press the Enter key. Then, the rest of the commands in your AUTOEXEC.BAT file will be executed. (If your original AUTOEXEC.BAT file contained a Date command, you'll see the date displayed a second time.)

   To delete the Date command, enter the Edlin command for the AUTOEXEC.BAT file again. Enter L to list the file and make sure the Date command is on line 1. If it is, enter this Delete command:

   1D

   If the Date command *isn't* on line 1, enter the appropriate line number instead of 1 in the Delete command.

   Now, enter L to see that the Date command has been deleted. Check the file contents against the printout you made in exercise 1 to make sure the file is in its original form. Then enter E to end the Edlin session and save the AUTOEXEC.BAT file.

Note: At this point, you may want to make some changes to your AUTOEXEC.BAT file. One word of caution: Don't delete or modify any commands in your AUTOEXEC.BAT file that you don't understand; they may have an important effect on your system. Stick to the commands that you've learned in this and previous chapters.

Section 3

Other essential DOS skills

The five chapters in this section present a variety of DOS skills that every PC user should have. In chapter 7, you'll learn how to use batch files to start your programs. Even if you never actually create a batch file of your own, this chapter is worth reading because it will give you a better understanding of how your PC works. However, you can read it at any time during your PC training; you don't have to read it right away.

In contrast, you should read the other four chapters in this section in order. In chapter 8, you'll learn how to manage the directories and files on your hard disk. In chapter 9, you'll learn how to work with diskettes. And in chapters 10 and 11, you'll learn how to back up the files on your hard disk to diskettes using the DOS Backup command and the DOS 6.0 Backup utility, Microsoft Backup. These are essential skills for all PC users, no matter what application programs they use. Although you can perform some of the functions presented in these chapters by using a shell or an application program like *WordPerfect*, you can do them more efficiently if you understand how to do them from the command prompt in DOS.

Chapter 7

How to use batch files to start your programs

As you learned in chapter 6, a batch file is a file that contains one or more DOS commands and has a file name with BAT as the extension. When you use a batch file, DOS gets its commands from the file instead of from the command prompt. As a result, the commands in the batch file are executed in the order in which they appear in the file. To execute a batch file other than the AUTOEXEC.BAT file, you just enter the name of the batch file at the command prompt without its BAT extension.

In this chapter, you'll learn to create simple batch files that make it easier to start your programs. First, you'll learn three techniques for starting an application program from a batch file. Next, you'll learn how DOS searches for batch files on a PC. Finally, you'll learn how to create batch files that accept parameters. Throughout this chapter, I assume that you already know how to create and change a batch file using the methods that I presented in chapter 6.

Three ways to start an application program from a batch file

Whether you're issuing commands at the command prompt or from a batch file, there are three methods you can use to start an application program, as shown in figure 7-1 (I presented the first two methods in chapter 4, so I'll just review them briefly here). As you will see, two of these methods can't be used for certain programs. But you should understand all three methods so you can select the one that's best for each of your programs.

Method 1: Set the default drive and current directory to the program directory before issuing the program name In the first example in figure 7-1, the first two commands set the default drive and the current directory to those that contain the program. Then, the third command starts the program. This method will work no matter what version of DOS you're using or what application program you're trying to start.

Method 1:	Set the default drive and current directory to the program directory before issuing the program name.
	`c:`
	`cd \wp51`
	`wp`

Method 2:	Enter the program's path along with the program name (DOS 3.0 or later). `c:\wp51\wp`
Method 3:	Include the program's directory in the Path command in the AUTOEXEC.BAT file and enter just the program name in the batch file. `wp`

Figure 7-1 Three ways to start an application program from a batch file

Method 2: Enter the program's path along with the program name (DOS 3.0 or later) If you're using a version of DOS that's 3.0 or later, you can code a program's path along with its program name. This is illustrated by the second example in figure 7-1. This command tells DOS to look on the C drive in the WP51 directory for a program named WP.

As I said in chapter 4, this method won't work with some application programs. For instance, some releases of *Lotus 1-2-3* require that the current directory be set to the program directory before the program is run. As a result, you have to use the first method in figure 7-1 for starting programs like these.

Method 3: Include the program's directory in the Path command in the AUTOEXEC.BAT file and enter just the program name With some programs, you can add the program directory to the Path command in your AUTOEXEC.BAT file. Then, DOS searches through the directories in the Path command list until it finds the program to be executed. To start the program, you enter just its command name. This is illustrated by the third example in figure 7-1.

In general, I recommend you use methods 1 and 2 rather than this method for starting your programs. That's because each directory you include in the Path command can cause DOS to spend more time searching directories whenever you run an external command or application program. Also, this method won't work for programs that require the current directory to be set to the program directory.

Example 1: The 123.BAT file

```
c:
cd \123
123
cd \
cls
```

The command the starts the 123.BAT file

```
C:\>123
```

Example 2: The WP.BAT file for use with DOS 3.0 or later

```
c:
cd \wp51\mma
\wp51\wp
cd \
cls
```

The command that starts the WP.BAT file

```
C:\>wp
```

Figure 7-2 Typical batch files for starting a spreadsheet and a word processing program

Two examples of batch files that start application programs

Figure 7-2 shows two examples of batch files, along with the commands you enter at the command prompt to start them. These batch files start a spreadsheet and a word processing program.

A batch file for starting *Lotus 1-2-3* The first batch file in figure 7-2 starts *Lotus 1-2-3*. Because some releases of this program require that the current directory be set to the program directory, this batch file uses the first method in figure 7-1.

Notice that this file contains two commands after the command that starts *Lotus 1-2-3*. These two commands aren't executed until the PC user exits from *Lotus*. Then, the first command changes the current directory to the root directory, and the second one clears the monitor screen. At that point, the batch file is finished executing, so DOS displays the command prompt and waits for the next command.

Also notice that the batch file name and the name for the command file that starts the program are the same. If this seems too confusing to you, you can give the batch file a different name, like 123GO.BAT. Then, to start the batch file, you would enter 123GO at the command prompt.

A batch file for starting *WordPerfect* The second batch file in figure 7-2 starts *WordPerfect* 5.1 using the second method in figure 7-1. Its file name is WP.BAT, so once again, the command you use to start the batch file is the same as the command you use to start the program itself.

The second command in this batch file sets the current directory to a data directory before starting the program. As a result, once the program is started, the current directory will be WP51\MMA. Then, when you use the *WordPerfect* Retrieve or Save function, *WordPerfect* will automatically access or save the file in WP51\MMA.

Unfortunately, you can't use this batch file with a version of DOS that precedes 3.0. That's because the third command specifies the path for the word processing program, and earlier versions of DOS don't let you do that.

How to make sure DOS can find your batch files

To execute the commands in a batch file, DOS needs to be able to find the file. As a result, you should store all your batch files in the same directory, and make sure that directory is included in the list established by the Path command in the AUTOEXEC.BAT file. If, for example, your batch files are stored in a UTIL directory that also includes some utility programs, your AUTOEXEC.BAT file should include a Path command like this:

```
path=c:\dos;c:\util
```

Then, DOS will be able to find the batch files in your UTIL directory.

Besides setting up the search path, you need to be aware of how DOS searches directories to locate batch files. DOS searches the current directory first, followed by the directories listed in the Path command. In each directory, DOS looks first for a COM file, then for an EXE file, and last for a BAT file.

If you use the same name for a batch file that is used for a COM or EXE file, this search order can cause a problem as illustrated by the batch file in figure 7-3. This file uses method 3 in figure 7-1 to start the program: it includes the program directory in the Path command of the AUTOEXEC.BAT file and uses just the program name, WP, in the batch file.

As you can see, the WP.BAT file is stored in the UTIL directory. Then, when the WP command is entered at the command prompt, DOS starts the batch file because it finds the WP.BAT file in the UTIL directory before it finds a WP.COM or WP.EXE file in another directory. After the second command in this batch file changes the current directory to WP51\MMA, the third command issues the WP command to start *WordPerfect*. That's when the problem starts.

First, DOS looks for a WP file in the current directory, C:\WP51\MMA. When it doesn't find one in this data directory, it starts searching the directories listed in the Path command. If you look at the Path command in the AUTOEXEC.BAT file, you can see that the UTIL directory is before the WP51 directory in the search list. That means that DOS finds the WP.BAT file before it finds the WP.EXE file when the WP command is executed. As a result, the WP command in this batch file starts the batch

---

The AUTOEXEC.BAT file

```
echo off
prompt $p$g
path=c:\dos;c:\util;c:\wp51
cls
```

The WP.BAT file in the UTIL directory

```
cd \wp51\mma
wp
cd \
cls
```

The command that starts the batch file

```
C:\>wp
```

Figure 7-3 A batch file that won't work correctly

file again, not *WordPerfect*. This starts a loop that will continue until you interrupt it by pressing Ctrl+C.

If you're using DOS 3.0 or later, the best way to solve this problem is to include the program's path along with its name in the batch file. For example, the third line of the WP.BAT file in figure 7-3 should be:

`\wp51\wp`

That's the way it is in the WP.BAT file in figure 7-2. Then, DOS looks for the program in the correct directory, and you get the result you want.

Another solution is to use a name for the batch file that is different from the name for the program's command file. If, for example, you name the batch file WPGO.BAT, the file will work the way you want it to.

A third solution is to change the current directory to the one that contains the program instead of the one that contains the data before you issue the program command. This, of course, is the solution you'll have to use if you have an early version of DOS.

Incidentally, it might seem logical to try and solve this problem by changing the Path command in the AUTOEXEC.BAT file as follows:

`path=c:\dos;c:\wp51;c:\util`

Then, the batch file would be able to find the WP.EXE file in the WP51 directory. The problem here is that if you entered WP at the command prompt to start your batch file, DOS would find the WP.EXE file in the WP51 directory instead of the WP.BAT file in the UTIL directory. So you would be starting *WordPerfect* instead of executing the batch file.

How to use parameters with a batch file

As you already know, many DOS commands accept parameters. The Directory command, for instance, accepts parameters that specify which drive and directory you want to display. And the Type command accepts a parameter that specifies the file you want to display.

Similarly, many application programs accept one or more parameters. When you start *WordPerfect*, for example, you can use a parameter to specify the name of the file that you want the program to retrieve, as in this example:

`C:\WP51>wp mma\c1figs`

Here, the file name specification includes the subdirectory the file is in. Then, after DOS loads the program, *WordPerfect* retrieves the file you specified (in this case, C:\WP51\MMA\C1FIGS). Many application programs provide for a retrieval parameter like this, and some programs provide for other parameters as well.

You can also specify a parameter like this when you use a batch file. To do that, you code a *replaceable parameter* in the appropriate command in the batch file. This parameter consists of the character %, followed by a number (*1* for the first replaceable parameter, *2* for the second one, and so on). Then, you enter the value for the replaceable parameter in the command that you use to execute the batch file.

For example, suppose you want to create a batch file named WP.BAT that starts *WordPerfect* and provides for a file name parameter. Figure 7-4 shows how you can do this. Notice the third line of the batch file:

`wp %1`

Here, the %1 is the replaceable parameter. When DOS executes this line of the batch file, it replaces the %1 with the value of the first parameter you entered when you started the batch file. So if you start the batch file using the command shown in the figure, DOS substitutes MMA\SLSRPT for %1 when it executes the third line. As a result, *WordPerfect* will retrieve the SLSRPT file in the MMA subdirectory of the WP51 directory as its initial document.

As I said before, you can use more than one replaceable parameter in a batch file. You just use %2 for the second parameter, %3 for the third parameter, and so on. Then, you enter the actual values as additional parameters on the command that starts the batch file. But although DOS lets you use as many parameters as you want, you'll rarely need more than one.

A batch file named WP.BAT that provides for one parameter

```
c:
cd \wp51
wp %1
```

A command that starts the batch file and specifies which file to retrieve

```
C:\>wp mma\slsrpt
```

Figure 7-4 How to use a replaceable parameter in a batch file

Some perspective on batch files

Once you know how to create and maintain a batch file, you should be able to set one up in just a few minutes. Although each batch file saves you just a few keystrokes each time you use it, this set-up time pays off because it simplifies your operational procedures. As a result, you don't have to remember as many DOS details in order to use your application programs.

Once you've set up a batch file for starting an application program, you can execute the batch file in several ways. If, for example, you want to start the same application program each time you turn on your PC, you can include the command for the batch file that starts the application in the AUTOEXEC.BAT file. In other words, a batch file can execute other batch files. You can also execute a batch file from the DOS shell or from another shell utility. And you can execute a batch file from the command prompt.

Although this chapter shows you how to use batch files just for starting application programs, you can also use them for simplifying DOS commands. In chapter 10, for example, you'll learn how to use a batch file to simplify the use of the Backup command. By using the batch file instead of entering the command, you don't have to remember the details of using the command.

With this in mind, you should consider using a batch file to simplify your operational procedures whenever you're bothered by the continual need to remember DOS details. Once you've got your batch files set up, you'll spend more time using your application programs and less time using DOS.

Terms replaceable parameter

Chapter 7

Objectives

1. Given the drive, directory, and command name for a program, list the commands for a batch file that will start the program. If the program lets you set the data directory to the one you want to use before you start the program, include the batch file commands that will provide for that.

2. Describe the search sequence that DOS uses when it looks for a batch file.

Exercises

1. Use the Directory command to look at your directories and see which (if any) contain batch files. You can do that using this wildcard specification in each Directory command:

    `*.bat`

    If, for example, you're looking in the UTIL directory on the C drive, you issue this command:

    `C:\UTIL>dir *.bat`

2. If you find directories that contain batch files, use the Print command to print a copy of each batch file. Then, examine the copy to understand what each command does. If you don't understand all of the commands, don't worry. But you should at least be able to identify the commands that I've presented so far in this book.

3. Now, create a batch file that starts one of your application programs based on the examples in figure 7-2. If you have batch files for all your programs, create a new one for one of them, but when you name the batch file, don't use the name of the existing file. If you do, you could lose the existing file by overwriting it. If you have a full-screen text editor, use it to create your batch file. Otherwise, you can use your word processing program if it has a text feature. If you have neither of these, you can always use Edlin, but it should be your last choice.

    When you create your batch file:

    - Start your batch file with the Echo-on command so you can see the commands as they're executed.
    - Remember to use the extension BAT in the file name.
    - Store your batch file in a directory that's appropriate for batch files. If none is, you can temporarily store the file in the root directory of drive C. Then, in the next chapter, you'll learn how to create and organize directories.

4. To test your batch file, enter the file name without the BAT extension at the command prompt. If your PC displays this message:

    `Bad command or file name`

    it means the directory you stored your batch file in isn't in the current path. In that case, use the Change-directory command to change the current directory to the one that contains your batch file. Then, enter the file name again.

Chapter 8

How to manage the directories and files on a hard disk

When you use a hard disk, its directories and files can quickly get out of control. If you use three or four different application programs for a year or two, it's not unusual to have more than one thousand files spread over a couple dozen directories. By that time, you're likely to have dozens of files that you no longer need and at least a few files that you need but can't find. That's why it's important that you learn how to do an effective job of managing your directories and files.

In this chapter, you'll learn how to use seven DOS commands to manage your directories and five commands to manage your files. Next, you'll learn how to use the two DOS wildcards within the commands for managing files. Then, you'll learn how to use the directory commands and file commands together for some common maintenance tasks. Last, you'll learn 12 guidelines that will help you manage your directories and files more effectively.

If you have DOS 5.0 or 6.0, you should use the DOS shell for most of these tasks. But you should also know how to manage directories and files from the command prompt for at least two reasons. First, you can perform some file management jobs more efficiently from the command prompt. Second, you'll be able to use the shell more effectively if you understand how the shell functions are done with DOS commands. All a shell program does is convert the functions that you request into DOS commands so you don't have to be concerned about the details of the commands.

Seven commands for working with directories

Figure 8-1 summarizes seven commands you can use for working with directories. In chapter 4, you learned how to use the first two, and you shouldn't have any trouble learning to use the others.

Name	Format	Function

Directory	`DIR [file-spec] [/P]`
	`[/W]`
	`[/O]`
	`[/S]`
		Displays a directory listing for the specified files. The /P switch causes a pause when a screen is full; the /W switch causes a wide display format; the /O switch, introduced in DOS 5.0, displays the listing in alphabetical order, with subdirectories first, followed by files; the /S switch, introduced in DOS 5.0, displays subordinate directories and their files.

Change directory	`CD [directory]`	Changes the current directory. If the parameter is omitted, this command displays the path of the current directory.
Make directory	`MD directory`	Makes a new directory.
Remove directory	`RD directory`	Removes a directory. However, a directory must be empty before it can be removed. As a result, you can't remove a directory when it's the current directory.
Tree	`TREE [drive] [/F]`	Displays the directory structure for a drive. The /F switch also causes a display of the files within each directory.
Move	`MOVE directory-1` `     directory-2`	New in DOS 6.0. Renames a directory. The drive and path in the second directory specification must be the same as in the first directory specification. You can't rename the current directory.
Delete tree	`DELTREE directory`	New in DOS 6.0. Deletes a directory with all its subdirectories and files. Use this command with caution.

Figure 8-1 Seven commands for working with directories

The Directory command   As you already know, this command displays a directory. But if you use DOS 5.0 or 6.0, you can use two other switches with the Directory command: the /O switch and the /S switch.

The /O switch displays the directory listing in alphabetical order, as shown in figure 8-2. The subdirectories are listed first in order, followed by the files. As you can imagine, it's much easier to find a file you're looking for in a listing like this than in an unsorted listing, especially when the directory contains dozens of files.

```
C:\>dir /o

 Volume in drive C has no label
 Volume Serial Number is 1983-5D30
 Directory of C:\

123          <DIR>        12-15-92   8:58a
DATA         <DIR>        12-15-92   9:03a
DOS          <DIR>        12-15-92   8:50a
QA4          <DIR>        12-15-92   8:57a
UTIL         <DIR>        12-15-92   9:03a
WP51         <DIR>        12-15-92   8:54a
AUTOEXEC BAT          120 12-15-92   2:26p
COMMAND  COM        53022 10-26-92   6:00a
CONFIG   SYS          137 12-15-92   9:05a
        9 file(s)      53279 bytes
                    25639160 bytes free

C:\>
```

Figure 8-2   The use of the /O switch in the Directory command for DOS 5.0 and later versions

When you use the /S switch, DOS not only displays the contents of the directory you've specified, but also displays the contents of any subdirectories that are subordinate to that directory. You'll probably use this switch most often for finding a file when you can't remember what subdirectory it's in. In that case, you enter the file name as part of the file specification in the command and DOS looks for the file name in the specified or current directory and all its subdirectories. Then, it displays a listing for each of the files it finds with that name.

In figure 8-3, for example, I used the /S switch to find the path for a file named ADV92. DOS looked through all of the directories on the C drive starting with the current directory (the root directory) and found two files with that name. The complete paths and file names for each one are:

```
123\FILES\ADV92.WK1
WP51\MKTG\ADV92
```

The Change-directory command   As you already know, you use this command to change the current directory. But there's another form of this command that is often useful:

```
cd ..
```

The two dots in the directory specification represent the parent directory. The parent directory is always the directory in the path that immediately precedes the current directory. So with this specification, you can change the current directory to the parent directory.

```
C:\>dir adv92 /s

 Volume in drive C is DRIVE_C
 Volume Serial Number is 1911-0C02

Directory of C:\123\FILES

ADV92        WK1       11818 12-16-92    1:25p
        1 file(s)       11818 bytes

Directory of C:\WP51\MKTG

ADV92                  2819 10-22-92    3:19p
        1 file(s)        2819 bytes

Total files listed:
        2 file(s)       14637 bytes
                   134680576 bytes free

C:\>
```

Figure 8-3   The use of the /S switch in the Directory command for DOS 5.0 and later versions

The Make-directory command   You use the Make-directory command to make a new directory. As you can see in figure 8-1, you enter a directory specification in this command to indicate the directory you want to create. This specification gives the name of the new directory, and it also locates the new directory within the directory structure of the drive. You'll learn how to use this command for directory maintenance tasks later in this chapter.

When you name a directory, you use the same naming rules that you use for files. Thus, a directory name can be up to eight characters long with an extension of up to three characters. In practice, though, it makes sense to create short, meaningful directory names with no extensions.

The Remove-directory command   You use this command to remove a directory. However, you can't remove a directory with this command if it contains any subdirectories or files. And you can't remove a directory if it's the current directory. You'll learn how to use this command for directory maintenance tasks later in this chapter.

The Tree command   If you have more than a few directories on your PC, it's hard to visualize the directory structure. The Tree command is designed to help you review that structure. It displays the directories on a disk drive. If you use the /F switch, it also displays the files in each directory.

```
C:\>tree

DIRECTORY PATH LISTING

Path: \DOS

Sub directories:   None


Path: \UTIL

Sub directories:   None


Path: \WP51

Sub directories:   MMA
                   PROJ1


Path: \123

Sub directories:   MMA
                   DOUG


Path: \QA4

Sub directories:   MMA
```

Figure 8-4   The output displayed by the Tree command in DOS versions before 4.0

To illustrate, figure 8-4 shows the output that's displayed by the Tree command for versions of DOS before 4.0. As you can see, this command displays a list of the directories and the subdirectories that they contain. Unfortunately, it's difficult to work with this information in this form, so this command isn't used much.

In contrast, figure 8-5 shows how the output of the Tree command is displayed for DOS 4.0 and later versions. With these versions, this command displays a graphic tree that gives you a quick view of the directory structure. In general, the more directories you have on your drives, the more valuable the graphic tree structure becomes and the less valuable the tree listing becomes.

The Move command (DOS 6.0)   The Move command, introduced in DOS 6.0, is designed to move files from one directory to another, as you'll see later in this chapter. However, it also lets you change the name of a directory, as in this example:

```
C:\>move \wp51\mma \wp51\rpts
```

```
C:\>tree
Directory PATH listing
C:.
├──DOS
├──UTIL
├──WP51
│   ├── MMA
│   └──PROJ1
├──123
│   ├──MMA
│   └──DOUG
└─ QA4
    └── MMA
```

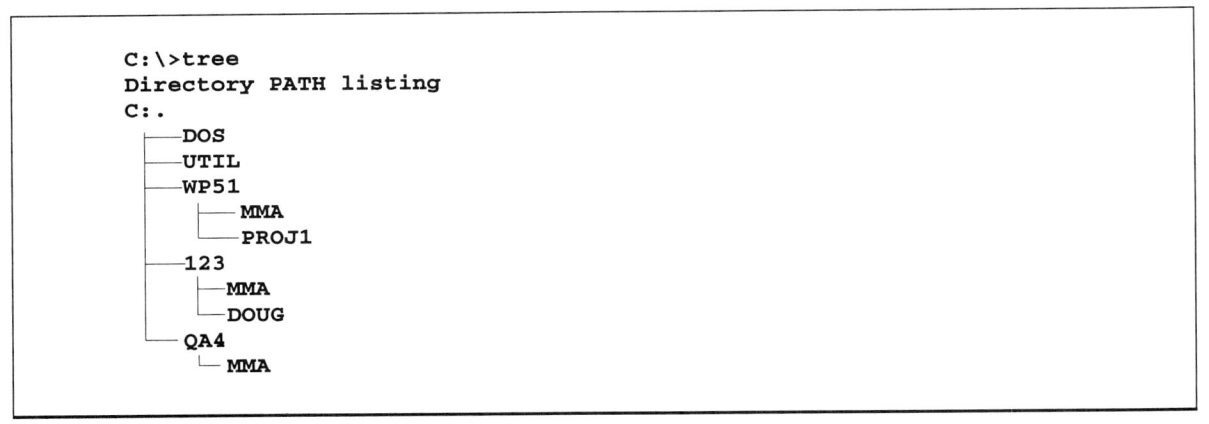

Figure 8-5 The output displayed by the Tree command for DOS 4.0 and later versions

Here, the subdirectory named MMA is renamed RPTS. Note that the directory you're renaming can't be the current directory.

As you'll see later in this chapter, you have to enter a whole series of commands to rename a directory without the Move command. So although you won't have to rename directories very often, you'll want to use this command whenever you do.

The Delete-tree command (DOS 6.0)   As I mentioned a moment ago, you can't use the Remove-directory command to delete a directory that contains any subdirectories or files. But in DOS 6.0, the Delete-tree command has been introduced for that purpose. When you enter the command, as in this example:

`C:\>deltree c:\wp51\mma`

DOS displays a message like this:

`Delete directory "c:\wp51\mma" and all its subdirectories? [yn]`

Then, if you enter *y*, DOS deletes the directory and all of its subordinates.

As you might imagine, you can do a lot of damage with this command, destroying months of work with just a few keystrokes. So don't use it unless you're sure you want to delete the entire directory, no matter what files and subdirectories it contains.

Five commands for working with files

Figure 8-6 summarizes five commands you can use for working with files. You can use all of these commands to operate on a single file or on multiple files. However, to operate on multiple files with the Copy, Delete, and Rename commands, you have to use wildcards. I'll show you how to use wildcards with these commands later in this chapter. For now, just concentrate on learning how to use these commands on single files.

Name	Format	Function
Copy	`COPY source-spec` `     [target-spec]`	Copies the file identified by the source specification to the path and file name given by the target specification. If the target specification is omitted, this command copies the source file to the current directory on the default drive using the source file name for the target file too.

Xcopy	`XCOPY source-spec`
	`      [target-spec]`
	`      [/S]`
		Copies the files identified by the source specification to the files identified by the target specification. The /S switch tells DOS to copy all the files and subdirectories in the source directory. This command is available in DOS 3.2 and later versions.

Delete	`DEL file-spec [/P]`	Deletes the file identified by the file specification. The /P switch, introduced in DOS 4.0, asks you for confirmation before the file is deleted.
Rename	`REN source-spec` `    target-spec`	Renames the file identified by the source specification with the name given in the target specification. You cannot specify a drive and directory in the target specification; you can only rename the file within the same directory.

Move	`MOVE source-spec-1`
	`     [source-spec-2]`
	`     target-spec`
		New in DOS 6.0. Moves the file or files specified by the source specifications to the target specification. If more than one file is specified, the target specification must be a directory name. If only one file is specified, you can also rename it by including a file name in the target specification.

Figure 8-6 Five commands for working with files

The Copy command You use the Copy command to copy files. You can use this command to copy files within a single directory, from one directory to another, from the hard disk to a diskette, or from a diskette to a hard disk. As a result, you're likely to use the Copy command frequently.

The format of the Copy command

```
COPY source-spec [target-spec]
```

Example 1:	A Copy command that copies the file named ADMGOALS.TXT in the current directory to a new file named ADMGOALS.BAK in the same directory.

```
C:\WP51\MMA>copy admgoals.txt admgoals.bak
```

Example 2:	A Copy command that copies the file named ADMGOALS.TXT in the current directory to a file with the same name in the WP51\MMA93 directory on the D drive.

```
C:\WP51\MMA>copy admgoals.txt d:\wp51\mma93
```

Example 3:	A Copy command that copies the file named ADMGOALS.TXT in the WP51\MMA directory on the C drive to a new file with the same name in the current directory on the default drive.

```
D:\DATA\MMA93>copy c:\wp51\mma\admgoals.txt
```

Example 4:	A Copy command that copies the file named ADMGOALS.TXT in the current directory to a file with the same name on a diskette in the A drive.

```
C:\WP51\MMA>copy admgoals.txt a:
```

Example 5:	An invalid Copy command that tries to copy a file within the current directory but doesn't give a name for the new file.

```
C:\WP51\MMA>copy admgoals.txt
```

Figure 8-7 The Copy command

If you look at the format of the Copy command shown in figure 8-6, you can see that it has two parameters. The first parameter is the file specification for the *source file*; the file that's going to be copied. The second parameter is the file specification for the *target file*; the file that's going to be created by the Copy command.

Figure 8-7 shows five examples of Copy commands along with explanations of what happens when they are executed. In all of these examples, the command prompt tells you what the default drive and current directory are. If you specify the drive, directory, and file name for both the source and target files, it doesn't matter what the default drive and the current directory are. But if you omit the drive specification for a file, the default drive is assumed. And if you omit the directory specification, the current directory is assumed.

The format of the Xcopy command

```
XCOPY source-spec [target-spec] [/S]
```

Example 1: An Xcopy command that copies all files from the MMA directory and its subdirectories on the C drive to the root directory on the D drive.

```
C:\>xcopy \mma d: /s
```

Example 2: An Xcopy command that creates an MMA directory on the D drive and then copies all files from the MMA directory and its subdirectories on the C drive to the MMA directory on the D drive.

```
C:\>xcopy \mma d:\mma\ /s
```

Figure 8-8   The Xcopy command

If you omit the file name for the target file, DOS uses the file name of the source file for the target file. Since that's frequently what you want, you'll often omit the target file name, whether or not you give a drive and directory specification. For instance, example 2 gives a drive and directory specification but no file name, and example 4 gives a drive specification but no file name.

When you use the Copy command, you must realize that it will replace an existing file if the file specification for the target file is the same as one for an existing file. Worse, DOS will replace the existing file without warning you that it's going to be replaced. If, for example, you copy a file named C1.DOC to a diskette that already has a file named C1.DOC on it, DOS will replace the existing file with the new file. Although that might be what you want, you must use the Copy command with care so you don't replace files accidentally.

The Xcopy command   The Xcopy command is similar to the Copy command, but it lets you copy all the files in a directory and its subdirectories at once. To do that, you enter the command with the /S switch, as shown in figure 8-8, and enter a directory name instead of a file name as the source specification. In example 1, DOS will copy all the files in the MMA directory and its subdirectories to the root directory of the D drive, using the same file and subdirectory names as they have on the C drive. In example 2, the target specification is a directory name, as indicated by the backslash at the end (if you forget the backslash, DOS will ask you if it's a file name or a directory name). Here, DOS will create a directory named MMA on the D drive and then copy all the files in the MMA directory and its subdirectories from the C drive to the D drive.

As I mentioned earlier, you can also copy multiple files with a single Copy command. But you can't copy an entire directory structure as you can with Xcopy.

The format of the Delete command

```
DEL file-spec [/P]
```

Example 1:	A Delete command that deletes the file named ADMGOALS.TXT from the current directory.

```
C:\WP51\MMA>del admgoals.txt
```

Example 2:	A Delete command that deletes the file named ADMGOALS.WK1 from the WK1 directory on the D drive.

```
C:\WP51\MMA>del d:\wk1\admgoals.wk1
```

Example 3:	A Delete command that asks you for confirmation before deleting the file named ADMGOALS.WK1 from the WK1 directory on the D drive.

```
C:\WP51\MMA>del d:\wk1\admgoals.wk1 /p

D:\WK1\ADMGOALS.WK1,  Delete (Y/N)?
```

Figure 8-9   The Delete command

What's more, Xcopy works by reading in as much data as it can, then writing files to the target. In contrast, Copy works on one file at a time. In some cases, this makes Xcopy faster, especially when you're reading or writing files from diskette. So you'll probably use Xcopy often when you're copying files.

The Delete command   You use the Delete command to remove a file from a directory. In this command, the file specification identifies the file that you want to delete. When you use the Delete command without the /P switch, you must be careful because it deletes the file you've specified without giving you any warning or a chance to cancel the command before the damage is done. (The /P switch was introduced in DOS 4.0, so it's not available to you if you have an earlier version of DOS.)

Figure 8-9 shows three examples of the Delete command. In example 1, the command deletes a file named ADMGOALS.TXT from the current directory. In example 2, the command gives a complete file specification to delete a file named ADMGOALS.WK1 from the WK1 directory on the D drive. In example 3, the /P switch causes DOS to ask you for confirmation before it deletes the file.

The Rename command   You use the Rename command to change the name of a file. In this command, the source specification identifies the file you want to rename, and the target specification gives the new name you want to use. Note,

How to manage the directories and files on a hard disk   **117**

The format of the Rename command

```
REN source-spec target-spec
```

Example 1: A Rename command that renames REVSUM.TXT in the current directory to REVSUM92.TXT.

```
C:\WP51\MMA>ren revsum.txt revsum92.txt
```

Example 2: A Rename command that renames REVSUM.WK1 in the WK1 directory on the D drive to REVSUM92.WK1.

```
C:\WP51\MMA>ren d:\wk1\revsum.wk1 revsum92.wk1
```

Example 3: An invalid Rename command that tries to rename a file in the current directory with a target file specification that's in another drive and directory.

```
C:\WP51\MMA>ren revsum.txt d:\wk1\revsum92.txt
```

Figure 8-10   The Rename command

however, that you can't specify a drive and directory in the target specification because this command can only rename a file; it can't move the file to another directory.

Figure 8-10 shows three examples of Rename commands. In example 1, the command renames a file named REVSUM.TXT in the current directory to REVSUM92.TXT. In example 2, the command renames a file named REVSUM.WK1 in the WK1 directory on the D drive to REVSUM92.WK1. In example 3, the command is invalid because its target specification includes drive and directory information.

The Move command (DOS 6.0)   You've already seen how to rename a directory with the DOS 6.0 Move command. You can also use this command to move one or more files on your system. And you can use it to rename a single file as you move the file.

Figure 8-11 shows six examples of Move commands. In example 1, the command moves a file named WP.BAT from the UTIL directory to the BAT directory. In example 2, the command moves a file named MONTHEND.WK1 from the C drive to the A drive. In example 3, the command moves a file named EOMJAN.WK1 down one step in the directory structure by moving it from the 123 directory on the C drive to the 123\92RECS directory. In example 4, the command moves a file from one drive and directory to another and changes its name at the same time. So the file that was named REVSUM92 is now called REVENUE.92. Example

---

The format of the Move command

```
MOVE source-spec-1 [source-spec-2] target-spec
```

Example 1: A Move command that moves the file named WP.BAT from the current directory to the BAT directory on the default drive.

```
C:\UTIL>move wp.bat \bat
```

Example 2: A Move command that moves the file named MONTHEND.WK1 from the current directory on the C drive to the A drive.

```
C:\123>move monthend.wk1 a:
```

Example 3: A Move command that moves the file named EOMJAN.WK1 from the 123 directory on the C drive to the 123\92RECS directory.

```
C:\>move 123\eomjan.wk1 123\92recs
```

Example 4: A Move command that moves the file named REVSUM92 from the current directory on the C drive to the DATA directory on the D drive and renames the file REVENUE.92.

```
C:\WP51\MMA>move revsum92 d:\data\revenue.92
```

Example 5: A Move command that moves two files, C1.DOC and C1FIGS.DOC, from the MMA directory on the C drive to the DOSBK directory.

```
C:\DOSBK\>move \mma\c1.doc \mma\c1figs.doc \dosbk
```

Example 6: A Move command that uses a period in the target specification to move two files to the current directory.

```
C:\DOSBK\>move \mma\c1.doc \mma\c1figs.doc .
```

Figure 8-11 The Move command

5 shows how to move two files at the same time. It moves the files named C1.DOC and C1FIGS.DOC from the MMA directory on the C drive to the directory named DOSBK. In this case, the target specification must be a directory name.

With what you know about the operation of the Copy command, you might expect that you could omit the target directory from the Move command in example 5 since the intended target directory is the current directory. You can't do that, however, because the Move command requires a target specification. If you omitted the target directory from the command in example 5, Move would assume that the second file specification was the target, and the command wouldn't work as you intended.

How to manage the directories and files on a hard disk 119

Wildcard	Meaning
*	One or more characters of any kind
?	One character of any kind

Example	Meaning
`*.*`	All files (any name, any extension)
`*.com`	All files with COM as the extension
`*.`	All files that don't have an extension
`c1.*`	All files named C1 no matter what the extension is
`c*.*`	All files with names that start with C
`c?.*`	All one- or two-character file names that start with C
`c?.com`	All one- or two-character file names that start with C and have an extension of COM
`c???????.`	All file names that start with C and that don't have an extension (same as c*.)
`????.exe`	All one-, two-, three-, or four-character file names that have an extension of EXE

Figure 8-12 The * and ? wildcards

Instead of entering the name of the current directory for the target specification as in example 5, you can use the shortcut illustrated in example 6. Here, I entered a period for the target specification. When you do that, DOS substitutes the current directory for the period.

Like the Copy command, the Move command will overwrite existing files in the target directory without warning. So be careful whenever you use it to move files into a directory that already has files in it.

How to use wildcards within a DOS command

DOS provides two *wildcards* that you can use within the file specifications of DOS commands. These wildcards are summarized in figure 8-12. When you use wildcards within a command, a single DOS command can operate on more than one file.

You already know a little bit about the * *wildcard* (asterisk wildcard). It represents one or more characters of any kind, and it is the wildcard that you'll use the most. Sometimes, this wildcard is called the *star wildcard*, and a specification like *.*

is referred to as "star-dot-star." This wildcard makes it easy for a single command to operate on all of the files within a directory or all the files in a directory that have a specific extension.

The *? wildcard* (question mark wildcard) represents one character of any kind. Although you may never need it, it can be useful once in a while. It's used to select files that have any character in each ? wildcard position. For instance, a specification like this

```
C?FIGS
```

includes files with names like C1FIGS, C2FIGS, and C9FIGS, but it excludes files with names like C19FIGS and C20FIGS.

Perhaps the best way to get comfortable with the use of the wildcards is to practice using them in Directory commands, as illustrated in figure 8-13. Here, the first command displays only the files with COM as the extension. The second command displays the files that have an extension of COM and that start with the letter M. The third command displays the files that have no extension and that start with the letter M. In this case, there aren't any files that meet this criteria, so DOS displays a "File not found" message. The fourth command uses ? wildcards to display file names of four or fewer characters that start with the letter M and that have COM as the extension. The fifth command uses ? wildcards to display file names of three or fewer characters no matter what the extensions are.

Once you're sure that you know how wildcards work, you can use them in Copy, Xcopy, and Rename commands as illustrated in figure 8-14. Here, the examples only show the use of * wildcards, but you can use ? wildcards whenever they are appropriate.

If you have any doubt about the way wildcards are going to work in Delete commands, I recommend that you use a two-step procedure like the one in figure 8-15. In step 1, you use the Directory command with the file specification for the files you want to delete. Then, if the correct files are displayed, use exactly the same file specification in a Delete command, as shown in step 2.

Remember that if you have DOS 4.0 or later, you can use the /P switch to avoid deleting the wrong files. When you use this switch, the Delete command asks you for confirmation before it deletes a file. If you respond with *y* when DOS asks you if you want to delete a file, the file is deleted. If you respond with *n*, the command proceeds to the next file specified by the command or ends the command if no other files are specified.

If you use the *.* specification to delete all the files in a directory, DOS asks you if you're sure you want to do that. But it doesn't ask you to confirm each file deletion individually. So again, if you have any doubts as to which files will be deleted, use a Directory command or the /P switch to check.

In DOS 6.0, you can also use wildcards with the Move command, but you can't use them as widely as you can in some of the other commands. Figure 8-16 gives you two examples. The first example works just as you've seen the wildcards work in other commands. The second example, however, is an invalid command because it

How to manage the directories and files on a hard disk

Example 1

A Directory command that displays all the files in the current directory that have an extension of COM.

```
C:\DOS>dir *.com /w

 Volume in drive C has no label
 Volume Serial Number is 1983-5D30
 Directory of C:\DOS

FORMAT.COM      KEYB.COM        SYS.COM         UNFORMAT.COM    CHOICE.COM
MIRROR.COM      DOSSHELL.COM    MODE.COM        GRAFTABL.COM    HELP.COM
EDIT.COM        MSHERC.COM      ASSIGN.COM      DISKCOMP.COM    DISKCOPY.COM
MORE.COM        GRAPHICS.COM    TREE.COM        DOSKEY.COM      LOADFIX.COM
VSAFE.COM       COMMAND.COM
       22 file(s)       327796 bytes
                      25636864 bytes free

C:\DOS>
```

Example 2

A Directory command that displays all the files in the current directory with names that start with the letter M and have an extension of COM.

```
C:\DOS>dir m*.com

 Volume in drive C has no label
 Volume Serial Number is 1983-5D30
 Directory of C:\DOS

MIRROR      COM      18169 04-09-91   5:00a
MODE        COM      23537 10-26-92   6:00a
MSHERC      COM       6934 04-09-91   5:00a
MORE        COM       2618 10-26-92   6:00a
        4 file(s)        51258 bytes
                      25636864 bytes free

C:\DOS>
```

Example 3

A Directory command that displays all the files in the current directory with names that start with the letter M and have no extension.

```
C:\DOS>dir m*.

 Volume in drive C has no label
 Volume Serial Number is 1983-5D30
 Directory of C:\DOS

File not found

C:\DOS>
```

Figure 8-13 The use of wildcards in Directory commands (part 1 of 2)

Example 4

A Directory command that displays all the files in the current directory with names that start with the letter M, that have four or fewer characters, and that have an extension of COM.

```
C:\DOS>dir m???.com

 Volume in drive C has no label
 Volume Serial Number is 1983-5D30
 Directory of C:\DOS

MODE        COM       23537 10-26-92   6:00a
MORE        COM        2618 10-26-92   6:00a
       2 file(s)        26155 bytes
                     25636864 bytes free

C:\DOS>
```

Example 5

A Directory command that displays all the files in the current directory that have file names of three or fewer characters.

```
C:\DOS>dir ???

 Volume in drive C has no label
 Volume Serial Number is 1983-5D30
 Directory of C:\DOS

.              <DIR>       12-15-92   8:50a
..             <DIR>       12-15-92   8:50a
EGA         SYS        4885 10-26-92   6:00a
EGA         CPI       58873 10-26-92   6:00a
SYS         COM       13440 10-26-92   6:00a
MSD         EXE      158428 10-26-92   6:00a
MEM         EXE       30470 10-26-92   6:00a
LCD         CPI       10753 04-09-91   5:00a
FC          EXE       18650 10-26-92   6:00a
XMA         TXT        5408 12-19-88  12:00a
      10 file(s)       300907 bytes
                     25636864 bytes free

C:\>DOS
```

Figure 8-13 The use of wildcards in Directory commands (part 2 of 2)

includes a wildcard in the target specification. Although you can code a Copy command like this, when you're moving multiple files the target specification must be a directory name, and the wildcard indicates a file name.

Example 1:	A Copy command that copies all of the files in the WP51\MMA directory on the C drive to a diskette in the A drive.
	`C:\>copy \wp51\mma\*.* a:`
Example 2:	A Copy command that copies all of the files on the diskette in the A drive to the current directory.
	`C:\DATA\123>copy a:*.*`
Example 3:	A Copy command and an Xcopy command that copy all of the files with an extension of WK1 in the current directory to a diskette in the A drive.
	`C:\DATA\123>copy *.wk1 a:` `C:\DATA\123>xcopy *.wk1 a:`
Example 4:	A Rename command that renames all files named PRSUM in the current directory, no matter what the extensions are, to PRSUM93.
	`C:WP51\MMA>ren prsum.* prsum93.*`
Example 5:	A Rename command that changes the extensions of all files in the current directory with the extension of WK1 to the extension of BAK.
	`C:\123\MMA>ren *.wk1 *.bak`

Figure 8-14 The use of wildcards in Copy, Xcopy, and Rename commands

Step 1:	Use the Directory command with the wildcard specification that you intend to use in the Delete command.
	`C:\>dir d:\wp51\mma\*.bak`
Step 2:	If the files that are displayed are the ones that you want to delete, use the Delete command with exactly the same wildcard specification that you used in step 1.
	`C:\>del d:\wp51\mma\*.bak`

Figure 8-15 How to use wildcards to avoid deleting the wrong files

Example 1:	A Move command that moves all of the files with an extension of 92 from the current directory to a diskette in the A drive.
	`C:\DATA\WP51>move *.92 a:`
Example 2:	A Move command that's invalid because it includes a wildcard in the target specification (the wildcard indicates a file name and the target specification must be a directory name when you're moving multiple files).
	`C:\DATA\WP51>move *.92 a:\*.old`

Figure 8-16 The use of wildcards in Move commands

Typical command sequences for managing directories and files

Although the versions of DOS before DOS 6.0 provide commands for making a new directory and removing an empty directory, they don't provide commands for renaming a directory, for removing a directory that contains files, or for moving a directory and its files from one point in the directory structure to another. To do these tasks, you have to use a combination of DOS commands. With DOS 6.0, you can use the Move command to rename a directory and you can use the Deltree command to delete a directory that contains files. But you still have to use a combination of commands to move a directory and its files.

When you use the DOS shell for managing directories and files, you can do most directory functions more easily than you can from the command prompt. For instance, the DOS shell provides specific functions for creating, renaming, and deleting directories. As a result, you don't have to know how to do these functions from the command prompt. However, the DOS shell doesn't provide a function for moving a directory and its files from one point in the directory structure to another. To do that, you must use the series of DOS commands that I'll describe in a moment. You can start these commands from the command prompt or from the shell, but you must understand what has to be done before you can do it.

How to make a new directory   Figure 8-17 shows you two ways to use the Make-directory command when you want to make a new directory. In example 1, the Change-directory command changes the current directory to the one that the new directory should be subordinate to. Then, the Make-directory command specifies only the new directory name as a parameter. In example 2, the Make-directory command gives a complete path for the new directory as a parameter.

How to delete a directory   The first part of figure 8-18 shows how to delete a directory in DOS 6.0. As you can see, all you have to do is issue a Deltree command

| **Example 1** | ```
C:\>cd \123
C:\123>md becky
``` |
| **Example 2** | ```
C:\>md \123\becky
``` |

Figure 8-17 Two ways to make a new directory named 123\BECKY

For DOS 6.0

```
C:\>deltree \qa4\college
Delete directory "\qa4\college" and all its subdirectories?[yn]y
Deleting \qa4\college...

C:\>
```

For versions of DOS before DOS 6.0

Step 1: Change the current directory to the one that you want to remove.

```
C:\>cd \qa4\college
```

Step 2: Delete all the files in the directory.

```
C:\QA4\COLLEGE>del *.*
All files in directory will be deleted!
Are you sure (Y/N)?y
```

Step 3: Change the current directory to the root directory.

```
C:\QA4\COLLEGE>cd \
```

Step 4: Remove the empty directory.

```
C:\>rd \qa4\college

C:\>
```

Figure 8-18 How to delete a directory named QA4\COLLEGE

for the directory and press *y* when DOS asks you for confirmation. Then, DOS will delete the directory and all its subdirectories.

Unfortunately, DOS versions prior to 6.0 don't have the Deltree command. So, to delete an entire directory using an older version of DOS, you must use the sequence of commands shown in the second part of figure 8-18. In step 1, you change the current directory to the one that you want to remove. In step 2, you delete all the files in the directory because a directory has to be empty before you can remove it. When you use wildcard specifications to delete all of the files in a directory, DOS displays this message

```
Are you sure (Y/N)?
```

to give you a chance to change your mind. If you are sure, you respond by entering *y*. In step 3, you use the Change-directory command to change the current directory to the root directory because you can't use the Remove-directory command to remove the current directory. And in step 4, you use the Remove-directory command to remove the empty directory.

This example assumes that the QA4\COLLEGE directory doesn't contain any subdirectories. But if a directory does contain subdirectories, you must first use this procedure to delete the files from each subdirectory and remove the subdirectory. Then, when the directory is completely empty, you can remove it.

If you like, you can simplify the procedure in figure 8-18 by specifying the directory path in the Delete command. Then, you can delete the files and remove the directory with just two commands:

```
C:\>del \qa4\college\*.*
All files in directory will be deleted!
Are you sure (Y/N)?y

C:\>rd \qa4\college
```

How to rename a directory The first part of figure 8-19 shows how to rename a directory in DOS 6.0. As you can see, all you have to do is enter a Move command that specifies the current directory name and the new name you want it to have. DOS makes all the adjustments needed to be able to identify the files in the directory according to their new path names.

In the versions of DOS before DOS 6.0, there's no single DOS command for renaming a directory, so you have to use the combination of commands shown in the second part of figure 8-19. In step 1, you use the Make-directory command to make a new directory with the new name that you want to use for the existing directory. In step 2, you copy all of the files in the existing directory to the new directory. In step 3, you delete all the files in the existing directory. In step 4, you remove the existing directory from the disk. The result is a renamed directory.

Unfortunately, in order to use this technique, you must have enough space on your hard disk to hold two copies of the files in the directory. If you don't have enough free disk space, you have to delete some files to free up some disk space

For DOS 6.0

```
C:\>move \123\mma 123\mma92
C:\123\MMA => C:\123\MMA92 [ok]

C:\>
```

For versions of DOS before DOS 6.0

Step 1: Make a new directory that has the name you want to rename the existing directory with.

```
C:\>md \123\mma92
```

Step 2: Copy the files from the old directory to the new directory using the Copy or Xcopy command.

```
C:\>copy \123\mma\*.* \123\mma92
BALSHEET.WK1
PROFORMA.WK1
SALARIES.WK1
MKTGEXP.WK1
ADMEXP.WK1
        5 File(s) copied
```

Step 3: Delete the files in the old directory.

```
C:\>del \123\mma\*.*
All files in directory will be deleted!
Are you sure (Y/N)?y
```

Step 4: Remove the old directory.

```
C:\>rd \123\mma

C:\>
```

Figure 8-19 How to rename a directory from 123\MMA to 123\MMA92

before you begin. In addition, the process is more complicated if the directory you want to rename has subdirectories. In that case, you must copy each of those subdirectories as well. (If you're using DOS 3.2 or later, you can use the Xcopy command with the /S switch instead of the Copy command to copy all the subdirectories with a single command.)

For DOS 6.0

Step 1: Use the Xcopy command to create a new directory in the location that you want to move the old directory to and copy the files from the old directory to it.

```
C:\>xcopy \123\mma\*.* \93recs\*.* /s
```

Step 2: Delete the old directory.

```
C:\>deltree \123\mma
Delete directory "\123\mma" and all its subdirectories?[yn]y
Deleting \123\mma...

C:\>
```

For versions of DOS from DOS 3.2 to DOS 5.0

Step 1: Use the Xcopy command to create a new directory in the location that you want to move the old directory to and copy the files from the old directory to it.

```
C:\>xcopy \123\mma\*.* \93recs\*.* /s
```

Step 2: Delete the files in the old directory.

```
C:\>del \123\mma\*.*
All files in directory will be deleted!
Are you sure (Y/N)?y
```

Step 3: Remove the old directory.

```
C:\>rd \123\mma
```

Figure 8-20 How to move a directory

How to move a directory   There's no single DOS command for moving a directory from one point in a directory structure to another. Also, as I mentioned earlier, the DOS 5.0/6.0 shell doesn't provide for this function. As a result, you have to use a combination of commands to move a directory, as shown in figure 8-20.

If you're using DOS 6.0, the procedure consists of two steps. In the first step, you use an Xcopy command to copy all the files from their current location to the directory you want to move them to. Here, the target specification, 93RECS, is a directory name and the /S switch is specified. So the Xcopy command creates a new directory called 93RECS subordinate to the root directory and copies all the files in 123\MMA and its subdirectories to 93RECS. Then, in step 2, you use the Deltree command to delete the old directory with all its subdirectories and files. If you're worried about having enough space to copy the files, you can use a three-step procedure instead: (1) make a new directory in the location you want to move the old directory to; (2) use the Move command to move all the files from the old directory to the new one; and (3) delete the old directory using a Deltree or Remove-directory command. In that case, you'll have to repeat the steps for any subdirectories the directory has.

If you're using a version of DOS from DOS 3.2 to DOS 5.0, the steps are basically the same as for renaming a directory, as you can see in the second part of figure 8-20. In step 1, you use the Xcopy command to create a directory in the new location and to copy all the files and subdirectories from the original location. In step 2, you delete all the files from the original directory. And in step 3, you remove the original directory from the disk. Again, if the directory contains subdirectories, you'll have to repeat steps 2 and 3 for each subdirectory before you can use them for the original directory.

If you're using a version of DOS before 3.2, you have to begin by issuing a Make-directory command to make a new directory in the location that you want to move the old directory to. Then, you use the Copy command instead of the Xcopy command to copy all the files from the old directory to the new directory. At that point, you delete the files in the old directory and remove the old directory. This procedure is like the one for renaming a directory shown in figure 8-19.

Twelve guidelines for managing your directories and files

Now that you've learned the commands for managing your directories and files, here are 12 guidelines that will help you do a better job of managing them, whether you use the DOS commands or a shell. Because these guidelines are all quite straightforward, I'll go through them quickly. They are summarized in figure 8-21.

Keep the number of files in the root directory to a minimum If you do this, it's easier to manage the directories and files on your system. In general, the root directory of each drive should contain only entries for subordinate directories. In addition, the root directory of the C drive must contain the COMMAND.COM, CONFIG.SYS, and AUTOEXEC.BAT files.

You can't always keep other files out of the root directory, though, because some application programs and utility programs put files of their own in the root directory of the default drive. Nevertheless, you shouldn't put any more files in your root directory than are required. Instead, you should store your files in directories that help you keep them organized.

Don't use more than two directory levels below the root directory
Sometimes, it's tempting to use more than two levels of directories below the root directory. For instance, you start by adding a directory (WP) for your word processing program that's subordinate to the root directory. Next, you add a data directory

1. Keep the number of files in the root directory to a minimum.
2. Don't use more than two directory levels below the root directory.
3. Use simple directory names.
4. Store DOS files in a DOS directory.
5. Store utility programs in a utility directory.
6. Store all batch files in one directory.
7. Store application programs in their own directories.
8. Store data files in logically organized data directories.
9. Keep your data directories small.
10. Don't keep files you don't need.
11. Use consistent file names.
12. Include the file name in the heading of each document that's prepared from a file.

Figure 8-21 Twelve guidelines for managing directories and files

(WP\PROJECTA) for the files you'll create as part of an extensive writing project. Then, because several of you are working on the project, you are tempted to add more directories that are subordinate to the PROJECTA subdirectory. That way, there's a directory for each person's work: WP\PROJECTA\DOUG, WP\PROJECTA\ANNE, and so on.

As tempting as this may be from an organizational point of view, you should resist doing this because it leads to paths that are too long for efficiency. After you enter the complete path specifications a few times, you'll be convinced of that. Also, you can get the same effect without going to a third structural level. Just make the directories for each person as well as the PROJECTA directory subordinate to the word processing directory. Or make the PROJECTA directory subordinate to the root directory instead of the word processing directory. Either way, by limiting yourself to two directory levels below the root directory, you'll simplify your directory and file management.

Use simple directory names You'll type directory and subdirectory names often as you use your PC, so keep them short and simple like the ones illustrated in this book. Don't use special characters in your directory names because they're more difficult to type than letters and numbers, and don't use extensions in your directory names either. For program directories, try to use the name suggested by the program's installation instructions. For data directories, try to use a short but meaningful name.

Store DOS files in a DOS directory DOS 5.0 and 6.0 automatically install themselves into a separate directory named DOS that's subordinate to the root directory on the C drive. With older versions of DOS, however, it's common to find all of the DOS files in the root directory. Rather than clutter up the root directory, I suggest that you move the DOS files (except for COMMAND.COM, CONFIG.SYS, and AUTOEXEC.BAT) to a directory named DOS. Then, add the DOS directory to the Path command in your AUTOEXEC.BAT file.

In moving your DOS files from the root directory, you may have to work around other files that are in the root directory. As a result, you'll need to perform six steps to move your DOS files to a DOS directory. First, create a DOS directory that's subordinate to the root directory. Second, copy all of the files from the root directory to the DOS directory. Third, delete all of the files in the root directory. Fourth, copy the COMMAND.COM, CONFIG.SYS, and AUTOEXEC.BAT files and any files that aren't DOS files from the DOS directory to the root directory. Fifth, delete the COMMAND.COM, CONFIG.SYS, and AUTOEXEC.BAT files and any files that aren't a part of DOS from the DOS directory. Sixth, add the DOS directory to the search list in the Path command in the AUTOEXEC.BAT file.

Store utility programs in a utility directory If you own any utility programs, I suggest you store them in a directory named UTIL. Then, add the UTIL directory to the Path command in your AUTOEXEC.BAT file. If you purchase a large utility that comes with many files, you can create a separate directory for that program.

Store all batch files in one directory I mentioned this in chapter 7, but it's worth repeating. To control the batch files on your system, you should store them in one directory. This can be the UTIL directory, or you can create a separate directory for them named BAT or BATCH. If you create a separate directory, be sure to add it to the search list in the Path command in your AUTOEXEC.BAT file.

Store application programs in their own directories Because most application programs require dozens of files, you should store each program in its own directory and make that directory subordinate to the root directory. If you look back to the tree in figure 8-5, you can see three directories for application programs: WP51 for *WordPerfect*; 123 for *Lotus 1-2-3*; and QA4 for *Q&A*.

Store data files in logically organized data directories Although some programs require it, you shouldn't store data files in program directories if you can avoid it. Otherwise, your program directories will quickly become unmanageable. Instead, you should store your data files in logically organized data directories.

Figure 8-22 illustrates five ways to organize data directories. In the first structure, word processing documents are stored in a directory called DOC, and spreadsheets are stored in a directory called WK1 (the normal extension for *Lotus 1-2-3* spreadsheets). This one-level structure is sensible if you don't have too much software or data on your system.

A one-level directory structure

```
├── DOS
├── UTIL
├── WP
├── 123
├── DOC
└── WK1
```

A two-level directory structure with all data directories subordinate to the DATA directory

```
├── DOS
├── UTIL
├── WP
├── 123
└── DATA ──┬── DOC
            └── WK1
```

A two-level directory structure with data organized by program

```
├── DOS
├── UTIL
├── WP ──┬── MEMOS
│        ├── LETTERS
│        └── REPORTS
└── 123 ──┬── CORP
          └── DEPT
```

A two-level directory structure with data organized by project

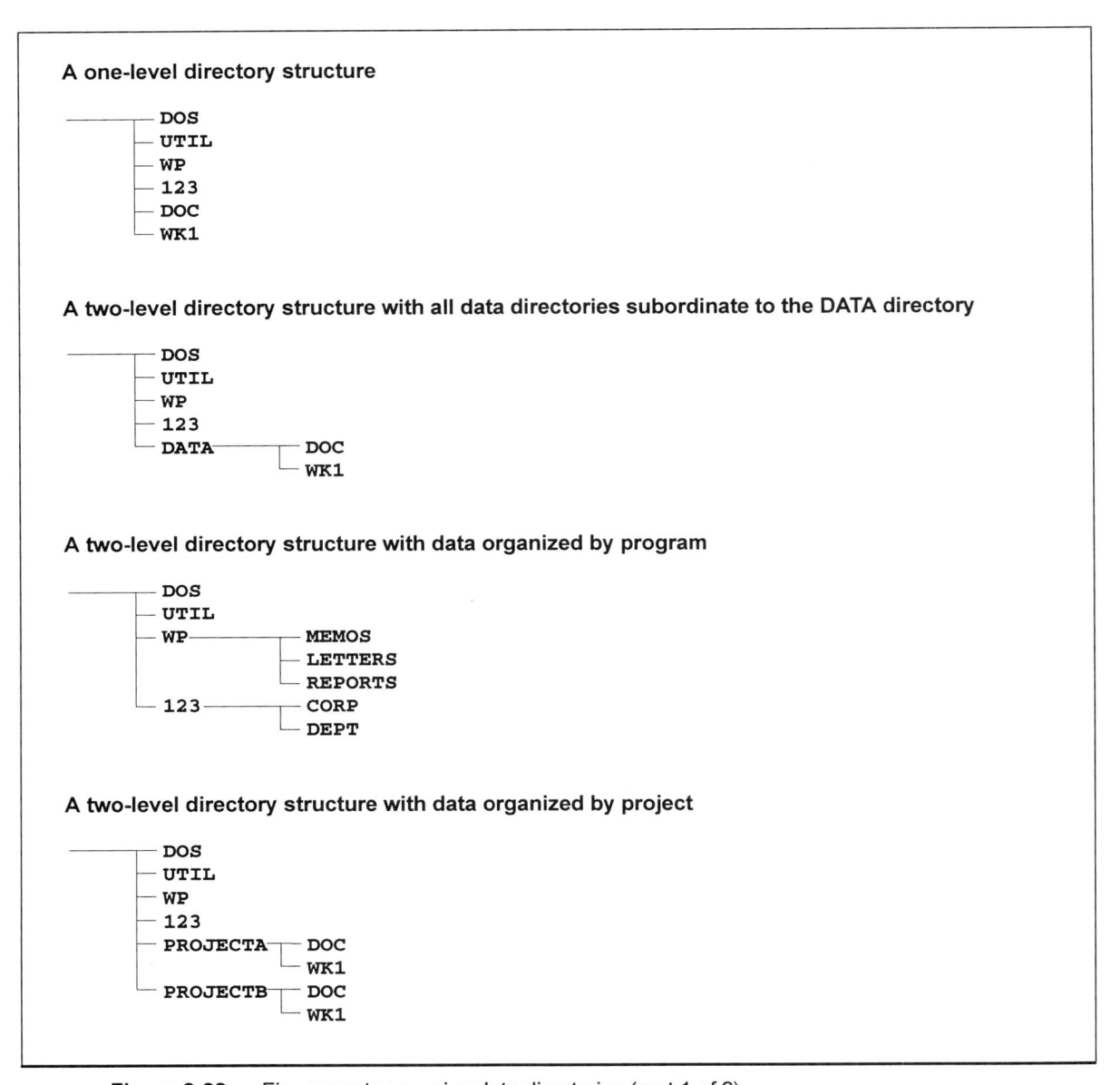

```
├── DOS
├── UTIL
├── WP
├── 123
├── PROJECTA ──┬── DOC
│              └── WK1
└── PROJECTB ──┬── DOC
               └── WK1
```

Figure 8-22 Five ways to organize data directories (part 1 of 2)

In the second structure in figure 8-22, the two data directories (DOC and WK1) are subordinate to a directory named DATA. And all of the program directories are subordinate to the root directory. As chapter 10 explains, this two-level structure can simplify your backup procedures.

A two-level directory structure with data organized by user

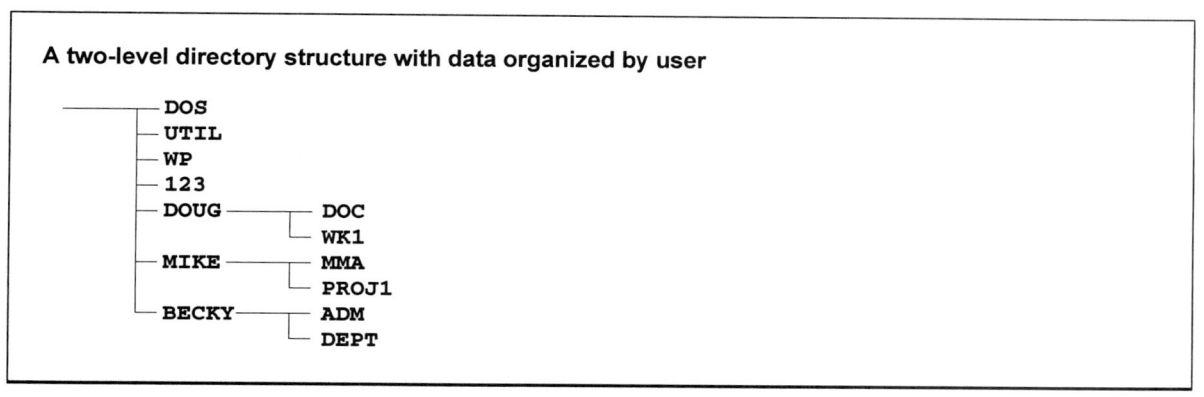

```
├── DOS
├── UTIL
├── WP
├── 123
├── DOUG ────┬── DOC
│            └── WK1
├── MIKE ────┬── MMA
│            └── PROJ1
└── BECKY ───┬── ADM
             └── DEPT
```

Figure 8-22 Five ways to organize data directories (part 2 of 2)

The third structure in figure 8-22 is a two-level structure that's organized by application program. Here, the data directories are subordinate to the program directories. As a result, you know that the MEMOS, LETTERS, and REPORTS directories contain word processing documents. And you know that the CORP and DEPT directories contain spreadsheets.

The fourth structure in figure 8-22 is a two-level structure that's organized by project. Here, the DOC directories contain word processing documents related to each of the two projects, and the WK1 directories contain spreadsheets related to the projects.

The last structure in figure 8-22 is a two-level structure that's organized by PC user. This is sensible when several people use the same PC. Then, the users decide how they want to organize their subdirectories.

The point I'm trying to make is that there should be some logic to the structure of your directories. If there is, it will be easier for you to manage your files. You'll also be able to find whatever files you're looking for.

Keep your data directories small   At some point, a data directory holds so many files that it becomes unmanageable. Then, it's time to delete files you no longer need. It may also be time to regroup the files into two or more subdirectories based on some logical structure. If you keep your data directories small, you'll be able to manage your files more effectively.

Don't keep files you don't need   This guideline is pretty obvious, and it's closely related to the previous one. However, I've included it as a separate guideline because most PC users don't follow it. Since they've usually got millions of bytes of free space on their disk drives, they just don't worry about a few unnecessary files. But the few files add up, and eventually the clutter makes it more difficult to manage the directories and files.

For instance, many PC users keep a copy of each letter they write on their systems. But they rarely refer to any of them. Similarly, they keep several versions of reports and proposals on their systems, but they only use the final versions. If you're guilty of either of these practices, delete the files you never use and you'll simplify file management.

To complicate matters, some programs automatically create files that you don't need. For instance, many programs create backup files for each file that you work on so you won't lose your work in case of a power failure. Normally, these files have a distinctive extension such as BAK or BK. Also, some programs create temporary files while you're using them. If you end the program normally, these files are deleted. But if you don't, these files with extensions like TMP, $$$, or 001 stay on your system. Occasionally, then, you should take a few minutes to delete the backup and temporary files that have accumulated. You can delete them by using a wildcard with an appropriate extension as in this command:

```
C:\WORD>del *.tmp
```

Use consistent file names   A good file name is one that is descriptive enough to tell you what's in the file, and distinct enough to distinguish it from other files with similar names. Unfortunately, you can't always create good file names with a limit of eight characters for the name and three for the extension. That's why it's so important that you organize your data files in logical directories and that you keep those directories small.

Within each data directory, you should try to create file names that are consistent. In a word processing directory, for example, you may want to use the extension RPT for reports, LTR for letters, and MEM for memos. If the program doesn't let you use your own extensions, you can start the file names with three-character identifiers. Similarly, you may want to start spreadsheet names with PF for proforma analyses, SLS for sales summaries, and FIN for financial summaries. Although this consistency may not help you find the exact file you're looking for, it will at least help you narrow down the possibilities.

Include the file name in the heading of each document that's prepared from a file   Because you can't always create distinctive file names, you should include the file name in the heading of any document or spreadsheet that's printed from a file. Then, if you want to modify the document, you look for a file with that name in the directory that's logically related to it. Usually, you don't need to include the path along with a file name in the heading, but if there's any chance for confusion, include the path too.

How a shell program can help you manage directories and files

If you follow the 12 guidelines I've just presented, you can do an effective job of managing your directories and files whether or not you use the DOS shell. If you're using an older version of DOS, though, you should probably consider upgrading to DOS 6.0 so you can use the DOS shell (and take advantage of the other DOS 6.0 features as well). Section 4 of this book covers the DOS shell in detail, and chapter 14 in particular shows you how to use it for managing directories and files.

From a practical point of view, it's usually best to use some combination of DOS commands and shell functions to manage your directories and files. If you want to carefully select files for deletion by reviewing their names and creation dates, the DOS shell is usually more efficient. But if you want to copy or delete entire directories or portions of directories that can be selected by wildcards, the DOS commands are usually more efficient.

Terms

source file
target file
wildcard

* wildcard
star wildcard
? wildcard

Objectives

1. Given a drive specification, use the Tree command to display the directory structure of the drive.

2. Given a directory specification, use the appropriate commands to move it, to rename it, to remove it, or to add a new directory of that name to your system.

3. Given file specifications, use the appropriate commands with or without wildcards to copy, delete, rename, or move one or more files.

Exercises

In these exercises, you'll use the commands presented in this chapter as well as some of the commands you've already learned. You'll delete files and directories, and move files and directories. Be careful when you use these commands; you don't want to accidentally delete a critical DOS file from your C drive. As a result, these exercises ask you to work with a diskette to avoid mistakes that might affect your C drive. And any commands that move, delete, or rename files or directories always specify the A drive.

1. To get comfortable using wildcards in your commands and to see how they work, change the current directory to the DOS directory. Then, enter Directory commands like these:

    ```
    dir *.exe /w
    dir *.com /w
    ```

    As you know from chapter 7, these are the command files for DOS. Next, enter this command:

    ```
    dir c*.*
    ```

You should see a list of all the files in the directory that begin with C, no matter what extension they have. Now, enter this command:

```
dir c*.c*
```

As you can see, this lists all the files that have file names beginning with C and extensions beginning with C. Now, enter this command:

```
dir c*.
```

This lists all the files that have file names beginning with C but no extension. Finally, experiment with the ? wildcard by entering this command:

```
dir ????.exe
```

You should see a list of files with names of four or fewer characters that have an extension of EXE.

2. Now that you're familiar with wildcards, make sure that the current directory is the DOS directory. Then, use wildcards to copy all the files that start with A from your DOS directory to an empty diskette in drive A. To do that, use this Copy command:

```
copy a*.* a:
```

Next, change the default drive to drive A. Then, use the Directory command to get a directory listing of the files in the current directory of the default drive. If you're using DOS 5.0 or later, use the /O switch to display the listing in alphabetical order.

3. To create a directory named COM on the diskette in drive A, use this Make-directory command:

```
md a:\com
```

Next, copy all the files in the DOS directory of the C drive that begin with A and have an extension of COM to the COM directory on the diskette. Use either a Copy or Xcopy command like this:

```
copy c:\dos\a*.com a:\com
xcopy c:\dos\a*.com a:\com
```

Now, copy the COM files in the DOS directory on the C drive that start with C and D to the COM directory using Copy or Xcopy commands. Then, use Directory commands to list the files in the DOS directory and the COM directory to make sure your commands worked correctly.

4. Use a single Rename command to rename all the files in the COM directory so the extensions are CBK:

```
ren a:\com\*.* *.cbk
```

Then, use a Directory command to list the files in the COM directory to make sure the Rename command worked correctly.

5. Change the name of the COM directory to CBK. To do that using DOS 6.0, use this command:

    ```
    move a:\com a:\cbk
    ```

    If you're using an earlier version of DOS, use this series of commands instead:

    ```
    md a:\cbk
    copy a:\com\*.* a:\cbk
    del a:\com\*.*        (Enter Y when DOS asks "Are you sure?")
    rd a:\com
    ```

    Use a Directory command to check the results.

6. Use the Make-directory command to create another directory on the A drive called CCOM. Then, move all the files that begin with C from the CBK directory to the CCOM directory. To do that using DOS 6.0, use these commands:

    ```
    md a:\ccom
    move a:\cbk\c*.* \ccom
    ```

    If you're using an earlier version of DOS, use this series of commands instead:

    ```
    md a:\ccom
    copy a:\cbk\c*.* a:\ccom
    del a:\cbk\c*.*       (Enter Y when DOS asks "Are you sure?")
    ```

    Again, use a Directory command to check the results.

7. Check the command prompt to make sure the current directory is the root directory on the A drive (change it if it's not). Now, remove the CBK directory from the diskette in the A drive. To do that using DOS 6.0, use this command:

    ```
    deltree a:\cbk
    ```

    If you're using an earlier version of DOS, use these commands instead:

    ```
    del a:\cbk\*.*        (Enter Y when DOS asks "Are you sure?")
    rd a:\cbk
    ```

    Then, use similar commands to delete the CCOM directory.

8. Use the Directory command to get a directory listing for the root directory on each drive of your hard disk. Do these directories contain acceptable numbers of files? Are the DOS files in the root directory of the C drive? Are any other programs in the root directory of the C drive? What directory and file reorganization do these listings suggest?

9. Run the Tree command for the C drive of your system to see what output you get. If you have other drives on your hard disk, run the Tree command for those drives too. How are the program directories on your system organized? How are the data directories organized? What directory and file reorganization is suggested by the current directory structure?

Chapter 9

How to work with diskettes

Since your PC has a hard disk, you won't have much need for diskettes. Most of the time, you'll retrieve the files you need from the hard disk, and you'll save the files you create on the hard disk.

Nevertheless, one diskette drive is an essential component of a hard disk system because the hard disk isn't removable. As a result, software for a hard disk system is usually delivered on diskettes. You often use diskettes when you want to transfer data from one PC to another. And the most common way to back up a hard disk is to transfer its data to diskettes.

In this chapter, you'll learn how to work with diskettes. First, I'll review the diskette characteristics I presented in the first chapter. Then, I'll present two DOS commands you can use when you work with diskettes. Last, I'll present three specific skills that are related to diskette use.

When you finish this chapter, you will know how to use diskettes for transferring data from one system to another. You will also know how to work with diskettes when you use them for backing up data as presented in the next two chapters. You need to have these skills whether or not you use a shell program on your PC.

A review of diskette characteristics

In chapter 1, I described the two types of diskettes that are in widespread use today: the 5-1/4 inch diskette and the 3-1/2 inch diskette. Each type of diskette (and every hard disk, too) has two sides that contain a given number of *tracks*, and each track is divided up into *sectors* that are used to store data. Although you don't need to know anything about how tracks and sectors are arranged on a disk, you may need to know how many tracks and sectors are on the diskettes you're using, especially if you're using an older version of DOS. So I've summarized that information in figure 9-1, along with some of the other characteristics of each type of diskette. Now, I'll briefly review each type.

5-1/4 inch diskettes   These diskettes are most commonly used with PCs, XTs, and ATs. The double-density capacity is 360KB; the high-density capacity is 1.2MB. Although a 1.2MB diskette drive can read and write both types of diskettes, a 360KB drive can only read and write double-density diskettes.

Size	Capacity	Common labelling notation	Tracks	Sectors per track
5-1/4"	360KB	5-1/4" Double-Sided Double-Density 5-1/4" DSDD	40	9
5-1/4"	1.2MB	5-1/4" Double-Sided High-Density 5-1/4" DSHD	80	15
3-1/2"	720KB	3-1/2" Double-Sided Double-Density 3-1/2" 2DD 3-1/2" 1.0M formatted capacity	80	9
3-1/2"	1.44MB	3-1/2" Double-Sided High-Density 3-1/2" 2HD 3-1/2" 2.0M formatted capacity	80	18
3-1/2"	2.88MB	3-1/2" Double-Sided Extended-Density 3-1/2" 2ED 3-1/2" 4.0M formatted capacity	80	36

Figure 9-1   A summary of diskette characteristics

Although 5-1/4 inch diskettes are tough, they're not indestructible. In fact, reading and writing errors often occur when you use this type of diskette. So to get the best results from them, you should handle them with care. That means you shouldn't write on them with a pencil or a ballpoint pen; you shouldn't touch the surface that's exposed through the diskette opening; you shouldn't get them close to anything magnetic (including paper clips that have been in a magnetic paper clip holder); and you shouldn't leave them anywhere that will expose them to extremes of heat or cold. You should also keep them in their protective sleeves when they're not in use.

3-1/2 inch diskettes   Although these diskettes were popularized by laptop computers and the PS/2s, you can now get a 3-1/2 inch drive for any type of PC. The double-density capacity is 720KB; the high-density capacity is 1.44MB; and the extended-density capacity is 2.88MB. Here again, a 2.88MB diskette drive can read and write diskettes of any capacity, a 1.44MB drive can read and write both double-density and high-density diskettes, and a 720KB drive can read and write only double-density diskettes.

These diskettes are more reliable than the 5-1/4 inch diskettes, so reading and writing errors rarely occur when you use them. Also, these diskettes don't require as much care. With sensible handling, you shouldn't have any problems with them.

Two commands for working with diskettes

Figure 9-2 summarizes the two commands you need for formatting and copying entire diskettes. Otherwise, you use the same file handling commands for diskettes that you use for hard disks, including the Copy, Xcopy, Delete, Rename, and Move commands. You can also use the directory commands covered in chapter 8, although the root directory is usually the only directory you need on a diskette.

The Format command   Before a diskette can be used, it has to be formatted. Although you can buy diskettes that are already formatted, you can also buy unformatted diskettes. If you do, you have to use the Format command to format them.

The Format command prepares the surface of the diskette so it can record information. It does this by defining the tracks on a diskette. The Format command also sets up the root directory for the diskette, and it checks the reliability of the diskette.

If you're using a version of DOS before 5.0 and you format a diskette that already has data on it, all of its data is destroyed. Similarly, if you unintentionally format your hard disk, all of its data is destroyed. To avoid this disaster, you should make sure that the drive specification in this command is always drive A or drive B. If you specify drive C, DOS will give you a warning message. But if you ignore it, the disaster is in progress.

If you're using DOS 5.0 or 6.0, DOS still gives you a warning message if you specify drive C. But even if you ignore the message, the data on the disk isn't destroyed. That's because beginning with DOS 5.0, the Format command does a *safe format*. With a safe format, DOS keeps the data needed to unformat a disk if you format it in error. Unformatting a hard disk is not a totally reliable procedure, however. So you still want to be careful when you use the Format command. (This book doesn't teach you how to unformat disks, but there's a full chapter on the subject in our advanced DOS book, *The Only DOS Book You'll Ever Need*.)

Figure 9-3 gives you several examples of the Format command. The first example shows you how to enter the command when the capacity of the diskette and the drive match up, as, for example, when you format a 3-1/2 inch high-density diskette in a 1.44MB drive. As you can see, no switches are required; the only parameter is the drive specification. Then, the command formats the diskette with the default format of the drive. If you get diskettes that are the right capacity for your diskette drive, this is the way you'll enter the command most of the time.

The next four examples in figure 9-3 show you how to enter this command when you want to use a drive with a higher capacity to format a diskette with a lower capacity. Here, the switches tell DOS what the formatting requirements are. In the second example, the /4 switch tells DOS the diskette capacity is only 360KB even though the drive capacity is 1.2MB. In the third example, the switches specify the number of tracks and sectors for a 720KB diskette. In the fourth and fifth examples, the /F switch that was introduced in DOS 4.0 simplifies the command syntax; you just specify the capacity of the diskette you're formatting, not the number of tracks and sectors it can contain. If you frequently use commands in any one of these forms, you

142   Chapter 9

The format of the Format command

```
FORMAT drive [/4] [/N:sectors] [/T:tracks] [/F:capacity] [/Q] [/S] [/U]
```

Function

This command formats a diskette for use by DOS. To format a diskette in the default format of the diskette drive, you don't need any switches. Otherwise, you must use one or more of the switches as illustrated in figure 9-3.

Switch meanings

Switch	Meaning
/4	Formats a 360KB diskette in a 1.2MB drive.
/N:sectors /T:tracks	DOS 3.2 and 3.3 switches used to format a double-density diskette on a higher-capacity drive.
/F:capacity	Replacement for the /N and /T switches, introduced in DOS 4.0.
/Q	Reformats a diskette quickly (only for use on previously formatted diskettes); introduced in DOS 5.0.
/S	Formats a system diskette that's used to boot DOS.
/U	Doesn't do a safe format. Although this saves formatting time, it prevents you from recovering the data on the diskette after it's formatted, so this switch is typically used only with unformatted diskettes. Introduced in DOS 5.0.

The format of the Diskcopy command

```
DISKCOPY source-drive target-drive
```

Function

This command copies an entire diskette including any directories and all of its files. It works most efficiently if you copy the diskette in one drive to a diskette in another drive. But you can also use this command when your PC has only one diskette drive.

Figure 9-2   Two commands for working with diskettes

may want to set up batch files for them so you don't have to remember how to enter the switches.

The sixth example in figure 9-3 shows how you can use the /Q switch introduced in DOS 5.0 to reformat a diskette quickly. When you use this switch, DOS doesn't format every track on the diskette. Instead, DOS just erases the directory and file entries on the diskette. This reduces the time required to reformat a previously

Example 1:	How to format a diskette in the default format of the drive
	`C:\>format a:`
Example 2:	How to format a 360KB diskette in a 1.2MB drive
	`C:\>format a: /4`
Example 3:	How to format a 720KB diskette in a 1.44MB drive (DOS 3.2 and 3.3)
	`C:\>format a: /n:9 /t:80`
Example 4:	How to format a 720KB diskette in a 1.44MB drive or a 2.88MB drive (DOS 4.0 and later versions)
	`C:\>format a: /f:720`
Example 5:	How to format a 1.44MB diskette in a 2.88MB drive (DOS 5.0 and later versions)
	`C:\>format a: /f:1440`
Example 6:	How to reformat a diskette quickly (DOS 5.0 and later versions)
	`C:\>format a: /q`
Example 7:	How to format a system diskette
	`C:\>format a: /s`
Example 8:	How to format a diskette without doing a safe format, so any data it contains is destroyed (DOS 5.0 and later versions)
	`C:\>format a: /u`

Figure 9-3 How to use the Format command

formatted diskette. However, you can't use the /Q switch to format an unformatted diskette. Because it doesn't do any actual formatting, it only works on previously formatted diskettes.

The seventh example in figure 9-3 shows you how to use the /S switch. When you use this switch with the Format command, it copies three DOS files from the hard disk to the diskette after it finishes formatting the diskette. One of the files is the COMMAND.COM file. The other two files are hidden files so they won't show up in a directory listing. When you use the /S switch, the default drive has to be the C drive, so DOS can find the three files it needs. After you format a diskette in this way, you can use it to boot DOS from the A drive. I'll explain more about this in a moment when I tell you about preparing a system diskette.

```
C:\>format a:
Insert new diskette for drive A:
and press ENTER when ready...

Checking existing disk format.
Saving UNFORMAT information.
Verifying 1.44M
Format complete.

Volume label (11 characters, ENTER for none)?

   1457664 bytes total disk space
   1457664 bytes available on disk

       512 bytes in each allocation unit.
      2847 allocation units available on disk.

Volume Serial Number is 3D39-12EE

Format another (Y/N)?n


C:\>
```

Figure 9-4 The operation of the Format command

The last example in figure 9-3 shows how you use the /U switch that was introduced with DOS 5.0. This switch causes all the data on the disk to be destroyed. With versions of DOS before 5.0, this was the default. With DOS 5.0 and 6.0, the default is to do a safe format, as I described earlier. Since a safe format protects you from destroying data unintentionally, you shouldn't use the /U switch for diskettes that have been used before. But when you're formatting unformatted diskettes, I recommend you use this switch because it reduces formatting time dramatically.

Figure 9-4 shows the Format command in operation. When you issue the command, DOS prompts you to insert the diskette to be formatted into the disk drive. After you insert the diskette and close the drive door (if it has a door), you press the Enter key to start the formatting. As DOS formats the diskette, it displays its progress. If you're using DOS 3.3 or earlier, it displays the track and side that's currently being formatted. If you're using DOS 4.0 or later, it displays the percent of the disk that has been formatted.

When DOS has completed the formatting operation, it displays storage information like that shown in figure 9-4. This information includes the total number of bytes on the diskette, the number of bytes in bad sectors (if any), and the number of bytes of available disk storage. If there are bad sectors on the diskette, you don't have to worry about them; DOS locks them out and doesn't use them to store data. In DOS 4.0 and later versions, DOS also displays information about the allocation units on the diskette.

After DOS has formatted one diskette, it asks if you want to format another. If you respond with *y* for yes, DOS repeats the process I just described. If you have just opened a box of diskettes, it's often worth taking the time to format all of them.

With some versions of DOS, the Format command displays a message that asks you to supply a *volume label* for the diskette that's going to be formatted. You can see this message displayed in the middle of figure 9-4. Because you don't need to assign a volume label to a diskette, you can just press the Enter key to ignore the message.

If you're using DOS 5.0 or 6.0, you'll also see the group of messages at the beginning of the Format operation in figure 9-4. The message I want you to notice in particular is the second one, "Saving UNFORMAT information." This means that DOS is performing a safe format, as I described earlier.

The Diskcopy command   Occasionally, you will want to make a copy of an entire diskette. Then, you can use the Diskcopy command. Because this command copies the entire *source diskette*, whether it's filled with data or not, all data on the *target diskette* is destroyed. So choose your target diskette carefully. You should also know that you can't use this command to copy a diskette of one capacity onto a diskette of another capacity.

If you have two drives on your system, you enter this command as shown in the first example in figure 9-5 (I've highlighted the Diskcopy commands in this figure so you can see them more easily). Then, DOS tells you to put the source diskette (the diskette you want to copy) in the A drive and the target diskette (the diskette you want to create) in the B drive. When the copy operation is finished, DOS asks if you want to copy another diskette.

If you have only one drive on your system, you enter the command as shown in the second example in figure 9-5. After DOS tells you to put the source diskette in drive A, this command reads as much data as it can from the source diskette into internal memory. If, for example, your PC has 640KB of memory and you're copying a 360KB diskette, this command reads the entire diskette into internal memory. Next, the command asks you to remove the source diskette from the drive and insert the target diskette. When you do that, the data in memory is copied onto the target diskette. If the entire diskette can't be read into internal memory all at once, the command repeats this procedure until all the data has been copied to the target diskette.

With some versions of DOS, you can use an unformatted diskette for the target diskette of a Diskcopy command. For instance, all versions of PC-DOS will automatically format the target diskette if it's not already formatted. However, the versions of MS-DOS before 4.0 require that you format the target diskette before you use this command.

The format of the Diskcopy command

```
DISKCOPY source-drive target-drive
```

Example 1: How to copy a diskette from one drive to another

```
C:\>diskcopy a: b:

Insert SOURCE diskette in drive A:

Insert TARGET diskette in drive B:

Press any key to continue . . .

Copying 80 tracks
18 sectors per track, 2 side(s)


Copy another diskette (Y/N)?n

C:\>
```

Example 2: How to copy a diskette using only one diskette drive

```
C:\>diskcopy a: a:

Insert SOURCE diskette in drive A:

Press any key to continue . . .

Copying 80 tracks
18 sectors per track, 2 side(s)

Insert TARGET diskette in drive A:

Press any key to continue . . .


Copy another diskette (Y/N)?n

C:\>
```

Figure 9-5   The operation of the Diskcopy command

Example 1: A Copy command that copies a file named PROJSUM.WK1 from the PROJECTB directory of the C drive to the diskette in the A drive.

```
C:\>copy \projectb\projsum.wk1 a:
```

Example 2: A Copy command that copies all the files in the BECKY directory on the C drive to the diskette in the A drive.

```
C:\>copy \becky\*.* a:
```

Example 3: A Copy command that copies all the files with the DOC extension from the current directory on the hard disk to the diskette in the A drive.

```
C:\DATA\MMA>copy *.doc a:
```

Figure 9-6 How to use the Copy command for copying selected files to a diskette

If you have two diskette drives, you can also use the Xcopy command to copy all of the files from one diskette to another. Xcopy can be faster than Diskcopy if the diskette doesn't have many files. And Xcopy lets you copy files between diskettes with different capacities as long as there's enough space on the target diskette to accommodate all of the files on the source diskette. What's more, Xcopy won't destroy the existing data on the target diskette the way Diskcopy does.

Three related skills

The Format and Diskcopy commands are the only new commands you need to know to work specifically with diskettes. Along with those commands, though, you should also know how to do the skills that follow.

How to use diskettes to transfer data from one PC to another To transfer data from one PC to another, you begin by copying the data from the hard disk to a diskette, as shown in figure 9-6. The first example shows you how to copy just one file; the second example shows you how to use wildcards to copy all the files in a directory; and the third example shows you how to copy just the files in a directory that have a specific extension. Once you have the data copied to a diskette, you can use the Copy command to copy the data to the hard disk of another PC.

You should realize, though, that you can't use the Copy command to copy a file that is larger than the capacity of a single diskette. Similarly, you can't use this command to copy all the files in a directory if the files require more bytes than are available on a single diskette. In either case, the Copy command is cancelled when it tries to copy a file that requires more bytes than are in the remaining capacity of the diskette. To get around this limitation, you can use the Backup command that is presented in chapter 10.

You should also be aware of the compatibility problems you can encounter when you transfer files from one PC to another. The most obvious problem is trying to read a high- or extended-density diskette in a drive with a lower capacity. Although that won't work, you should remember that a higher-capacity drive is able to read a lower-capacity diskette. As a result, you shouldn't have any trouble transferring data from a PC with a lower-capacity drive to a PC with a higher-capacity drive.

When you want to transfer data from a higher-capacity drive to a lower-capacity drive, you should use the lower-capacity drive to do the formatting whenever possible. If the diskettes are formatted by the higher-capacity drive, they may be incompatible with the lower-capacity drive due to some technical differences in how the two types of drives do the formatting.

How to write-protect a diskette   Occasionally, you may want to protect the files on a diskette so no one can delete them, overwrite them, or destroy them by reformatting the diskette. You can provide this protection by *write-protecting* the diskette. Then, DOS can read data from the diskette, but it can't change the data on the diskette in any way.

Figure 9-7 shows how to write-protect a diskette. For a 5-1/4 inch diskette, you cover the notch on the diskette with one of the write-protect tabs that come with a box of diskettes. For a 3-1/2 inch diskette, you slide the plastic tab on the diskette to open the write-protect window.

When you use a program or command that tries to write on a write-protected diskette, DOS displays a message like this:

```
Write protect error writing drive A
Abort, Retry, Fail?
```

If that happens, you can remove the write protection, put the diskette back in the drive, and reply with an *r* for retry. Or, you can reply with an *a* for abort. But you should never replace the write-protected diskette with another diskette and reply with an *r* for retry. If you do, the data won't be written in the right location on the replacement diskette. Although DOS won't alert you to the problem, it won't be able to retrieve the file correctly later on.

How to prepare a system diskette   Normally, when you start your PC, it boots the DOS files it needs from the hard disk. Sometimes, though, you will want to boot your PC from a diskette. If, for example, something goes wrong with the hard disk, you may have to boot from a diskette to get your PC started again. For this purpose, you need a special type of diskette called a *system disk*, or *system diskette*. This diskette contains the files that DOS needs for getting itself started.

If you have DOS 3.3 or an earlier version, the easiest way to prepare a system diskette is to use the Diskcopy command to make a copy of the system diskette that DOS came with. For most versions of DOS, you'll use the diskette labelled "DOS diskette" or "DOS Operating Diskette."

Attach a write-protect tab to a 5-1/4 inch diskette.

Slide the tab to expose the write-protect window on a 3-1/2 inch diskette.

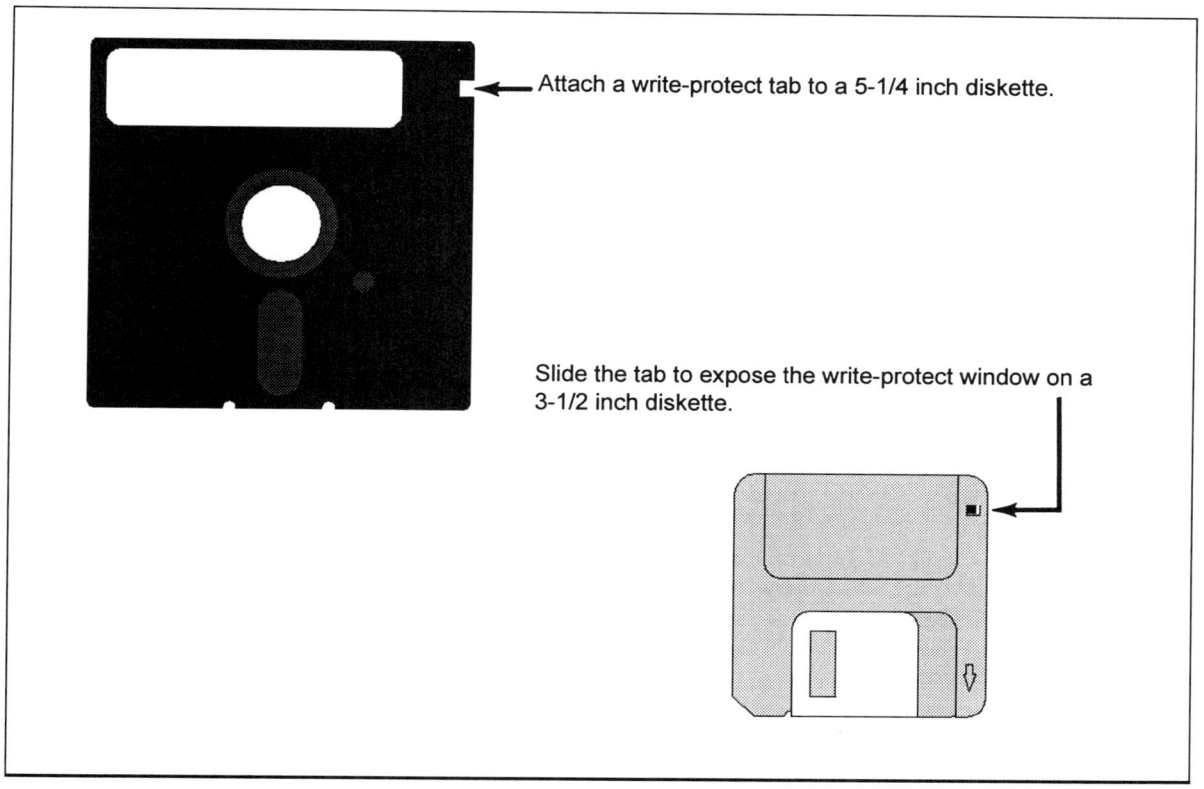

Figure 9-7 How to write-protect a diskette

If you have a later version of DOS, you can't use the Diskcopy command to copy the system diskette that comes with DOS. And even with earlier versions, you may want to customize your system diskette instead of making an exact duplicate of the DOS system diskette. For example, you may want to put just a few of the DOS commands on the diskette. Then, you'll have room on the diskette for a small program. In these cases, you can create a system diskette by using the Format command with the /S switch (and any of the other switches you have to use), as shown in the seventh example in figure 9-3. Then, DOS copies three files onto the diskette: the COMMAND.COM file and two hidden files. After that, you can copy whatever DOS command files you want to use from the hard disk. You can also copy the program files for any programs that you want to put on the diskette. This procedure works with all versions of DOS.

Some perspective on diskettes for hard disk users

As I said at the start of this chapter, you shouldn't have much need for diskettes if you have a hard disk system. However, they're still the best medium for transferring data from one PC to another (unless your PC is connected to a network). And, as you'll learn in chapter 10, they're still the least expensive medium for backing up the data on a hard disk.

Terms

track
sector
safe format
volume label
source diskette

target diskette
write protection
system disk
system diskette

Objectives

1. Describe the differences between diskettes in terms of diskette size and capacity.
2. Given a double-density, a high-density, or an extended-density diskette, format it on a drive of the same or a higher capacity.
3. Given a diskette of any capacity, copy it in its entirety using one or two drives.
4. Given the specifications for one or more files that can be stored on a single diskette, transfer them from one PC to another. You should be able to do this even if one of the PCs has a higher-capacity drive than the other one.
5. Given any type of diskette, write-protect the data on it.
6. Use the Format command to create a system diskette.

Exercises

Before you start these exercises, remember that the Format command can destroy data. So to make sure that you don't accidentally format one of your hard drives, always specify a diskette drive with this command.

1. Find a diskette that is unformatted or that doesn't contain any files you need. Use the Directory command to make sure it doesn't have any files you need to keep before you continue with this exercise.
   Use the Format command to format the diskette in the default format of your A drive:

   `format a:`

   If DOS asks you for a volume label, just press the Enter key. When it asks you if you want to format another diskette, press *n*. Then, use the Directory command again to display the directory of the newly formatted diskette.

If you get an error message when you execute the Format command, it may mean the capacity of your diskette and of your drive are incompatible. Exit from the command (if your version of DOS doesn't exit from it automatically). Then, look at what type of diskette you have and check its capacity in figure 9-1. Now, look at figure 9-3 to decide which form of the Format command you need to use. Then try the command again. Be sure to enter A as the drive you want to format, and check the result with the Directory command. If the command still doesn't work, get help.

Note to users of DOS 5.0 and later versions: As the Format command starts to execute, you may get an error message that tells you there's insufficient space for the MIRROR image file and that ends by asking you if you want to proceed with formatting. This means there isn't enough space on the diskette to do a safe format. Since you're sure you want to format this diskette, enter *y* to continue.

2. Use the Copy command to copy all of the files in a directory on the hard disk to the diskette you just formatted. If possible, choose a directory that exceeds the capacity of the diskette (the copy operation will end when there's no more room on the diskette). Use the Copy command in example 2 of figure 9-6 as a model.

    When the command is finished, use the Directory command to display the directory of the diskette.

3. Use the Diskcopy command to copy the files on the diskette you've just created to another diskette on the same drive. To do this, first use the Directory command to find a diskette that's empty or that doesn't contain any files you need and that's the same capacity as the diskette you're copying. Then, enter a Diskcopy command like this one:

    ```
    diskcopy a: a:
    ```

    When DOS prompts you for the source diskette, insert the diskette you created in exercise 2 into the drive and press any key to continue. When DOS prompts you for the target diskette, insert the empty diskette into the drive. You may have to switch the diskettes in and out of the drive several times.

    When the command asks you if you want to copy another diskette, enter *n* to end the operation. Then, use Directory commands to check the contents of both diskettes.

4. If you're using DOS 5.0 or later, use the /Q switch in a Format command like this:

    ```
    format a: /q
    ```

    to quickly reformat the diskette you created in exercise 3. Otherwise, use this Delete command:

    ```
    del a:*.*
    ```

    to delete all the files on the diskette you created in exercise 3 (when DOS asks if you want to continue, check that you entered A for the drive in the Delete command and then press *y*).

Now, use a Copy command like the one in example 1 of figure 9-6 to copy one file from your hard disk to the diskette. Then, write-protect the diskette, as shown in figure 9-7: if it's a 5-1/4 inch diskette, put a write-protect tab over the notch; if it's a 3-1/2 inch diskette, slide the plastic tab to expose the write-protect window.

Now, use another Copy command to try to copy a second file from your hard disk to the diskette. When DOS displays the message about a write-protect error, enter *a* for abort. Now, re-enter the same Copy command. This time, when DOS displays the write-protect message, take the diskette out of the drive, remove the write-protect tab or slide the tab to cover the write-protect window, insert the diskette back into the drive, and press *r*. Now, DOS will copy the second file to the diskette. Use a Directory command to check the results.

5. (If you have access to another PC with a diskette drive of the same or higher capacity as yours) Take the diskette you created in exercise 4 and transfer the data to another PC. Insert the diskette into the drive of the second PC and use a Copy command like this one to copy the files to the root directory of the PC's hard disk:

    ```
    copy a:*.* c:\
    ```

    Use a Directory command to check the contents of the root directory. Then, use the Delete command to delete the two files you copied to the root directory.

6. Use a Format command like this one to create a system diskette from your hard disk:

    ```
    format a: /s
    ```

    Be sure to include the /4, /N, /T, and /F switches as needed. Then, with the system diskette in the A drive, restart the PC to make sure that the diskette works.

Chapter 10

How to back up a hard disk using the Backup command

Eventually, the hard disk on your PC will fail, and all of the data on it will be lost. This could happen the first month you have the disk drive, or it could happen after five years of heavy use. But even before it fails, you can lose all the data on the disk through an operational error, like someone accidentally reformatting drive C. You can also lose all the data due to theft, fire, or vandalism.

Sooner or later, you'll also lose one or more of the files on your hard disk due to a programming or an operational error. If, for example, you're working on two proposals at the same time and you replace the first one on the disk with the second one, the first one is lost. Or, if while using the Delete command, you accidentally delete all the files in the current directory when you meant to delete all of the files on the diskette in the A drive, dozens of files may be lost. Mistakes like that happen to even the most proficient PC users.

So think about it right now. Can you afford to lose all of the data on your hard disk? Can you afford to lose one of your largest and most important files? If you can't, you should protect yourself by *backing up* your hard disk to diskettes. Then, if a disaster happens, you can recover from it by *restoring* the diskette files to the hard disk.

In this chapter, you'll learn how to back up and restore the files on your hard disk using the DOS Backup and Restore commands that come with all versions of DOS before DOS 6.0. Since many PC users don't back up their disks regularly because backup takes too long, the emphasis will be on efficient backup procedures. After you learn how to use the Backup and Restore commands, you'll learn three ways to design your backups and six guidelines that will help you do your backups as quickly and as effectively as possible. Then, you'll learn about two hardware improvements and one software improvement that can make your backups even more efficient.

In DOS 6.0, the Backup and Restore commands have been replaced by a backup utility called *Microsoft Backup*. If you upgrade to DOS 6.0 from an earlier version of DOS, the installation procedure will retain the Backup command on your system. But if you get DOS 6.0 on a new PC, you won't get the Backup command at all. That's no problem, though, because Microsoft Backup is far easier to use than the DOS commands. And, if you still need the Backup command, you can get it by purchasing the DOS 6.0 supplemental program diskette that's available from Microsoft. (DOS 6.0 does include the Restore command. So if you've been backing up your data with the Backup command, you can still use the Restore command under DOS 6.0 to restore it.)

I'll show you how to use Microsoft Backup in the next chapter. Before you read that chapter, though, you need to read this one. You can skim over the details of using the DOS commands if you like, but you need to know the backup concepts and guidelines presented in this chapter, regardless of how you back up your system.

Two types of backup

The key to efficient backups is realizing that there are two kinds of backups. These are illustrated in figure 10-1. Here, the system is backed up on Monday using a *full backup*. On the other days of the week, the system is backed up using an *incremental backup*.

Full backup Most computer users think of a full backup as a backup of every file on a drive. And, in fact, the term *full backup* is used quite often to mean just that. But a full backup doesn't have to include all the files on a drive. For example, it may consist of only the files in a single directory, or it may even consist of a single file. What distinguishes a full backup from other types of backups is that all the files you specify are backed up whether or not they've changed since the last backup. This will make more sense in a minute when I describe incremental backups. For now, keep in mind that when a hard disk fails, the full backup is the starting point for recovery.

In general, full backups are time consuming, particularly if they include all the files on a drive as in figure 10-1. If, for example, you have 20MB of files on a hard disk and you're using 1.2MB or 1.44MB diskettes, a full backup can take 30 minutes. And it will take even longer if you're using 360KB or 720KB diskettes. That's why you'll want to use some combination of full and incremental backups.

Incremental backup In contrast to a full backup, an incremental backup is a backup of just the files that have been created or changed since the last backup. This is illustrated in figure 10-1 by the procedures for Tuesday through Friday. Even if you have hundreds of files on your system, you probably use only a few files each day. As a result, incremental backups are much faster than full backups. On my PC, for example, I do an incremental backup each day before I leave the office, and that procedure takes less than 30 seconds.

Incremental backups are possible because the directory entry for each file on a DOS system has an *archive bit*. This bit indicates whether or not the file needs to be backed up. Whenever you create or change a file, this bit is set so the Backup command knows that the file should be backed up during an incremental backup. Then, when the Backup command is executed, all of the archive bits are reset so the files won't be backed up the next time. Usually, when you use an application

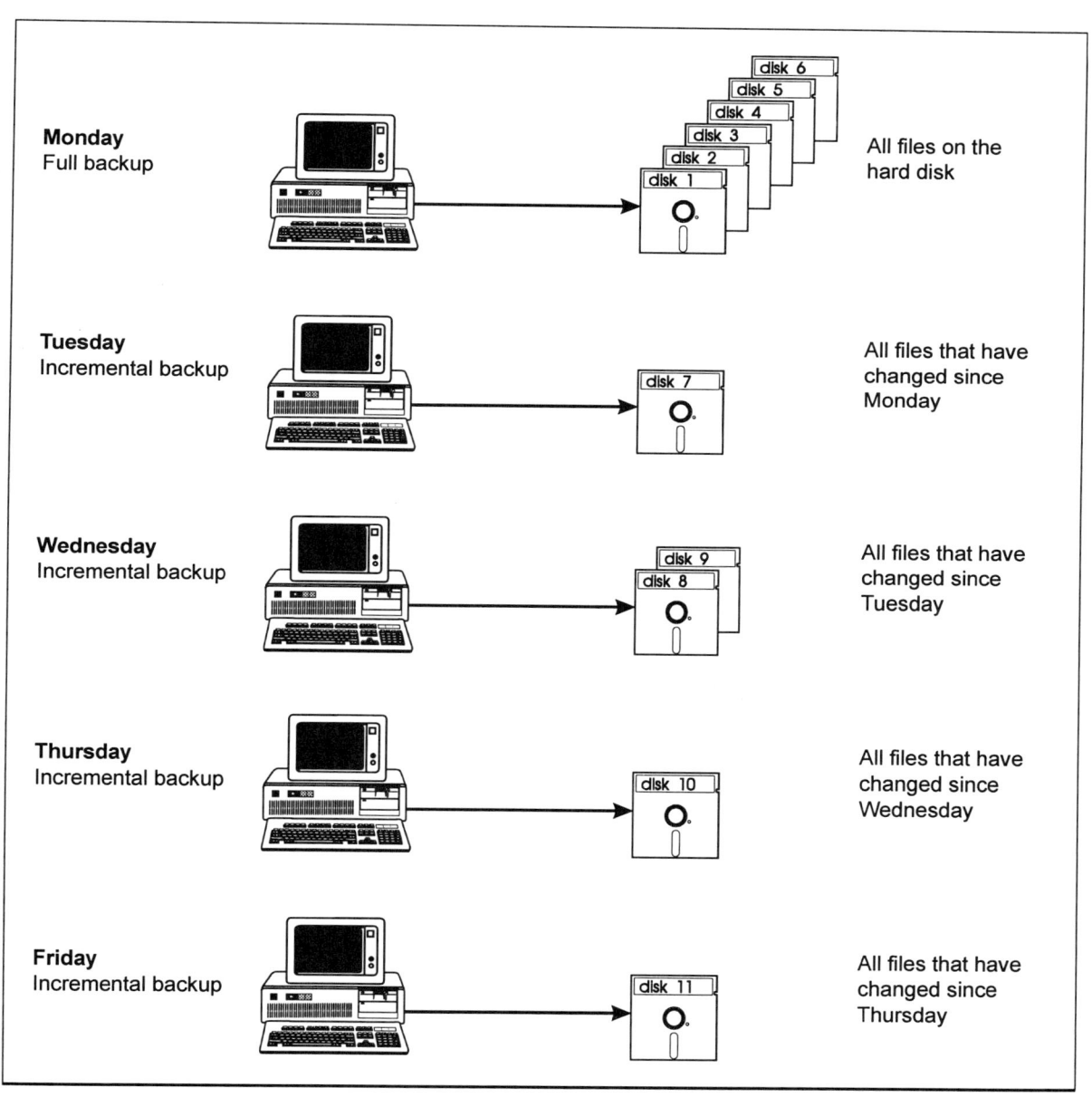

Figure 10-1 A weekly schedule of full and incremental backups

program, only the data files that you work on are changed, so your program files aren't included in an incremental backup.

If you look again at figure 10-1, you can see that each incremental backup is directed to a new diskette. This type of backup is called a *separate incremental backup*. Starting with DOS 3.3, you can also do *appended incremental backups*, as shown in figure 10-2. In this case, the backed up files are added to last diskette in the backup set, so you don't need as many diskettes.

Two commands for backing up data and restoring it

Figure 10-3 summarizes the two DOS commands for backing up and restoring a hard disk. Although you should use the Backup command frequently, you only use the Restore command when you need to restore data to your hard disk.

The Backup command If you study the Backup command in figure 10-3, you can see that this command backs up the files in the source specification to the target specification. When you use this command, the source specification is for one or more files on the hard disk, while the target specification is a diskette drive. When the command is run, the files in the source specification are backed up to the diskette drive. Any data on the diskette in the drive is lost; it's overwritten by the backup data.

If you use the /S switch with the Backup command, the files in the source specification are backed up, and so are all the files in the directories that are subordinate to the source specification. If, for example, the source specification is the root directory of a drive, all the files on that drive are backed up because all the directories are subordinate to the root directory.

Whether or not the /S switch is on, the /M switch provides for an incremental backup. If the /A switch is specified with the /M switch, the Backup command does an appended incremental backup. Otherwise, it does a separate incremental backup.

Figure 10-4 shows how to use the Backup command. Here, the first example does a full backup of the C drive. In this case, the /S switch is required because it tells DOS to include the files in all the subdirectories of the source specification. If the /S switch wasn't included, only the root directory would be backed up.

When a backup is in progress, DOS displays messages that tell you which diskette to insert into the drive next. For instance, a message like this is displayed when the command needs diskette number 3:

```
Insert backup diskette 03 in drive A:
WARNING! Files in the target drive
A:\ root directory will be erased
Press any key to continue . . .
```

As a result, you need to label and number your backup diskettes so you can keep them organized. Also, if you're using a version of DOS before DOS 4.0, you need to make sure the diskettes are formatted before you use them (starting in DOS 4.0, the Backup command formats the diskettes properly as long as they match the default size of the diskette drive).

How to back up a hard disk using the Backup command **157**

Monday Full backup	→	All files on the hard disk
Tuesday Appended incremental backup	→	All files that have changed since Monday
Wednesday Appended incremental backup	→	All files that have changed since Tuesday
Thursday Appended incremental backup	→	All files that have changed since Wednesday
Friday Appended incremental backup	→	All files that have changed since Thursday

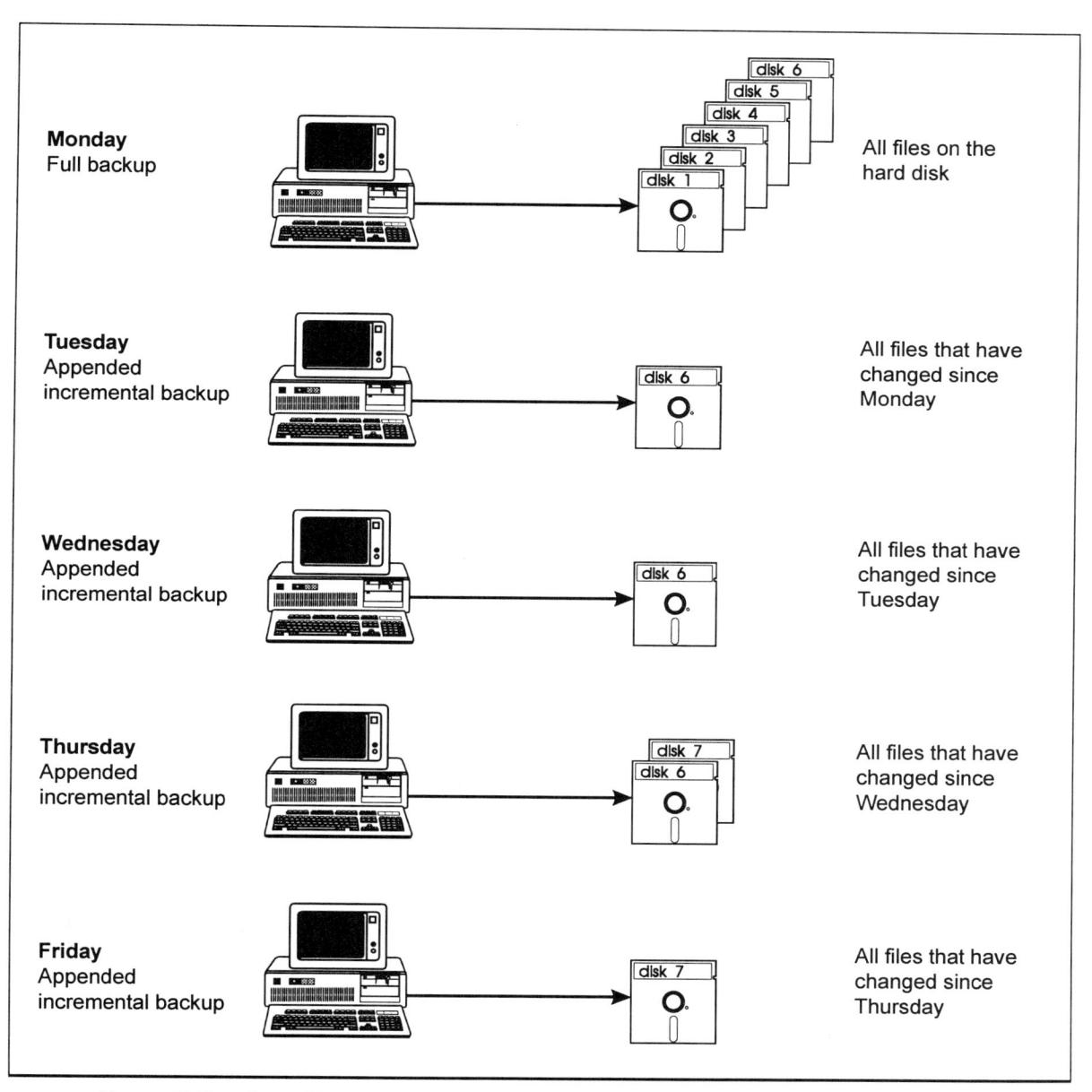

Figure 10-2 A weekly schedule of full and appended incremental backups

---

The format of the Backup command

```
BACKUP source-spec target-spec [/S] [/M] [/A]
```

Switch meanings

/S	Includes files that are in the subdirectories of the specified directory.
/M	Backs up only those files that have been modified since the last backup.
/A	Adds the new files to the files that are already on the backup diskette (DOS 3.3 or later).

The format of the Restore command

```
RESTORE source-spec target-spec [/S]
```

Switch meaning

/S	Restores all files in all subdirectories.

Figure 10-3 The Backup and Restore commands

The second example in figure 10-4 shows how to use the Backup command for an incremental backup of all the files on the C drive. Here, the /S switch tells DOS to include subdirectories, and the /M switch tells it to do an incremental backup. Since the /A switch isn't specified, the backed up files will be directed to a new diskette, as illustrated in figure 10-1.

The third example in figure 10-4 shows the use of the /A switch to do an appended incremental backup. When it is used, DOS prompts you to insert the last backup diskette into the drive, and then the backed up files are added to this diskette. Since this saves diskettes, you usually want to use this switch for incremental backups. Remember, though, that you can only do appended backups with a version of DOS that's 3.3 or later.

The last example in figure 10-4 shows you how to back up just one directory on a hard disk. This is useful when you work on the files in only one directory. And it's usually better than the DOS Copy command because the Backup command will use as many diskettes as are needed for the backup operation. It will also back up a single file that is so large it can't be stored on a single diskette. In contrast, the Copy command stops as soon as the first diskette is full.

The format of the Backup command

```
BACKUP source-spec target-spec [/S] [/M] [/A]
```

Example 1: A Backup command that backs up all the files on a drive whether or not they've been changed since the last backup (a full backup).

```
C:\>backup c:\*.* a: /s
```

Example 2: A Backup command that backs up only those files on the drive that have been changed since the last backup (a separate incremental backup).

```
C:\>backup c:\*.* a: /s /m
```

Example 3: A Backup command that does an appended incremental backup of the files on a drive (DOS 3.3 or later).

```
C:\>backup c:\*.* a: /s /m /a
```

Example 4: A Backup command that backs up all the files in one data directory.

```
C:\>backup c:\123\mma\*.* a:
```

Figure 10-4 How to use the Backup command

If you use the Directory command to display the root directory of a backup diskette, you'll realize that the Backup command doesn't work at all like a Copy command. Instead of one entry for each file that has been backed up, you'll find just two directory entries for an entire backup diskette. One entry is for a file named BACKUP; the other is for a file named CONTROL. The first file contains all the files that have been backed up to the diskette; the second one contains control information that is required for the proper operation of the Backup and Restore commands.

Both backup file names have a 3-digit extension that identifies the sequence of the backup diskette. For example, on the first backup diskette, the file extensions are .001; on the second diskette, .002; and so on. If you do appended incremental backups, these sequence numbers are continued when you use a new diskette. But each separate incremental backup begins again with sequence 001. One way DOS uses these file extensions is to make sure that you insert the backup diskettes in the correct sequence when you're restoring files.

The Restore command Because of the special format used by the Backup command to store data, you must use the Restore command to restore files that have been backed up. You can't use the Copy command.

The first example in figure 10-5 shows you how to use the Restore command if you want to restore all of the files from a full backup of the C drive. Because the /S switch is used, this command will restore the files in all of the subdirectories. If you insert all of the backup diskettes in the sequence in which they were created, this command restores all the files from a full backup as well as all the files from the appended incremental backups that were done after the full backup. If the incremental backups are on separate diskettes, however, the restore operation stops at the end of the full backup. Then, you have to issue the same Restore command again for each separate incremental diskette to restore the most recent versions of all your files.

The second example in figure 10-5 shows you how to use this command if you want to restore the files from just one directory of a backup. Because this command is entered in an unusual way, you should take a moment to study it. As you can see, the A drive is given as the source drive, just as you would expect. However, the directory that you want restored from the A drive is given in the target specification. In this example, all the files in the QA4\DATA directory are restored. Note that the *.* designation is included in the target specification so that DOS knows the target is a directory name, not a file name. Also note that you must specify the directory you want to restore whether the backup consists of all the files on the drive or only the files from one directory, as in this example. When the Restore command is executed, the restored files are always stored in the directory that they were backed up from.

If you've done appended incremental backups, a Restore command for a directory will restore all the files in the directory from the full backup as well as any applicable files from the incremental backups. However, if the incremental backups are on separate diskettes, you'll have to issue additional Restore commands for those diskettes. That way, you'll be sure you've restored the most recent versions of all the files in the directory.

The third example in figure 10-5 shows you how to use the Restore command if you want to restore just one file from a full backup. As you can see, the A drive is given as the source drive, and the path and name of the file that you want restored from the A drive are given in the target specification. Again, the restored file is always stored in the directory that it was backed up from.

Whether you restore one file or many, the Restore command has you insert each diskette from your set of backup diskettes. As a result, if you're restoring only one file, you may spend several minutes inserting diskettes before you get to the one that has the file you want.

When you're restoring a single file, the Restore command works a little differently than it does when you're restoring a full directory or drive. Even if you use appended incremental backups, DOS doesn't look on all the backup diskettes for the file you're restoring. Instead, it stops the restore operation when it comes to the end of the first diskette that contains the file. Even though that diskette may contain more than one version of the file, it may not contain the most recent version. To make sure you get the most recent version, you have to issue a Restore command for each incremental diskette in the order in which they were backed up. If you used appended

> **The format of the Restore command**
>
> ```
> RESTORE source-spec target-spec [/S]
> ```
>
> **Example 1:** A Restore command that restores all of the files from a full backup.
>
> ```
> C:\>restore a: c:\*.* /s
> ```
>
> **Example 2:** A Restore command that restores all of the files from a backup of the QA4\DATA directory on the C drive.
>
> ```
> C:\>restore a: c:\qa4\data\*.*
> ```
>
> **Example 3:** A Restore command that restores a single file from a full backup.
>
> ```
> C:\>restore a: c:\account\dist5.dbf
> ```

Figure 10-5 How to use the Restore command

incremental backups, that means you'll start each restore operation with a diskette other than the first one. As a result, DOS will display a message telling you that the diskette is out of sequence. However, this is only a warning message. To continue with the diskette, just press the Enter key.

Even if it takes several minutes to restore a file, you'll be delighted to discover that the file has been restored and you haven't lost all the hard work that went into it. If you ever have to restore hundreds of files, you'll be thankful indeed that you took the time to do an effective job of backing up your hard disk.

Three ways to back up your hard disk

To make your backups as tolerable as possible, you should design them so they're as efficient and easy as possible. That almost certainly means you should use incremental backups in combination with full backups. But that can also mean you should do two different sets of backups: one for program files and one for data files.

Here, then, are three practical ways to run your backups. If you're like most PC users, one of these methods will be appropriate for your system. If you don't use your system often enough to justify daily backups, you can use the same methods on a less frequent backup schedule.

Daily backup of all files   If you want to keep your backups as simple as possible, don't distinguish between program and data files. Then, you can back up your hard disk by doing a full backup of all the files on the first day of each month or each week and an incremental backup of all the files on the other days of the month or week. That way, all the files on your hard disk are backed up daily.

However, because program files usually don't change, you spend more time doing backups than you need to when you use this method. If, for example, your hard disk has 6MB of files on it but only 2MB of data files, you're backing up 4MB of files unnecessarily. To improve the efficiency of your backups, you can use one of the two methods that follow.

Daily backup of data drive and periodic backup of program drive On my PC, all the program files are stored on drive C, and all the data files are stored on drive D. Then, I do a full backup of drive C once a month, and I don't do daily incremental backups for this drive. In contrast, I do a full backup for drive D on every Monday, and I do daily incremental backups for this drive the rest of the week. By using separate backup procedures for the program drive and the data drive, my total backup time for the month is less than 30 minutes.

If your hard disk is already divided into a C and D drive, this is probably the backup method you should use. If it isn't, it's probably not worth the effort to set up separate drives. So you should consider a different backup method.

Daily backup of data directories and periodic backup of program directories If you commonly work within several data directories, you can sometimes simplify your backup procedures by reorganizing your directories. If, for example, all of your data directories are subordinate to one data directory as shown in figure 10-6, you can back them up using one command for a full backup and another one for an incremental backup. By combining a backup procedure for the entire hard disk with a backup procedure for the DATA directory and its subdirectories, you can reduce the time you spend doing your daily backups.

Six guidelines for simple and reliable backups

Now that you know how to back up your hard disk, here are six guidelines for simple and reliable backups. They are summarized in figure 10-7.

Set a schedule for your backups Because backing up a hard disk takes time away from your other activities, it's always tempting to skip your backup procedure for a day, a week, or a month. Even if you're doing incremental backups that take less than a minute each, it's tempting to skip them. Before long, you won't even remember the last time you did a backup.

That's why it's important to set a schedule for your backups. How often should you do them? That depends on how much you use your system. If, for example, you use your system more than four hours a day, you should probably do daily backups. If you use your system just an hour or two a day, you can perhaps get by with weekly backups, but you're going to be better off with daily backups. As a rule of thumb, you should schedule your backups so you'll never lose more work than you can afford to lose when a disk failure occurs. Then, you should stick to your schedule.

Directory structure with all data directories subordinate to the DATA directory

```
├── DOS
├── UTIL
├── WP
├── 123
├── QA4
└── DATA ─┬─ WPMEMOS
          ├─ WPLTTRS
          ├─ WPRPTS
          ├─ WK1MMA
          └─ QAFILES
```

Backup command for a full backup of the data directories

```
C:\>backup c:\data\*.* a: /s
```

Backup command for an appended incremental backup of the data directories

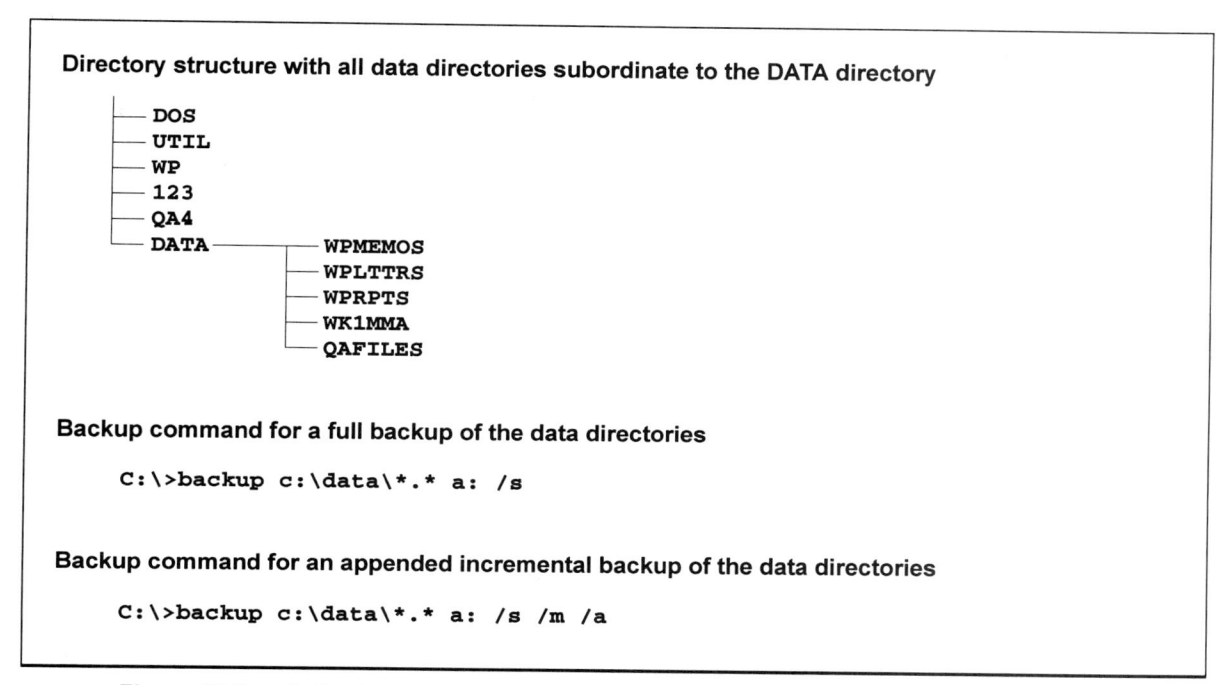

```
C:\>backup c:\data\*.* a: /s /m /a
```

Figure 10-6   A directory structure that can simplify backups

---

1. Set a schedule for your backups.
2. Use batch files to automate your backups.
3. Delete unnecessary files before you do a full backup.
4. Keep your diskettes organized.
5. Keep a log of your backups.
6. Consider keeping two sets of backups.

Figure 10-7   Six guidelines for simple and reliable backups

Example 1:	A batch file named BACKFULL.BAT that does a full backup of drive C.
	`backup c:\*.* a: /s`
Example 2:	A batch file named BACKINC.BAT that does an appended incremental backup of drive C.
	`backup c:\*.* a: /s /m /a`

Figure 10-8   Two batch files for backups

If you do one backup for program files and one for data files, you should set a separate schedule for each type of backup. For instance, you can schedule program backups once a month and data backups daily.

If you want to schedule both full and incremental backups, you can set full backups for a day like the first day of each month, the first day of each week, the last day of each month, or the last day of each week. Just schedule your full backups on days that usually provide the free time you need for this task. Then, schedule incremental backups on the other days. But if you don't want to schedule days for full backups, you can just do them whenever the number of diskettes you've used for incremental backups gets unwieldy.

Use batch files to automate your backups   Once you've designed and scheduled your backups, you should put the commands in batch files to make them easier to use. In figure 10-8, for example, you can see one batch file for a full backup of the C drive, and one for an incremental backup. Once you create these files, you don't have to remember the details for entering the Backup command each time that you do a backup. Instead, you can execute these batch files from the command prompt or from the DOS shell.

Delete unnecessary files before you do a full backup   Often, it's quicker and easier to delete unnecessary files than it is to back them up. So before you start a full backup, it's worth taking a few minutes to see if your hard disk has any directories or files that you no longer need. If you find some and delete them, your backups will run more quickly, and your directories and files will be more manageable.

Keep your diskettes organized   This is obvious, but I think it's worth mentioning. By all means keep your diskettes organized by labelling and numbering your backup diskettes and your diskette boxes. That way, you'll be able to run your backups as efficiently as possible. Also, if you ever have to use the Restore command, you'll be able to present the diskettes in the proper sequence so that the command will work the way you want it to.

In general, the label for a backup diskette should indicate the drive or directory that the backup is for. It should also give the sequence number of the diskette within the backup procedure. However, a diskette label shouldn't indicate whether it is for a full or incremental backup. If, for example, the full backup ends with diskette 6 and the first incremental backup starts with diskette 7, you shouldn't indicate this on the diskette labels. And you shouldn't write the date of the backup on the labels. Instead, because this information is likely to change with each backup you do, you should record it in a backup log.

Keep a log of your backups   When you use more than one type of backup, you can easily lose track of what type of backup you should be doing and which diskette you should start with. That's why you should keep a log of the backups you run. You don't need anything elaborate for this, so a simple form like the one in figure 10-9 will do.

In this log, you can see that the PC user does a full backup of the C drive on the last work day of the month. That backup includes both program and data directories, so it protects against a complete failure of the hard disk. For the rest of the month, the user does a full backup of just the data directories on each Monday and incremental backups of just the data directories on the other days of the week. By using a separate procedure for backing up data files, the user can keep backup time to a minimum and never be in danger of losing more than a day's work. But without a backup log, a system like this can get out of control.

Consider keeping two sets of backups   As you use diskettes, occasionally you'll find that one you've used in the past without any trouble has become unreadable. If that happens to one of the diskettes in your backup set, it means you can't restore the data from that diskette. So you may want to keep two backup sets for your hard drive. When you have two complete sets of backups, you alternate the sets each time you do a backup. If, for example, you do full backups weekly and incremental backups daily, you use a different backup set each week. Then, you'll never lose more than a week's worth of work.

If you decide to keep a second complete set of backups, the label for each diskette should indicate which backup set it's a part of. And you should record which set you're using for each backup on your backup log. It's also a good idea to keep each backup set in a different place. For example, you can keep one set in your desk, and the second set in the office safe. Then, if one whole set is destroyed, you still have the second set.

Chapter 10

Backup Log			
Date	Drive/Path	Backup type	Last disk
3/30	C:	Full	12
4/2	C:\data	Full	2
4/3	"	Incremental	3
4/4	"	"	3
4/5	"	"	3
4/6	"	"	4
4/9	C:\data	Full	2
4/10	"	Incremental	3
4/11	"	"	3
4/12	"	"	4
4/13	"	"	4
4/16	C:\data	Full	2
4/17	"	Incremental	3
4/18	"	"	3
4/19	"	"	3
4/20	"	"	3
4/23	C:\data	Full	2
4/24	"	Incremental	3
4/25	"	"	3
4/26	"	"	3
4/27	"	"	3
4/30	C:	Full	12
5/1	C:\data	Full	2
5/2	"	Incremental	3
5/3	"	"	4
5/4	"	"	4

Figure 10-9   A simple backup log

Two hardware improvements that can simplify backups

If your backups take so long that you often skip them, you should do whatever you can to make them quicker and easier. One way to make an improvement in your backup procedures is to add a new hardware component to your system. Two components that can help are a high-capacity diskette drive and a backup tape drive.

A high-capacity diskette drive   If you don't already have a high-capacity diskette drive on your system, buying one can quickly improve backups. Since the 1.2MB diskettes have about four times the capacity of the 360KB diskettes, you only have to use one-fourth as many diskettes. Similarly, you only have to use one-half as many diskettes if you add a 1.44MB diskette drive to a PC with only a 720KB drive, and a 2.88MB drive will cut that number by half again. At a price of about $100 for a 1.44MB drive or $225 for a 2.44MB drive, this purchase can simplify your backups so you're more likely to do them as scheduled.

A backup tape drive   Backup tape drives are becoming more and more popular all the time. That's because they're faster and have far larger capacities than diskettes. In fact, if you get a tape drive with a large enough capacity, you can run a full backup unattended because you don't have to insert diskettes as the backup runs. You can also set up the backup procedure so it runs automatically after you've gone home.

A backup tape drive records data on a special high-capacity tape enclosed in a removable cartridge. Most tape drives fit in the space allocated for a diskette drive in the systems unit of a PC. The two most common tape drives for individual PCs are 120MB drives, available for about $200, and 250MB drives, for about $300. At these prices, a tape drive can easily justify its cost by reducing the time and trouble of doing regular backups.

The only drawback to tape is that Microsoft Backup, the backup utility in DOS 6.0, doesn't support it. However, most tape drives come with their own backup utility. And most commercial backup utilities support tape drives.

How a commercial backup utility can improve backups

If your backup requirements are simple, the DOS Backup and Restore commands may be all that you need. For most PC users who don't have DOS 6.0, however, a commercial *backup utility* like *Central Point Backup*, *Fastback Plus*, or *Norton Backup* will pay for itself in less than a year. In general, backup utility programs are much faster than the DOS commands, and they're also easier to use. But, as with hardware improvements, the most important benefit of a backup utility is not the time you save by using one. It's the fact that you're far more likely to do scheduled backups because they take less time.

As you'll see in the next chapter, the DOS 6.0 backup utility, Microsoft Backup, is far more flexible and easy to use than the DOS Backup and Restore commands. But

Chapter 10

it still isn't as fast as most commercial backup utilities, and it doesn't support tape backup. So even if you have DOS 6.0, you may still be interested in getting a commercial backup utility. You'll be better able to decide that after you've learned to use Microsoft Backup in the next chapter.

If you don't have DOS 6.0 but you're thinking about getting a commercial backup utility, I suggest you read the next chapter on Microsoft Backup, too. It will give you some idea of what a backup utility has to offer. And, if you're considering upgrading to DOS 6.0 for some of its other features, you may decide that Microsoft Backup will be an adequate backup utility for you.

Terms

backing up a hard disk
restoring a hard disk
full backup
incremental backup

archive bit
separate incremental backup
appended incremental backup
backup utility

Objectives

1. Explain the difference between a full backup and an incremental backup.
2. Explain the difference between a separate incremental backup and an appended incremental backup.
3. Use the Backup command to do a full backup of a specified drive or directory, with or without subdirectories.
4. Use the Backup command to do an incremental backup of a specified drive or directory, with or without subdirectories.
5. Use the Restore command to restore an entire backup set, a directory, or a file.
6. Describe an efficient method of backup for your PC and your work habits.
7. Explain how a commercial backup utility can improve backup procedures.

Exercises

1. Locate several diskettes that are new or that don't contain any data you need to keep. If you're using a version of DOS before 4.0, make sure they've been formatted. Then, use a Backup command like the one in example 4 of figure 10-4 to do a full backup of one of the data directories on your hard disk. The size of the directory will determine the number of diskettes you need, and DOS will prompt you to insert each diskette into the diskette drive. Be sure to number and label the diskettes; you'll need them for the next two exercises.

   Now, use the Directory command to display the directory of one of the backup diskettes. Note that there are only two files on the diskette: BACKUP and CONTROL.

2. Modify one of the data files that you backed up in exercise 1, but not a file that you can't afford to lose. Then, do an incremental backup of all the files in the directory that you backed up in exercise 1.

   To do that if you're using a version of DOS before DOS 3.3, enter the same Backup command that you used in exercise 1, but add the /M switch to it. Then, insert a new diskette into your diskette drive when DOS prompts you for it, and press any key to continue.

   If you're using DOS 3.3 or later, enter the same Backup command that you used in exercise 1, but add both the /M and the /A switches to it. Then, insert the last diskette that you used in exercise 1 into the diskette drive when DOS prompts you for it, and press any key to continue.

3. Delete the file that you modified in exercise 2 from your hard disk. Then, use a Restore command like the one in example 3 of figure 10-5 to restore the modified version of the file. DOS will prompt you to insert each diskette into the diskette drive as needed.

   If you did a separate incremental backup: When DOS prompts you for the first diskette in the backup set, insert the *incremental* diskette in the drive. DOS will find the modified version of the file there and will restore it. Then, check the contents of the file on the hard disk to make sure it's the modified version. If it isn't, it means you inserted the first diskette of the full backup when the Restore command was executed instead of the incremental diskette. In that case, issue the Restore command again for the incremental diskette.

   If you did an appended incremental backup: When DOS prompts you for the first diskette in the backup set, insert the *last* diskette you used when you did the incremental backup in exercise 2. If DOS tells you that this diskette is out of sequence, press any key to continue. Then, DOS will find the modified version of the file and restore it. Look at the contents of the file on the hard disk to make sure it's the modified version. (Note: If both the original and the modified versions of the file were backed up on the same diskette, the messages on the screen will show you that DOS has restored the file twice. The first message is for the original version of the file; that version is overwritten when DOS finds and restores the modified version of the file. So the only version of the file on your hard disk will be the modified version.)

4. Run a full backup of all the drives on your hard disk and record the time that it takes. Also, record the details of the backup using a simple backup log like the one in figure 10-9.

5. Using the methods and guidelines given in this chapter, evaluate your backup needs and establish backup procedures for your system. If you've read chapter 7, create batch files for the Backup commands required by your procedures.

Chapter 11

How to back up a hard disk using Microsoft Backup (DOS 6.0)

The DOS Backup command is both hard to use and slow. That's why backup utilities have become popular. As I said in the last chapter, these utilities let you back up your hard disk in a fraction of the time that it takes when you use the DOS Backup command. They're also easier to use than the Backup command, and the backups they do are more reliable than those done by the Backup command.

The most important benefit of a backup utility, though, is the fact that you're more likely to do regular backups when they take only a minute or two a day. Then, whether you lose just one file, all the files in a directory, or all the files on your hard disk, it won't be a disaster. Instead, you'll be able to restore whatever files you've lost.

Prior to DOS 6.0, the only way to get a backup utility was to purchase one. The most popular of these utilities are *Central Point Backup* by Central Point Software and *Norton Backup* by Symantec. With DOS 6.0, Microsoft includes a backup program called *Microsoft Backup*. Microsoft Backup is actually a scaled-back version of *Norton Backup*. Although it's not as fast and sophisticated as *Norton Backup* or *Central Point Backup*, it's so much better than the DOS Backup command that you shouldn't even consider using the DOS Backup command if you have DOS 6.0.

So in this chapter, I'll introduce you to the major features of Microsoft Backup. First, I'll point out the main differences between Microsoft Backup and the DOS Backup command. Next, I'll show you the operational details of using this full-screen utility, including how to use the mouse to activate functions. Then, I'll show you how to use the four main functions of Microsoft Backup to get your system set up right, to back up data, to restore data, and to verify the accuracy of your backups.

Why Microsoft Backup is better than the Backup command

Microsoft Backup provides many of the features of other popular backup utilities, as listed in figure 11-1. Its main advantages over the DOS Backup command are improved speed, ease of use, and file compression capabilities.

Features of Microsoft Backup

- Full, incremental, and differential backups
- Faster backups
- Saved backup configurations
- File compression

Figure 11-1 Features of the DOS 6.0 backup utility, Microsoft Backup

Speed Figure 11-2 gives you some idea of how Microsoft Backup can improve on the speed of the DOS Backup command. Although this chart just summarizes the data from an informal test on my own system, I think the message is clear. Microsoft Backup can reduce the time you take for backups by 75 percent or more. This means a backup that takes 20 minutes when you use the DOS Backup command will probably take less than 5 minutes when you use Microsoft Backup.

To operate at increased speed, Microsoft Backup uses an advanced hardware feature called *DMA*, or *Direct Memory Access*. Because Microsoft Backup doesn't use DMA as aggressively as commercial backup utilities, such as *Central Point Backup* and *Norton Backup*, these programs are even faster than Microsoft Backup.

Ease of use As you learned in the last chapter, the switches of the Backup command make it difficult to use. In contrast, Microsoft Backup provides features that make it easy to use. For instance, it provides menus you use to select options. In addition, it lets you create saved backup configurations. That means that you can save the specifications for a backup procedure after you get it set up the way you want it. Then, you can run the backup procedure the next time just by loading the saved configuration.

File compression Microsoft Backup gives you the option of *compressing* the data in the files that it backs up. This means the files take up less space on the diskettes than they do on the hard disk. In the chart in figure 11-2, you can see the number of diskettes required by Microsoft Backup compared to the Backup command.

Although file compression isn't an essential feature of a backup utility, it can increase backup speed because it reduces the amount of data that has to be written on the backup diskettes. Also, it provides a minor savings in diskette costs. Because data files can be compressed more than program files, this feature means the most when you're backing up data files. In general, the more data you have on your hard disk, the more useful this feature becomes.

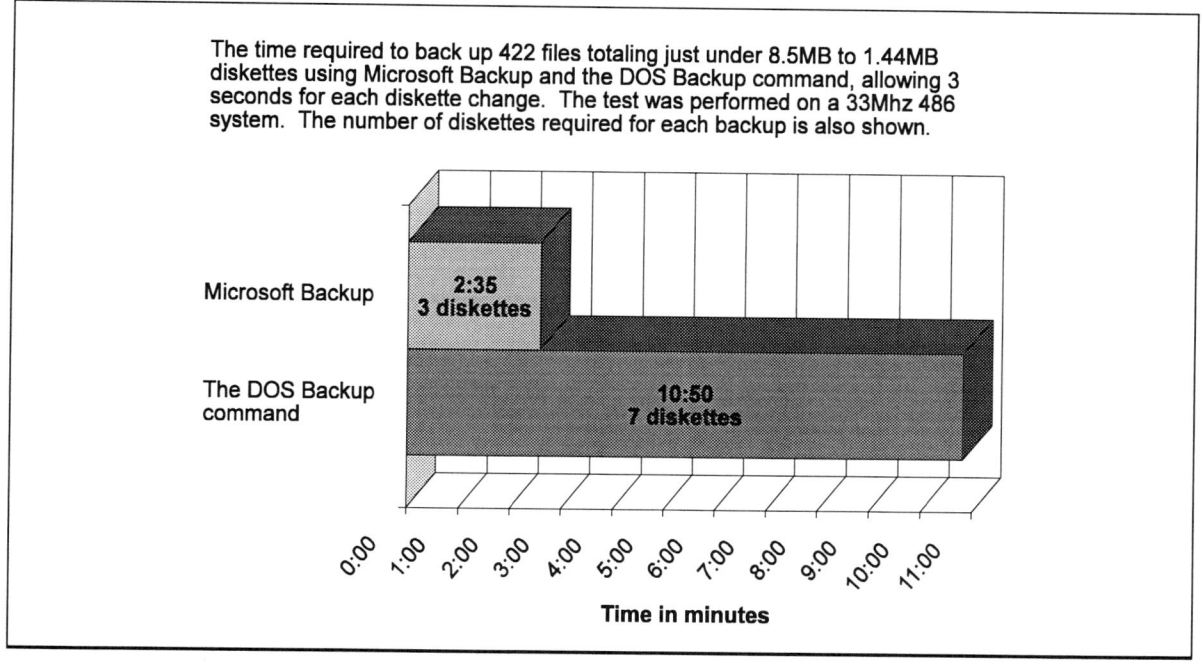

> The time required to back up 422 files totaling just under 8.5MB to 1.44MB diskettes using Microsoft Backup and the DOS Backup command, allowing 3 seconds for each diskette change. The test was performed on a 33Mhz 486 system. The number of diskettes required for each backup is also shown.
>
> Microsoft Backup: 2:35, 3 diskettes
> The DOS Backup command: 10:50, 7 diskettes
>
> Time in minutes

Figure 11-2   A performance comparison of Microsoft Backup and the DOS Backup command

Three types of backups: Full, incremental, and differential

In the last chapter, I introduced you to the two major types of backups, full and incremental. Both of these are supported by Microsoft Backup, as well as the DOS Backup command. I also presented the concept of appended incremental backups, supported by DOS 3.3 and later versions of DOS. Unfortunately, Microsoft Backup does *not* support appended incremental backups. So you'll have to use a separate diskette each time you do an incremental backup, as shown in figure 11-3. Now, I want to introduce you to one other type of backup that is supported by Microsoft Backup: differential backup.

Differential backups   As I said in chapter 10, when you do an incremental backup, the archive bit on each file is turned off, indicating that the file has been backed up. In contrast, the archive bit isn't turned off during a *differential backup*. As a result, a differential backup is a backup of all the files that have been created or changed since the last full backup even if they have been backed up in a previous differential backup. You can't do this type of backup with the DOS Backup command.

174   Chapter 11

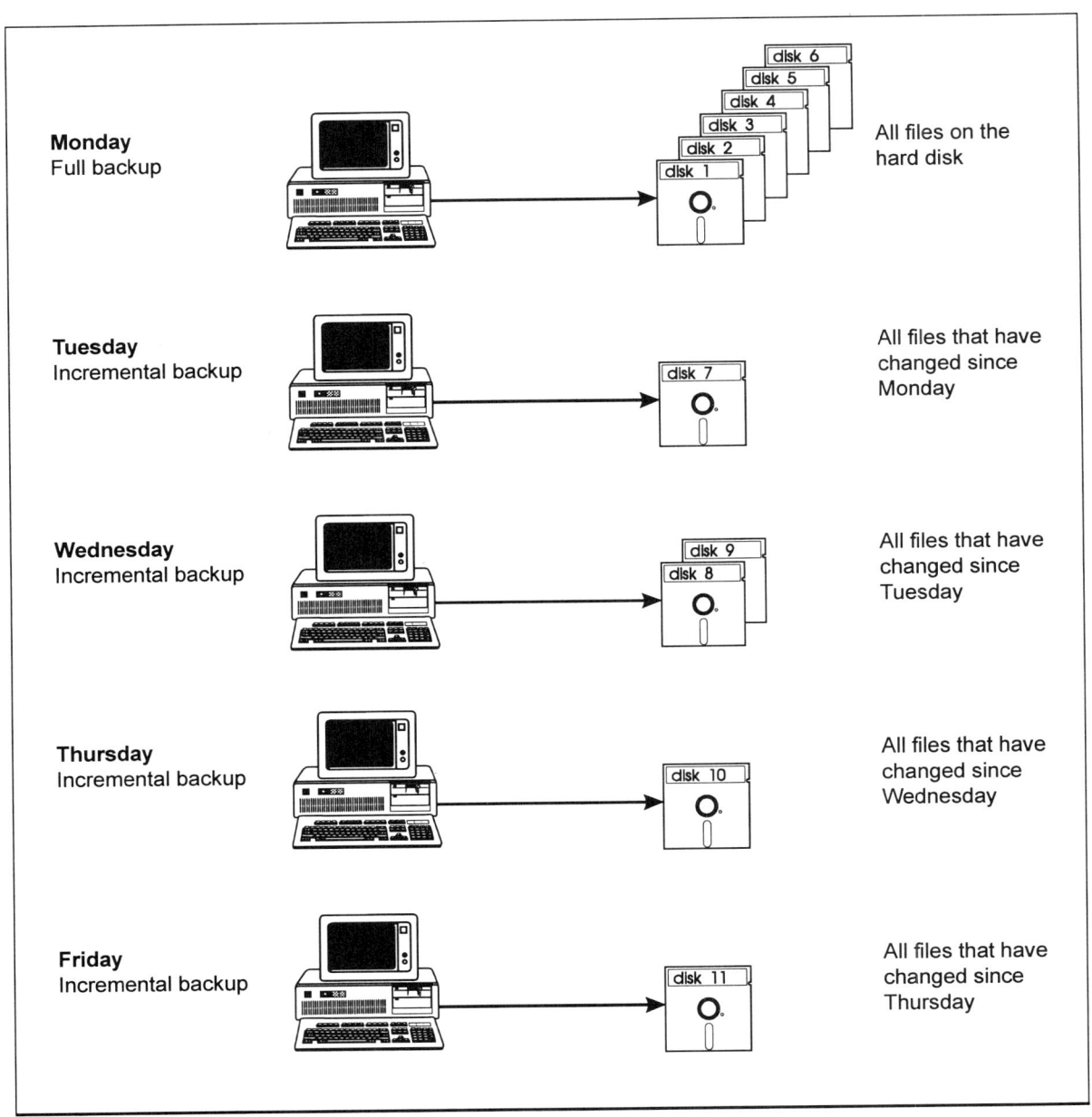

Monday Full backup	🖥️ →	disks 1–6	All files on the hard disk
Tuesday Incremental backup	🖥️ →	disk 7	All files that have changed since Monday
Wednesday Incremental backup	🖥️ →	disks 8, 9	All files that have changed since Tuesday
Thursday Incremental backup	🖥️ →	disk 10	All files that have changed since Wednesday
Friday Incremental backup	🖥️ →	disk 11	All files that have changed since Thursday

Figure 11-3   A weekly schedule of full and separate incremental backups

To illustrate how you can use differential backups, figure 11-4 shows a weekly schedule of one full and four differential backups. As you can see, each differential backup requires only diskette 7. Since the diskettes for a differential backup include only one version of each backed-up file, a schedule of differential backups is likely to require fewer diskettes than a schedule of separate incremental backups. However, the differential backups will take longer on the average than the incremental backups. That's because you have to back up more files each time, unless you're working on the same files every day.

If you do work on the same files each day, you may want to consider differential backups because they will be just as fast as incremental backups, and they won't require as many diskettes. You should be aware, though, that if you use the same diskette for each differential backup as shown in figure 11-4, you can lose a whole week's work if the diskette goes bad. So it's a good idea to alternate between diskettes for each differential backup. Then, if one diskette goes bad, you'll only lose one day's work.

An overview of Microsoft Backup

To start Microsoft Backup, you enter the program name MSBACKUP at the command prompt. When you do, the screen in figure 11-5 is displayed. As you can see, Microsoft Backup provides four functions: Backup, Restore, Compare, and Configure. I'll show you how to use all of these functions in this chapter. But first, I'll show you how to activate functions from Microsoft Backup, how to use the pull-down menus, and how to get Help information.

How to activate Backup functions
The rectangles that contain the Backup functions are called *buttons*. To activate one of these functions, move the mouse cursor to the button and press the left mouse button. This is referred to as *clicking the mouse*. If you don't have a mouse, you can activate a function by pressing its *shortcut key*. The shortcut key is the letter in the function name that's highlighted. If you're using a color monitor, the shortcut key is in a contrasting color. If you're using a black and white monitor, the shortcut key is in reverse video. For example, the shortcut key for the Backup function is *b*.

You can also activate a function by pressing the Tab key until the function is selected, then pressing the Enter key. A selected function is identified by two arrowheads on the left and right ends of the button. If you're using a color monitor, the selected function is also highlighted. Notice that when a function is selected, a brief description of the function appears on the bottom line of the screen.

Once you've activated a function, you can exit from it by pressing the Esc key. If the function has a Cancel button, you can also exit by selecting that button. To exit from Microsoft Backup, select the Quit button.

176 Chapter 11

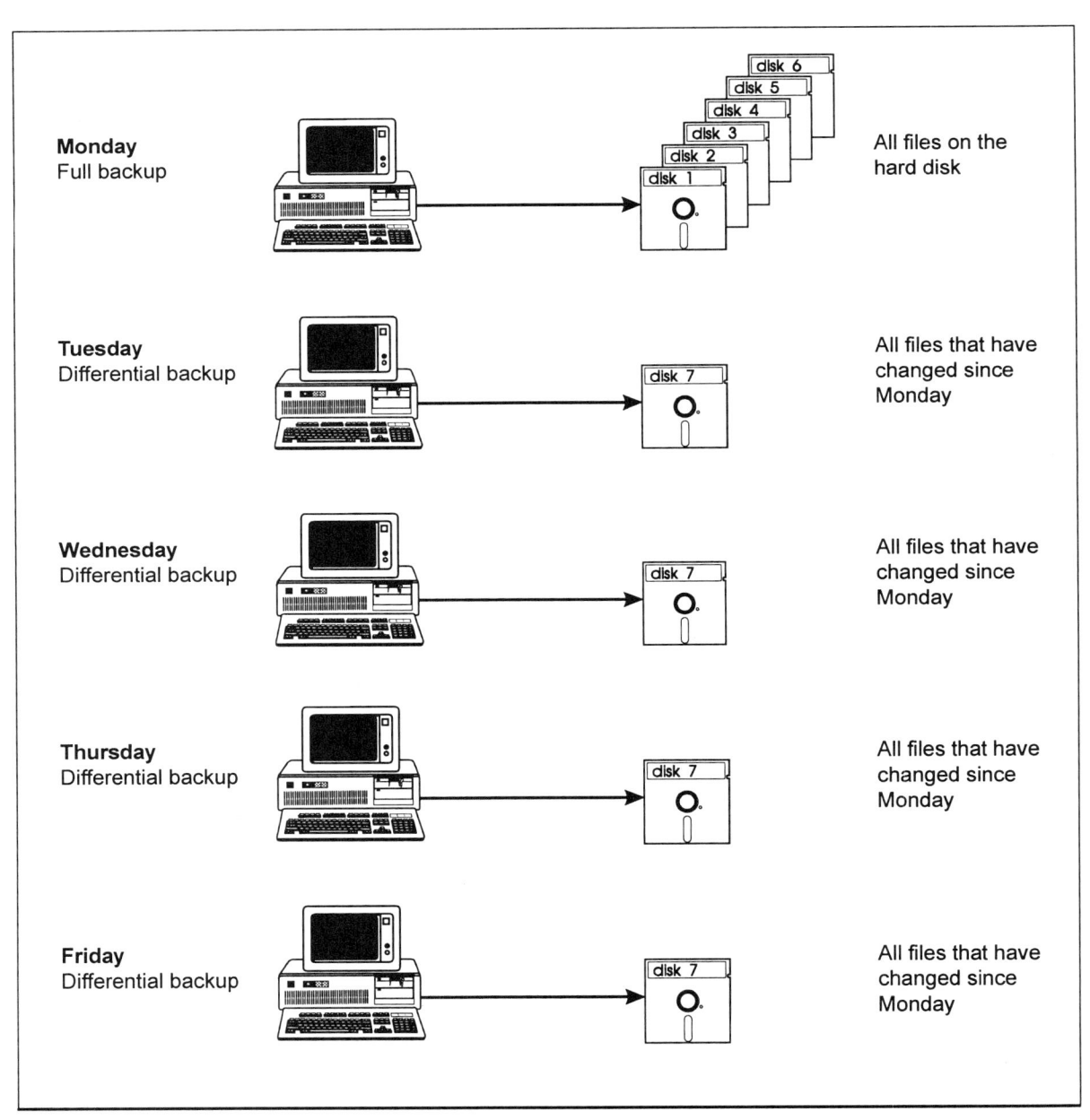

Figure 11-4 A weekly schedule of full and differential backups

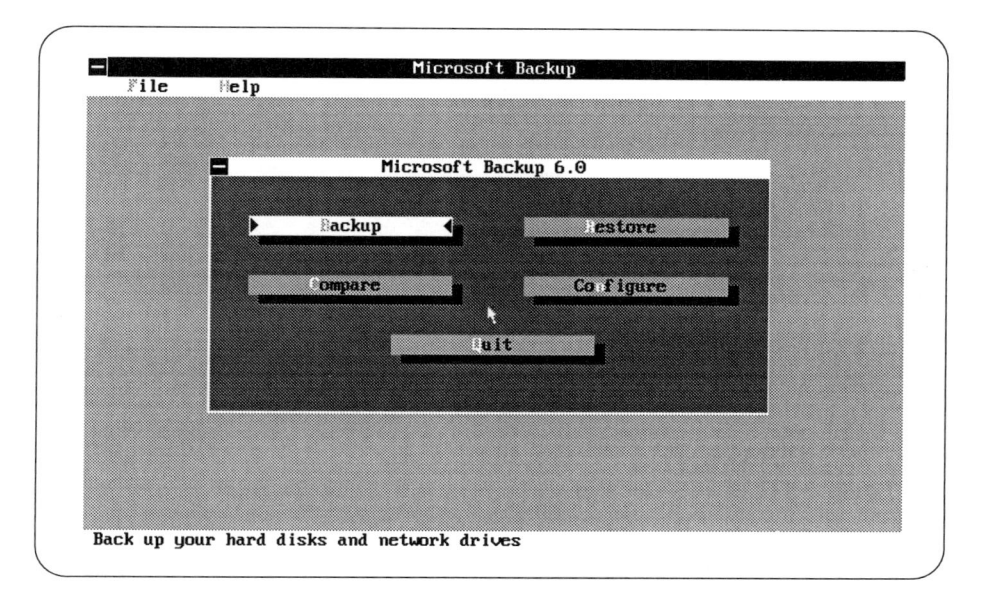

Figure 11-5 The opening screen for Microsoft Backup

How to use the pull-down menus You can also activate functions from the *menu bar* at the top of the screen. The menu bar on all the screens in Microsoft Backup contains only two menu items: File and Help. To activate one of these menu items, you click the mouse on it. When you do that, a *pull-down menu* is displayed. For example, figure 11-6 shows the pull-down menu that's displayed when you activate the File menu item. As you can see, this menu has seven functions. To activate one of these functions, you just point to it with the mouse cursor and click again.

If you don't have a mouse, you can activate a menu item using its shortcut key. In this case, you must hold down the Alt key while pressing the shortcut key. You can also press F10 to activate the File menu. Then, you can activate a function from the menu by pressing its shortcut key, or you can use the cursor control keys to highlight the function and then press the Enter key.

How to get Help information Whenever you're using Microsoft Backup, you can get information from the Help facility by pressing the F1 key. This information is displayed in a *window* as shown in figure 11-7, and it's *context-sensitive help*, which means it always relates to whatever you're trying to do at the time. For example, I pressed F1 when the Backup button was selected to get the Help information in figure 11-7.

To scroll through the Help text, you can use the cursor control keys or the Page-up and Page-down keys. If you're using a mouse, you can also scroll using the

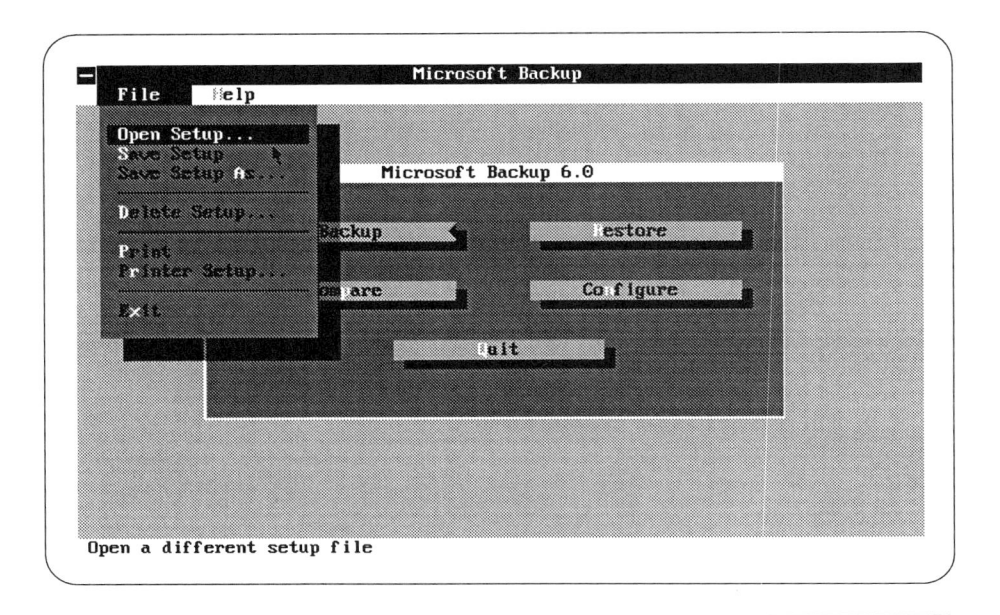

Figure 11-6 The File pull-down menu

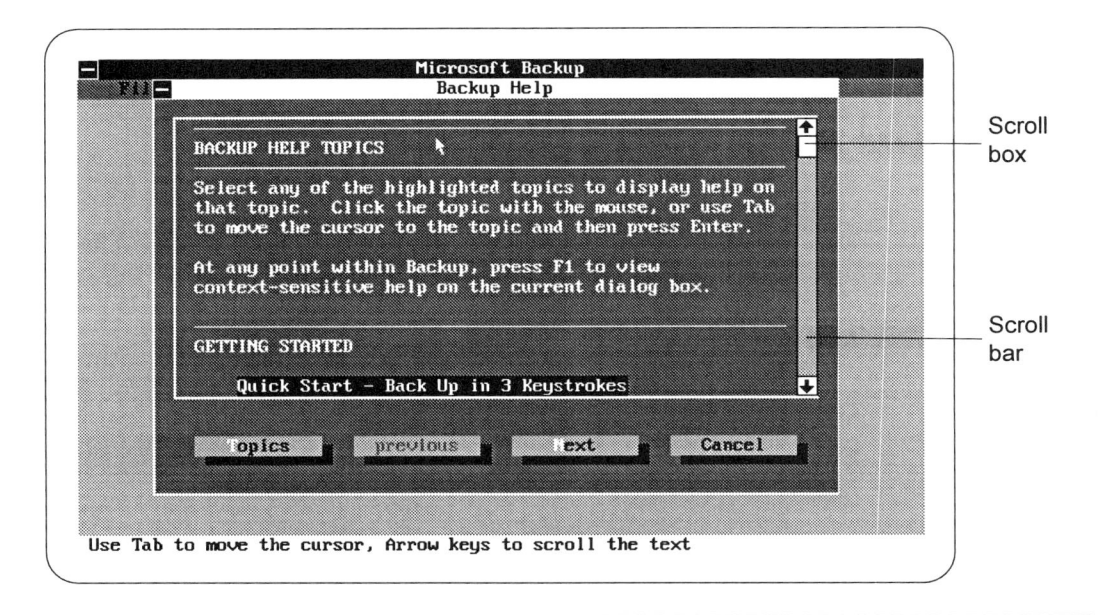

Figure 11-7 One of the Help facility windows that's displayed when you press the F1 key

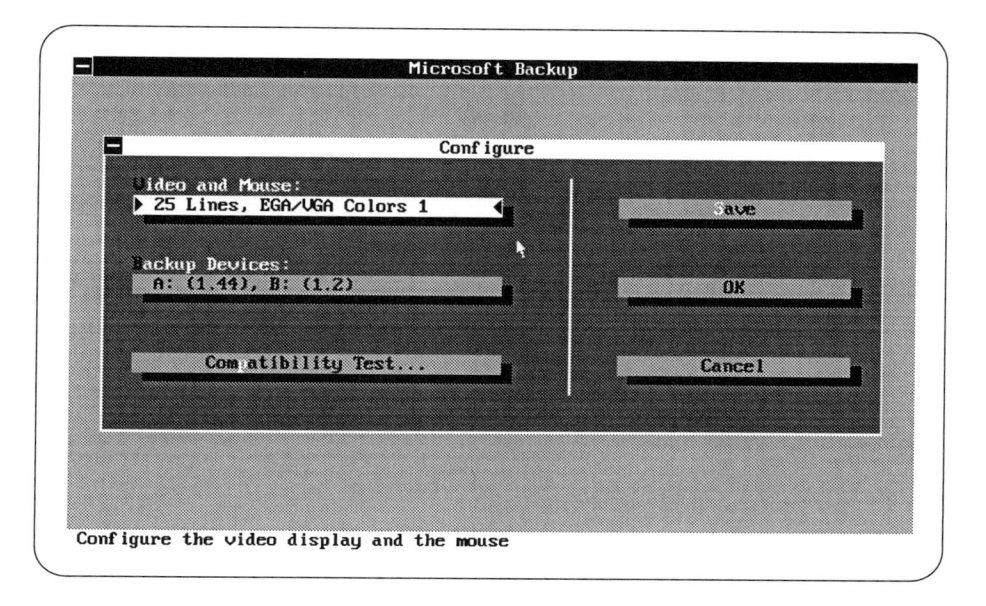

How to back up a hard disk using Microsoft Backup (DOS 6.0) **179**

Figure 11-8 The Configure screen

scroll bar at the right of the Help window. You can scroll one line at a time by clicking on the arrow at the top or bottom of the scroll bar. Or, you can scroll through varying numbers of lines using the portion of the scroll bar called the *scroll box*.

The scroll box reflects the position of the screen information relative to the full text. For example, when the scroll box is at the top of the scroll bar, as in figure 11-7, the screen displays the beginning of the Help text. When the scroll box is near the middle of the scroll bar, the screen displays the middle part of the Help text. To scroll through the text, move the mouse cursor to the scroll box, then hold down the left mouse button while you move the scroll box to a new position. As you move the mouse, the Help text scrolls to its new position.

To use one of the button functions at the bottom of the Help screen, you click on it with the mouse. You can also start one of these functions by using the Tab key and the cursor control keys to move the cursor to the desired button and then pressing the Enter key. The Topics button displays the Help index. The Previous button displays the previous Help topic. The Next button displays the next Help topic. And the Cancel button exits from Help.

How to use the Configure function before you run your first backup

Figure 11-8 shows the Configure screen that's displayed when you select the Configure function from the opening screen of Microsoft Backup. The first time you

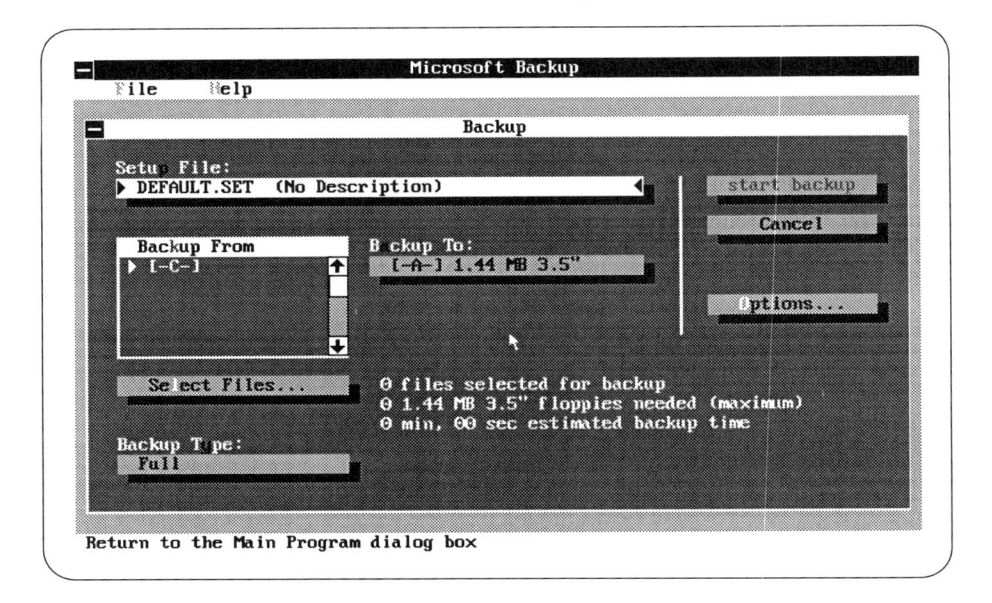

Figure 11-9 The Backup screen

use this utility, you should make sure that the video, mouse, and backup devices options are set correctly for your system. They should be set up properly, but if you ever need to change one of these options, simply click the mouse anywhere in the box that contains the option. Then, a *dialog box* appears that allows you to select the right value for the option. To display these dialog boxes using the keyboard, highlight the option box using the Tab key, then press the Enter key.

You should also run the compatibility test once for each backup device you use on your system (I'll show you how to select the backup device in a moment). You start the compatibility test by clicking on its button or by highlighting it and pressing the Enter key. The compatibility test makes sure that Microsoft Backup is compatible with the backup device you're using.

How to use the Backup function to back up data

When you select the Backup function from the opening screen, the Backup screen in figure 11-9 is displayed. From this screen, you can select the type of backup you want to do, the files to be backed up, the drive where the files are to be backed up, and a setup file that contains the specifications for the backup. The settings you see in figure 11-9 are the defaults provided by Microsoft Backup the first time you use it. This screen also tells you the number of files selected for the backup, the number of diskettes that will be required for the backup, and the estimated time to perform the backup. As you can see, there are no files currently selected for the backup. You can also select the Options button from this screen to set backup options. And you can select the Start-backup button to start a backup. To use Microsoft Backup efficiently, you need to know how to use all of these features.

How to set backup options Before you start a backup, you should set the backup options. To do that, you select the Options button from the Backup screen. Then, the dialog box in figure 11-10 is displayed. To select or deselect an option, click the mouse on the box to the left of the option. Or, use the cursor control keys to move to a box and press the Space bar. When an option is selected, a check mark appears in the box.

In figure 11-10, I've set the options the way I think you'll use them most often. If you look at the option descriptions in the figure, you'll see that the first two options I've set provide for file compression and data-recovery safeguards; the third one causes Microsoft Backup to beep whenever you need to provide information to the backup operation. Usually, you will set these options just once so they'll be used in all your backup procedures.

How to do a full backup Figure 11-11 shows you how to do a full backup once you've specified the backup options. In part 1 of the figure, the default settings for the backup are in effect, so no files are selected for the backup. The first thing you need to do, then, is select the files you want to back up.

The Backup-from box displays all the drives on your hard disk. To include or exclude an entire drive from the backup, click the right mouse button on the drive designator in this box (you can also double-click the left mouse button) or highlight the drive designator using the Tab key or the cursor control keys and press the Space bar. For example, if you click on the designator for drive C, an "All files" message appears, indicating that all the files on drive C are selected. Values for the three messages to the right of the Select-files box also appear, as shown in part 2 of figure 11-11. If you click on the C drive designator again, the "All-files" message and the values disappear. You can also select specific files and directories to be backed up. I'll show you how to do that later in this chapter.

If you want to change the drive where the data will be backed up, click the mouse on the Backup-to option box or highlight the box and press the Enter key. Then, a dialog box is displayed that lists all the backup drives so you can select the right one.

Once you're ready to start the backup, you select the Start-backup button, and a dialog box like the one in part 3 of figure 11-11 is displayed. This tells you to insert the first diskette into the backup drive. After you insert the diskette, press the Enter key or click on the Continue button.

During the backup, you'll see a screen like the one in part 4 of figure 11-11. This screen shows you the files and directories as they're backed up as well as the progress of the backup.

When a backup diskette becomes full, Microsoft Backup displays a message like the one in part 5 of figure 11-11. (The message is to the right of the drive letter at the

The Disk-backup-options dialog box

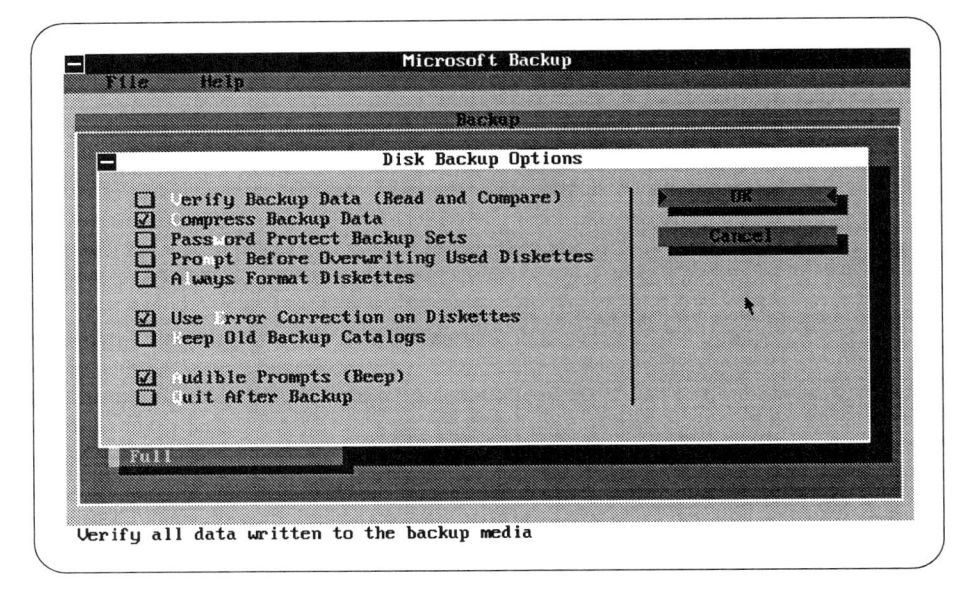

```
┌─────────────────────────────────────────────────────────┐
│ ─                    Microsoft Backup                   │
│  File    Help                                           │
│ ┌─────────────────────────────────────────────────────┐ │
│ │                     Backup                          │ │
│ │ ┌─────────────────────────────────────────────┐     │ │
│ │ │ ─            Disk Backup Options            │     │ │
│ │ │                                             │     │ │
│ │ │  ☐ Verify Backup Data (Read and Compare)    │     │ │
│ │ │  ☑ Compress Backup Data              ►  OK  ◄│    │ │
│ │ │  ☐ Password Protect Backup Sets             │     │ │
│ │ │  ☐ Prompt Before Overwriting Used Diskettes │     │ │
│ │ │  ☐ Always Format Diskettes          Cancel  │     │ │
│ │ │                                             │     │ │
│ │ │  ☑ Use Error Correction on Diskettes        │     │ │
│ │ │  ☐ Keep Old Backup Catalogs                 │     │ │
│ │ │                                             │     │ │
│ │ │  ☑ Audible Prompts (Beep)                   │     │ │
│ │ │  ☐ Quit After Backup                        │     │ │
│ │ │                                             │     │ │
│ │ │  Full                                       │     │ │
│ │ └─────────────────────────────────────────────┘     │ │
│ │ Verify all data written to the backup media         │ │
│ └─────────────────────────────────────────────────────┘ │
└─────────────────────────────────────────────────────────┘
```

Option	Function
Verify Backup Data	Causes Microsoft Backup to verify the data written to the backup diskettes. Because this nearly doubles the time required for a backup, we recommend you select the Use-error-correction-on-diskettes option instead.
Compress Backup Data	Minimizes the number of diskettes and the time required for a backup. Use this option for your backups.
Password Protect Backup Sets	Allows you to assign a password to your backup diskettes.
Prompt Before Overwriting Used Diskettes	Causes Microsoft Backup to warn you if you insert a backup diskette that contains data. Because this option requires you to confirm every diskette you reuse, it adds to your backup time. So if you always use the same sets of diskettes for backups and know you aren't destroying any data that you need, you won't want to select this option.

Figure 11-10   How to set the backup options (part 1 of 2)

Option	Function
Always Format Diskettes	Formats each backup diskette before data is written to it. Since this is time-consuming, you usually won't select this option. Then, only unformatted diskettes are formatted.
Use Error Correction on Diskettes	Writes information to each backup diskette that can help recover the data from the diskette if it's damaged. Use this option instead of the Verify-backup-data option.
Keep Old Backup Catalogs	Keeps a record of previous backups. Since this isn't usually necessary, you probably won't select this option.
Audible Prompts	Causes your workstation to beep whenever Microsoft Backup requires your attention (for example, when you need to insert the next backup diskette).
Quit After Backup	Causes Microsoft Backup to end automatically when the backup is complete.

Figure 11-10 How to set the backup options (part 2 of 2)

top of the Diskette-progress box.) Then, when you insert the next diskette, the backup continues. If you don't respond by inserting the next diskette within a few seconds, a dialog box like the one I showed you in part 3 of the figure is displayed. Then, after you insert the next diskette, you have to press the Enter key or click on the Continue button.

Part 6 of the figure shows the type of summary information you get when the backup procedure is finished. Here, you can see that the backup time for almost 23MB of data was only 6 minutes and 17 seconds. You can also see that the file compression for these files was 2.5 percent, so only 7 diskettes were required for the backup.

How to do an incremental or differential backup The procedure for doing an incremental or differential backup is almost identical to the procedure for a full backup. The only difference is that you have to change the Backup-type option on the Backup screen. To do that, click the mouse on the Backup-type option box or highlight it and press the Enter key. When you do, a dialog box like the one in figure 11-12 is displayed. Then, select the option you want by clicking on it with the mouse or by pressing the Space bar. Once you've selected the backup type, you're ready to start your backup.

Part 1:

To back up an entire drive, move the cursor to the drive designator in the Backup-from box and press the Space bar or click the right mouse button.

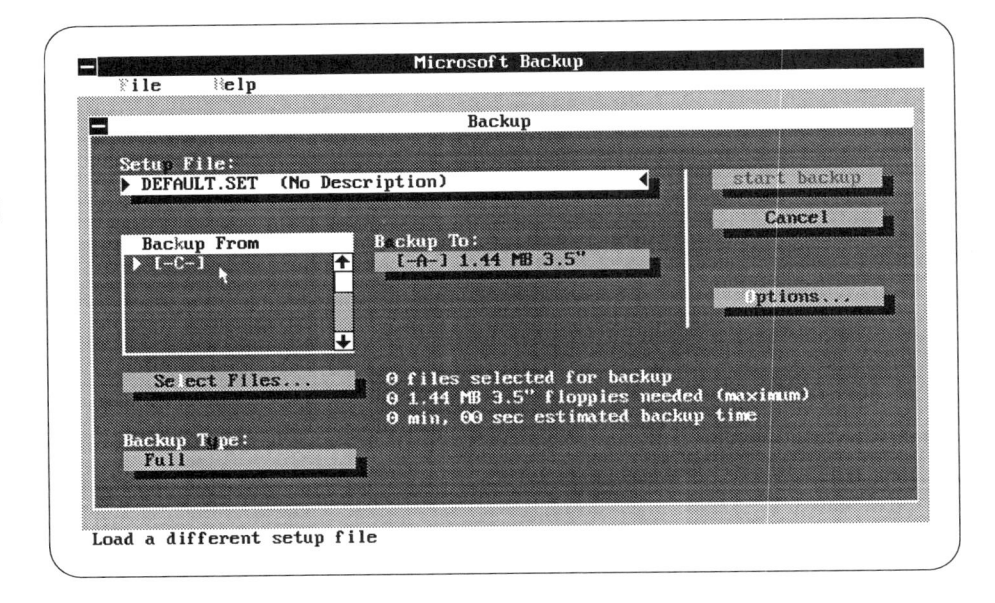

Part 2:

The "All files" message appears in the Backup-from box and the messages to the right of the Select-files box tell you how many files will be backed up, how many diskettes the backup will require, and the estimated backup time. Select the Start-backup button to begin the backup.

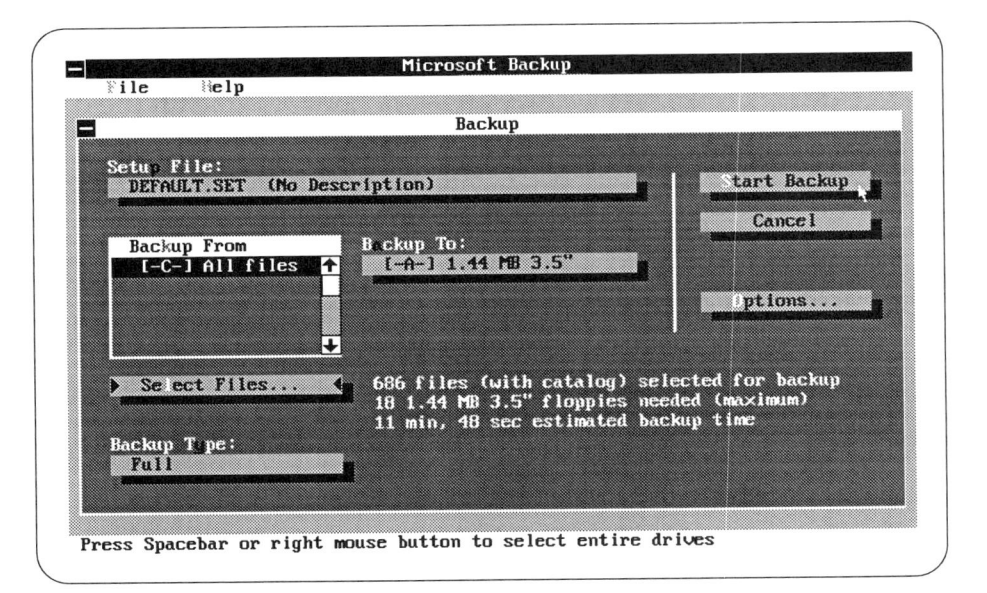

Figure 11-11 How to do a full backup (parts 1 and 2 of 6)

How to back up a hard disk using Microsoft Backup (DOS 6.0)

Part 3:

Before the backup starts, Microsoft Backup prompts you for the first diskette. After inserting the diskette, press the Enter key or click on the Continue button.

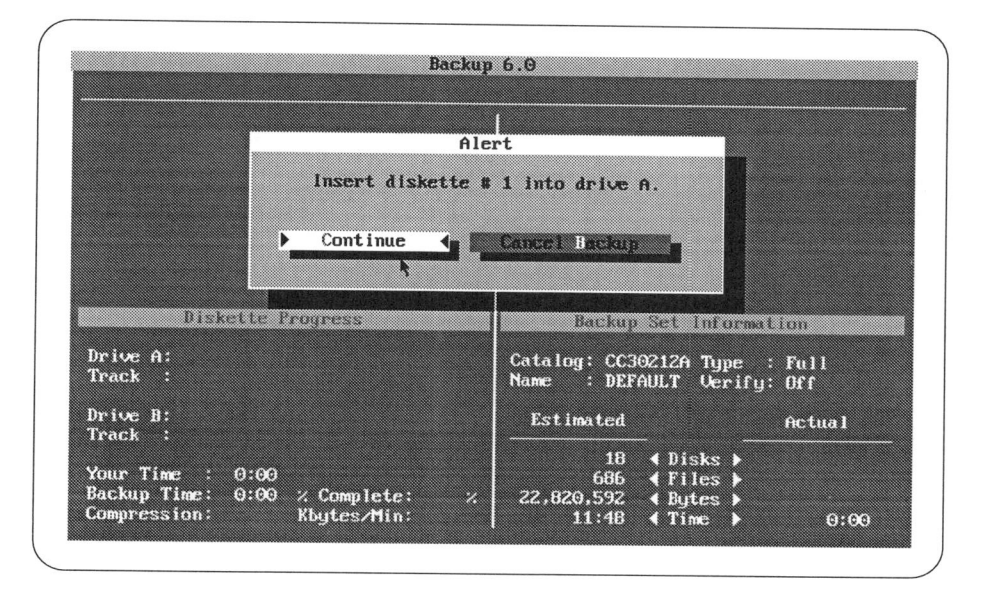

Part 4:

While Microsoft Backup is working, the values in the Diskette-progress and Backup-set-information boxes change to show you how the backup is progressing.

Figure 11-11   How to do a full backup (parts 3 and 4 of 6)

Part 5:

When a diskette becomes full, Microsoft Backup prompts you to insert the next diskette.

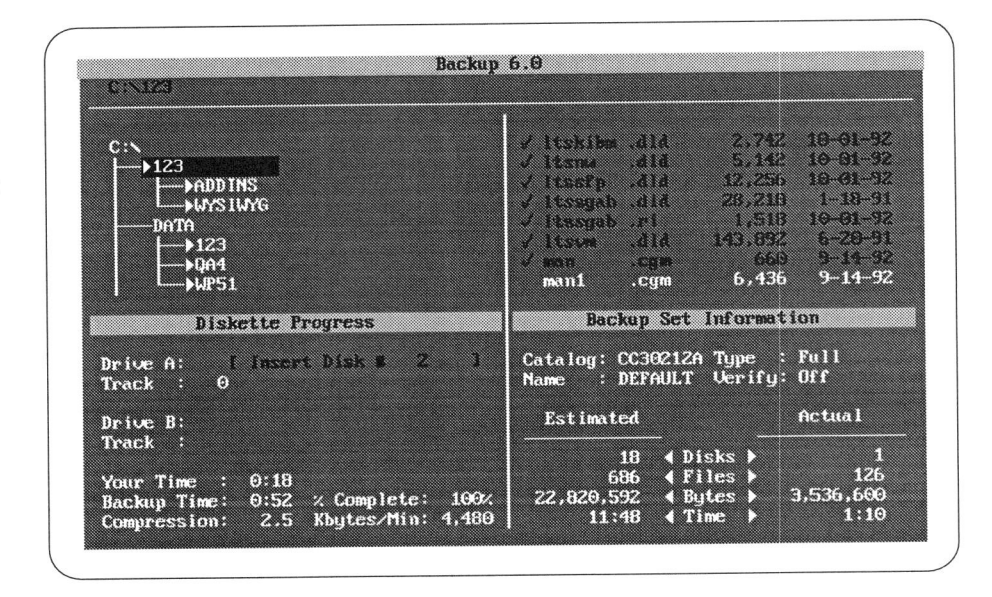

Part 6:

At the end of the backup, Microsoft Backup gives you summary information. Press the Enter key or click on the OK button to return to the opening Backup screen shown in figure 11-5.

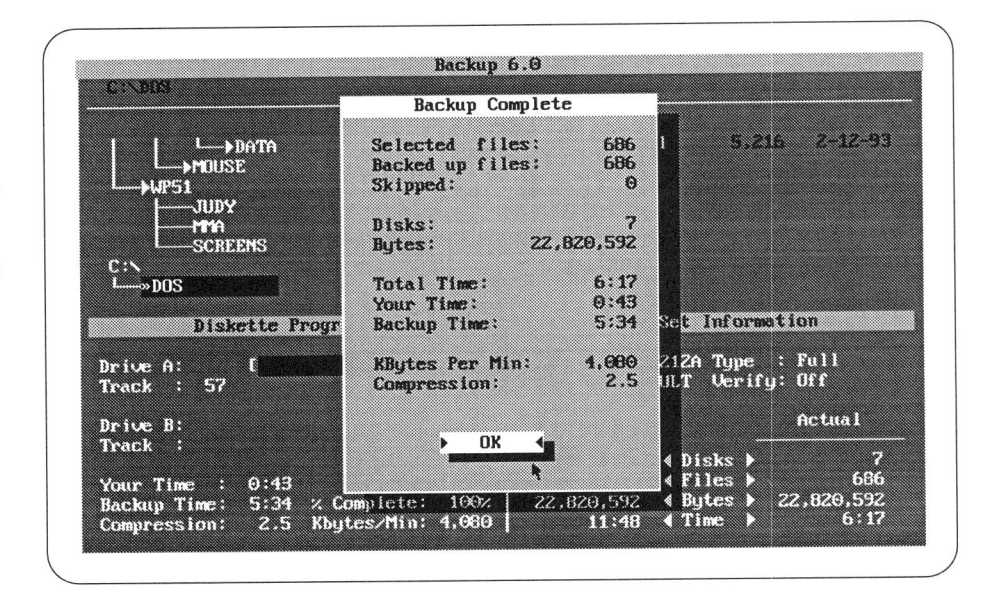

Figure 11-11 How to do a full backup (parts 5 and 6 of 6)

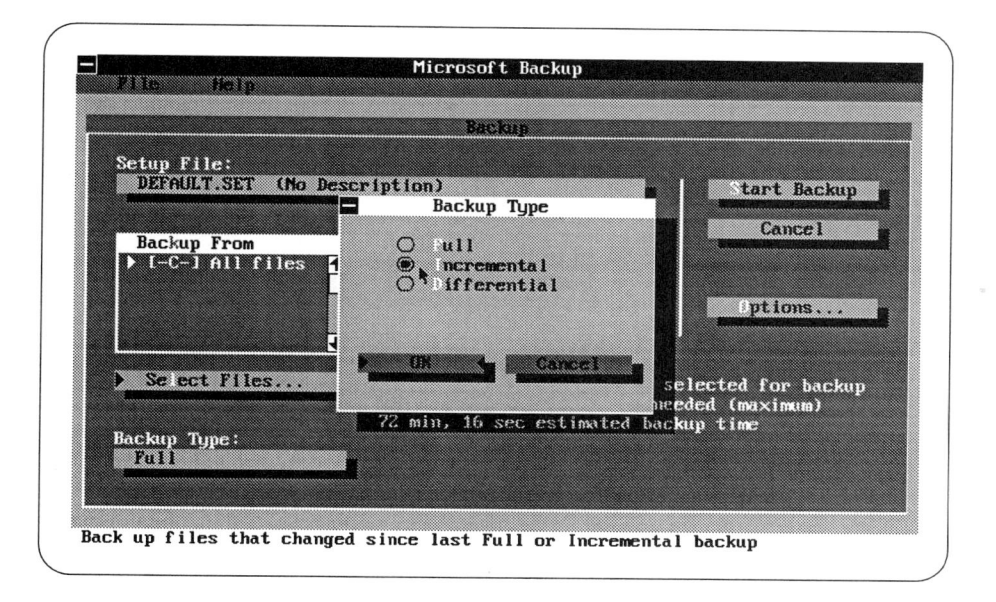

[Screenshot of Microsoft Backup dialog showing Backup Type selection with Full, Incremental, and Differential options]

Figure 11-12   How to select the backup type

How to select files for a backup   In the last chapter, I showed you how you can simplify backups by organizing your directories so that all data directories are subordinate to one directory. Then, you can do a periodic backup of the program directories and a daily backup of the data directories. To do that, you'll need to select the directories you want to back up. Figure 11-13 shows you how to back up a single data directory.

In part 1, you can see that no files are selected for the backup. The current drive is C, indicated by the arrowhead to the left of the drive designator. To change the current drive, click on it with the mouse. Or, tab to the Backup-from box, then use the cursor control keys to highlight the drive you want.

Next, select the Select-files option. When you do, the screen in part 2 of the figure is displayed. Here, the left side of the screen contains the directory structure of the drive and the right side of the screen contains a list of the files in the current directory. If a directory is selected for the backup, it has an arrowhead pointing to it. If a file is selected, it has a check mark in front of it.

As you can see in part 2, no directories are selected. To select a directory, click the right mouse button on it or highlight the directory and press the Space bar. In part 3, you can see that I've selected all the directories subordinate to the DATA directory. I didn't select the DATA directory itself because it doesn't contain any files. Note that if you select a directory that contains subdirectories, the subdirectories are *not* automatically selected. You have to select each directory individually.

Part 1:

If you don't want to back up an entire drive, select the Select-files function to specify which files or directories should be backed up.

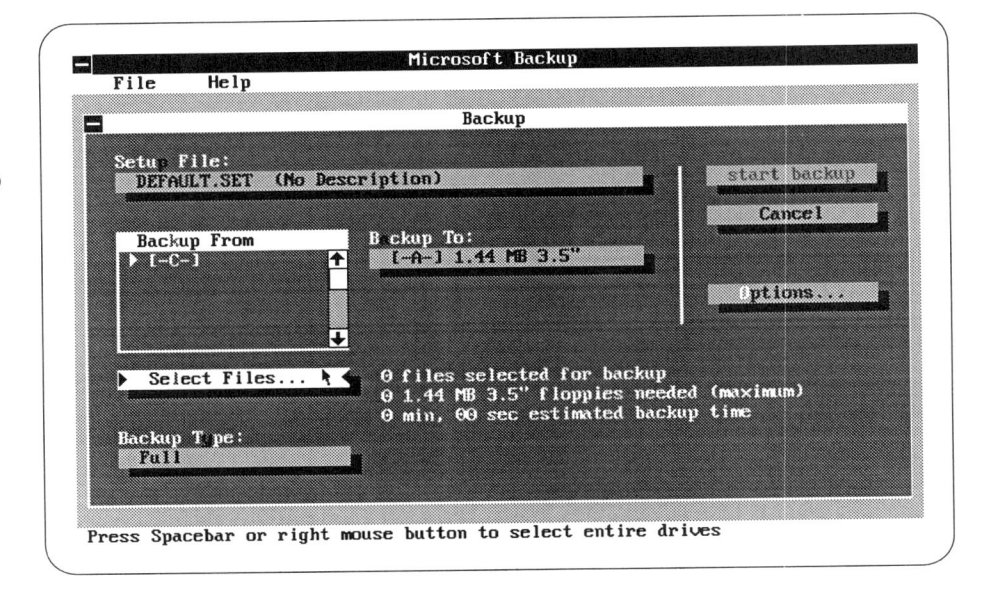

Part 2:

The Select-files screen displays a listing of all the files on the selected drive. The left part of the screen shows the directory structure, while the right part of the screen shows the files in the highlighted directory.

Figure 11-13 How to select files for a backup (parts 1 and 2 of 4)

How to back up a hard disk using Microsoft Backup (DOS 6.0) **189**

Part 3:

Move the cursor to the directory you want to back up, and press the Space bar or click the right mouse button to select all the files in it. To select only certain files, move the cursor to the file names and select them individually. When you've selected the files, select the OK button or press the Enter key to return to the Backup screen.

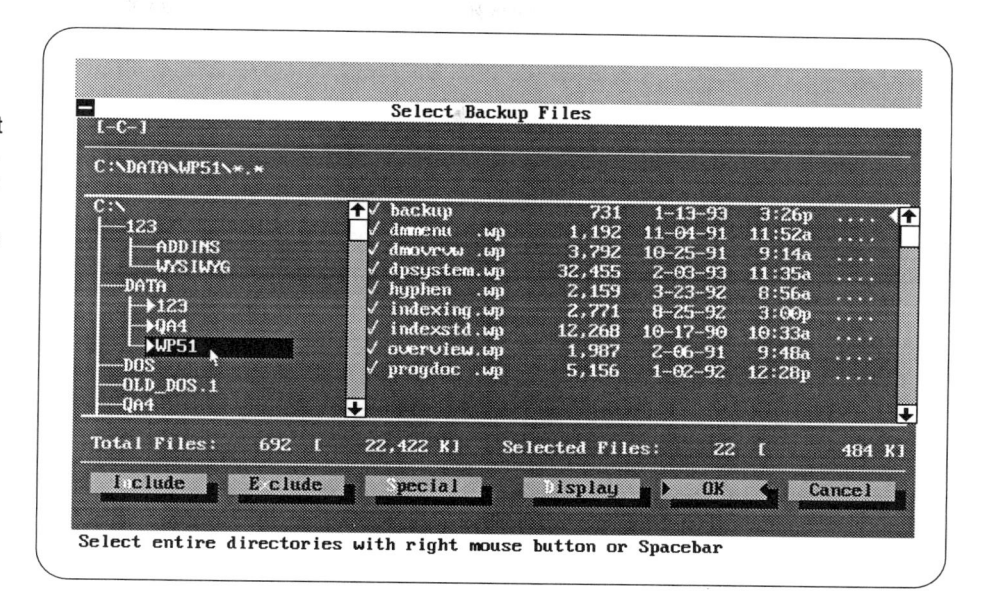

Part 4:

The messages to the right of the Select-files box show how many files have been selected and what the backup requirements are.

Figure 11-13 How to select files for a backup (parts 3 and 4 of 4)

If you don't want to back up all the files in a directory, you can select individual files. First, move the cursor to the appropriate directory. The files in that directory are then displayed on the right of the screen. To select a file with the keyboard, press the Tab key to move the cursor to the file list; then, use the cursor control keys to move through the list and the Space bar to select a file. If you're using a mouse, select the directory, then click on the file. To deselect a file, move the cursor to the file and press the Space bar or click the right mouse button.

After you select the files you want to back up, select the OK button at the bottom of the screen. This returns you to the Backup screen shown in part 4 of figure 11-13. Here, you can see information about the number of files to be backed up and the number of diskettes and the amount of time the backup requires. Now, you're ready to start the backup. But if the settings you just specified are for a backup that you'll do regularly, you should first save those settings in a setup file. I'll show you how to do that next.

Before I show you how to create a setup file, though, I want to mention the buttons that appear at the bottom of parts 2 and 3 of figure 11-13. The Include and Exclude buttons let you select specific files or groups of files to be included in or excluded from the backup. The Special button lets you select the files to be backed up by date. And the Display button lets you control how the files are displayed on the screen. For example, you can display the files by date order rather than alphabetical order. Most of the time, you don't need the functions these buttons provide to do your backups, so I'm not going to present them in detail here. But I want you to know they're available in case you ever need them.

How to use a setup file   To simplify your backup procedures, you can save the specifications for a backup in a *setup file*. Then, you don't have to select the functions and options for a specific backup procedure the next time you want to repeat the backup. Instead, you just load the setup file for the backup and start the backup. Microsoft Backup lets you save a backup configuration using the Save-setup and Save-setup-as functions of the File menu, shown in part 1 of figure 11-14. You use the Save-setup function to change a setup file you saved previously. You use the Save-setup-as function to create a new setup file.

After you've configured a backup by setting the drives, directories, and options the way you want them, you select the Save-setup-as function. When you do, a dialog box like the one in part 2 of figure 11-14 lets you name the setup file and enter a description for it. Here, I've used the name DATAC for a backup of the data on drive C. In part 3, you can see that the configuration file has been saved in the file named DATAC.SET.

To load a setup file, you can use the Open-setup function of the File menu, or you can select the Setup-file option box to display a list of setup files like the one in figure 11-15. After you select the file you want, you're ready to start the backup. Because this simplifies the use of Microsoft Backup, I recommend that you save one setup file for each backup procedure that you run.

Part 1:

To save a new setup file, set the backup specifications on the Backup screen. Then, open the File menu and select the Save-setup-as function.

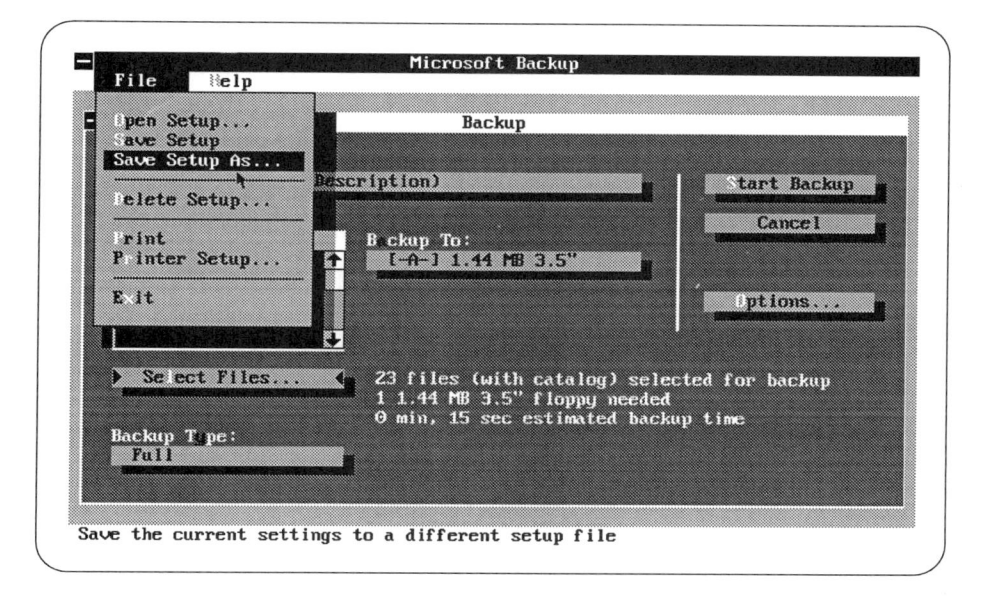

Part 2:

In the dialog box, enter the file name of the new setup file and a file description if desired. Then, select the Save button.

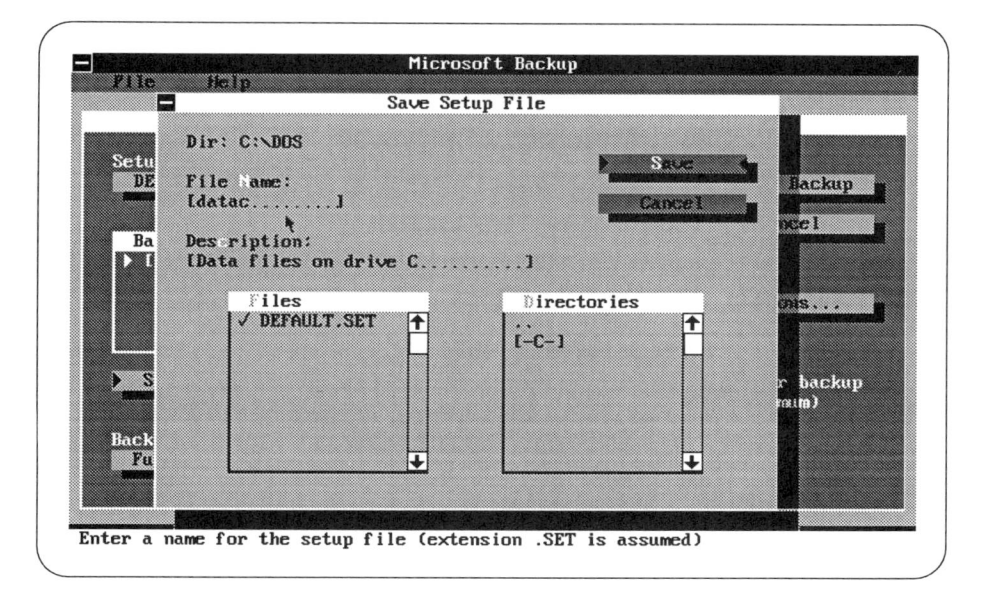

Figure 11-14 How to save the specifications for a backup in a setup file (parts 1 and 2 of 3)

Part 3:

Microsoft Backup saves the backup specifications in the setup file and returns to the Backup screen. The Setup-file box shows the new setup file name.

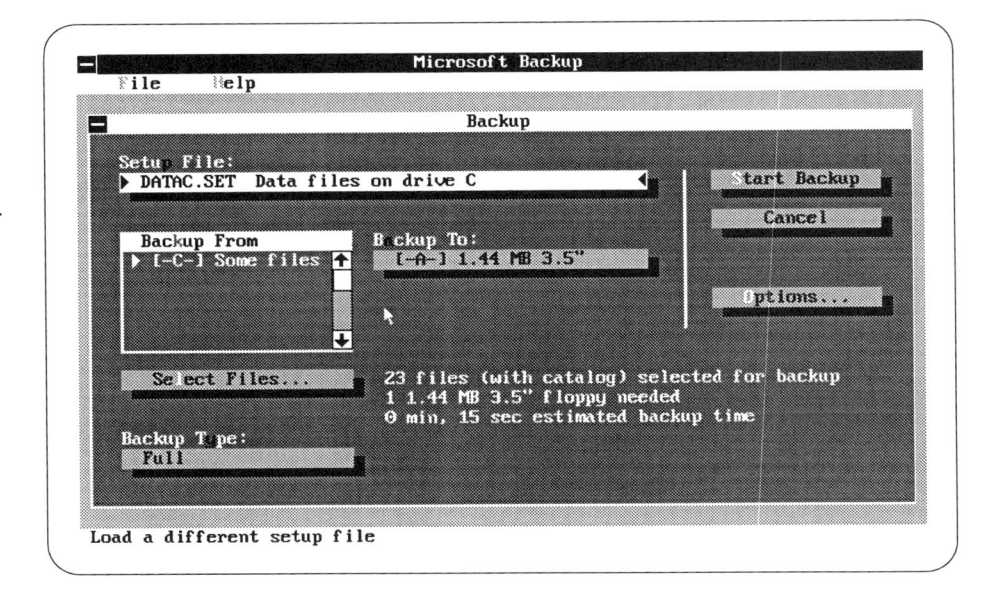

```
┌─────────────────────── Microsoft Backup ───────────────────────┐
│  File   Help                                                    │
│  ┌───────────────────────── Backup ────────────────────────┐   │
│  │ Setup File:                                              │   │
│  │ ▶ DATAC.SET  Data files on drive C        ◀  Start Backup│   │
│  │                                              Cancel      │   │
│  │  Backup From         Backup To:                          │   │
│  │  ▶ [-C-] Some files  [-A-] 1.44 MB 3.5"                  │   │
│  │                                              Options...  │   │
│  │                                                          │   │
│  │   Select Files...   23 files (with catalog) selected for backup
│  │                     1 1.44 MB 3.5" floppy needed         │   │
│  │                     0 min, 15 sec estimated backup time  │   │
│  │  Backup Type:                                            │   │
│  │   Full                                                   │   │
│  └──────────────────────────────────────────────────────────┘   │
│  Load a different setup file                                    │
└─────────────────────────────────────────────────────────────────┘
```

Figure 11-14   How to save the specifications for a backup in a setup file (part 3 of 3)

You can also load a setup file automatically when you start Microsoft Backup. To do that, specify the name of the setup file following the program name at the command prompt, like this:

`C:\>msbackup datac`

Since MSBACKUP is the name of Microsoft Backup, this command starts the program using DATAC as the name of the setup file that should be used for the backup.

If you use setup files, it's best if you use the same file for all types of backups of the same data. For example, I use the DATAC setup file for both full and incremental backups of my data files. Because I have the backup type set to incremental in the setup file, that means I have to change it to full whenever I do a full backup. Although this is a slight inconvenience, it makes restoring the data easier, as you'll see in a moment.

How to use the Restore function to restore files

Before you use the Restore function of Microsoft Backup, you need to understand how it uses catalogs to keep track of the directories and files that are backed up. So, I'll begin this section by describing those catalogs. Then, I'll show you how to load a catalog for a restore operation, how to select files for the restore, and how to set restore options.

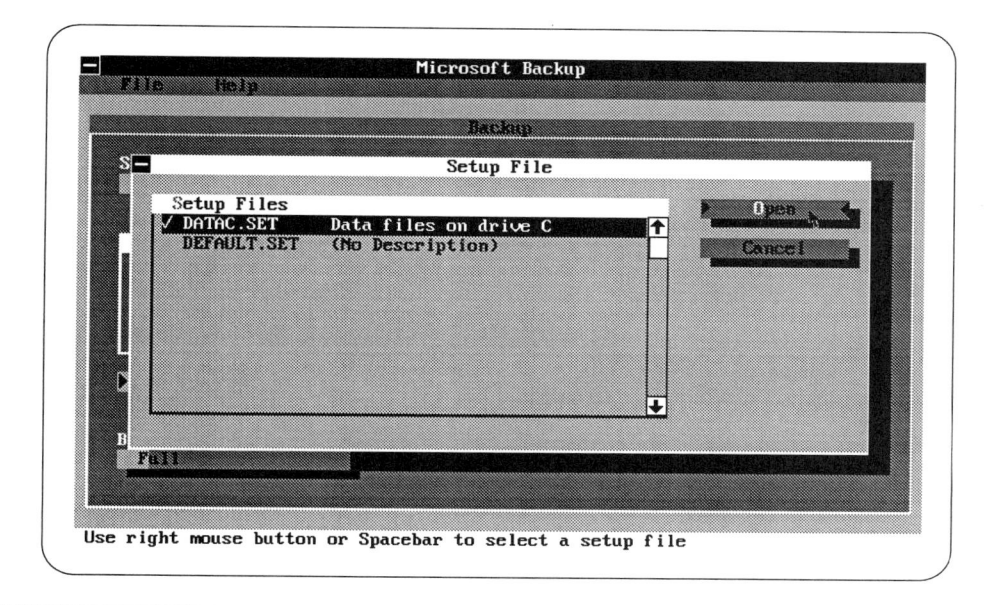

How to back up a hard disk using Microsoft Backup (DOS 6.0)   **193**

Figure 11-15   The dialog box for the Setup-file option

Catalogs   When you use Microsoft Backup, it automatically keeps track of the directories and files that have been backed up in a *backup catalog*. Microsoft Backup keeps this history information on the hard disk as well as on the last diskette of a *backup set*. That way, if the catalog on the hard disk is damaged, you can retrieve the catalog from the backup set.

The name that's given to a backup catalog consists of the drive indicators, date, sequence of the backup, and type of backup. Specifically, a catalog name has the format illustrated in figure 11-16. So, a catalog named CC21123A.FUL is for the first full backup of data on drive C done on 11/23/92.

When you do a full backup, Microsoft Backup creates a *master catalog* in addition to the backup catalog. The master catalog keeps track of all of the backups in a *backup cycle*. A backup cycle consists of a full backup plus any intermediate backups done up until the next full backup. For example, if you do a full backup of your data every Monday and incremental backups Tuesday through Friday, the backup cycle consists of the full backup and all four incremental backups. When you do another full backup the following Monday, a new backup cycle begins. Note that all the backups in a cycle must use the same setup file. That's why you should use the same setup file for both full and incremental backups, as I explained earlier. The name of the master catalog is the same as the setup file, with the extension CAT. So the file named DATAC.CAT is a master catalog for all backups done using the setup file named DATAC.

Position	Description
1	The first drive backed up
2	The last drive backed up
3	The last digit of the current year
4-5	The current month
6-7	The current day
8	The sequence of the backup for the day, if more than one backup is done of the same data
Extension	FUL for full backup; INC for incremental backup; DIF for differential backup

Example

CC21123A.FUL	The first full backup of data on drive C done on 11/23/92.

Figure 11-16 The format of the file name for a backup catalog

How to load a catalog Figure 11-17 shows the Restore screen for Microsoft Backup. The default catalog is the one for the most recent backup. In this case, it's the incremental backup of drive C done on 2-14-93. To select a different catalog, press Enter or click on the Backup-set-catalog option. When you do, the dialog box in figure 11-18 is displayed, showing you all the catalogs on the hard disk. Here, the list contains four catalogs. The first one, DATAC.CAT, is the master catalog for the backup of data files on drive C. The second one, CC30212A.FUL, is for a full backup of the data files on drive C. And the third and fourth catalogs, CC30213A.INC and CC30214A.INC, are for incremental backups of the data on drive C. To select a catalog, click on it with the right mouse button or use the cursor control keys to highlight the catalog and press the Space bar.

Normally, you'll restore from the master catalog. When you do, Microsoft Backup restores each backup set in the backup cycle in order. For example, if you load the DATAC master catalog in figure 11-18, the full backup, CC30212A.FUL is restored, followed by the two incremental backups. Without the master catalog, you'd have to restore each backup set in a separate operation. So the master catalog simplifies the restore process.

Another way to select a backup catalog is by activating the Catalog button on the Restore screen. In addition to listing the catalogs on the hard disk, this function gives you some additional options for recovering a catalog if it isn't on the hard disk or on

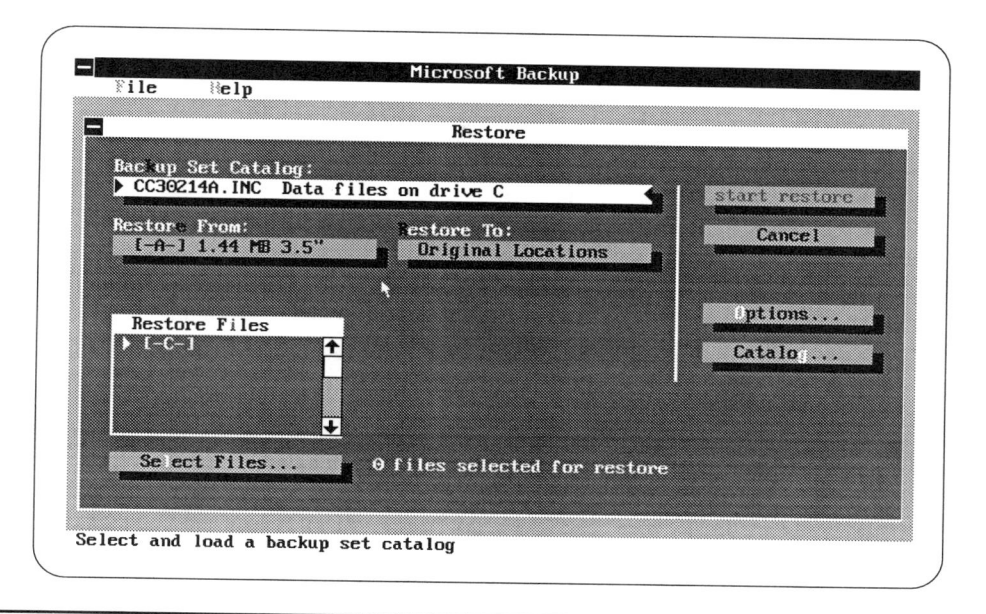

Figure 11-17 The Restore screen

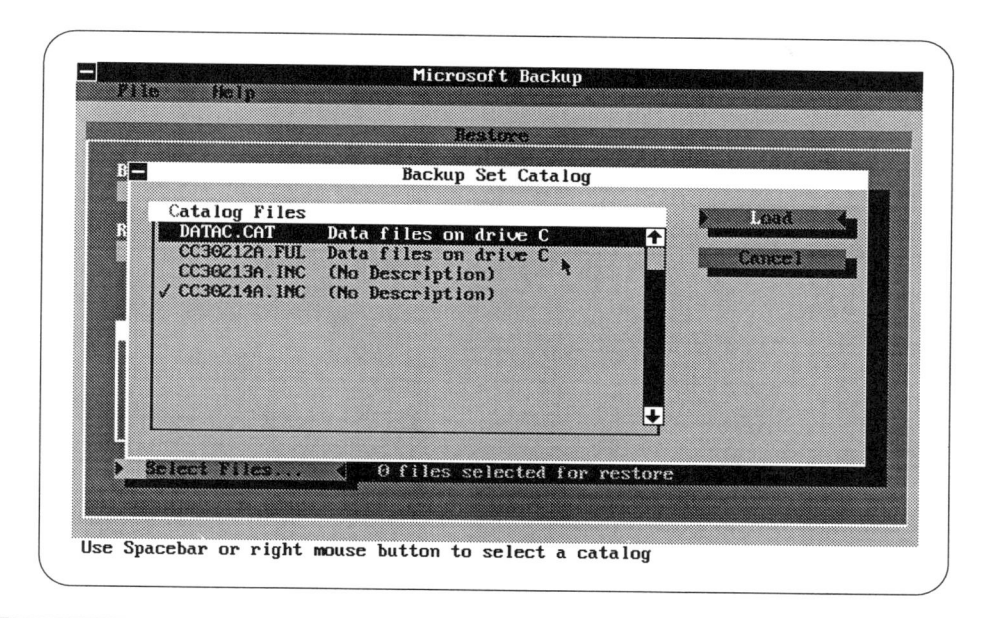

Figure 11-18 The dialog box for the Backup-set-catalog option

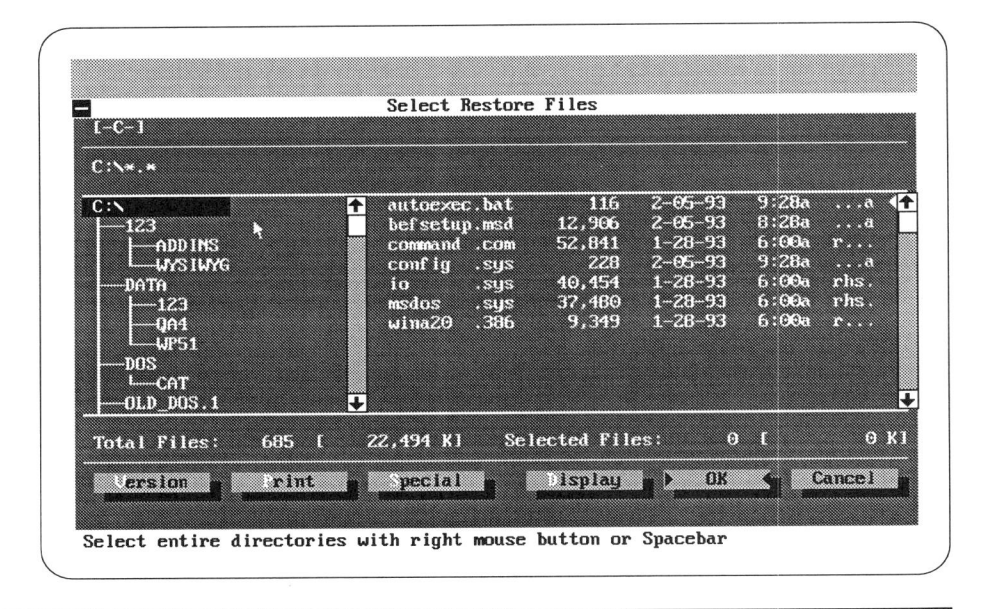

Figure 11-19 The Select-files screen for the Restore function

the backup set. These options are beyond the scope of this book, though. So for now, you can select the catalog just by using the Backup-set-catalog box.

How to select the files to restore   After you select the catalog for the restore, you select the files you want to restore. You select files the same way you do for a backup. So to restore all the files in the specified catalog, click the right mouse button on the drive designator, or highlight the drive designator and press the Space bar, and the "All files" message will appear. To restore selected files, select the Select-files option, and mark the files you want to restore.

When you select the Select-files option, a screen like the one in figure 11-19 is displayed. This screen is identical to the Select-files screen for the Backup function except for the first two functions at the bottom of the screen. The Print function lets you print the catalog file you've selected, and the Version function lets you select the version of the file you want to restore.

By default, Microsoft Backup restores the most recent version of a file. But occasionally, you may need to restore an earlier version of a file. For example, if a file becomes damaged and you don't realize it until after you've made one or more backups of the damaged file, you may want to restore an undamaged version of the file from an earlier backup.

To use the Version function, you must select a master catalog for the restore operation so that all the versions of files in the backup cycle are available. Then, you

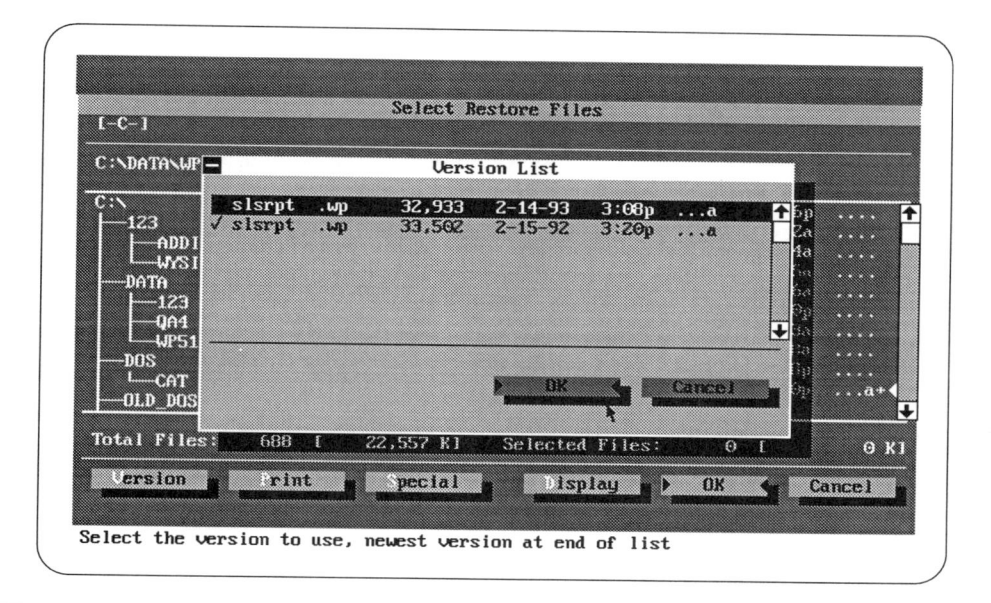

Figure 11-20 How to restore a version of a file other than the most recent one

highlight the file on the Select-files screen and select the Version function. When you do, a dialog box like the one in figure 11-20 is displayed. From this dialog box, you can select a version by clicking the right mouse button on it or by highlighting the version and pressing the Space bar. Note that the dates and times in this display are when the file was created or modified last, not when the file was backed up.

How to set restore options Before you do a restore for the first time, you should make sure the options are set the way you want them. Figure 11-21 shows the Disk-restore-options screen you see when you select the Options button on the Restore screen; it also gives you a brief description of each option. Once you've set these options, they stay in effect until you change them. But you'll probably want to check them whenever you restore files to make sure they're appropriate for the type of restore operation you're doing.

You should also make sure the Restore-to option on the Restore screen is set properly before you begin a restore. Typically, you'll restore the data to its original location. But you can also restore to another drive or another directory, something you can't do with the DOS Backup command.

The Disk-restore-options dialog box

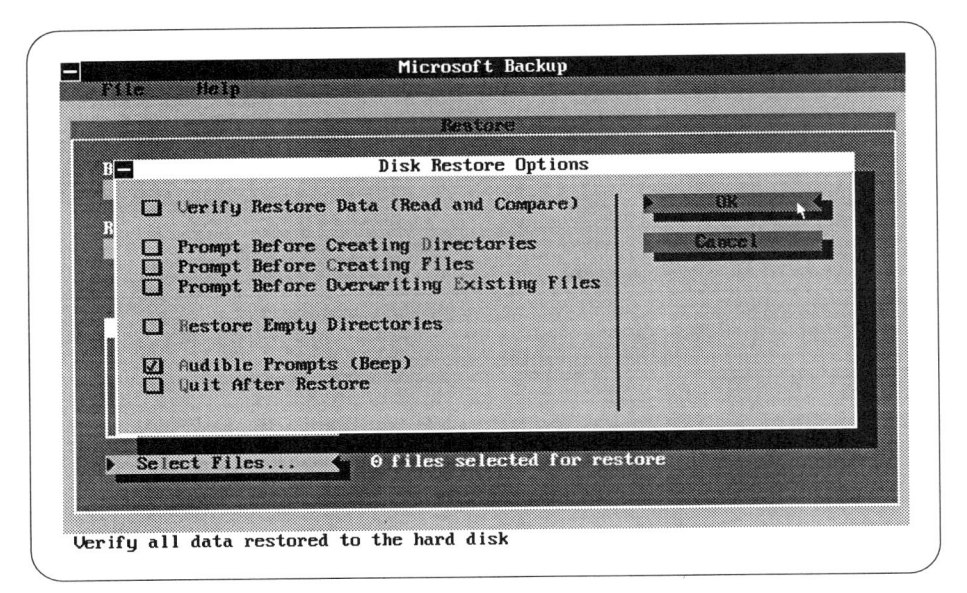

[Screenshot of Microsoft Backup Disk Restore Options dialog showing checkboxes for: Verify Restore Data (Read and Compare), Prompt Before Creating Directories, Prompt Before Creating Files, Prompt Before Overwriting Existing Files, Restore Empty Directories, Audible Prompts (Beep) [checked], Quit After Restore. OK and Cancel buttons on the right. Status bar reads: "Verify all data restored to the hard disk"]

Option	Function
Verify Restore Data	Causes Microsoft Backup to verify the data restored to the hard disk. This adds a lot of time to the restore operation, but you may want to select this option, depending on what files you're restoring.
Prompt Before Creating Directories	Asks you for verification before creating a directory that doesn't already exist on the hard disk.
Prompt Before Creating Files	Asks you for verification before creating a file that doesn't already exist on the hard disk.
Prompt Before Overwriting Existing Files	Warns you if there's already an existing copy of the file you're restoring on the hard disk. You can either skip the file or restore it at that point.
Restore Empty Directories	Restores a complete directory structure, including directories that don't have any files selected for the restore. So if the restore operation comes to a directory that doesn't exist on the hard disk, it restores that directory; it doesn't restore any files in the directory, though, unless they're selected.

Figure 11-21 How to set the restore options (part 1 of 2)

Option	Function
Audible Prompts	Causes your workstation to beep whenever Microsoft Backup requires your attention (for example, when you need to insert the next backup diskette).
Quit After Restore	Causes Microsoft Backup to end automatically when the restore operation is complete.

Figure 11-21 How to set the restore options (part 2 of 2)

How to use the Compare function to verify a backup

The Compare function is similar to the Restore function, as you can see from the Compare screen in figure 11-22. The main difference is that instead of restoring selected files from a backup, it compares the backed up files to the original. If the Compare function doesn't detect any errors, you know that the backup worked correctly.

Because the Compare function takes extra time, you won't want to run it each time you do a backup. But you may want to run it occasionally to assure yourself that your backups are reliable.

Some perspective on Microsoft Backup

At this point, you may be wondering if Microsoft Backup is really easier to use than the DOS Backup command. After all, you only have to enter a few keystrokes to use the Backup command, whereas Microsoft Backup has dozens of options you need to know about. These options, though, give you a lot more control over your backups than you have with the Backup command. So even if they seem confusing right now, I think you'll appreciate the flexibility they provide once you try them out. And remember, many of these options need to be set only once, so you won't have to worry about them after that.

Of course, if you haven't used a full-screen utility like Microsoft Backup before, the operational details may add to your difficulties at first. But I'm confident that once you've had some practice using the keyboard or a mouse to move around the screen and choose options, you'll wonder how you ever thought the Backup command could be easier to use than Microsoft Backup.

If you're using *Windows*, I want you to know that DOS 6.0 also includes a *Windows* version of this program called *Microsoft Backup for Windows*. Aside from the differences that result from the *Windows* user interface, the *Windows* version of Microsoft Backup is nearly identical to the DOS version. As a result, you should have no trouble applying what you've learned in this chapter to the *Windows* version.

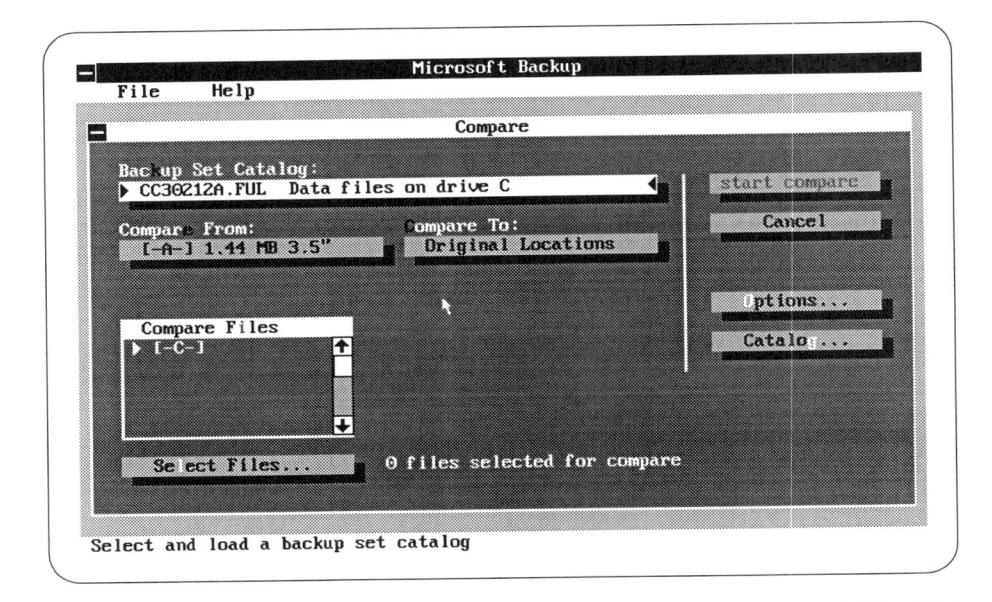

Figure 11-22 The Compare screen

Because Microsoft Backup provides for so many options, it's adequate for most PC users. But if your backup needs are extensive, you may want to consider purchasing a commercial backup utility. In general, commercial utilities have three advantages over Microsoft Backup: (1) they're even faster than Microsoft Backup; (2) they support backups to tape drives; and (3) you can set up a backup to run automatically. If any of these capabilities are essential to your backup strategy, then by all means consider purchasing a commercial utility.

Terms

DMA
Direct Memory Access
file compression
differential backup
button
click the mouse
shortcut key
menu bar
pull-down menu
window

context-sensitive help
scroll bar
scroll box
dialog box
setup file
backup catalog
backup set
master catalog
backup cycle

Objectives

1. Explain the difference between a differential backup and an incremental backup.
2. Use Microsoft Backup to do a full backup of a specified drive or directory.
3. Use Microsoft Backup to do an incremental or differential backup of a specified drive or directory.
4. Use Microsoft Backup to restore an entire backup set, a directory, or a file.
5. Establish backup procedures for your system using Microsoft Backup.

Exercises

1. Start Microsoft Backup by entering the program name MSBACKUP at the DOS command prompt. Then, experiment with the Tab key and the cursor control keys or the mouse to move from one button to another on the opening screen of the program.

    With the cursor on the Backup button, press F1. This takes you to the Help information for the Backup function. Use the cursor control keys and the Page-up and Page-down keys to scroll through the text to see what kind of information is available to you. If you're using a mouse, click on the up and down arrows in the scroll bar to scroll up or down through the text one line at a time. Then, put the mouse cursor on the scroll box, hold down the left mouse button, and move the scroll box to a new position in the scroll bar to scroll through the text more quickly.

    When you're finished experimenting with the Help feature, press the Esc key or click on the Cancel button to return to the opening screen of Microsoft Backup.

    In the exercises that follow, you'll select options on the screen. To do that using a mouse, move the mouse cursor to your selection and click the left mouse button. To do that using the keyboard, use the cursor control and Tab keys to move to your selection and press the Enter key. If one of the letters in the option is highlighted, you can also select it by pressing that key, the shortcut key.

2. In this exercise, you'll run the compatibility test for the backup device you'll use most often, to make sure your backups will work properly with that device. If someone else has set up Microsoft Backup for you and has run the compatibility test, you can skip this exercise.

    Before you start the compatibility test, though, you need to make sure that your system is configured correctly. So select the Configure button on the opening screen of Microsoft Backup. Then, check the values given for your monitor, mouse, and backup devices. If you're not sure they are set properly, ask for help or look in the hardware manuals that came with your system to find the specifications.

    Now, select the Compatibility-test button. The first screen that's displayed gives you some information, and says you'll need two diskettes to run the test. Because the test does an actual backup, be sure you use diskettes that are compatible with the backup device you're testing and that they don't contain any data you need to keep. If the diskettes are new, you don't need to format them; Microsoft Backup will do that automatically.

Select the Start-test button to begin the test. As the test progresses, you'll see various backup screens displayed on your monitor. When you get a message that says the test will pause at the Backup-to window, select the Continue button. Then, when the test pauses at the Backup-to window, check the backup device that's selected. If this isn't the device you want to use, move the cursor to the correct device and press the Space bar. If you're using a mouse, click on the correct device with the right mouse button. When the backup device is set correctly, select the OK button to continue.

As the test continues, you'll be prompted for each backup diskette. At the prompt, insert the appropriate diskette in the drive and press the Enter key. When the backup is done, Microsoft Backup displays information that summarizes the backup operation. At this screen, select the OK button to continue.

Next, the test performs a Compare operation to make sure the backup worked properly. Once again, Microsoft Backup prompts you for the appropriate diskette. At the end of the compare operation, it displays summary information.

When the test is over, a message appears on your screen saying that the test was successful. Then, select the OK button to return to the Configure screen; and select the Cancel button or press the Esc key to return to the opening screen of Microsoft Backup.

If the test didn't run successfully, ask for help before you continue with the rest of the exercises.

3. To start the backup procedure, select the Backup button on the opening screen of Microsoft Backup. Then, at the Backup screen, practice moving from one box to another using the Tab and cursor control keys.

Now, select the Options button and press the Space bar three times or click the mouse three times on the first option. A check mark appears in the box when the option is on and disappears when the option is off. Then, set the options as shown in figure 11-10. After you have them set, select the OK button to save the options and return to the Backup screen.

Note what the backup device is in the Backup-to box, and then select that option. This will give you a dialog box listing all the backup devices on your system. Experiment with the Space bar or the mouse to see how you can choose a different device. Then, select the device you ran the compatibility test on in exercise 2 and select the OK button to return to the Backup screen.

Next, select the Backup-type option, the Full option, and the OK button. If the Backup-type was Full to begin with, you can also select the Cancel button or press the Esc key to return to the Backup screen.

Move the cursor to the Backup-from box and press the Space bar or click the right mouse button to select and deselect the entire drive. Did you notice how the messages to the right of the Select-files box changed? End by deselecting the drive so that no files are selected.

Now, select the Select-files option. When the directory structure appears on your monitor, use the Up-arrow and Down-arrow keys to move to different directories to see how the file list at the right of the screen changes. If you're using a mouse, click on one of the directories and see how the file list area shows all the files in that directory.

Next, select one of your data directories to back up by highlighting it and pressing the Space bar or by clicking on it with the right mouse button. Then, select the OK button to confirm your selection and return to the Backup screen. Note the messages to the right of the Select-files box and how they differ from those for backing up the entire drive.

To save the selections you just made so you can use them later in these exercises, open the File menu by clicking on it with the mouse. Or, if you're using the keyboard, press the Alt+F key combination or the F10 key. Then, select the Save-setup-as function. When the dialog box appears, enter the file name PRACTICE for the setup file and enter a description that gives the name of the directory you're backing up. Finally, select the Save button to save the file and return to the Backup screen. On this screen, you'll see the description you just entered in the Setup-file box.

4. On the Backup screen, you can see a message to the right of the Select-files box that tells you how many diskettes you need for the backup and what size and capacity they should be. If the diskettes aren't new, make sure they don't contain any data you need to keep (if they're new, you don't need to format them; Microsoft Backup will do that).

   To start the backup, select the Start-backup button. Microsoft Backup will do a full backup of the directory you selected in exercise 3. Whenever Microsoft Backup prompts you for a diskette, insert the proper diskette into the drive and press the Enter key. After noting the summary information in the Backup-complete box at the end of the operation, select the OK button to return to the opening screen of Microsoft Backup. Then, select the Quit button to return to DOS.

5. To see how an incremental backup works, modify one of the data files that you backed up in exercise 4, but not a file you can't afford to lose. Then, begin the backup procedure by entering MSBACKUP at the command prompt. Next, select the Backup button. If the setup file that's displayed isn't PRACTICE, select the Setup-file option and select the PRACTICE file. Next, select the Open button. Now, select the Backup-type option, change the type from Full to Incremental, and select OK to return to the Backup screen. Note the messages to the right of the Select-files box and how they differ from those for the full backup of the directory. As you can see, two files are selected: the file you changed and the catalog file for the backup.

   To run the backup, select the Start-backup button from the Backup screen. When the program prompts you for a diskette, be sure to use a different diskette for the backup than the ones you used in exercise 4. Once the backup is finished, note how the summary information differs from that for the full backup of the directory. Then, return to the opening screen of Microsoft Backup and select the Quit button to exit to DOS.

6. To see how the Restore operation works, delete the file that you modified in exercise 5 from your hard disk. Then, start Microsoft Backup at the command prompt. From the opening screen, select the Restore button. Now, look at the catalog entry in the Backup-set-catalog box. If the catalog isn't the one for the incremental backup you just ran as indicated by the description and the INC extension, you'll have to select it. To do that, select the Backup-set-catalog option to display a list of backup catalogs; then, select the appropriate INC catalog.

   Next, move to cursor to the Restore-files box and use the Space bar or the mouse to select all the files in the backup catalog. The message to the right of the Select-files box will show that only one file has been selected, since there's only one file in the incremental catalog.

   Now, select the Options button and set the options as shown in figure 11-21. Then, return to the Restore screen.

   Check that the Restore-from drive is the one you backed up to and that the Restore-to box indicates that file is to be restored in its original location. Now, start the restore by selecting the Start-restore button. When prompted, insert the incremental backup diskette in the drive and press the Enter key. At the end of the restore operation, exit to DOS and check to see that the file was restored properly.

7. Using the guidelines given in chapter 10 and the methods taught in this chapter, evaluate your backup needs and establish backup procedures for your system using Microsoft Backup. Then, create setup files that are appropriate for your backups.

Note: To return Microsoft Backup to the way it was before you started these exercises, you should delete the PRACTICE setup file. To that, start Microsoft Backup, select the Backup button, open the File menu, and select the Delete-setup function. Then, select PRACTICE.SET from the dialog box that appears, and select the Delete button; then, select the Delete button again when Microsoft Backup asks you for confirmation. Next, select the Cancel button to return to the opening screen of Microsoft Backup and the Quit button to return to DOS.

Section 4

How to use the DOS 5.0 or 6.0 shell

Since the introduction of the IBM PC and DOS in 1981, users have complained that DOS is hard to use. To a large extent, that's why *shell programs* have become popular. These programs let you perform many of the functions provided by DOS commands without forcing you to know the details of the commands themselves.

Beginning with DOS 4.0, Microsoft included a shell program with DOS called the *DOS shell*. With DOS 5.0, Microsoft significantly improved the shell program. And the DOS 6.0 shell is nearly identical to the DOS 5.0 shell. Although some commercial shell programs still provide advanced features that aren't found in the DOS 5.0 and 6.0 shells, the 5.0/6.0 shell provides most of the shell features you're likely to want. It also includes a few features that aren't found in any commercial shell programs. And it's easy to use. So if you have DOS 5.0 or 6.0 on your PC and you aren't already using another shell, I definitely recommend that you use the DOS shell.

If you have DOS 5.0 or 6.0, the four chapters in this section will show you how to use the DOS shell. In chapter 12, you'll be introduced to the basic functions of the shell. In chapter 13, you'll learn how to use the shell to create and use menus to start your application programs. In chapter 14, you'll learn how to use the shell to manage the directories and files on your hard disk. And in chapter 15, you'll learn how to use the task switching capabilities of the shell to quickly switch between application programs. When you finish this section, you'll be able to use the DOS shell for most DOS functions.

If you don't have DOS 5.0 or 6.0 on your PC, you can read this section to see what the shell can do and how it works. Then, you can decide for yourself whether upgrading to DOS 6.0 is worth the effort. If you like the idea of using a shell, but you don't want to upgrade to DOS 6.0, you can consider the purchase of a commercial shell program.

Chapter 12

An introduction to the DOS shell

In this chapter, I'll introduce you to the DOS shell by presenting a brief overview of its menu and file-management functions. Then, in chapters 13 and 14, I'll show you how to use these shell functions in detail. In chapter 15, I'll present the task-switching functions that the DOS shell provides.

As you will soon see, the quickest way to learn how to use a shell is to experiment with it. That's why the chapters in this section don't present detailed instructions for using the shell. Instead, they present general operational procedures for using the shell, and they introduce you to the capabilities of the shell. Once you have this background, you shouldn't have much trouble using the shell because most of its operations are self-explanatory.

If your PC has a mouse, you'll want to use it with the DOS shell because it simplifies some of the operations. However, you can also use the shell with the keyboard. Throughout this section of the book, I'll show you how to perform a function using both a mouse and the keyboard.

An overview of the DOS shell

Before you learn how to use the DOS shell, you should know that it provides functions you can use for three distinct purposes. First, it provides a program-list function that lets you start your application programs by selecting choices from a menu rather than by typing commands. Second, it provides file-management functions that let you manage your directories and files without remembering the details of DOS command formats. Third, it provides task-switching functions that let you load several programs into memory at once and switch from one to another with just a few keystrokes.

How to start the DOS shell If you want to start the DOS shell every time you start your computer, you should include the Dosshell command in your AUTOEXEC.BAT file. Dosshell is the name of the program file that starts the shell. If your shell isn't started by the AUTOEXEC.BAT file, you can start it any time by entering the Dosshell command at the prompt.

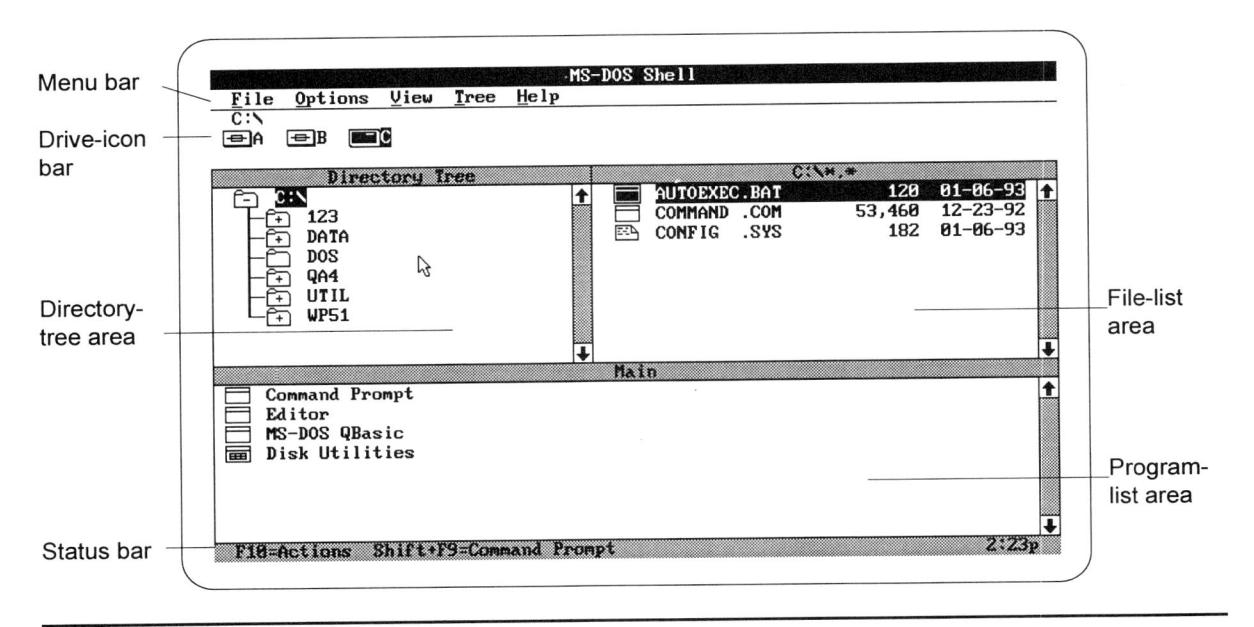

Figure 12-1 The first screen of the DOS 5.0/6.0 shell

The DOS shell display When you start the shell, it displays the screen shown in figure 12-1. This is the standard display, but you should know that you can select other display options. If you or someone else has used the shell previously and selected another display option, your screen won't look like this one. In just a moment, I'll show you how to reset your display to the one shown here.

In figure 12-1, you can see that the DOS shell displays a *menu bar* at the top of the screen. You use this menu bar to select DOS shell functions. Below the menu bar are the *drive icons* in the *drive-icon bar*. These icons represent each disk drive on your system, and you use them to select the drive you want to use. Below the drive icons, the display is divided into two areas: the *directory-tree area* and the *file-list area*. You use these two areas to manage your files and directories. The next area is the *program-list area*. You use it to start DOS utilities and application programs. At the bottom of the screen, the *status bar* displays the current time and indicates any function keys or keystroke combinations you can use to perform functions.

If you're using DOS 6.0 and DoubleSpace has been installed on your system, you may notice that the DOS shell displays more drive letters than you'd expect in the drive-icon bar. In the most common case, you'll see an H drive in addition to the A, B, and C drives. This H drive is the DoubleSpace *host drive*, which DoubleSpace uses to store compressed data from your C drive. It does *not* represent a separate disk drive, and you shouldn't use it to store files.

An introduction to the DOS shell 209

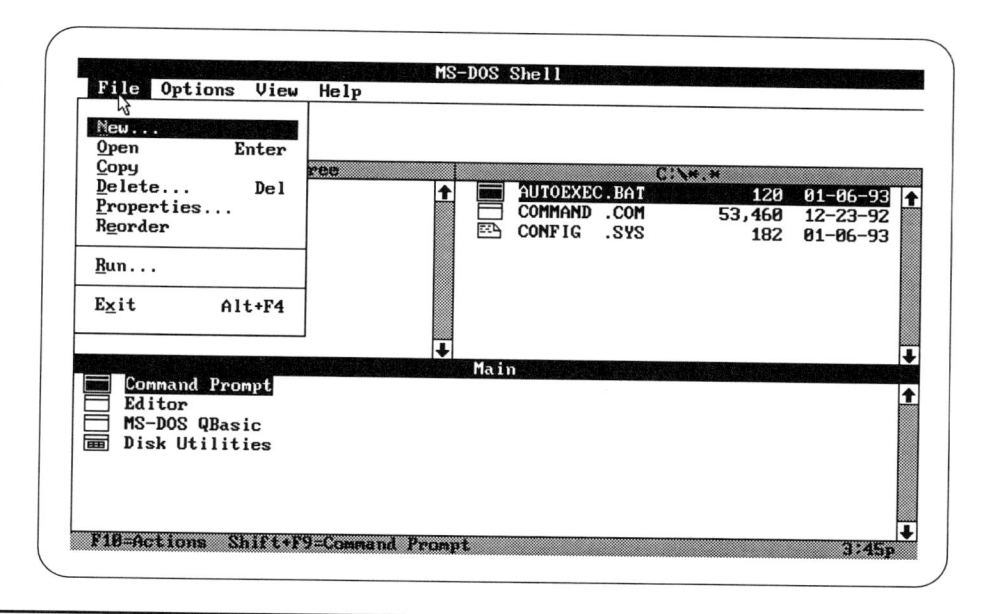

```
                              MS-DOS Shell
    File  Options  View  Help
    ┌──────────────────────┐
    │ New...               │
    │ Open          Enter  │ree                    C:\*.*
    │ Copy                 │
    │ Delete...     Del    │↑    AUTOEXEC.BAT       120  01-06-93 ↑
    │ Properties...        │     COMMAND .COM    53,460  12-23-92
    │ Reorder              │     CONFIG   .SYS      182  01-06-93
    │                      │
    │ Run...               │
    │                      │
    │ Exit        Alt+F4   │
    │                      │
    └──────────────────────┘↓
                                  Main
    ┌─ Command Prompt ─┐
    │  Editor          │                                          ↑
    │  MS-DOS QBasic   │
    │  Disk Utilities  │

    F10=Actions   Shift+F9=Command Prompt                    3:45p
```

Figure 12-2   The File menu when the program-list area is active

If the DOS shell display on your PC uses the same basic layout, but it looks slightly different from the one in figure 12-1, you're probably using a different monitor than the one I used for the figures. Also, I used the shell in *graphics mode* because it uses some graphics symbols. So if you're running the shell in *text mode*, your screen won't look exactly like the one in figure 12-1.

When you use the DOS shell, only one of the areas on the display is active at a time. If you're using a color monitor, the DOS shell identifies the active area by using a different color in the area's title bar. If you're using a monochrome monitor, the DOS shell identifies the active area by placing a small arrow next to the current item within the area.

To use one of the areas of the DOS shell, you must first make that area active. If you have a mouse, you just move the mouse cursor to the area you want to activate and press the left mouse button. This is referred to as *clicking the mouse*. If you don't have a mouse, you use the Tab key to move from one area to the next. Each time you press the Tab key, the next screen area is activated. As a result, you sometimes have to press the Tab key several times to activate the area you want.

How to use the pull-down menus   The menu bar in figure 12-1 contains five menu items: File, Options, View, Tree, and Help. To select one of these menu items, just click on it with the mouse. When you do that, a *pull-down menu* is displayed. For example, figure 12-2 shows the pull-down menu that's displayed when you click on the File menu item when the program-list area is activated. As you can see, this menu has eight functions: New, Open, Copy, Delete, Properties, Reorder, Run, and Exit. To select one of these functions, you just point to it with the mouse cursor and click again.

If you don't have a mouse, you can use three techniques to use the pull-down menus. One, you can activate the menu bar by pressing the F10 key. Then, you can pull down a menu by pressing the underlined letter of the menu you want (*f* for File, *o* for Options, and so on). Two, you can press the F10 key to activate the menu bar and then use the cursor keys to move the highlight to the menu you want and press the Enter key. Three, you can hold down the Alt key while pressing the underlined letter of the menu you want.

Once you've pulled a menu down, you can use the keyboard to select a function by pressing the underlined letter of the function you want (for example, *o* for Open). Or you can use the cursor control keys to move the highlight to the function and then press the Enter key.

You can also execute some of the functions on the pull-down menus by using the *shortcut keys*. If a function has a shortcut key, it's listed to the right of the function name on the pull-down menu. In figure 12-2, the pull-down menu shows shortcut keys for the Open, Delete, and Exit functions. So, for example, instead of selecting the File menu and then selecting the Exit function to exit from the DOS shell, you can simply press Alt+F4.

Although the shortcut keys can be useful, particularly if you use a function frequently, I won't present them for most of the DOS shell functions. Instead, I'll show you how to execute functions using the pull-down menus. Once you become familiar with the functions available from the pull-down menus, you can use the shortcut keys if you choose to.

If you're running the DOS shell on your PC as you read this chapter and if the DOS shell display is different than the one in figure 12-1, take a moment now to change the display. First, select the View menu from the menu bar. Then, select the Program/File-lists view from the menu. Now, your display should match the figures in this chapter.

When you use the DOS shell, you'll probably notice that the items in the menu bar change as you move from one area to another. When the program-list area is active, for example, the Tree menu is removed from the menu bar. In addition, the functions that appear in the pull-down menus vary depending on which area of the shell is active. In some cases, menu functions are displayed in grey to show that they're unavailable because they don't apply to the area that's active. (On a monochrome monitor, these functions aren't displayed at all.) When you're using the directory-tree area, for example, the Copy function of the File menu isn't available because you can't copy a directory.

How to get Help information from the DOS shell Whenever you're using the DOS shell, you can get information from the Help facility by pressing the F1 key. This information is displayed in a *window* as shown in figure 12-3, and it's

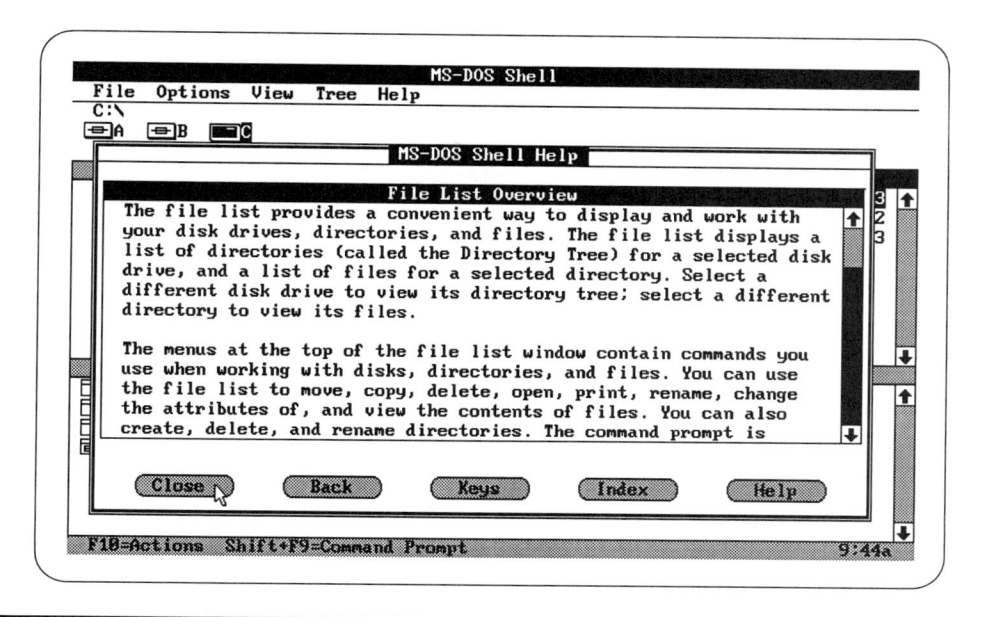

Figure 12-3 One of the Help facility windows that's displayed when you press the F1 key

context-sensitive help, which means it always relates to whatever you're trying to do at the time. If, for example, you press the F1 key while you're using the file-list area, you get the information shown in this figure. As you can see, the Help information explains what the file list does.

The five ovals at the bottom of the Help window are called *buttons*. To use any one of the button functions, you click on it with the mouse. You can also start one of these functions by using the Tab key to move the cursor to the desired button and then pressing the Enter key. For instance, you can cancel the Help function by clicking the mouse on the Close button, or you can move the cursor to it and then press the Enter key.

The Help button in figure 12-3 provides information about how to use the Help facility. The Index button displays an index of topics within the Help facility. By using it, you can skip directly to any Help subject that's available. The Keys button displays a list of all the functions that can be performed by keyboard and function keys when you're using the DOS shell. And the Back button moves you to the previous Help screen.

How to exit from the DOS shell You can exit from the DOS shell in two different ways. To exit from the shell completely and return to the DOS prompt, you select the Exit option from the File menu or press the F3 key. If you want to start the DOS shell again after you use this command, you must enter *dosshell* at the command prompt.

Chapter 12

Menu bar ─────────────

Program-list title bar ─────
Program list ─────────

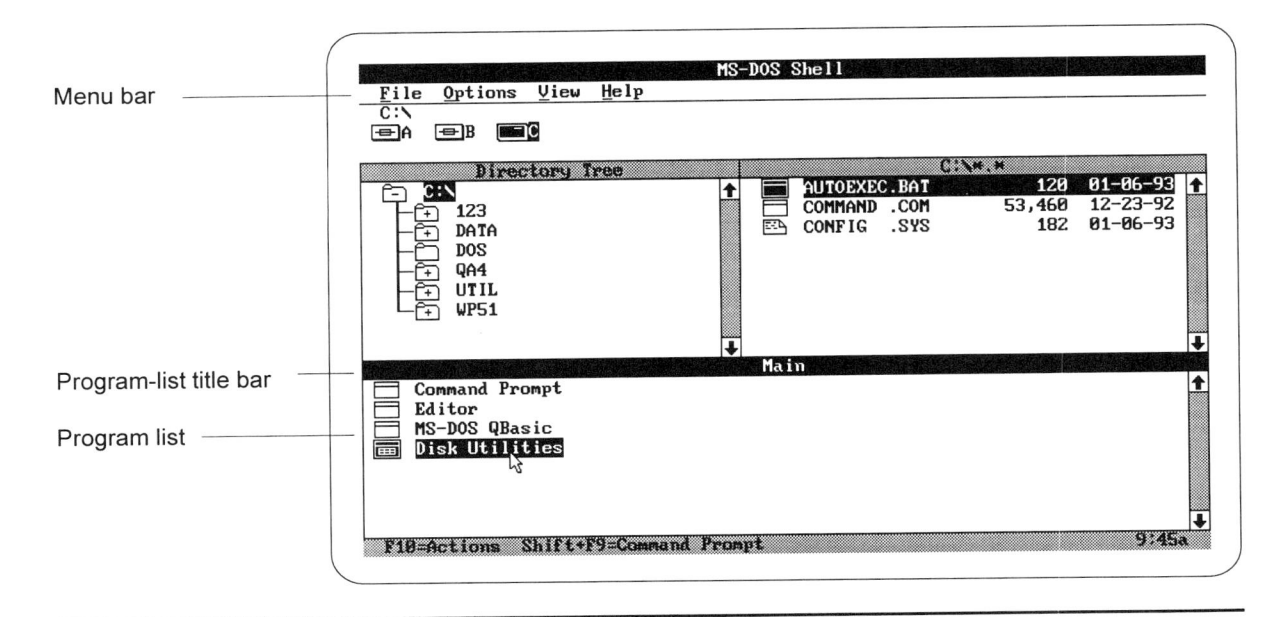

```
                              MS-DOS Shell
    File  Options  View  Help
    C:\
     A    B    C
    ┌──────────── Directory Tree ────────────┬──── C:\*.* ────┐
    │  ┌─ C:\                              ↑ │ AUTOEXEC.BAT      120  01-06-93 ↑│
    │  │  ├─ 123                             │ COMMAND  .COM  53,460  12-23-92 │
    │  │  ├─ DATA                            │ CONFIG   .SYS     182  01-06-93 │
    │  │  ├─ DOS                             │                                 │
    │  │  ├─ QA4                             │                                 │
    │  │  ├─ UTIL                            │                                 │
    │  │  └─ WP51                            │                                 │
    │                                      ↓ │                               ↓ │
    ├──────────────────── Main ──────────────────────────────────────────────┤
    │ ▫ Command Prompt                                                     ↑ │
    │ ▫ Editor                                                               │
    │ ▫ MS-DOS QBasic                                                        │
    │ ▫ Disk Utilities                                                       │
    │                                                                      ↓ │
    └────────────────────────────────────────────────────────────────────────┘
     F10=Actions  Shift+F9=Command Prompt                              9:45a
```

Figure 12-4   The components of the shell that provide the program-list functions

If you just want to exit from the shell temporarily, you can press the Shift+F9 key combination as indicated by the status bar, or you can select the Command-prompt option from the Main program list. Either way, the DOS command prompt is displayed. To return to the DOS shell, you just type the word *exit* at the prompt and press the Enter key.

An introduction to the program-list functions of the shell

A *program list* is a menu that you can use for starting your application programs or DOS utilities. When you first install the DOS shell, the program-list area contains a program list with just a few options that let you execute some of the more useful DOS commands. In this chapter, I'll show you how to use the default program list provided with the DOS shell. In the next chapter, you'll learn how to customize that program list by adding options to it that start your application programs.

The components of the DOS shell that provide the program-list functions
Figure 12-4 identifies the components of the DOS shell you use to perform program-list functions. The menu bar displays the menu choices that are available when you're working with the program list: File, Options, View, and Help. The *program-list title bar* shows the name of the program list that's currently displayed. Here, the *Main program list* is active and it has four options displayed in the program-list area: Command Prompt, Editor, MS-DOS QBasic, and Disk Utilities.

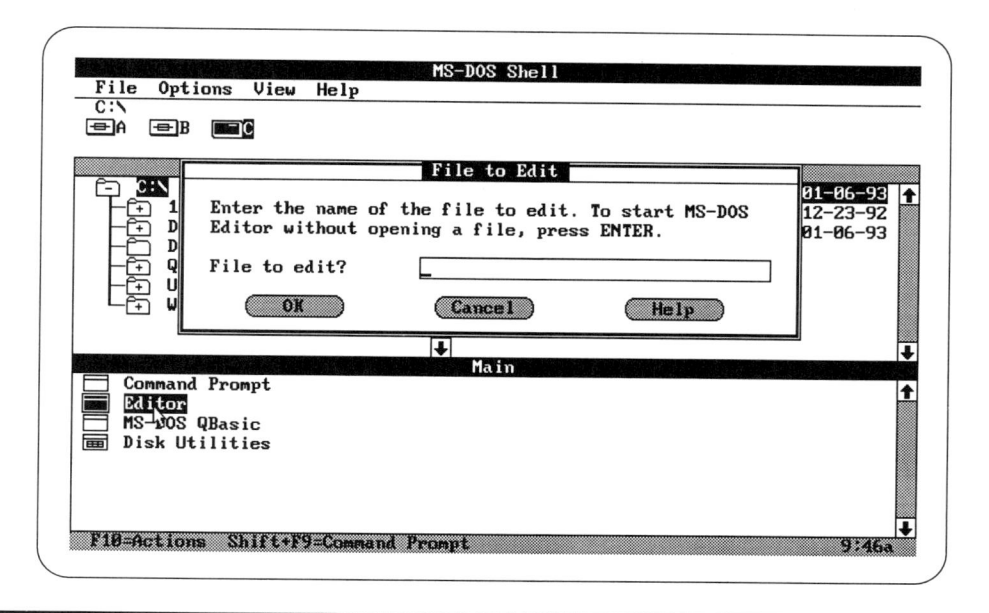

Figure 12-5 The dialog box for the Editor option of the main program list

In figure 12-4, you can see that the first three options of the Main program list have plain boxes to the left of them. That means these options start programs or functions. The last option, however, has a box with a pattern of smaller boxes in it. That means it leads to another program list. You can think of the Main program list and its subordinate program lists as a multi-level menu system. And you can think of the options in these program lists as menu choices. You'll understand how these two types of program lists work before you complete this chapter. (By the way, if you're using the shell in text mode instead of graphics mode, there won't be any boxes to the left of the options in the Main program list. But an option that leads to another program list will be bracketed.)

How to select an option from the Main program list To select one of the options on the Main program list, you move the mouse cursor to it and press the left mouse button twice in rapid succession. This is referred to as *double-clicking the mouse*. If you don't have a mouse, you must first press the Tab key one or more times to activate this area of the shell. Then, you use the cursor control keys to highlight your selection, and you press the Enter key to execute it.

How to start the Edit command The Editor option starts the Edit command that I showed you how to use in chapter 6. This full-screen text editor makes it easy to edit batch files. When you select the Editor, the DOS shell starts by displaying the *dialog box* shown in figure 12-5. After you type in the file specification and press the Enter key, DOS starts the Edit command and loads the file you specified.

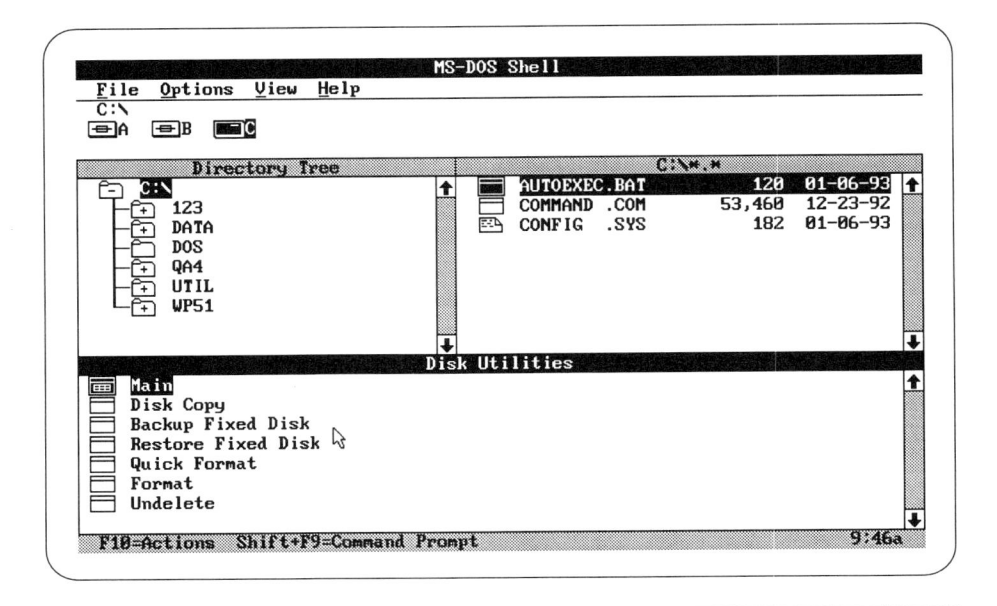

```
                              MS-DOS Shell
    File  Options  View  Help
    C:\
     ⊟A    ⊟B    ■C
    ┌─────────────────────────────────────────────────────────────┐
    │         Directory Tree                    C:\*.*            │
    │  ┌─ C:\                    ↑    ▄ AUTOEXEC.BAT   120 01-06-93│↑
    │  ├─⊞ 123                        ▄ COMMAND  .COM 53,460 12-23-92│
    │  ├─⊞ DATA                       ▄ CONFIG   .SYS    182 01-06-93│
    │  ├─⊞ DOS                                                    │
    │  ├─⊞ QA4                                                    │
    │  ├─⊞ UTIL                                                   │
    │  └─⊞ WP51                                                   │
    │                            ↓                                │↓
    │         Disk Utilities                                      │
    │  ▄ Main                                                    ↑│
    │  ▄ Disk Copy                                                │
    │  ▄ Backup Fixed Disk                                        │
    │  ▄ Restore Fixed Disk  ☒                                    │
    │  ▄ Quick Format                                             │
    │  ▄ Format                                                   │
    │  ▄ Undelete                                                 │↓
    │ F10=Actions  Shift+F9=Command Prompt              9:46a    │
    └─────────────────────────────────────────────────────────────┘
```

Figure 12-6   The Disk-utilities program list for the DOS 5.0 shell

How to use the Disk-utilities program list   When you select the Disk-utilities option from the Main program list, the DOS shell displays a list of utilities that varies depending on whether you're using DOS 5.0 or 6.0. Figure 12-6 shows the DOS 5.0 Disk-utilities program list. Here, the Disk-copy option runs the DOS Diskcopy command, the Backup-fixed-disk options runs the DOS Backup command, and so on. Figure 12-7 shows the DOS 6.0 version of the Disk-utilities program list. It's the same as the DOS 5.0 version, except that the outdated Backup and Restore options have been replaced by options that run the newer DOS 6.0 Anti-Virus and Backup utilities. (Incidentally, if you upgraded from DOS 5.0 to 6.0, the DOS shell will probably continue to display the DOS 5.0 version of the Disk-utilities program list.)

When you select one of these options, a dialog box asks for parameters. To illustrate, figure 12-8 shows the dialog box you get when you select the Format option. Here, the default drive is drive A. So if you want to format a 720KB diskette in drive B, which is a 1.44MB drive, you have to type in the following information:

    b: /f:720

These are the parameters I presented in chapter 9 when I showed you how to format a diskette using the Format command at the DOS prompt. So even though you're using the DOS shell, you have to know the details of the command.

An introduction to the DOS shell **215**

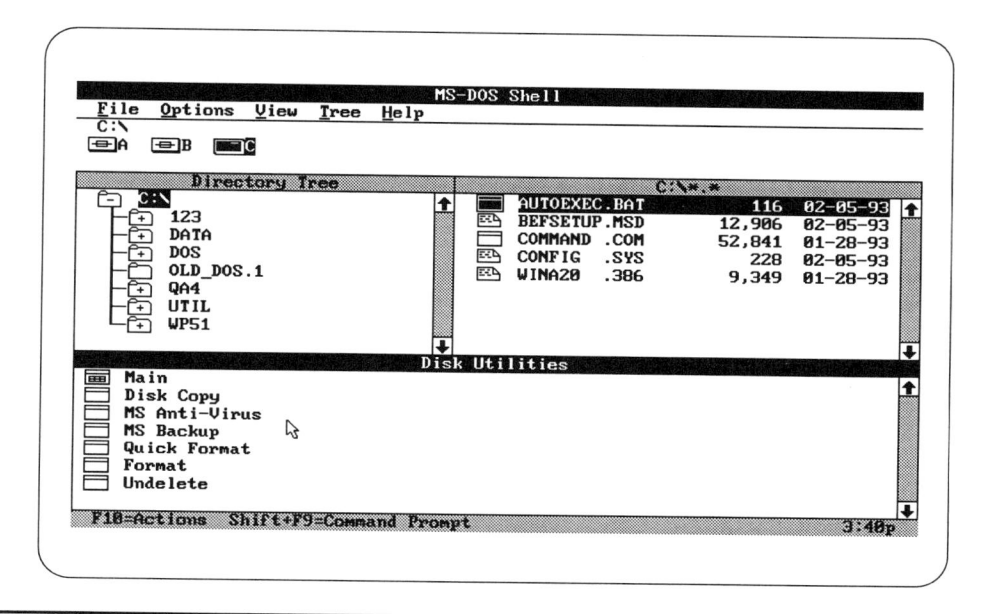

Figure 12-7 The Disk-utilities program list for the DOS 6.0 shell

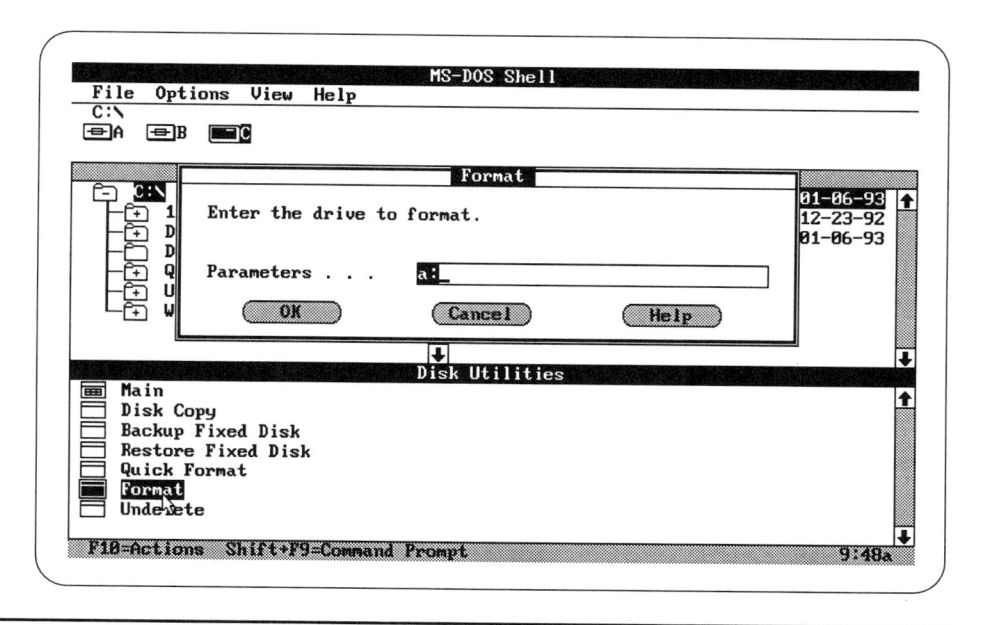

Figure 12-8 The dialog box for the Format option in the Disk-utilities program list

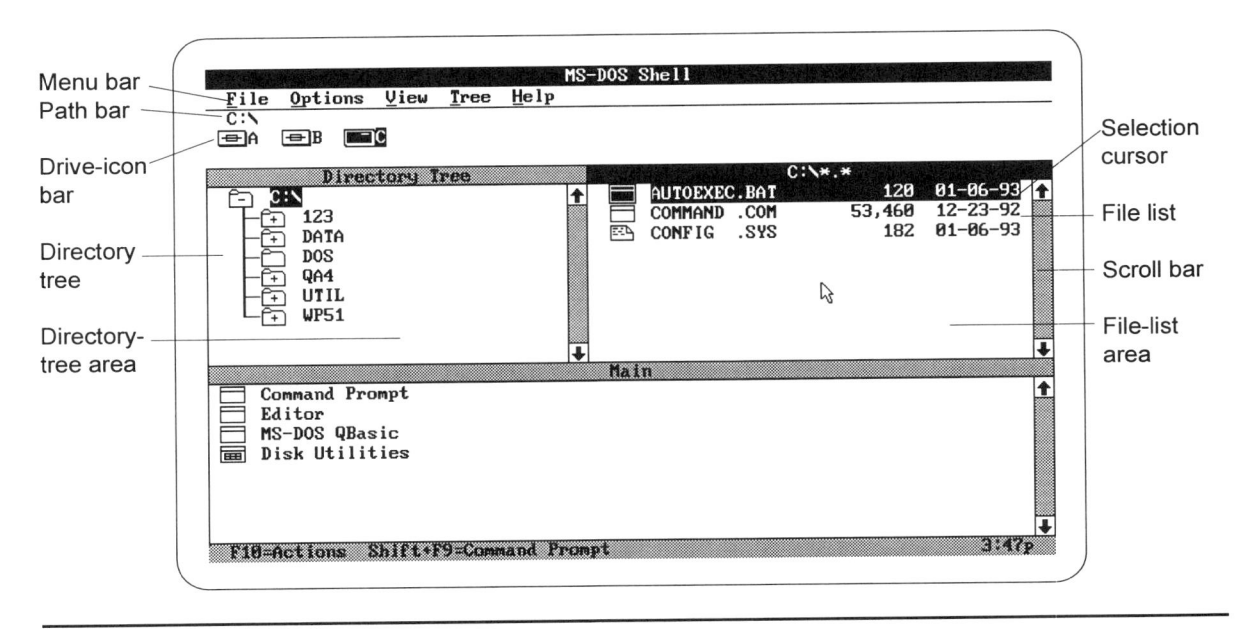

Figure 12-9 The components of the shell that provide the file-management functions

An introduction to the file-management functions of the shell

When you use the DOS shell to manage files, you use the directory-tree and file-list areas of the screen. After I introduce you to these and other components, I'll show you how to change the default drive, change the current directory, scroll through a file list, scroll through a directory tree, and select files. I'll also show you the functions available from the File menu for managing files.

The components of the DOS shell that provide file-management functions

Figure 12-9 identifies the components you use to manage files. You're already familiar with the menu bar. If the directory-tree or file-list area is active, the menu bar displays five choices for pull-down menus: File, Options, View, Tree, and Help.

The drive-icon bar displays the drives and highlights the default drive. If your monitor is in graphics mode, the shell uses a symbol to indicate whether a drive is a diskette drive or a hard drive. In addition, the *path bar* displays the default drive and path. In figure 12-9, this bar specifies the root directory on the C drive.

The directory-tree area presents a *directory tree*, which is a graphic representation of the default drive's directory structure. If your monitor is in graphics mode, folders represent directories, and plus signs on those folders identify directories that have subdirectories that aren't displayed. One directory is highlighted to identify it as the current directory.

The file-list area displays a *file list*, which is a list of the files of the current directory in a format that is similar to one displayed by the Directory command. In graphics mode, a symbol next to each file indicates whether the file is a program file, like AUTOEXEC.BAT, or a data file, like CONFIG.SYS. This symbol is called a *file icon*. The *selection cursor* is a bar in this area that's used to select files by highlighting them.

How to change the default drive   To change the default drive, you can use the mouse to click on the drive you want in the drive-icon bar. If you don't have a mouse, you can hold down the Ctrl key while you press the letter of the drive you want. Or you can press the Tab key until the drive-icon bar becomes active. Then, you can use the cursor control keys to highlight the drive that you want and press the Enter key.

How to change the current directory   To change the current directory, you can use the mouse to click on the directory you want. If you don't have a mouse, you must first use the Tab key to activate the directory-tree area. Then, you use the cursor control keys to highlight the directory you want and press the Enter key.

How to scroll through a file list   If a directory has more files than can be displayed in the file-list area at one time, you can scroll through the list to view all of the files. The easiest way to do that is by using the cursor control keys to move through the list one line at a time, or by using the Page-up and Page-down keys to move through the list one screen at a time.

You can also scroll through the list with a mouse by using the *scroll bar* to the right of the file list. You can scroll down one line at a time by clicking on the arrow at the bottom of the scroll bar. Similarly, you can scroll up one line at a time by clicking on the arrow at the top of the scroll bar.

To scroll through varying numbers of lines with the mouse, you move the mouse cursor to the portion of the scroll bar called the *scroll box*, as illustrated in part 1 of figure 12-10. Then, you hold down the left mouse button while you move the scroll box to the new position. As you move the mouse, the file list scrolls to its new position, as illustrated in part 2 of figure 12-10. Notice that the file named ATTRIB.EXE, which was at the bottom of the file list in part 1, has been scrolled off of the list in part 2.

To help you gauge your position when you use the scroll bar, the height of the scroll box indicates the relative size of the file list. For instance, the scroll box in figure 12-9 occupies the entire scroll bar, which means that all of the files in the directory are displayed. In contrast, the scroll box in figure 12-10 indicates that about one-fifth of the files in the directory are displayed. In part 1, the position of the scroll box within the scroll bar indicates that the files in the first part of the directory are displayed. In part 2, the position of the scroll box indicates that the files in the middle part of the directory are displayed.

Chapter 12

Part 1:

Put the mouse cursor on the scroll box.

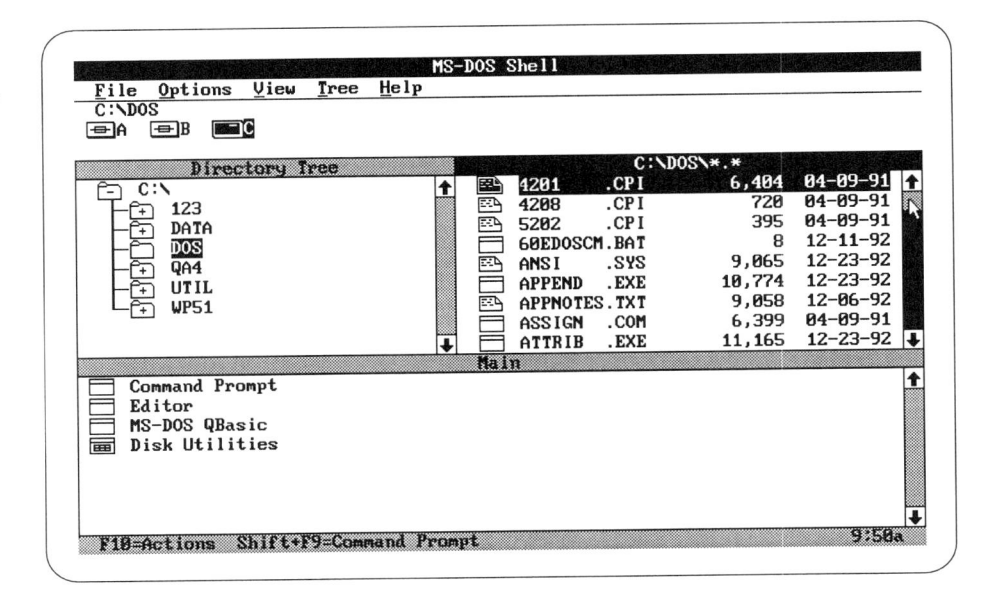

Part 2:

While holding down the left mouse button, drag the scroll box to the new file position.

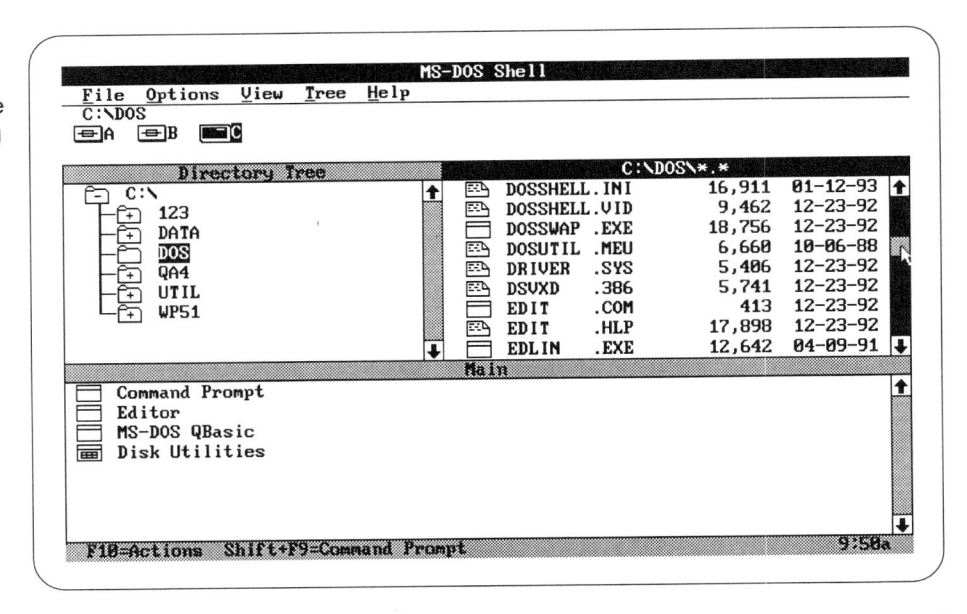

Figure 12-10 How to use the scroll bar to scroll through the file list

How to scroll through a directory tree   If a drive has more directories than can be displayed in the directory-tree area at one time, you can scroll through the directory tree just as you can the file list. Again, the easiest way to do that is by using the cursor control keys to move the tree display one line at a time or by using the Page-up and Page-down keys to move the tree one screen at a time.

You can also scroll through the directory tree with a mouse by using the scroll bar to the right of the directory tree. You can scroll up or down one line at a time by clicking on one of the arrows at the top or bottom of the scroll bar. And you can scroll varying amounts by moving the scroll box.

Figure 12-11 shows how the shell displays a typical directory structure. Here, plus signs (+) on folders indicate that these directories have at least one subdirectory. To expand a directory so you can see these subdirectories, you move the mouse cursor to the directory folder as shown in part 1. When you click the mouse, the directory is *expanded* to display any subdirectories as shown in part 2. To use the keyboard to expand a directory, you press the Tab key to activate the directory-tree area. Then, you use the cursor control keys to move to the desired directory. When you press the Plus sign key, the DOS shell expands the directory.

When a directory has been expanded, a minus sign (-) is displayed in the directory folder to indicate that you can *collapse* the directory. To collapse an expanded directory using a mouse, you just click on the folder. To collapse a directory using the keyboard, you move the highlight to the folder and press the Minus sign key.

The DOS shell also provides commands you can use to expand and collapse directories. You access these commands from the Tree menu. With them, you can expand one directory or all of the directories on the tree, and you can collapse a directory.

How to select files   When you use DOS commands, you enter the names of the files you want to process as parameters. In contrast, when you use the DOS shell, you don't enter file names. Instead, you select the files you want to process before you start a command. Then, when you select the command that you want from a menu, all the files you selected are processed. To delete files, for example, you first select all the files you want to delete. Next, you select the Delete command from the File menu. All the selected files are then deleted.

You can use three techniques to select files using a mouse. First, you can select a single file by moving the mouse cursor to the file in the file list and clicking on it. After you select a file, it's highlighted.

Second, you can select several files by holding down the Ctrl key as you click on each file. If you click on a file that's already selected while holding down the Ctrl key, the file is deselected. With this technique, you can select any number of files from anywhere in the file display as shown in figure 12-12.

Third, you can select a group of files that are listed together. First, you move the mouse cursor to the first file in the group and click on it, as shown in part 1 of figure 12-13. Next, you move the mouse cursor to the last file in the group you want to

Chapter 12

Part 1:

Move the mouse cursor to the folder of the directory you want to expand and click the mouse.

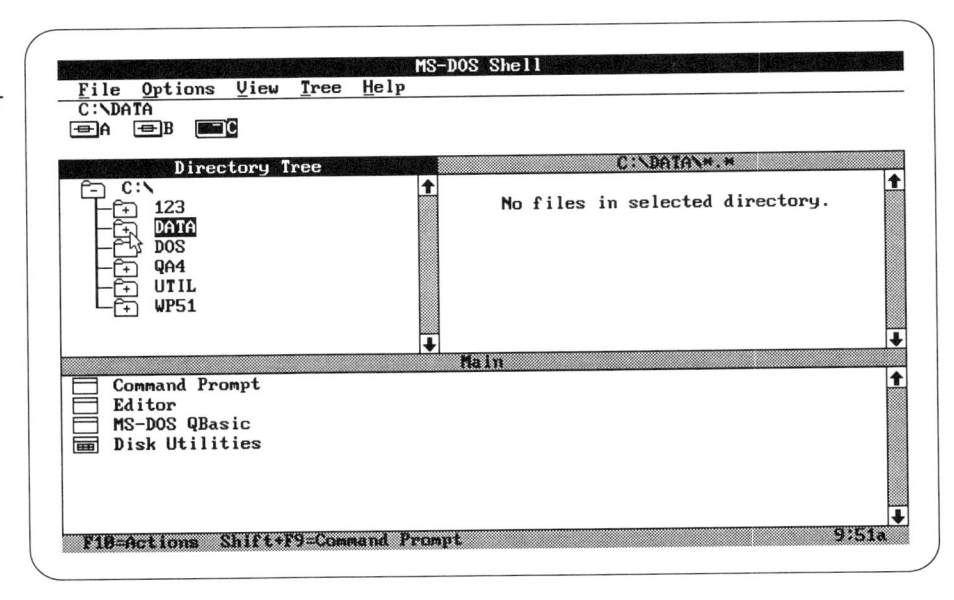

Part 2:

The expanded directory is then displayed.

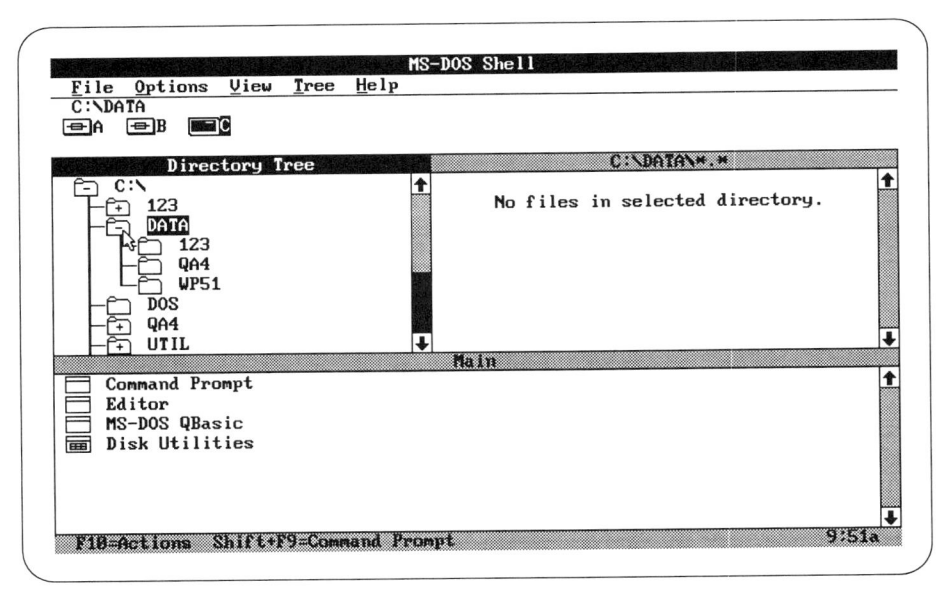

Figure 12-11 How to expand a directory using a mouse

An introduction to the DOS shell **221**

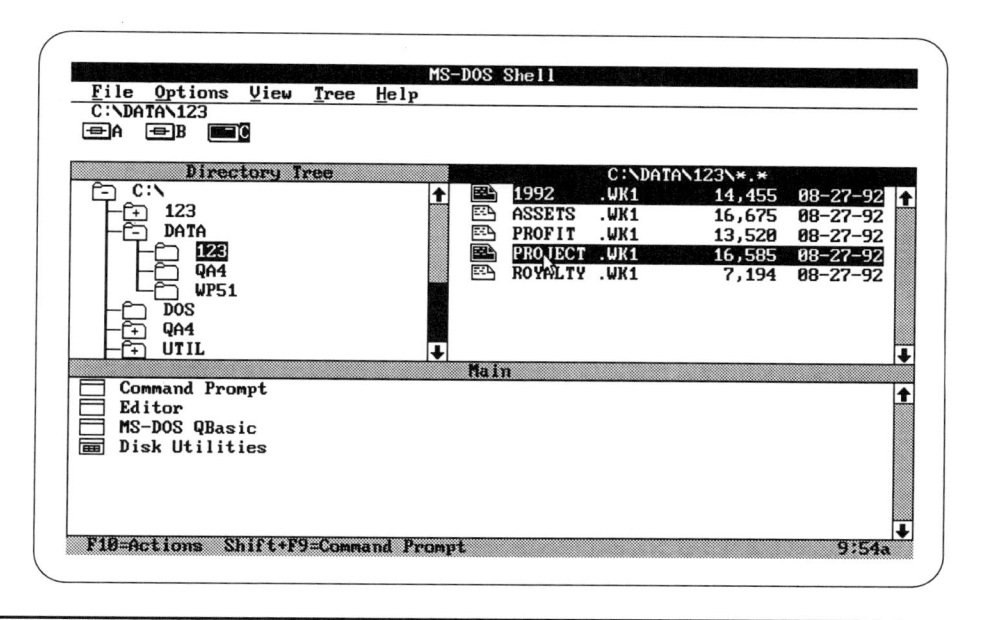

```
┌─────────────────────────────────────────────────────────────┐
│                        MS-DOS Shell                         │
│  File  Options  View  Tree  Help                            │
│  C:\DATA\123                                                │
│  [=]A  [=]B  [=]C                                           │
│ ┌─────── Directory Tree ──────┬──────── C:\DATA\123\*.* ───┐│
│ │  ┌─ C:\                   ↑ │  1992    .WK1   14,455 08-27-92 ↑│
│ │  ├─ 123                     │  ASSETS  .WK1   16,675 08-27-92 │
│ │  ├─ DATA                    │  PROFIT  .WK1   13,520 08-27-92 │
│ │        ├─ 123               │  PROJECT .WK1   16,585 08-27-92 │
│ │        ├─ QA4               │  ROYALTY .WK1    7,194 08-27-92 │
│ │        └─ WP51              │                                 │
│ │  ├─ DOS                     │                                 │
│ │  ├─ QA4                     │                                 │
│ │  └─ UTIL                  ↓ │                               ↓ │
│ ├──────────────────── Main ─────────────────────────────────┤│
│ │  Command Prompt                                         ↑ ││
│ │  Editor                                                   ││
│ │  MS-DOS QBasic                                            ││
│ │  Disk Utilities                                           ││
│ │                                                         ↓ ││
│ │ F10=Actions  Shift+F9=Command Prompt              9:54a   ││
└─────────────────────────────────────────────────────────────┘
```

Figure 12-12   Two files selected by holding down the Ctrl key as you click the mouse on each file

select. Then, you hold down the Shift key as you click on the file. All the files in the group are then selected, as shown in part 2 of figure 12-13. If you need to cancel all the files you've selected, just click the mouse on any file.

To select a single file with the keyboard, you use the cursor control keys to move the selection cursor to the file. To select several files, you press the Shift+F8 key combination to turn on Add mode. Then, you use the cursor control keys to move to each file you want to select and press the Space bar. If you press the Space bar on a file that's already selected while Add mode is on, the file is deselected. To turn Add mode off, you press the Shift+F8 keys again. To select a group of files, you hold down the Shift key and use the cursor control keys to select the group. If you need to cancel all the files you've selected, just press the Space bar.

Functions available from the pull-down menus   If you look again at figure 12-9, you can see that when the file-list area is active, the menu bar contains these five selections: File, Options, View, Tree, and Help. The pull-down menu you'll use the most as you work with files and directories is the File menu, shown in figure 12-14. As you can see, it provides several groups of functions. Many of these functions correspond to familiar DOS commands, such as Copy, Delete, and Rename. Other functions, such as Associate, are unique to the shell. You'll learn how to use many of these functions in chapter 14.

Part 1:

Select the first file in the group, then move the mouse cursor to the last file in the group.

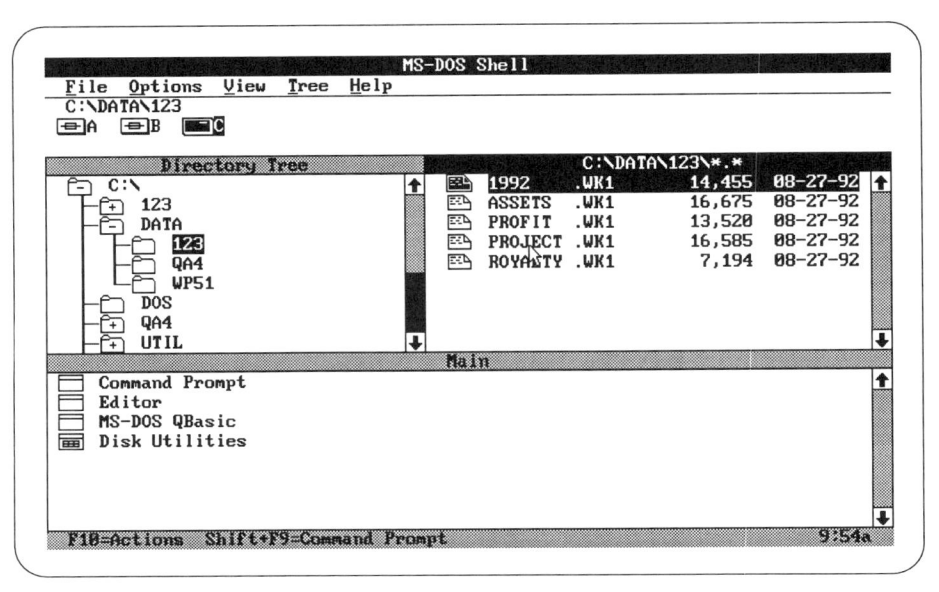

Part 2:

Select the group by holding down the Shift key while you click the mouse on the last file.

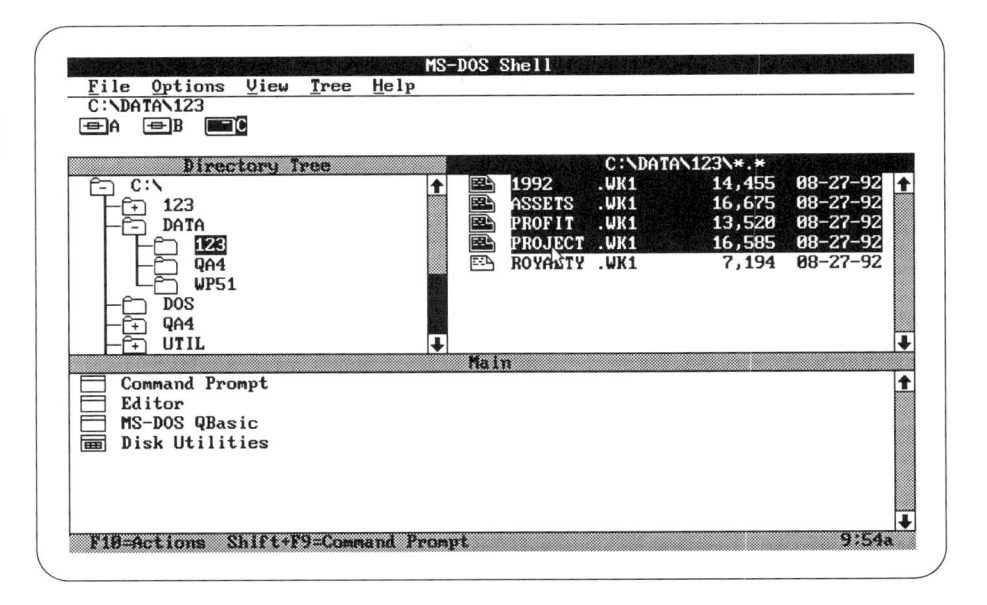

Figure 12-13 How to select a group of files using a mouse

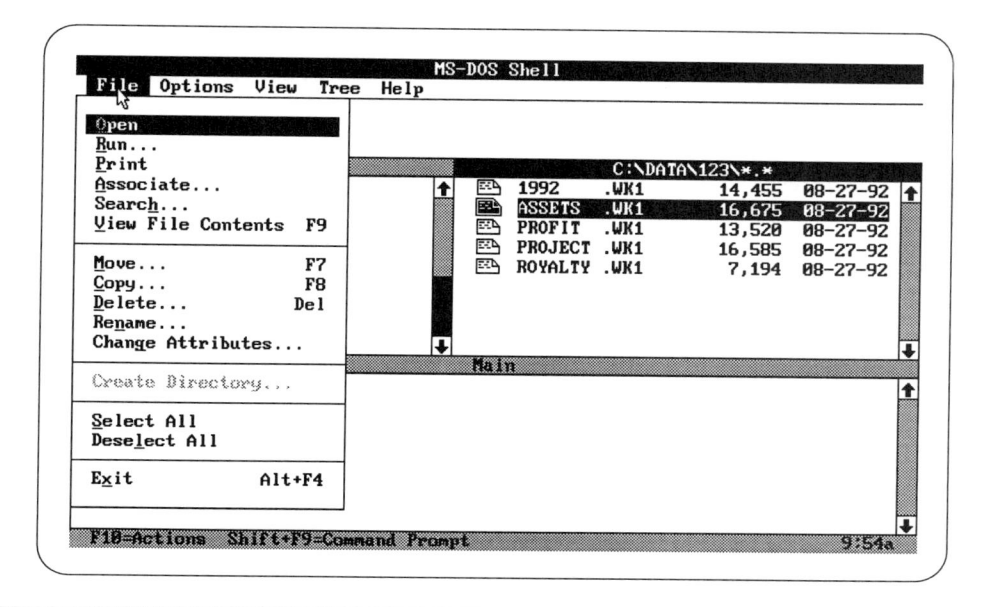

Figure 12-14 The File menu when the file-list area is active

How to start a command or program from the file-list area

When you use the DOS shell, you can start any command or program from the file-list area. To do this with a mouse, you double-click on the command or program file in the file list. To do this with the keyboard, you use the cursor control keys to highlight the command or program file and then press the Enter key.

Since you can use this method to start any file with a COM or EXE extension, you can start any of the external DOS commands in this way. You can also start batch files this way. If, for example, you have already stored one batch file for each of your application programs in the UTIL directory, you just change the current directory to UTIL, select the batch file you want to execute, and start the batch file using one of the techniques I just mentioned.

Some perspective on the DOS shell

If you use the DOS shell only for starting commands and programs, you won't get much benefit from it. In fact, if you already use batch files to start your application programs, you can probably start them faster from the command prompt than you can from the shell. Similarly, if you already know how to use the DOS commands, you can probably run them faster from the command prompt than you can from the Disk-utilities program list in the shell.

In the next chapter, though, you'll learn how to use the DOS shell to create and use menus to start your application programs. Then, in chapter 14, you'll learn how to use the shell to manage directories and files. After you finish these chapters, you'll have a better idea of how the DOS shell can help you work more efficiently.

Terms

shell program	button
DOS shell	program list
menu bar	menu bar
drive icon	program-list title bar
drive-icon bar	main program list
directory-tree area	double clicking the mouse
file-list area	dialog box
program-list area	path bar
status bar	directory tree
graphics mode	file list
text mode	file icon
clicking the mouse	selection cursor
pull-down menu	scroll bar
shortcut key	scroll box
window	expand a directory
context-sensitive help	collapse a directory

Objectives

1. Start a program or function from the program-list area.

2. Given file specifications for one or more files, select the files from the file-list area.

3. Start a command or program from the file-list area.

Chapter 13

How to use the DOS shell to create and use menus

The program-list functions of the DOS shell make it easy for you to create menus for starting your application programs. Once you create the menus, you can start your application programs more easily from a program list than you can from the file list. All you have to do to start a program is double-click the mouse on the selection you want. Or if you don't have a mouse, you just highlight the selection you want and press the Enter key.

In this chapter, you'll learn how to use the program-list functions to create your own menus. You'll also learn how to customize the items on a menu so they start your programs the way you want them to. Since you've already learned the general techniques for using the DOS shell, this chapter should be easy to follow. When you finish this chapter, you should be able to set up menus for your own programs in just a few minutes.

The menu structure of the program-list area

The program-list area in figure 13-1 shows the Main program list. When you install DOS 5.0 or 6.0, this screen automatically has the four options shown here: Command Prompt, Editor, MS-DOS QBasic, and Disk Utilities. As you can see, the first three options have plain boxes to the left of them to indicate that they start programs. The last option, however, has a box with a pattern of smaller boxes in it. This symbol indicates that this option leads to another program list. If you're not using the shell in graphics mode, the Disk-utilities option is bracketed to show that it leads to another program list.

When you use the DOS shell, you can create a multi-level menu system. The Main program list can lead to other program lists, and those program lists can lead to still others. For most users, though, a two-level menu structure is adequate. So the menu structure consists of just the Main program list and the program lists that it leads to.

If you use just two or three application programs, it's probably best to add them to the Main program list shown in figure 13-1. If, on the other hand, you use several

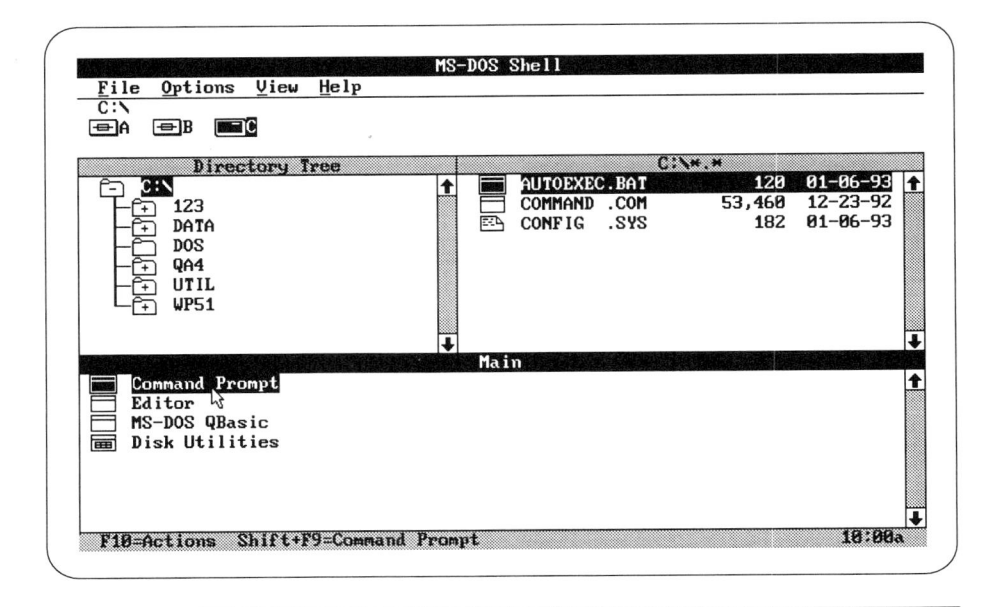

```
                        MS-DOS Shell
 File  Options  View  Help
 C:\
  ▣A    ▣B    ■C
┌─────────────────────────┬──────────────────────────────────┐
│      Directory Tree     │              C:\*.*              │
│  ┌─ C:\              ↑  │   AUTOEXEC.BAT    120   01-06-93 │
│  ├─ 123                 │   COMMAND .COM  53,460  12-23-92 │
│  ├─ DATA                │   CONFIG  .SYS     182  01-06-93 │
│  ├─ DOS                 │                                  │
│  ├─ QA4                 │                                  │
│  ├─ UTIL                │                                  │
│  └─ WP51                │                                  │
│                      ↓  │                                ↓ │
├─────────────────────────┴──────────────────────────────────┤
│                           Main                             │
│  ▣ Command Prompt                                        ↑ │
│  ▤ Editor                                                  │
│  ▤ MS-DOS QBasic                                           │
│  ▦ Disk Utilities                                          │
│                                                          ↓ │
│ F10=Actions  Shift+F9=Command Prompt           10:00a      │
└────────────────────────────────────────────────────────────┘
```

Figure 13-1 The Main program list

programs, it's probably best to create a program list for them that's subordinate to the Main program list. You can call this something like "Applications."

How to add a program list to the Main program list

To add a program list to the Main program list, you activate the program-list area and pull down the File menu as shown in figure 13-2. As you can see, it provides eight functions: New, Open, Copy, Delete, Properties, Reorder, Run, and Exit. In this chapter, I'll show you how to use only the New and Properties functions because all the others are easy to use once you know how to use these two.

Figure 13-3 shows the dialog boxes that appear when you select the New function from the File menu. The dialog box in part 1 lets you specify whether you want to add a new *program group* or a new *program item* to the current list. In this case, I've selected the Program-group option to add a subordinate program list to the Main program list. Here, *program group* is just another name for a program list.

The dialog box in part 2 lets you enter information to identify the new program list. The Title entry is the name of the list that will be added to the Main program list. This entry can be up to 23 characters long, and it's the only required entry for this dialog box.

The Help-text entry can be used if you want Help information to be available for the program group. If you make an entry, the text is displayed when the PC user

How to use the DOS shell to create and use menus **227**

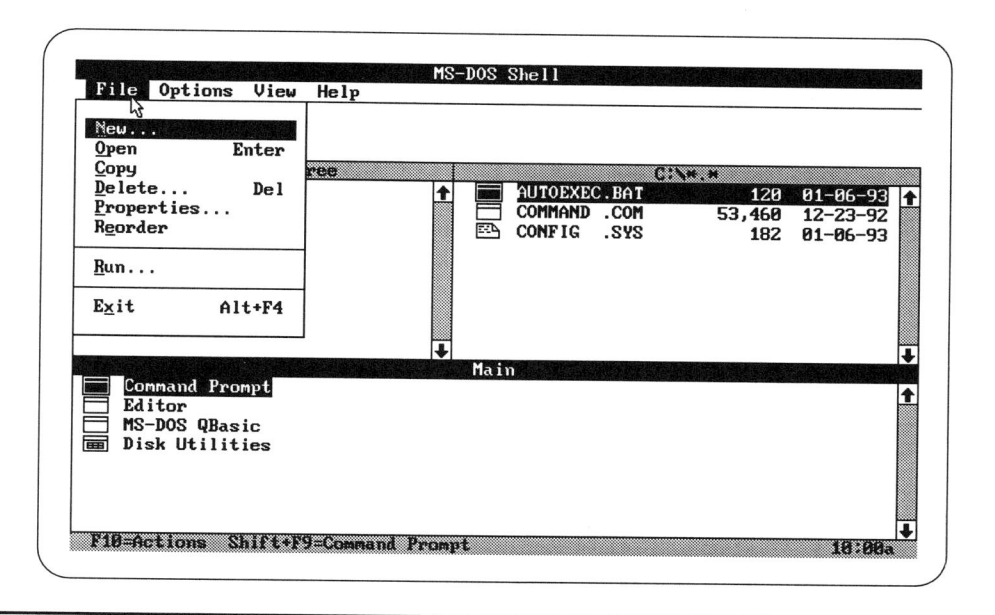

Figure 13-2 The File menu when the program-list area is active

presses the F1 key while the group is highlighted. Usually, though, the purpose of a program group is obvious so there's no reason to include a Help-text entry.

The Password entry can be used if you want to restrict access to the new program list. Then, only a PC user who knows the password can use the programs in the program list. Since passwords have a limited use, you usually leave this entry blank.

After you've completed the entries in this dialog box, use the OK button to add the program list to the Main program list. In figure 13-4, you can see how the Title entry in figure 13-3 is displayed after this list has been added to the Main program list.

As you can see in figure 13-4, the Applications option has a box with a grid of smaller boxes in it to indicate that it leads to another program list. When you select the Applications option before you add any programs to the new list, you get the screen in figure 13-5. Notice the change in the program-list title bar; it now tells you that you're in the Applications program list.

How to add a program to a program list

To add a program to a program list, you select the program list in the Main program list that you want to add a program to. If, for example, you want to add a program to the Applications program list, you first select the Applications program list from the Main program list. Then, the shell displays the screen shown in figure 13-5. Here, the Applications program list is empty except for the option that takes you back to the Main program list.

Part 1:

First, you select the New function from the File menu. Then, you choose the Program-group option in the first dialog box.

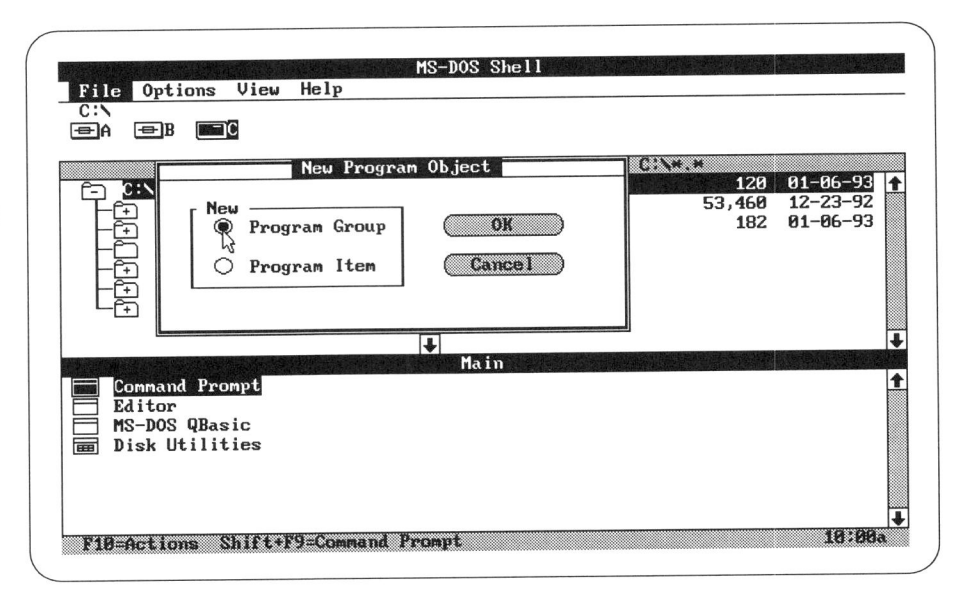

Part 2:

Next, you fill in the entries in the second dialog box that create and identify the new program list.

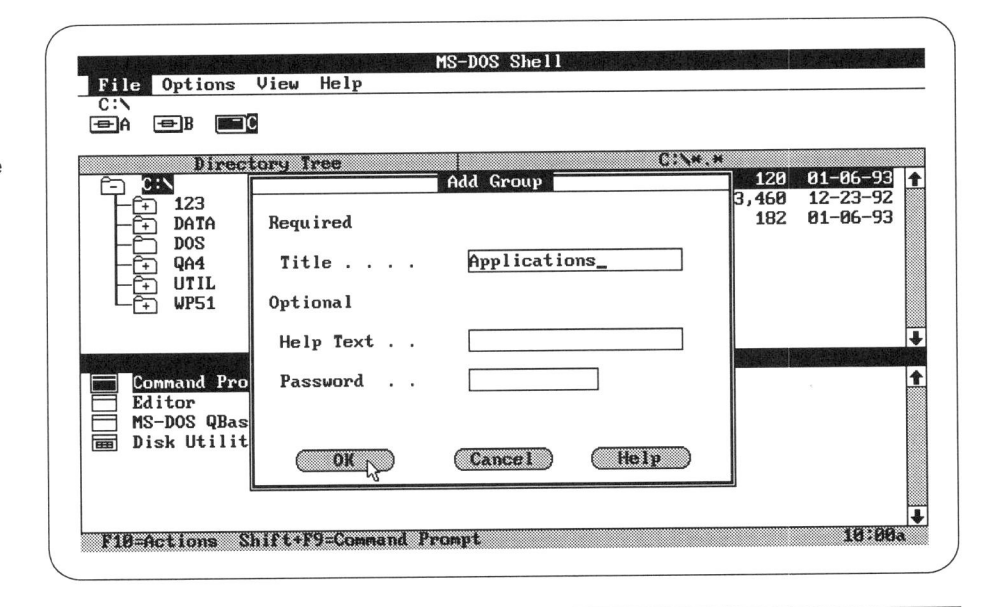

Figure 13-3 How to add a program list to the Main program list

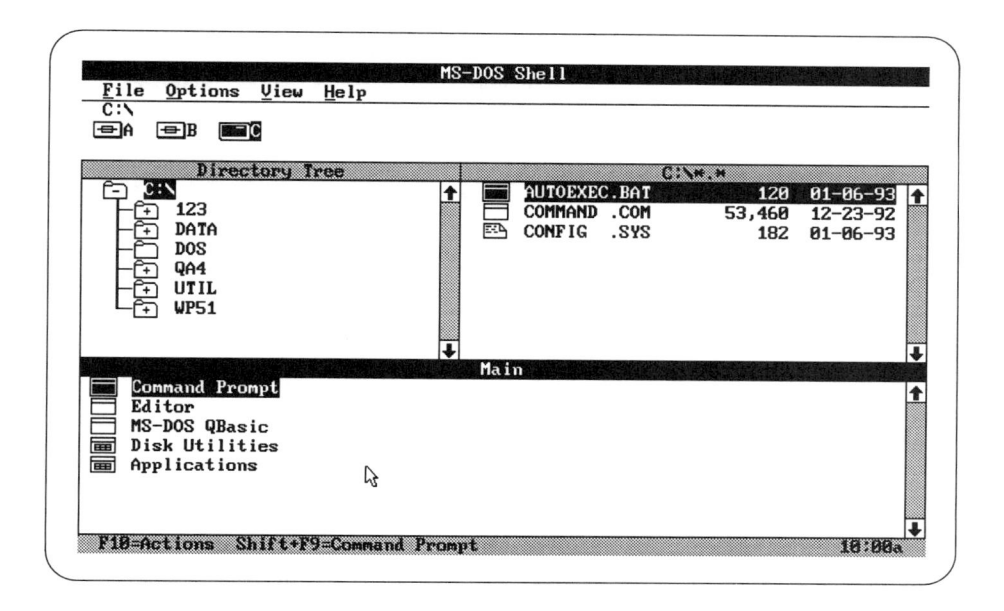

How to use the DOS shell to create and use menus **229**

Figure 13-4 The Main program list with the Applications option created by the dialog boxes in figure 13-3

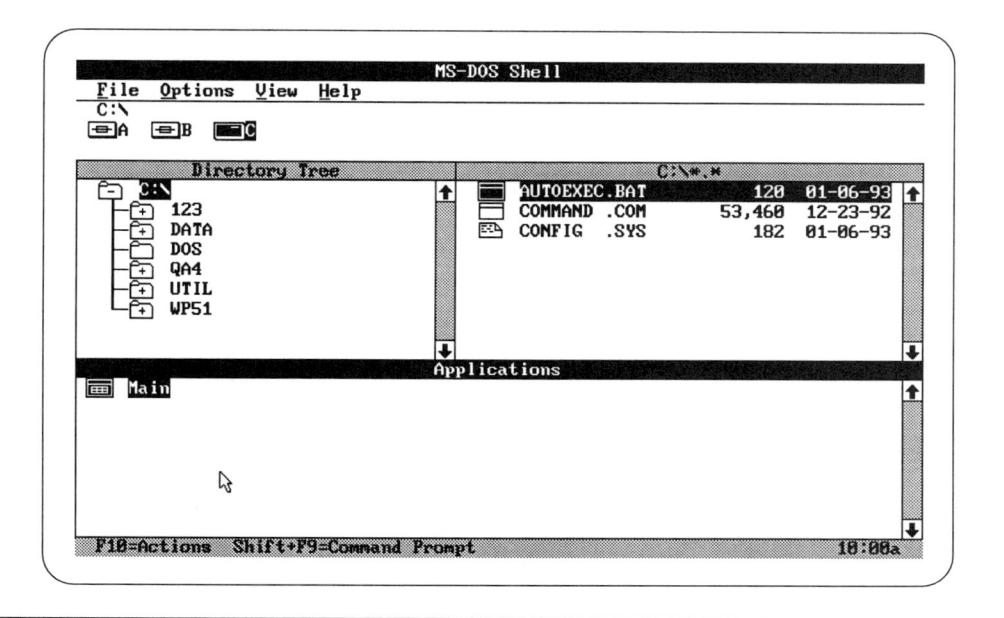

Figure 13-5 The empty program list of the Applications option

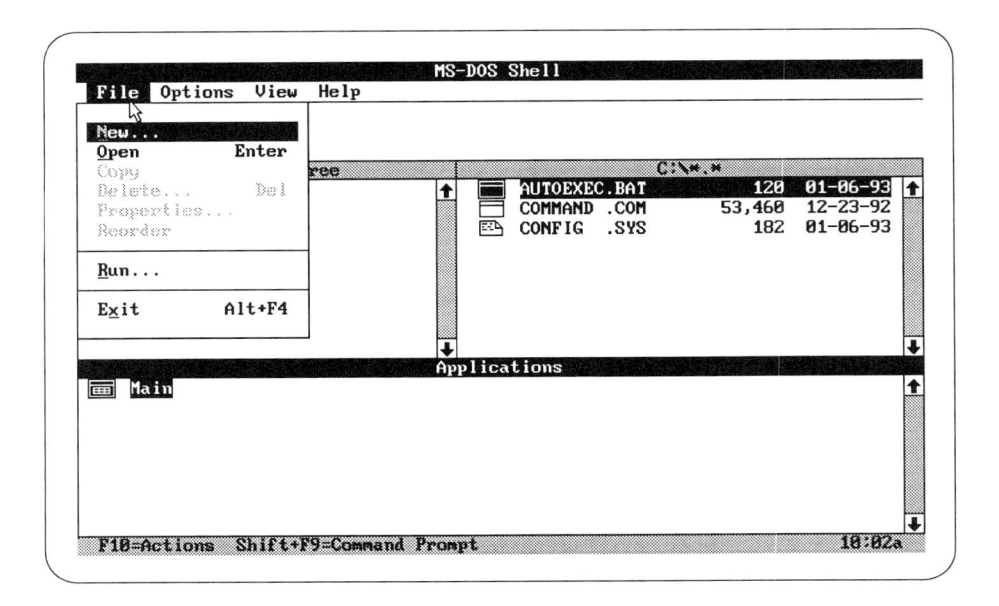

Figure 13-6 The File menu that's displayed for an empty program list

Next, you pull down the File menu as shown in figure 13-6. Because the Applications program list is empty, only four functions are available on the menu. Now, you select the New function. Figure 13-7 shows the dialog boxes that appear.

The dialog box in part 1 of figure 13-7 lets you specify whether you want to add a new program group or program item to the current list. In this case, I've selected the Program-item option to add a program to the program list. Here, the term *program item* just refers to the menu item that will start the program that's being added to the program list.

The dialog box in part 2 lets you enter information that's needed to start the program. The first required entry is the Title entry. This establishes the title that will be used in the Applications program list. In this example, the title that will appear on the program list is *Lotus 1-2-3*.

The second required entry is the Commands entry. For this entry, you can enter one or more commands, provided you don't exceed 256 characters. When you enter more than one command, you separate each command with a space, a semicolon (;), and another space. In part 2 of figure 13-7, you can see that the Commands entry contains these three DOS commands:

    c: ; cd \123 ; 123

The first command changes the default drive to the C drive; the second command changes the current directory to the 123 directory; and the third command starts

Part 1:

After you select the program list that you want to add a program to, you select the New function from the File menu. Then, you choose the Program-item option in the first dialog box.

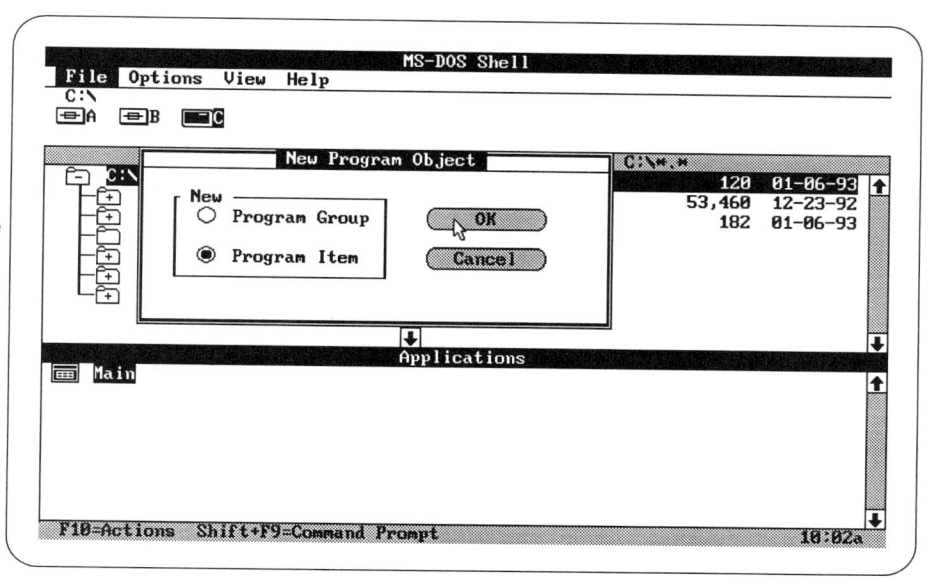

Part 2:

Next, you fill in the entries in the second dialog box that will identify and start the application program.

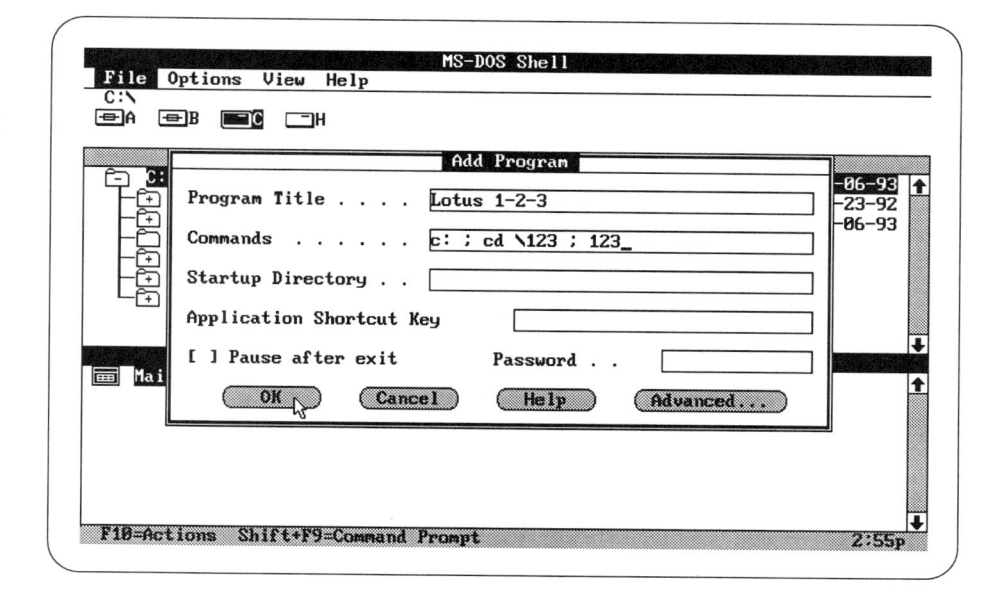

Figure 13-7 How to add a program to a program list

Lotus 1-2-3. If you already have a batch file set up for starting *Lotus 1-2-3* that contains these three commands, you can simplify your Commands entry by entering only the command for the batch file.

As you can see, the last three entries are optional. The Startup-directory entry lets you specify the data directory that you want to use with the program. However, this doesn't work with many programs. The Application-shortcut-key entry lets you assign a special keystroke combination to an application program. I'll show you how to use this entry in chapter 15 when I explain the task switching capabilities of DOS 5.0 and 6.0. The Pause-after-exit entry lets you pause after you exit from an application program and press a key before you return to the shell, instead of returning to the shell immediately. And the Password entry lets you assign a password that restricts access to the program. Most of the time, you'll leave these entries blank.

After you've added one application program to a program list, you'll see how easy it is. Then, you can add the other application programs you use to the list. If you want to reorder the program items in a list, you put the highlight on the program item you want to move, and you execute the Reorder function from the File menu. When I finished adding programs to my Applications group, it looked like the one in figure 13-8.

How to set up a customized dialog box for a program item

If the command that starts an application program accepts parameters, you can set up a customized dialog box so you can enter the parameter when you start the program. For instance, you can set up a dialog box for *WordPerfect* that accepts the file name for the first document to be processed by the program.

Figure 13-9 shows you how to create a customized dialog box. First, you highlight the application program in the program list. Then, you select the Properties function from the File menu to get the dialog box shown in part 1 of figure 13-9. Next, you enter a replaceable parameter in the command that starts the program. Here, the replaceable parameter (%1) after the WP command lets you enter a file name when you start *WordPerfect*. In this example, I've used the Startup-directory entry to specify a starting data directory because this works with *WordPerfect*.

Part 2 of figure 13-9 shows the dialog box that the DOS shell displays next. You use the Window-title entry to identify the customized dialog box. You use the Program-information entry to explain how you use the box. You use the Prompt-message entry to prompt for the parameter. And you use the Default-parameters entry to specify a default parameter (if you want one).

After you set up a dialog box like this one, the DOS shell displays it every time you use the program list to start the program. Figure 13-10, for example, shows the dialog box that's displayed as a result of the entries in figure 13-9. Here, the box prompts you for the file you want to use with *WordPerfect* and offers the file named *letter* as a default. At this box, you can either accept the default file specification or type in the one for the file you want to use. After you use the OK button, the DOS shell starts *WordPerfect* and loads the file you specified.

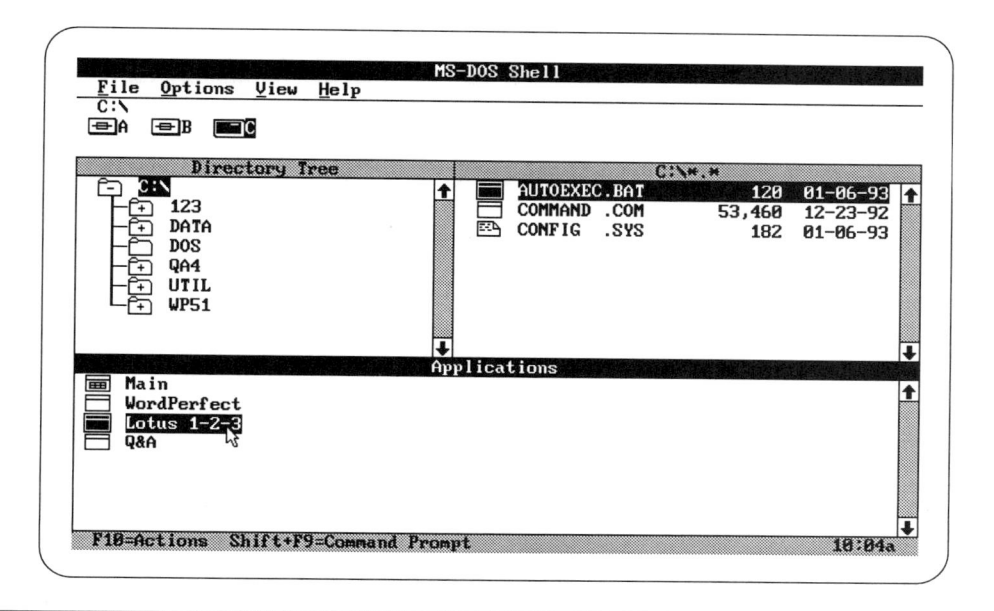

Figure 13-8 The options of the Applications program list

How to modify a program item in a program list

The DOS shell makes it easy for you to modify program items after you've created them. First, you highlight the item you want to change. Then, you select the Properties function from the File menu. The same dialog boxes you used to create the item are then displayed so you can change any of the entries. The new settings are put into effect as soon as you complete the process.

Some perspective on the DOS shell

Without much trouble, you should now be able to set up the menus you need for starting all of your application programs. This can simplify the operation of your PC. And it can be particularly valuable if your PC is used by several people who have trouble starting programs from the DOS prompt.

If you compare the use of the program lists of the DOS shell to the use of batch files, you'll realize that you can start programs just as fast from batch files at the command prompt as you can from the shell. However, you can usually add a program to a program list faster than you can create a batch file for starting a program. Also, program lists make the PC easier to use because you don't have to remember the names of batch files. As a result, the menu capability of the DOS shell is clearly an improvement upon the capabilities of earlier versions of DOS.

Part 1:

After you select the program from the program list, pull down the File menu and choose the Properties function so you can type a replaceable parameter in the command line of the dialog box.

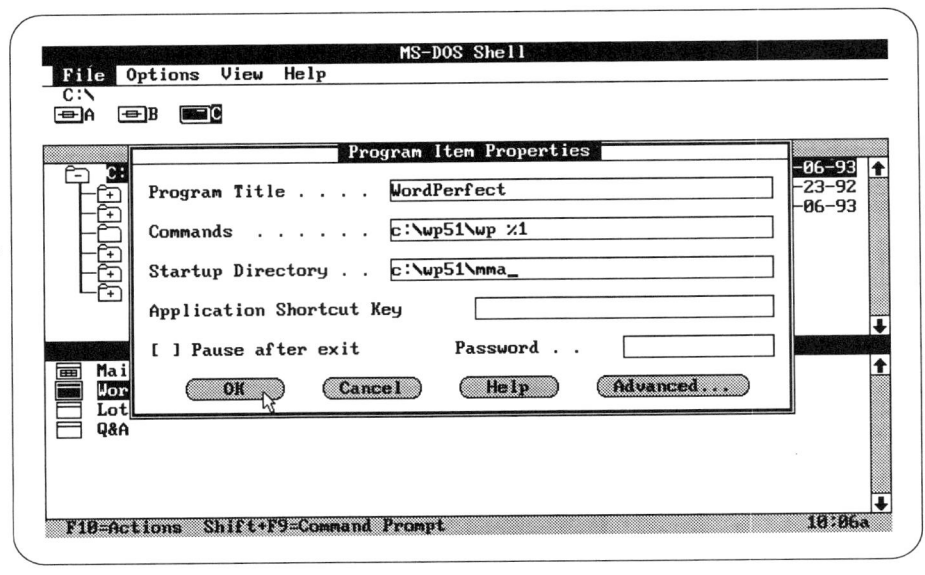

Part 2:

In the second dialog box, you create the text of the customized box and the default value for the replaceable parameter.

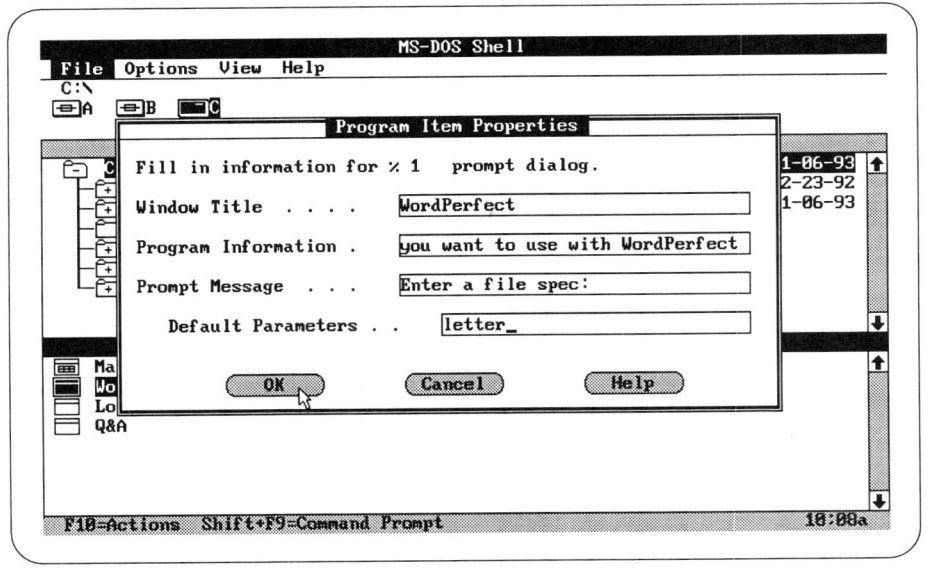

Figure 13-9 How to create a customized dialog box for a program item

How to use the DOS shell to create and use menus   **235**

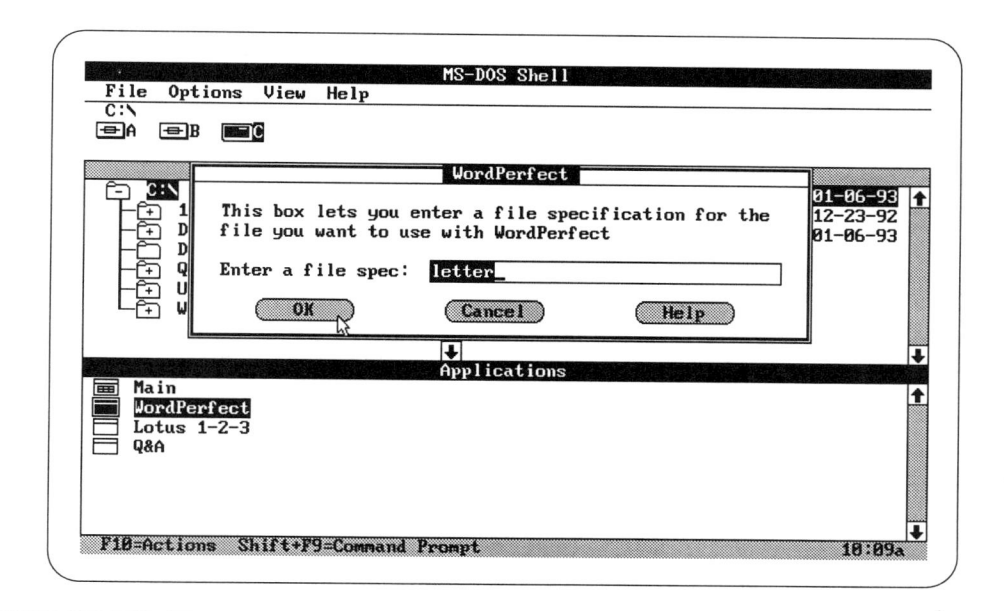

Figure 13-10   The customized dialog box created by the entries in figure 13-9

Terms

program group
program item

Objectives

1. Set up your program-list area so that it includes all the application programs you run regularly.
2. If any programs in your program-list area let you enter parameters when you start them, set up a customized dialog box for them.

Chapter 14

How to use the DOS shell to manage directories and files

In this chapter, you'll learn how to use the DOS shell to manage directories and files. First, I'll review how you use the directory-tree and file-list areas to select files for a function. Then, I'll show you how to use the most useful functions of the pull-down menus for these areas. Because you learned the basic techniques for using the DOS shell in chapter 12, you should be able to move quickly through this chapter.

How to use the directory-tree and file-list areas to select files

Before you perform a function on a file or group of files from the DOS shell, you have to select the files. To review how you do that, figure 14-1 shows the DOS shell screen. To select a file using a mouse, you first click on the directory that contains the file or files you want to select. If required, you click on the appropriate directory folder to expand the directory listing. Then, to select a single file, you just click on that file in the file list. To select several files, you hold down the Ctrl key as you click the mouse. If you click on a file that's already selected while holding down the Ctrl key, the file is deselected. And to select a group of files, you select the first file of the group. Then, you move the cursor to the last file in the group and hold down the Shift key as you click the mouse. To cancel your selection, just click the mouse on another file and start the selection process again.

To select a file using the keyboard, you use the cursor control keys to highlight the file. To select several files, you press the Shift+F8 key combination to turn on Add mode. Then, you move to each file you want to select and press the Space bar. If you press the Space bar on a file that's already selected while Add mode is on, the file is deselected. And to select a group of files, you hold down the Shift key as you press the cursor control keys. If you change your mind after you have selected files, you can cancel the selection by pressing the Space bar. After you select a file, it's highlighted in the file list as shown in figure 14-2. Here, two files have been selected.

238   Chapter 14

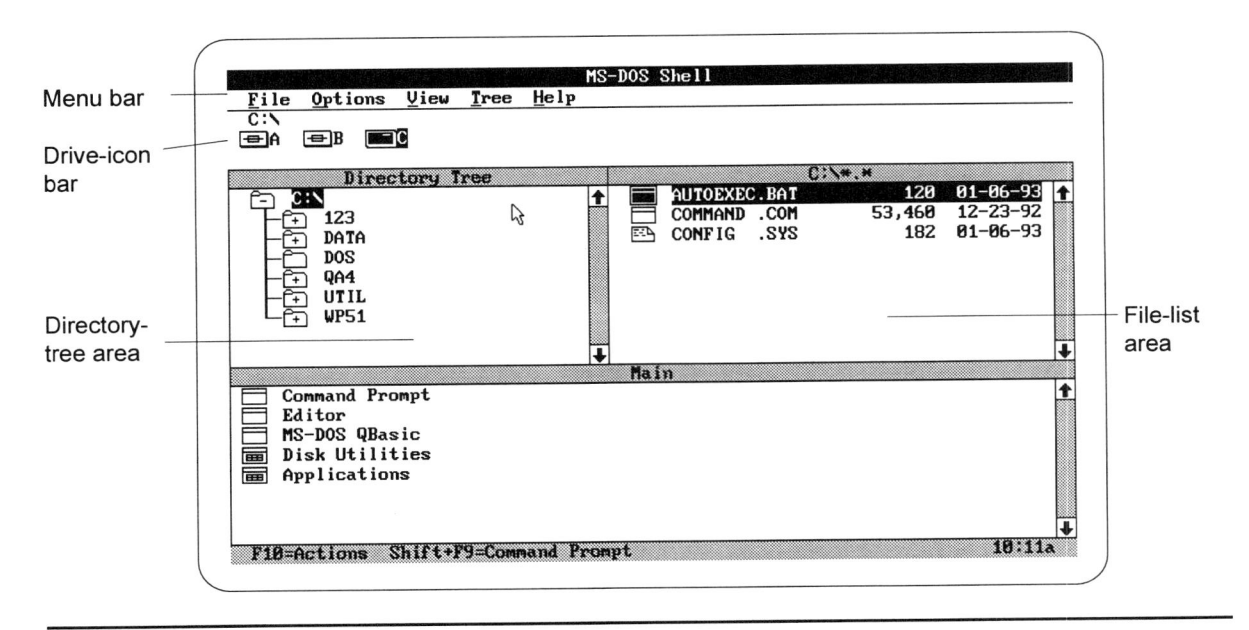

```
                          MS-DOS Shell
          File  Options  View  Tree  Help
          C:\
           [=]A   [=]B   [=]C
                Directory Tree                    C:\*.*
           ┌─ C:\                          AUTOEXEC.BAT    120  01-06-93
              ├─ 123                       COMMAND  .COM 53,460  12-23-92
              ├─ DATA                      CONFIG   .SYS    182  01-06-93
              ├─ DOS
              ├─ QA4
              ├─ UTIL
              └─ WP51

                                Main
           ┌─ Command Prompt
           ├─ Editor
           ├─ MS-DOS QBasic
           ├─ Disk Utilities
           └─ Applications

          F10=Actions  Shift+F9=Command Prompt              10:11a
```

Menu bar — (points to File Options View Tree Help)
Drive-icon bar — (points to A B C icons)
Directory-tree area
File-list area

Figure 14-1   The four components of the DOS shell you use to manage directories and files

How to use the most useful functions of the File menu for the file-list area

Figure 14-3 shows the File menu for the file-list area. When you pull this menu down while the file-list area is active, the menu offers the 14 functions shown. Now, I'll present the eight functions you use to manage files, and I'll present the functions you use most frequently first.

The Move function   The Move function copies files, and then it deletes the originals. To use the Move function, you first select the files you want to move. Then, when you select this function from the File menu, a dialog box like the one in figure 14-4 is displayed. The From field lists the file or files you've selected, and the To field lets you specify the path for the new location. Here, I've entered C:\DATA\123\ as the destination for the file.

If you're working in graphics mode and you have a mouse, you can also use another technique to move files. Figure 14-5 illustrates how you move files using this technique. First, select the files you want to move. Then, put the cursor on the file icon next to one of the selected files, press the left mouse button, and hold it down. While you hold down the button, *drag* a copy of the icon to the directory where you want to move the files, as shown in part 2. When you release the mouse button, the DOS shell displays the dialog box shown in part 3. At this box, you can confirm or cancel the move function.

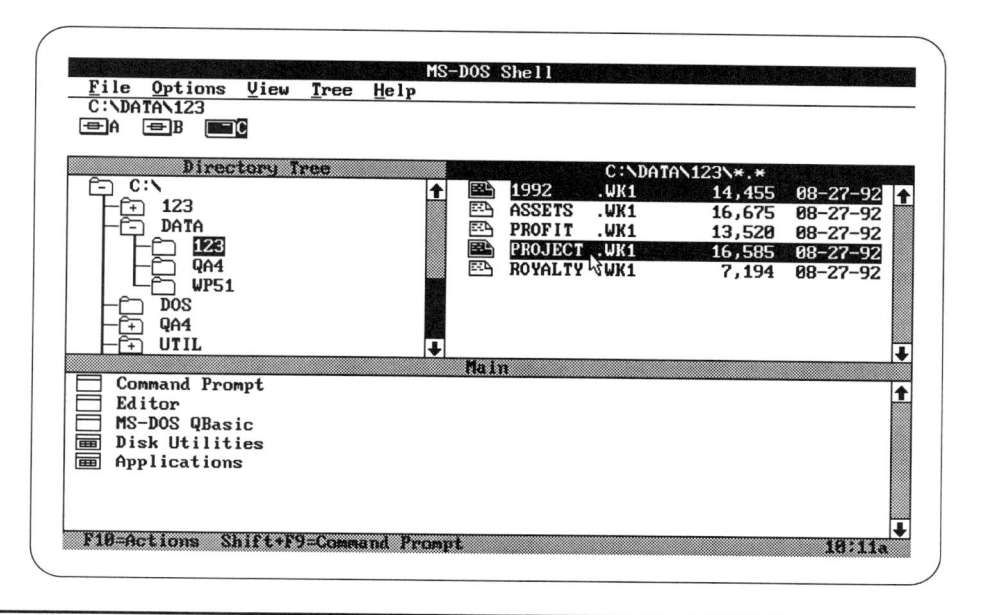

How to use the DOS shell to manage directories and files **239**

Figure 14-2 Two files selected from the file list

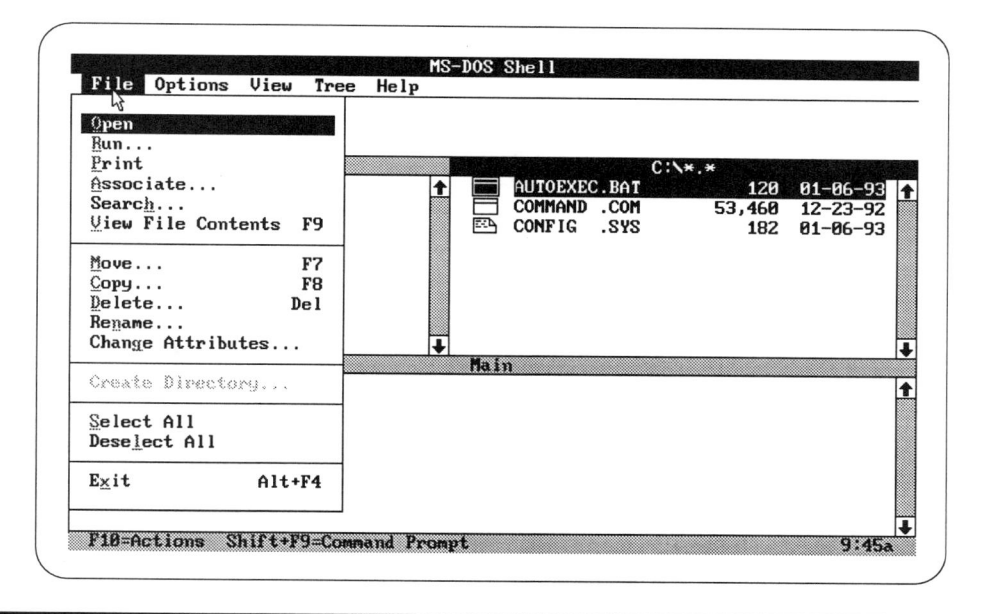

Figure 14-3 The File menu when the file-list area is active

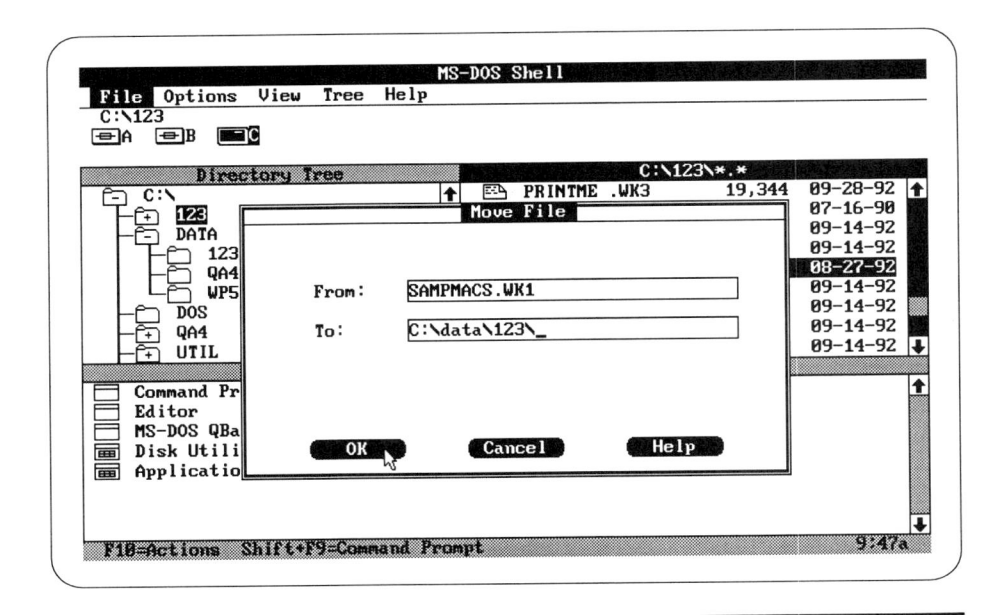

Figure 14-4   The dialog box for the Move function for moving files

The Copy function   The Copy function works much like the Move function. After you select the files you want to copy and select the Copy function, it displays a dialog box so you can specify where you want to copy the files. Then, it makes copies of the files in the new location.

You can also use the mouse technique to copy files if you're working in graphics mode. First, select the files you want to copy. Then, after you place the mouse cursor on one of the file icons, hold down the left mouse button and the Ctrl key and drag the icon to the drive or directory you want to use. When you release the mouse button, the DOS shell displays a dialog box like the one it uses for the Move function so you can either confirm the function or cancel it.

The Delete function   To use the Delete function, you first select the files you want to delete. Then, after you select the Delete function from the File menu, dialog boxes like the ones in figure 14-6 are displayed. The box shown in part 1 lists the files you selected. Here, you can confirm that you want to delete these files, or you can cancel the Delete function.

If you select OK from the first dialog box, a dialog box like the one in part 2 is displayed for each file. Then, you can delete the file, skip the file, or cancel the Delete function for the remaining files. In a moment, you'll learn how to use the Confirmation function of the Options menu to activate or deactivate this second dialog box.

How to use the DOS shell to manage directories and files   241

Part 1:

Select the file, then click the mouse cursor on the file icon and hold down the left mouse button.

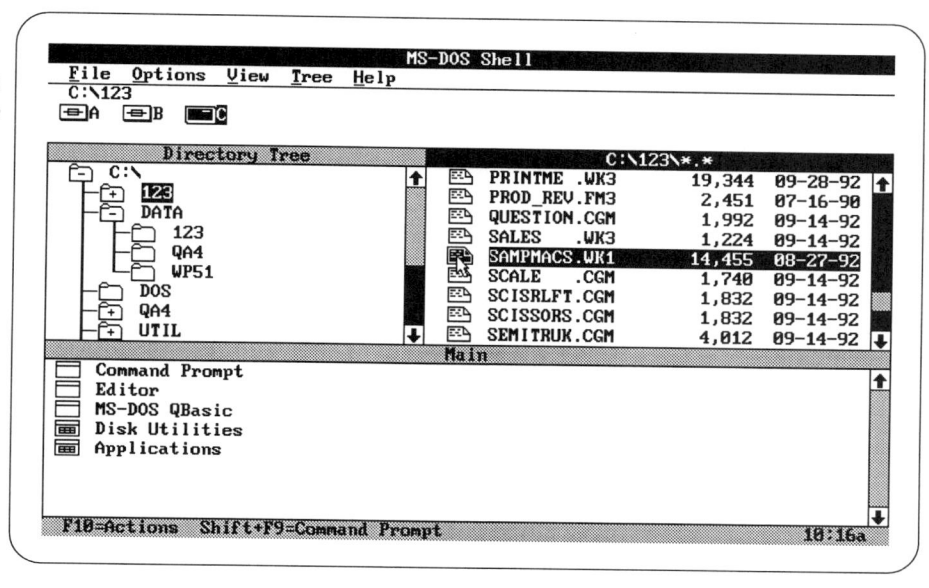

Part 2:

Drag the file icon to the directory you want to move the file to and release the mouse button.

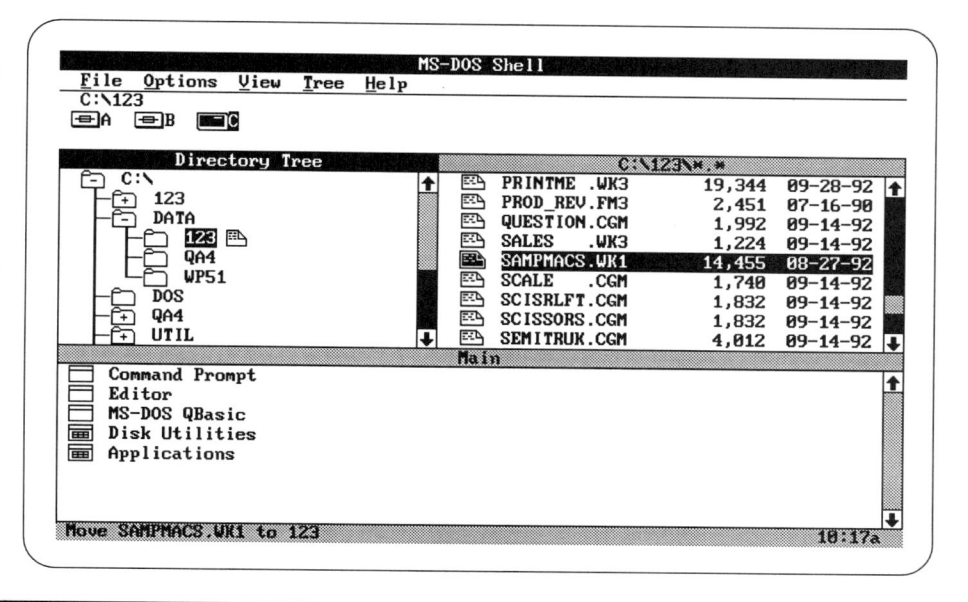

Figure 14-5   How to use the mouse to move a file (parts 1 and 2 of 3)

Part 3:

Use the dialog box to confirm the move or cancel the function.

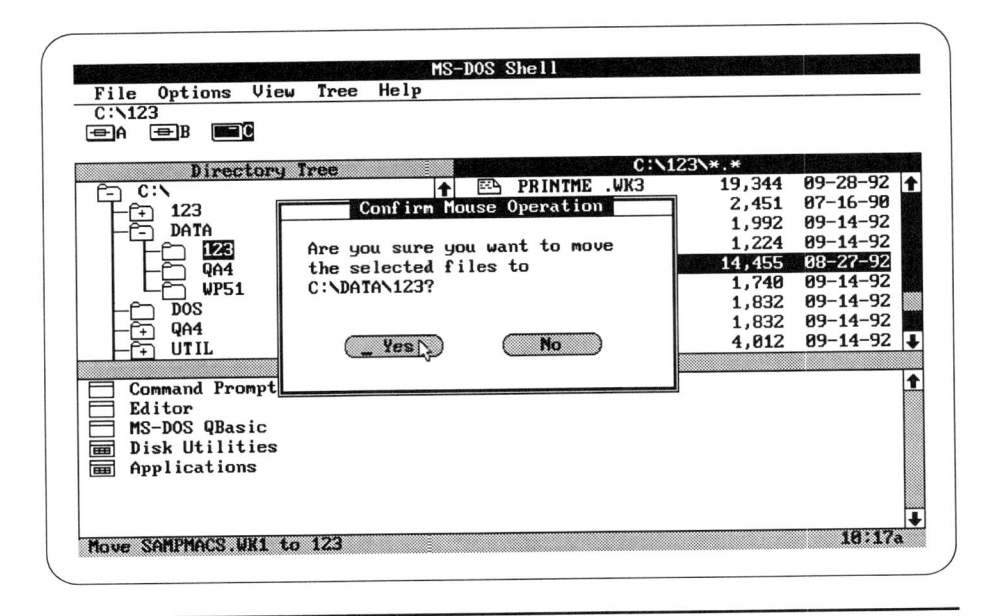

Figure 14-5 How to use the mouse to move a file (part 3 of 3)

The Rename function   To rename one or more files within a directory, you first select the files you want to rename. Then, after you select the Rename function from the File menu, a dialog box like the one in figure 14-7 is displayed for each file you've selected. Here, you can enter the new name for the file or cancel the function for the remaining files.

The Search function   The Search function makes it easy to find files. It lists all the files on a disk drive that match the file name you specify, and it shows the directory for each file. This command also accepts wildcards.

Figure 14-8 shows the Search function in use. Part 1 shows the dialog box that the DOS shell displays when you select the Search function. At this box, you type in the name of the file you want to find. Here, for example, I entered a file specification to find all the spreadsheet files on the disk. The screen in part 2 shows the list of files that match the file specification in part 1.

The View-file-contents function   The View-file-contents function displays the contents of a selected file. You can use it to help you verify that a file in the list is in fact the one you want. If the file is a text file, this function displays its contents as shown in figure 14-9. Here, the contents of the CONFIG.SYS file are displayed. Since batch files are text files, you can use this function to display their contents.

How to use the DOS shell to manage directories and files **243**

Part 1:

After you select the files, you can confirm or cancel the Delete function.

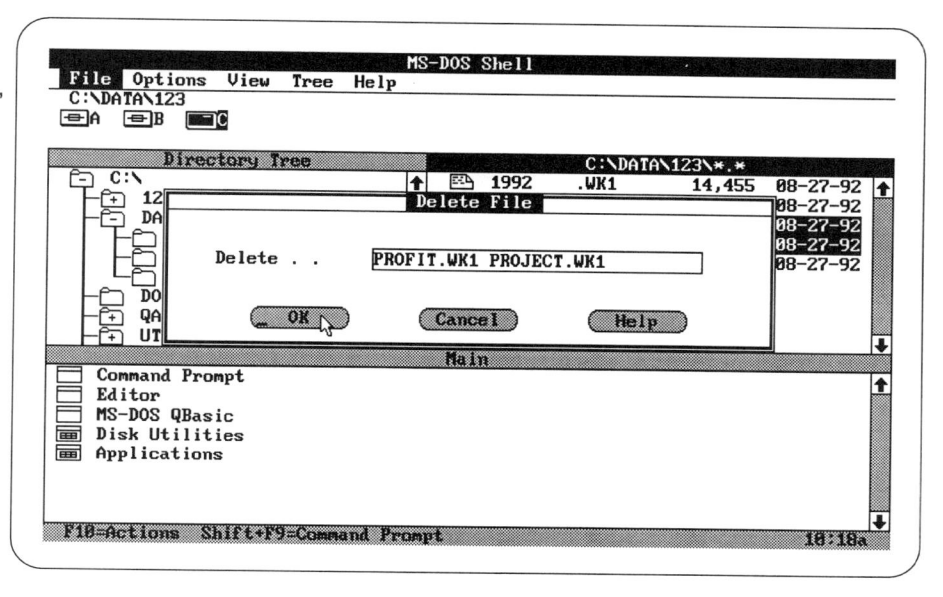

Part 2:

Confirm or cancel the Delete function for each selected file.

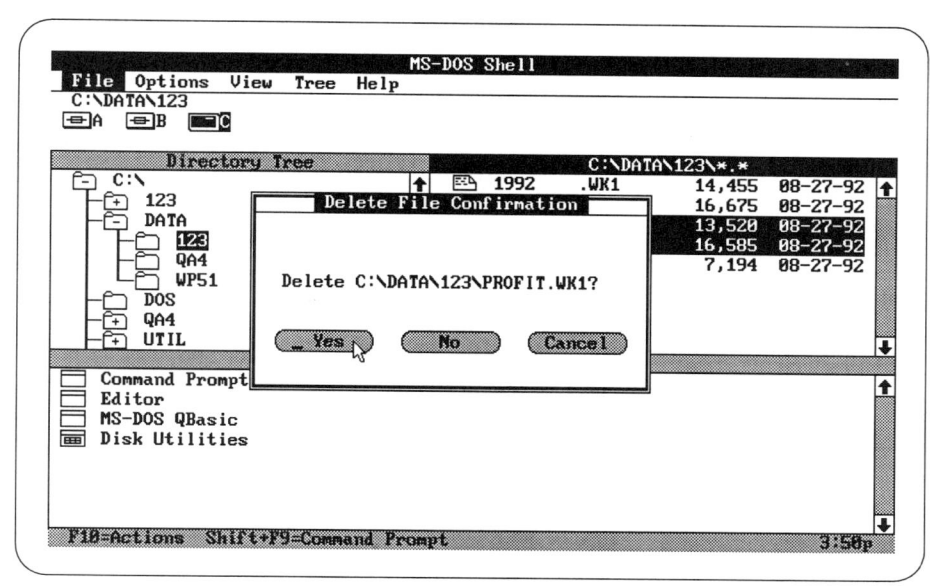

Figure 14-6 How to use the Delete function for deleting files

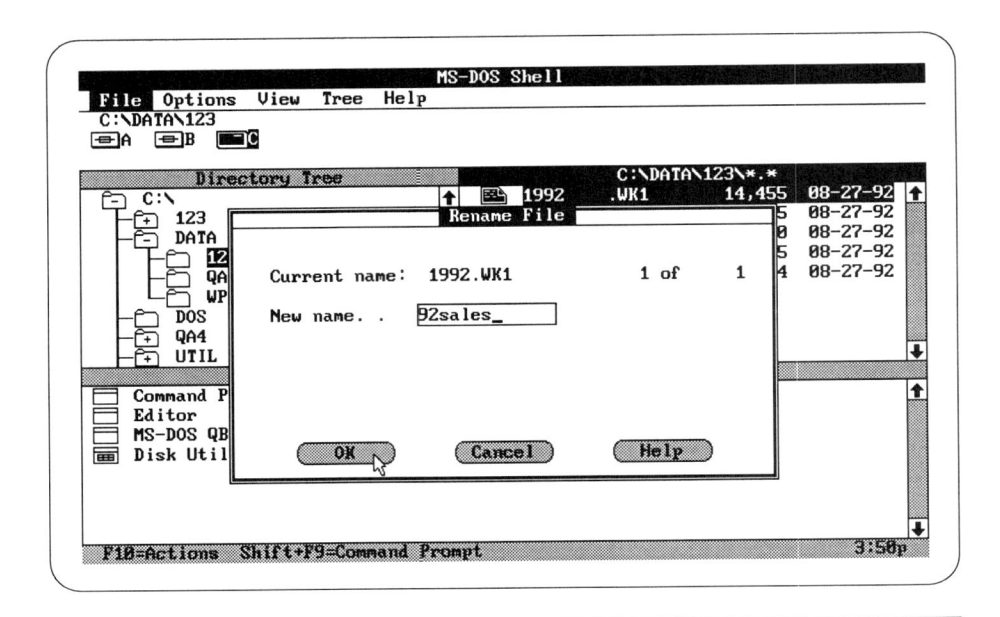

Figure 14-7 The dialog box for the Rename function for renaming files

If a file isn't a text file or the DOS shell doesn't recognize it as such, this function displays the file contents in *hex code*. Even if you're familiar with this code, this display format usually doesn't help you identify a file. As a result, this function is useful only for text files.

The Select-all and Deselect-all functions When you use the Select-all function, all the files in the file list are selected. That way, you don't have to select the files one at a time. This saves you time when the file list is long and fills several screens. You can use this function when you want to move, copy, or delete all of the files in a directory.

When you use the Deselect-all function, all the selected files are deselected. Since it's usually easier to deselect files using the mouse or the keyboard, you probably won't use this function often. But it can be useful if the Select-across-directories function is on. Then, you can deselect all the selected files, no matter what directory they're in. I'll present the Select-across-directories function later in this chapter.

How to use the DOS shell to manage directories and files **245**

Part 1:

Type in the file specification for the search.

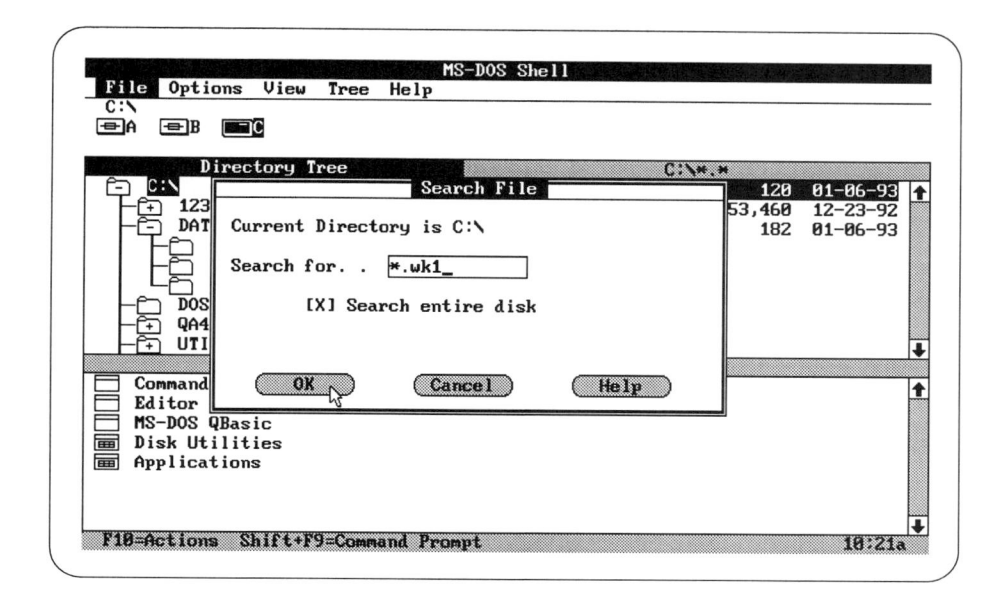

```
                             MS-DOS Shell
 File  Options  View  Tree  Help
 C:\
  ⊜A    ⊜B    ■C
              Directory Tree                    C:\*.*
   ┌ C:\                    ┌─ Search File ─┐    120   01-06-93
   ├ 123                    │                │  53,460  12-23-92
   ├ DAT  Current Directory is C:\           │    182   01-06-93
   ├                        │                │
   ├      Search for. . [*.wk1_]             │
   ├ DOS                    │                │
   ├ QA4        [X] Search entire disk       │
   ├ UTI                    │                │
   │                        │                │
   │           ( OK )   ( Cancel )  ( Help ) │
   ├ Command                └────────────────┘
   ├ Editor
   ├ MS-DOS QBasic
   ├ Disk Utilities
   ├ Applications

 F10=Actions  Shift+F9=Command Prompt              10:21a
```

Part 2:

The list of files that match the search specification is displayed.

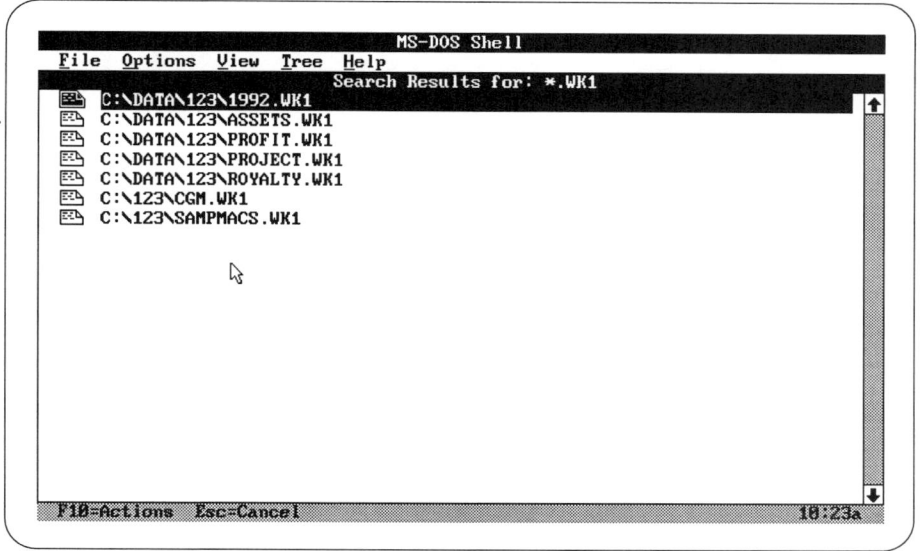

```
                             MS-DOS Shell
 File  Options  View  Tree  Help
                      Search Results for: *.WK1
    C:\DATA\123\1992.WK1
    C:\DATA\123\ASSETS.WK1
    C:\DATA\123\PROFIT.WK1
    C:\DATA\123\PROJECT.WK1
    C:\DATA\123\ROYALTY.WK1
    C:\123\CGM.WK1
    C:\123\SAMPMACS.WK1




 F10=Actions  Esc=Cancel                           10:23a
```

Figure 14-8 How to use the Search function

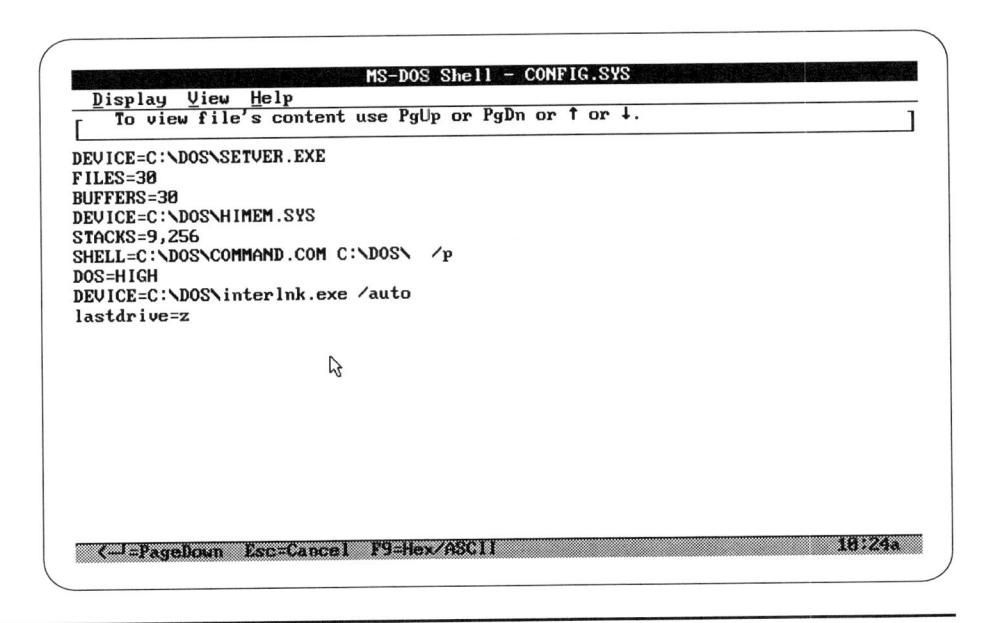

```
                      MS-DOS Shell - CONFIG.SYS
    Display  View  Help
  ┌──  To view file's content use PgUp or PgDn or ↑ or ↓.                    ┐
  DEVICE=C:\DOS\SETVER.EXE
  FILES=30
  BUFFERS=30
  DEVICE=C:\DOS\HIMEM.SYS
  STACKS=9,256
  SHELL=C:\DOS\COMMAND.COM C:\DOS\  /p
  DOS=HIGH
  DEVICE=C:\DOS\interlnk.exe /auto
  lastdrive=z



                                  ↳




  ◄─┘=PageDown  Esc=Cancel  F9=Hex/ASCII                              10:24a
```

Figure 14-9 How the View-file-contents function displays a text file

How to use the most useful functions of the File menu for the directory-tree area

Figure 14-10 shows the File menu that's available when the directory-tree area is active. Here, I'll show you how to use the three functions you use to manage your directories: the Delete, Rename, and Create-directory functions. Even though the Delete and Rename functions are the same names assigned to functions on the File menu of the file-list area, they perform different functions when the directory-tree area is active.

The Delete function   To delete a directory, you first select the directory you want to delete. Next, you select the Delete function from the File menu. The DOS shell then displays the dialog box shown in figure 14-11. At this box, you can confirm the function or cancel it.

If the directory you're trying to delete isn't empty, the DOS shell displays the dialog box shown in figure 14-12. That's because you can't delete a directory that contains files or subdirectories.

The Rename function   To rename a directory, you first select the directory you want to rename. Next, you select the Rename function from the File menu. The DOS shell then displays the dialog box shown in figure 14-13. At this box, you can

How to use the DOS shell to manage directories and files **247**

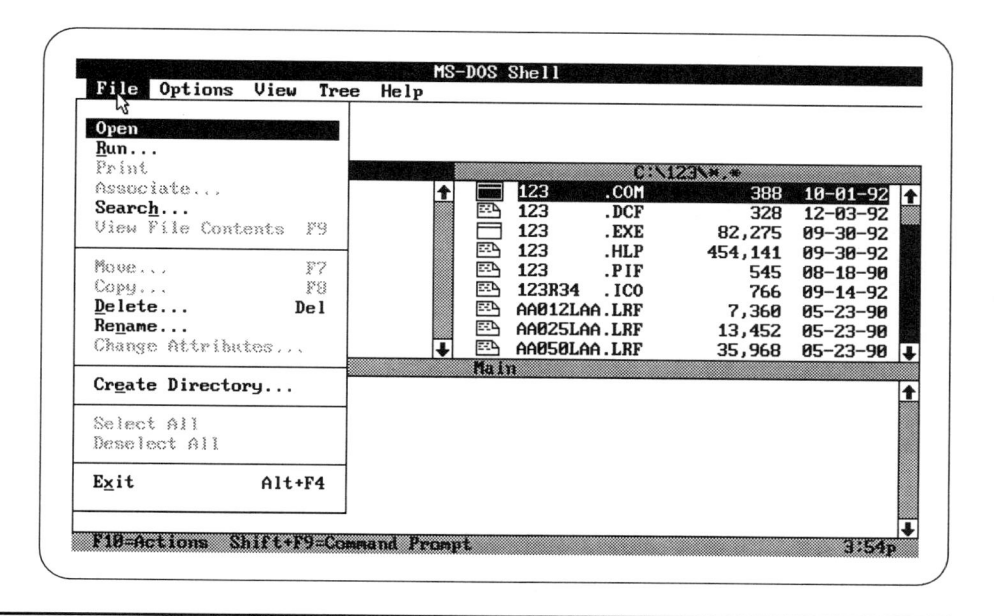

Figure 14-10 The File menu when the directory-tree area is active

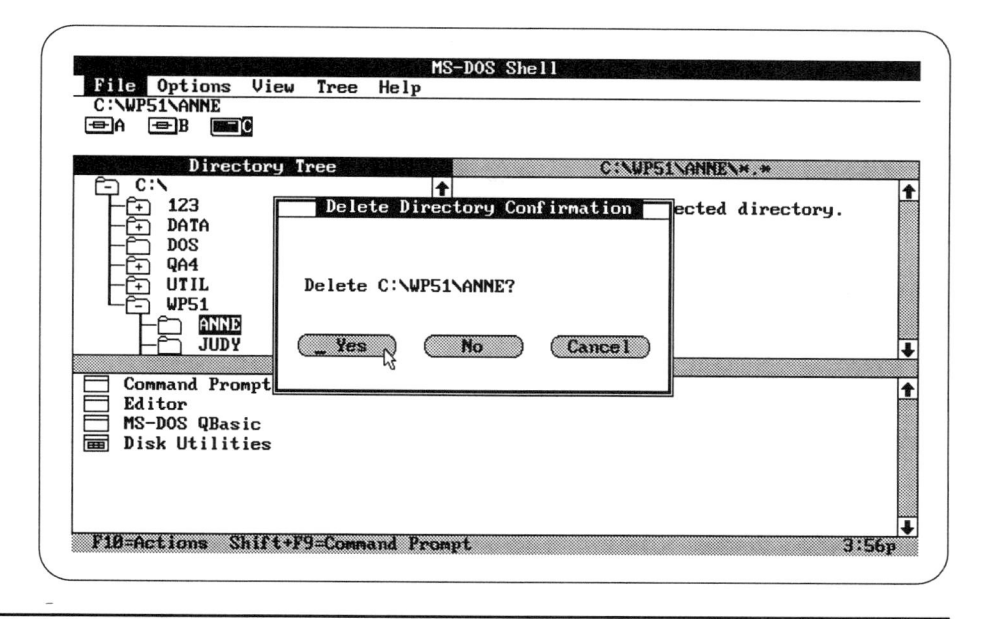

Figure 14-11 The dialog box for the Delete function for deleting directories

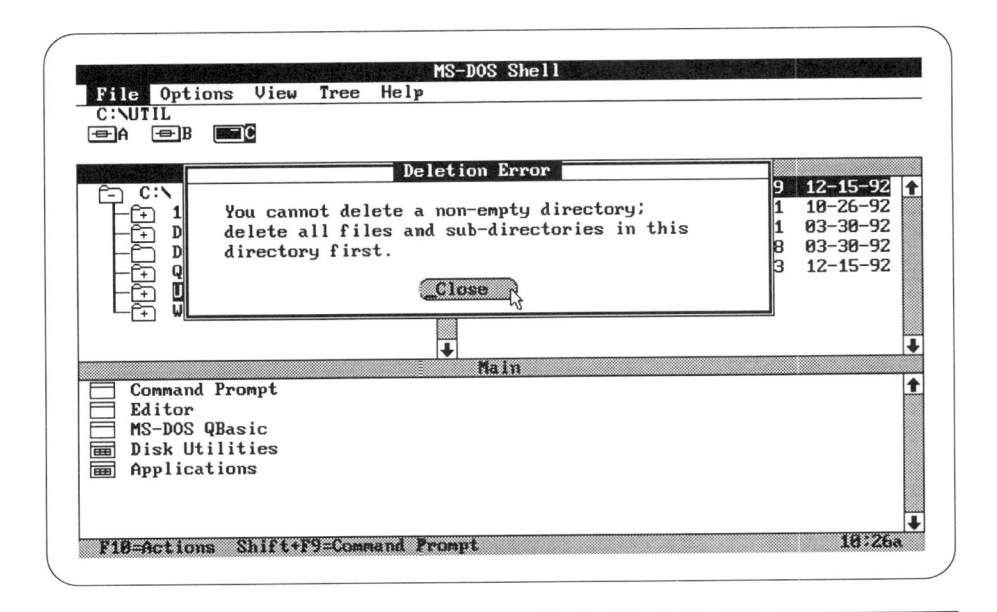

Figure 14-12 The dialog box that's displayed when you try to delete a directory that isn't empty

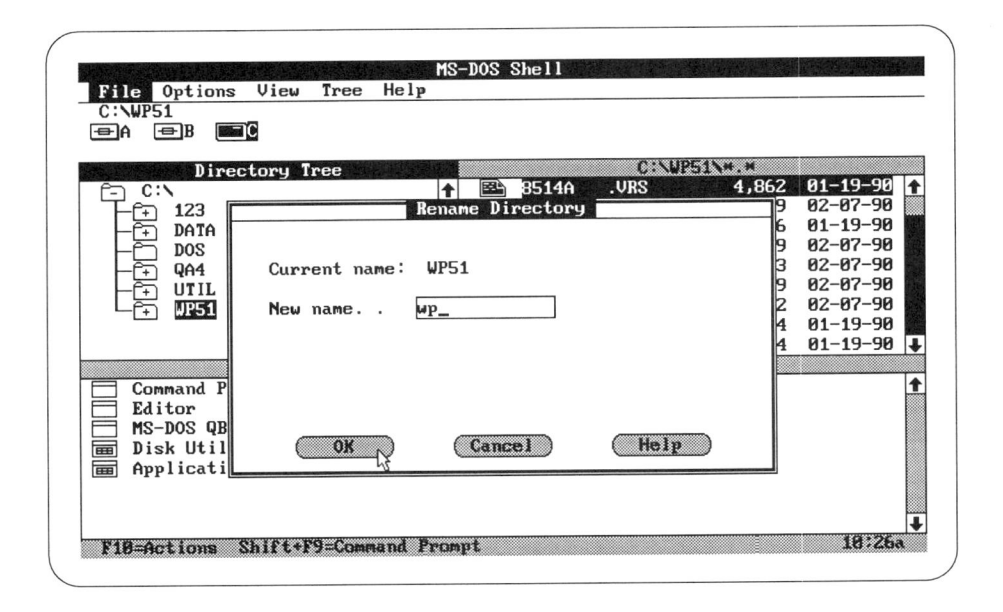

Figure 14-13 The dialog box for the Rename function for renaming directories

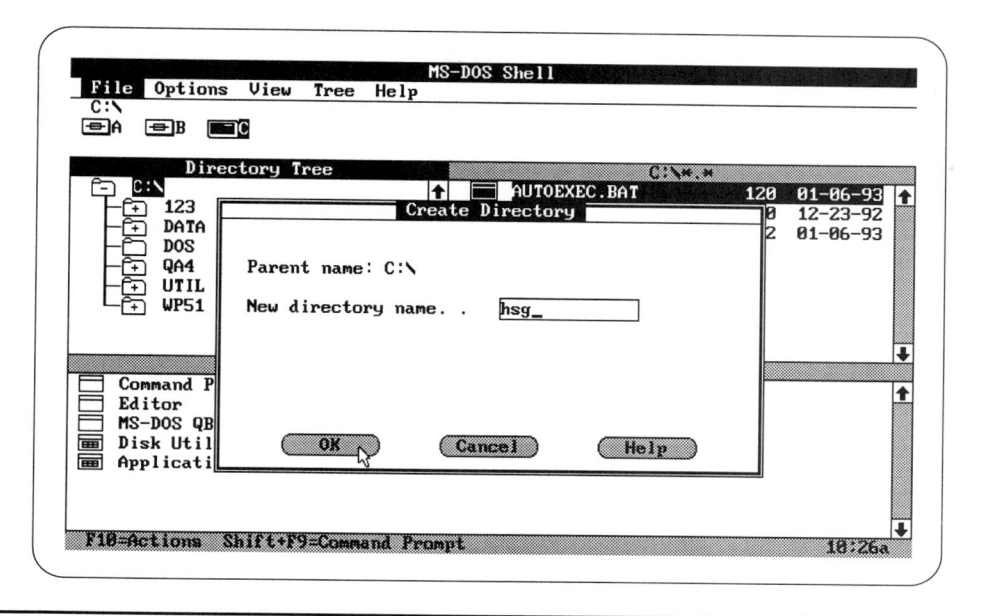

Figure 14-14 The dialog box for the Create-directory function

type in a new name for the directory. If you're using DOS 5.0, this is a valuable function because there isn't a DOS 5.0 command that lets you rename a directory. With DOS 6.0, however, you can rename a directory using the Move command.

The Create-directory function To create a directory, you first select the appropriate drive. Then, you select the directory you want the new directory to be subordinate to. If you're creating a top-level directory, you'll select the root directory. Next, you select the Create-directory function from the File menu. The DOS shell then displays the dialog box shown in figure 14-14. At this box, you enter the name of the new directory. After the function in figure 14-14 is executed, a directory named HSG will be created in the root directory.

How to use the most useful functions of the Options menu

Figure 14-15 shows the Options menu. When you pull down this menu, it offers the seven functions shown here. Generally, you use these functions to set up the DOS shell so it works the way you want it to. Although you probably won't need to do that often, you may occasionally want to change one of these options. So I'll explain when and how to use the most useful functions in this chapter. Then in the next chapter, I'll show you how to use the Enable-task-swapper function.

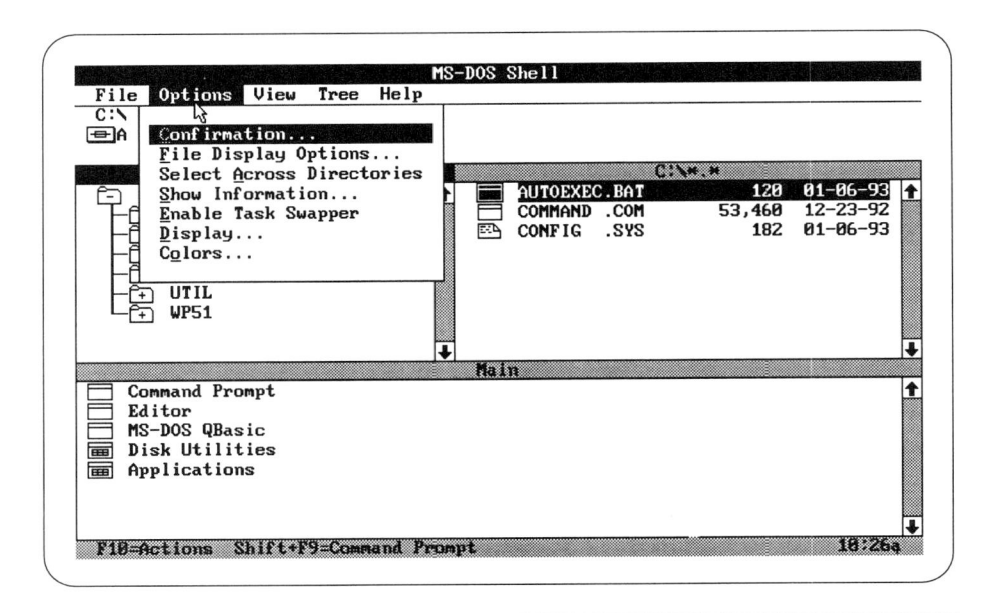

Figure 14-15 The Options menu

The Confirmation function Figure 14-16 shows the dialog box that's displayed when you select the Confirmation function from the Options menu. Here, an *X* next to the option indicates it's on. To turn an option on or off, you click on it with a mouse. With the keyboard, you use the cursor control keys to move the highlight from one option to the next, and you use the Space bar to turn an option on or off.

The Confirm-on-delete option specifies whether the DOS shell should ask for confirmation before it deletes a file. If this option is on, a dialog box like the one in part 2 of figure 14-6 is displayed each time a file is about to be deleted by the Delete function. As a general rule, you should leave this option on so you won't accidentally delete any files. However, as you become more familiar with the DOS shell, you may want to turn this option off.

The Confirm-on-replace option helps protect files from being accidentally replaced when you use the Copy and Move functions. When this option is on, a Copy or Move function asks for confirmation before replacing an existing file with a new file. In contrast, the DOS Copy and Move commands replace existing files without asking for confirmation. Although this option should be on most of the time, you may want to turn it off when you are deliberately replacing existing files with new ones of the same name.

The Confirm-on-mouse-operation option specifies whether the DOS shell should ask for confirmation before it executes a move or copy operation that you perform

How to use the DOS shell to manage directories and files   **251**

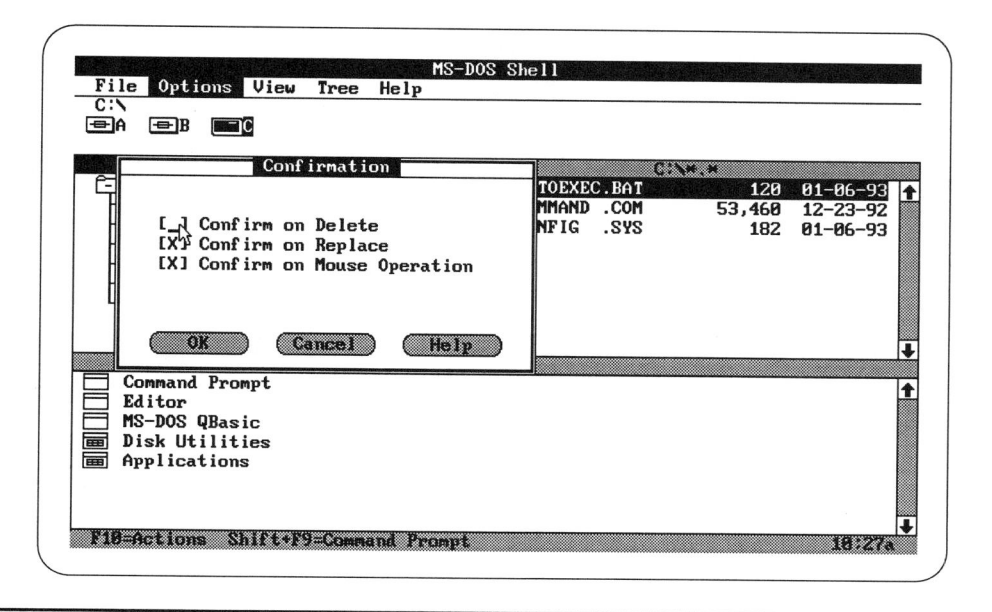

Figure 14-16   The dialog box for the Confirmation function

using the mouse techniques I showed you earlier. If this option is on, a dialog box is displayed before the function is executed. This box tells you whether you're copying or moving a file, and it gives you a chance to cancel the function. So I recommend that you keep this option on.

The File-display-options function   Figure 14-17 shows the dialog box that's displayed when you select the File-display-options function. The default setting for the Name field is *.*. That means all of the files in the current directory are displayed in the file-list area. However, you can change this default setting by entering a file name using wildcards. Here, for example, I entered *.COM to display only the files with an extension of COM. Figure 14-18 shows how the file list looks with this setting in effect.

If you want the files of a directory to be displayed in sequence by name, extension, date, size, or location in the directory, you can use the Sort-by fields in the dialog box. To select one of these fields with a mouse, you just click on the appropriate button. To select a field with the keyboard, you use the Tab key to activate the Sort-by portion of the dialog box. Then, you use the cursor control keys to select the field you want.

If you want to copy, move, rename, or delete files based on a wildcard specification, you can use this function to enter the wildcard specification. Then, you

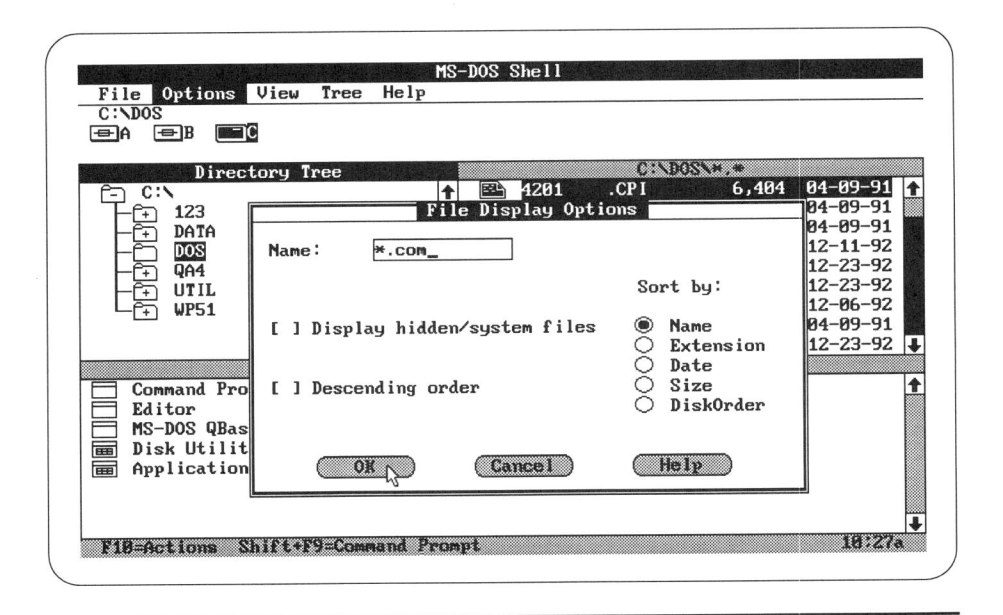

Figure 14-17 The dialog box for the File-display-options function

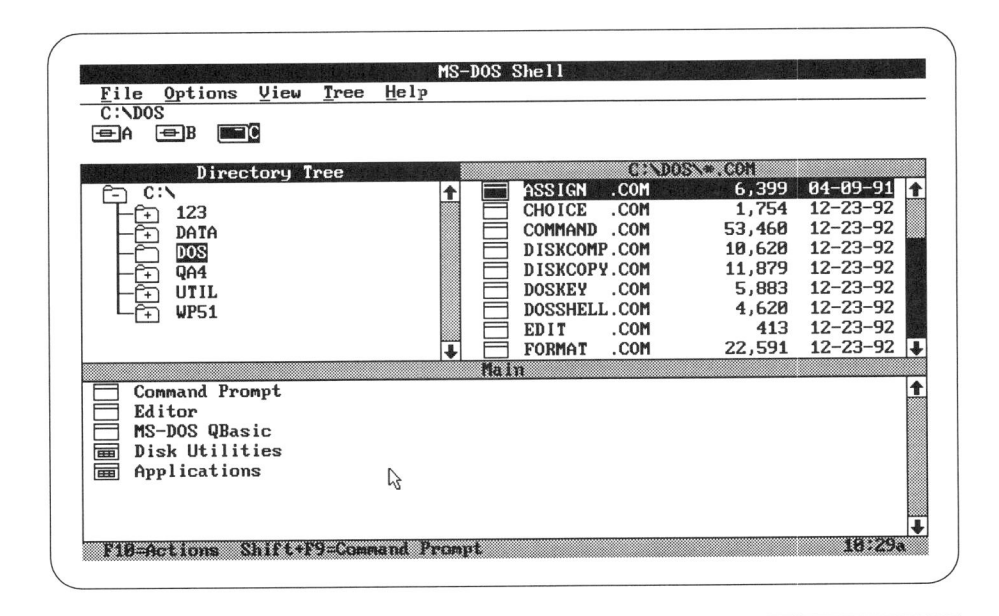

Figure 14-18 The file-list display that results from the selections in figure 14-17

How to use the DOS shell to manage directories and files   **253**

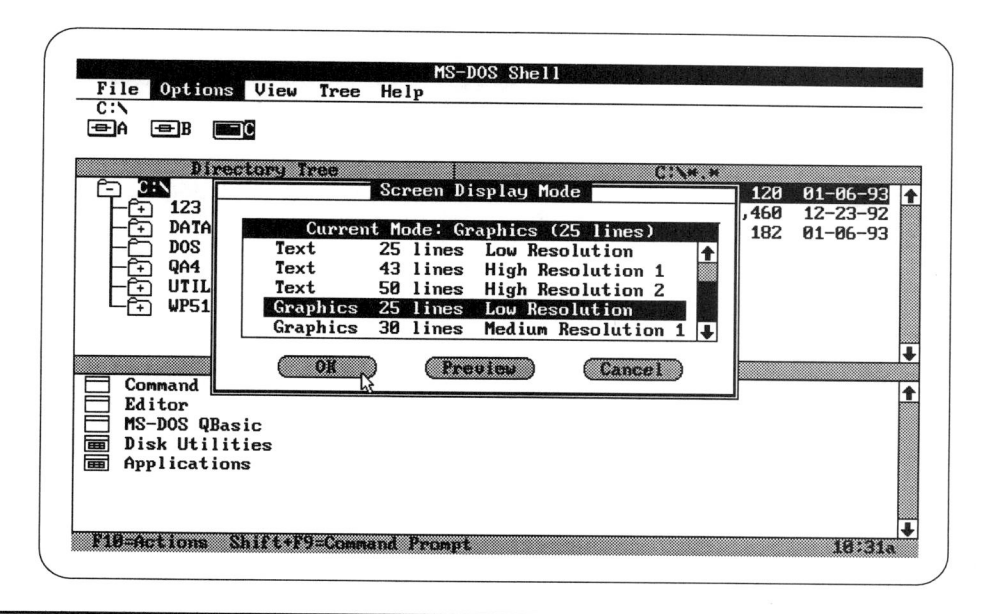

Figure 14-19   The dialog box for the Display function

can use the Select-all function of the File menu to select all the files that match the wildcard.

The Select-across-directories function   This function controls what happens to selected files when you change directories. If this function is off, all selected files are deselected when you change from one directory to another. That way, files from only one directory at a time can be selected. If this function is on, files are not deselected when you change directories. As a result, you can select files from more than one directory on your hard disk.

To turn on the Select-across-directories function, you execute it from the Option menu using either the mouse or the keyboard. When you do, a small dot appears next to the function name to show that it is on. To turn this function off, you execute it again. Although the Select-across-directories function should be off most of the time, you may want to use it occasionally for simplifying file maintenance.

The Display function   Figure 14-19 shows the dialog box that's displayed when you select the Display function. This box lets you specify whether you want to use *text* or *graphics mode* for the DOS shell screen. If your monitor can display graphics, you'll generally want to select this option because it can make the DOS shell easier to use. You can also specify the number of lines you want to display on your screen.

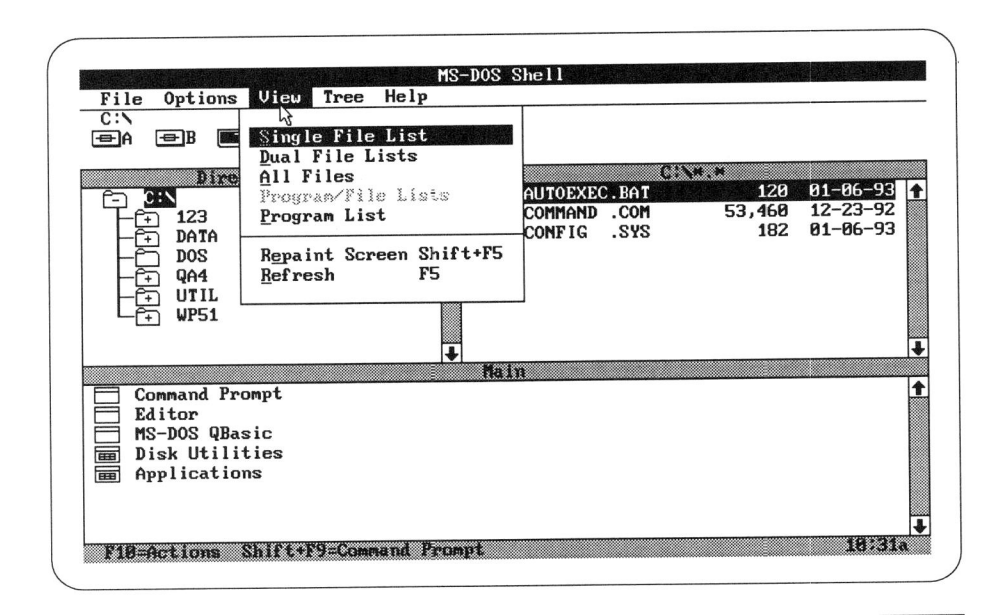

Figure 14-20 The View menu

The options that are available in figure 14-19 depend on the type of monitor you have. The options shown here, for instance, are the ones available with a VGA monitor. So if you have a different type of monitor, the DOS shell will offer you some different options.

How to use the most useful functions of the View menu

Figure 14-20 shows the seven functions available from the View menu. The first five functions change the format of the DOS shell screen. These different screen formats are called *views*. I'll present only four of the views here. I won't present the All-files view because it's too hard to use.

Before I present these views, you should know that if you change views, the new view remains in effect until you select another view. Even when you exit from the DOS shell and start it again, it won't return to the default view. Instead, it will use the view that was active when you last exited from the DOS shell.

The Single-file-list view Figure 14-21 shows the Single-file-list view. This view displays the directory-tree and file-list areas, but not the program-list area. As a result, you can see more files and directories on the screen than you can using the default view. Sometimes, this is helpful when you perform maintenance tasks that involve many files or directories.

How to use the DOS shell to manage directories and files   **255**

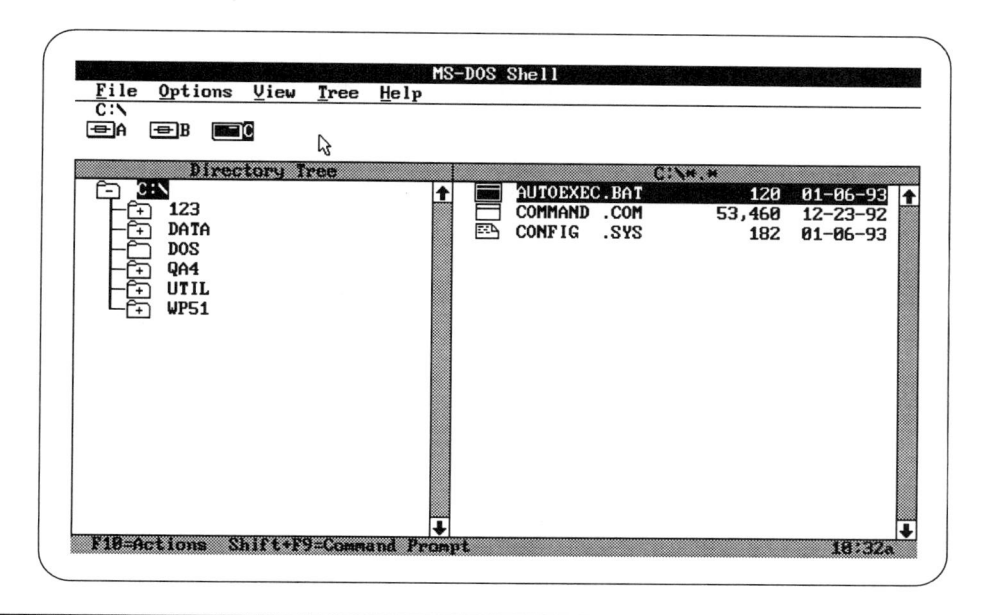

```
                          MS-DOS Shell
       File  Options  View  Tree  Help
       C:\
       [=]A   [=]B   [■]C
                   Directory Tree                        C:\*.*
          C:\                         ↑    AUTOEXEC.BAT      120   01-06-93  ↑
             ├─[+] 123                     COMMAND  .COM  53,460   12-23-92
             ├─[+] DATA                    CONFIG   .SYS     182   01-06-93
             ├─[+] DOS
             ├─[+] QA4
             ├─[+] UTIL
             └─[+] WP51




                                         ↓                                  ↓
       F10=Actions  Shift+F9=Command Prompt                          10:32a
```

Figure 14-21   How the screen looks in Single-file-list view

The Dual-file-lists view   Figure 14-22 shows the Dual-file-lists view. This view lets you display the files from two directories at the same time. As a result, the Dual-file-lists view makes it easier for you to compare the files in two directories and to copy or move files from one directory or drive to another.

The Program/File-lists view   Figure 14-23 shows the Program/File-lists view. You should already recognize this view because it's the one I've used throughout this section. It's also the default view, so it's the one that's active when you start the DOS shell for the first time.

The Program-list view   Figure 14-24 shows the Program-list view. As you can see, it displays only the program-list area. As a result, this view is most useful if you want to set up a PC for other people to use, and you don't want them to manage the files and directories on the hard disk.

The Refresh and Repaint functions   The Refresh and Repaint functions on the View menu perform operations that help keep the shell working correctly. The Refresh function causes the DOS shell to rescan the disk to find out what directories and files are on the disk. You may need to use this function in three situations: (1) if you exit temporarily from the DOS shell to get to the command prompt and enter a command that changes the directories or files; (2) if you execute a program or

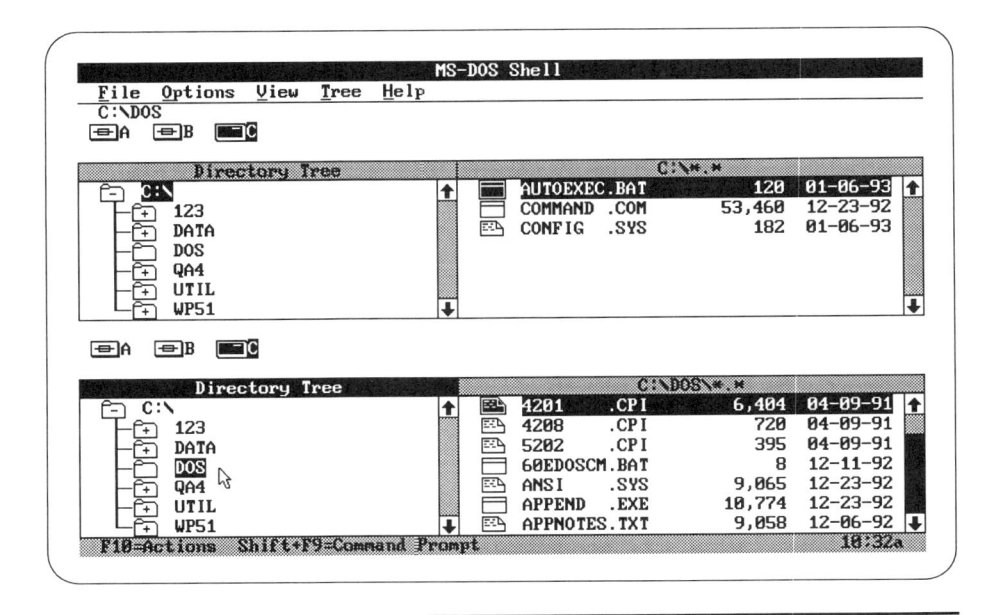

Figure 14-22 How the screen looks in Dual-file-lists view

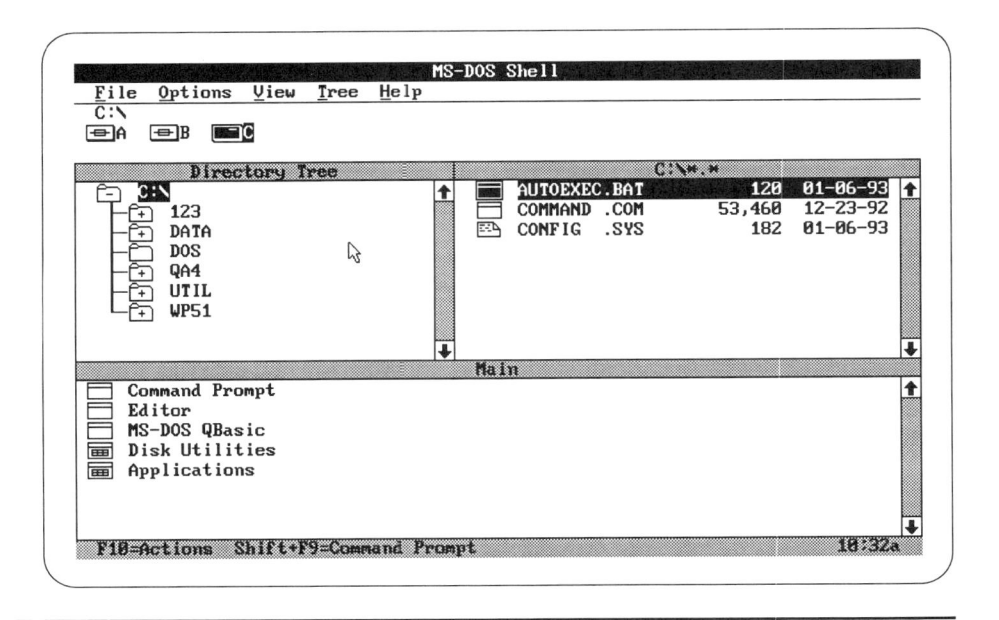

Figure 14-23 How the screen looks in Program/File-lists view

How to use the DOS shell to manage directories and files   **257**

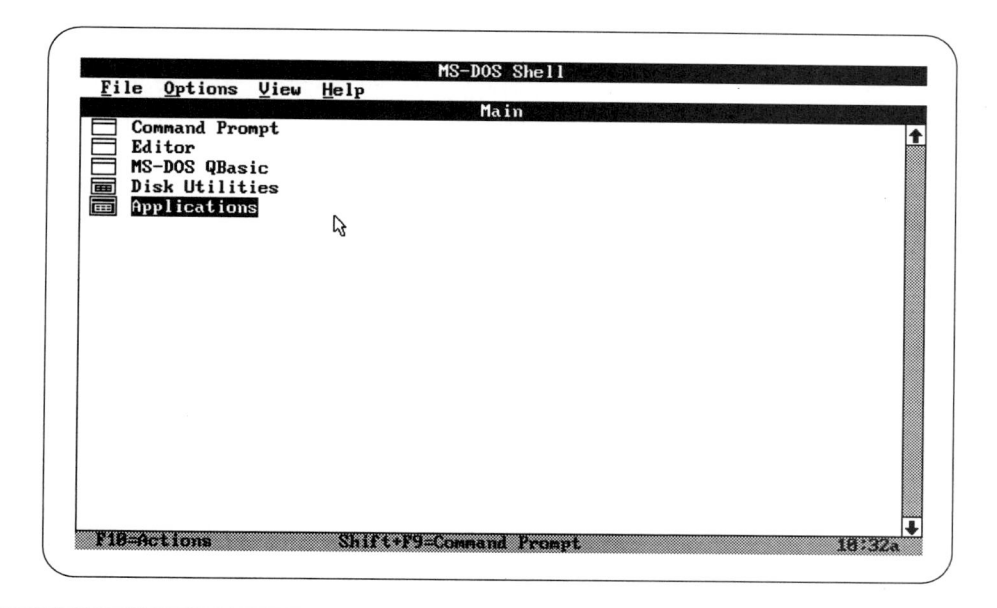

```
                              MS-DOS Shell
        File  Options  View  Help
                                 Main
           Command Prompt
           Editor
           MS-DOS QBasic
           Disk Utilities
           Applications


   F10=Actions          Shift+F9=Command Prompt              10:32a
```

Figure 14-24   How the screen looks in Program-list view

command from the file or program list that changes the directories or files; and (3) if the current drive is a diskette drive and you change the diskette. You need to refresh the display in these situations because the shell doesn't know that the information on the disk has changed. That's because even though the shell may be active when these functions are performed, the functions are actually performed outside of the shell.

The Repaint function redraws the DOS shell screen in the event that the screen is corrupted by unwanted characters. Since this should happen rarely, you won't have to use this function as often as you use the Refresh function.

Some perspective on the DOS shell

If you compare the capabilities that are provided by the DOS shell for managing directories and files with the DOS commands that are available at the command prompt, you'll realize that the shell can make it easier for you to manage your directories and files. The directory-tree area makes it easy for you to see, modify, and use the structure of your directories. The selection techniques make it easy for you to select the files for a function. And the pull-down menus make it easy for you to start functions after you've selected the files. As a result, it's easy to create, delete, and rename directories when you use the DOS shell. It's also easy to copy, move, delete, and rename files.

In practice, though, you'll probably use some combination of shell functions and DOS commands for managing directories and files. If, for example, you want to delete all of the files in a directory, you can do so by entering just one Delete command at the DOS prompt. And if you want to copy all of the files in a directory to a diskette, you can do so by entering just one Copy command at the DOS prompt.

Terms

dragging a mouse
hex code
text mode
graphics mode
view

Objectives

1. Use the functions of the Options and View menus to set up the DOS shell so it works the way you want it to.

2. Given file specifications, use the appropriate functions of the File menu to move, copy, delete, or rename one or more files.

3. Given a directory specification, use the appropriate functions of the File menu to delete it, rename it, or create it.

Chapter 15

How to use the DOS shell to switch between programs quickly

If you frequently switch from one program to another, the DOS shell provides a feature called the Task Swapper that can help you switch between programs more quickly. The capability this feature provides is commonly referred to as *task switching* or *task swapping*. This feature isn't available with earlier versions of DOS, and you can use this feature only through the DOS shell. Also, this feature may not work with older versions of some application programs, so there's a chance that you won't be able to use it with all of your application programs.

In this chapter, you'll learn how to use the Task Swapper. First, I'll explain how the Task Swapper works. Next, you'll learn how to activate the Task Swapper and switch between application programs. Then, you'll learn how to set up and use the Task Swapper to switch between programs more efficiently. Because you've already learned the basic techniques for using the DOS shell, you should be able to move quickly through this chapter.

An introduction to the Task Swapper

When you use the Task Swapper, you can load two or more application programs and switch between them without having to exit from one program before you switch to the next. Each program that's running under the Task Swapper is called an *active task*. You can, for example, start *WordPerfect* and begin work on a report. Then, you can start *Lotus 1-2-3* and load a spreadsheet file to review some data. When you use the Task Swapper to switch back to *WordPerfect*, it returns you to the place where you were last working on the report. As a result, you don't have to start *WordPerfect*, load the report, and find your place again.

Figure 15-1 illustrates how this process works. When the first task is active, *WordPerfect* and a working document are loaded and are running in internal memory, while the files for the second task, *Lotus 1-2-3* and a spreadsheet, are stored on disk.

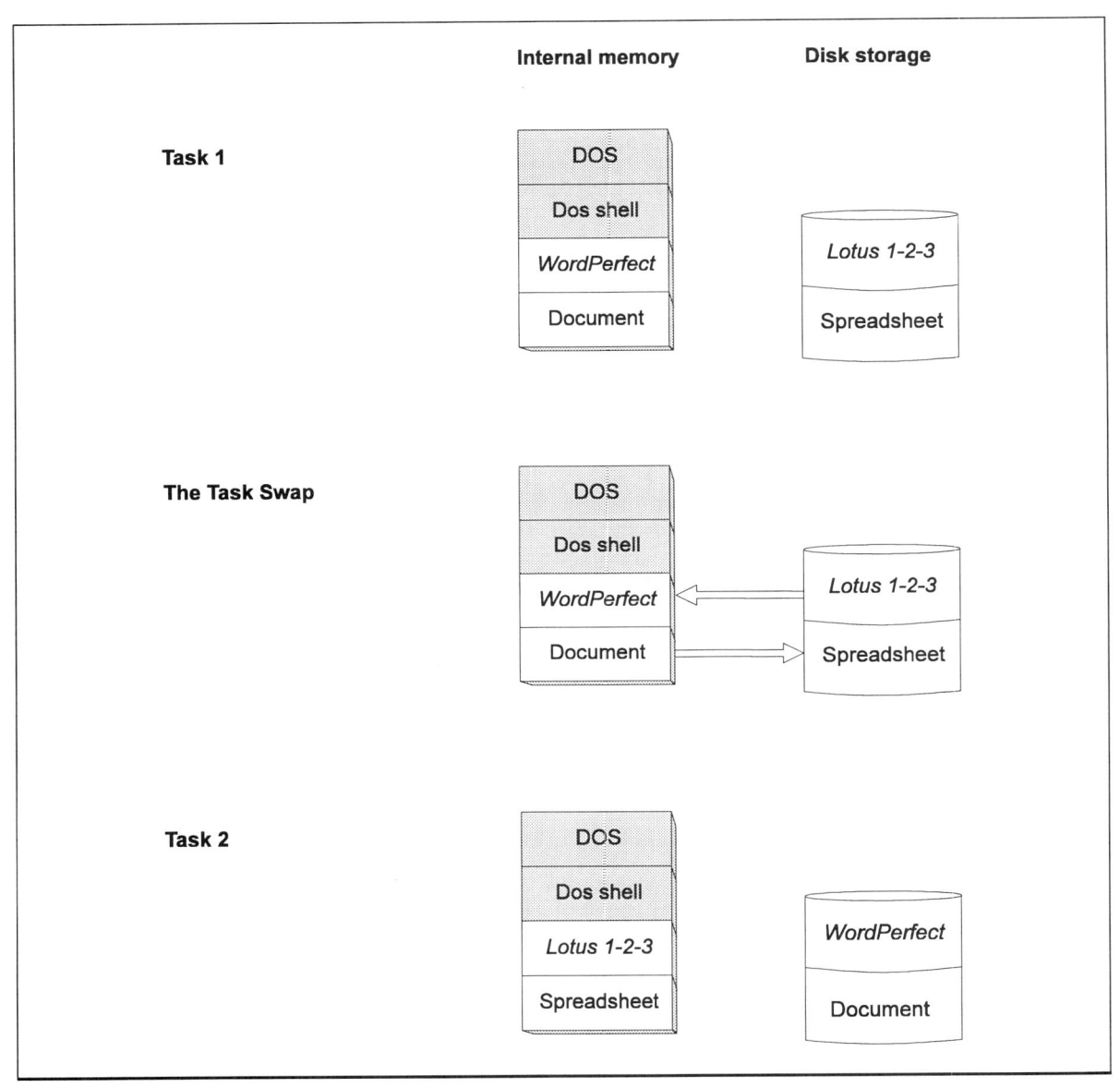

Figure 15-1 How the Task Swapper uses internal memory and disk storage to switch between two programs

When you perform the task swap, *WordPerfect* and the working document are transferred to disk storage, and *Lotus 1-2-3* and the current spreadsheet file are transferred to internal memory. When you switch back to *WordPerfect*, the process is repeated.

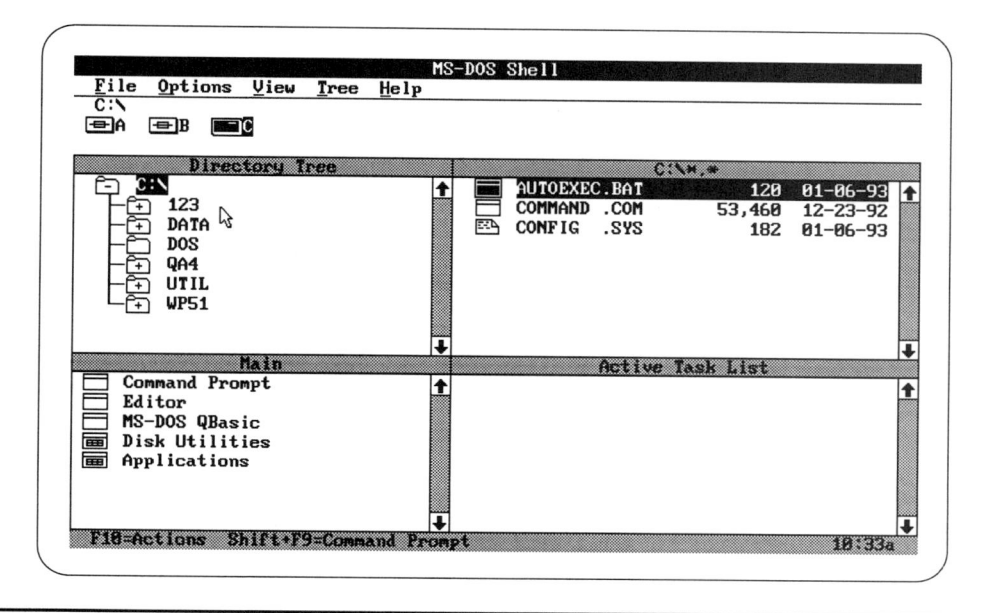

Figure 15-2 The DOS 5.0/6.0 shell with the Task Swapper enabled

How to use the Task Swapper

To use the Task Swapper, you begin by enabling it. Next, you load your application programs so they become active tasks. Then, after you learn a few keystroke combinations to switch between active tasks, you're ready to use the Task Swapper.

How to enable the Task Swapper To enable the Task Swapper, you select the Enable-task-swapper function from the Options menu. The DOS shell then displays an *active task list* in the bottom right portion of the screen, as shown in figure 15-2. After the Task Swapper is enabled, you can load your application programs into it.

How to load programs and switch between them In figure 15-3, you can see that two application programs have been loaded into the active task list. To load a program, you start it from the program list. If you have a mouse, just double-click on the appropriate program in the program list. Or if you're using the keyboard, highlight the appropriate program and press the Enter key. The DOS shell then starts the program and automatically adds it to the active task list. To load another program, you first use the Ctrl+Esc keystroke combination to switch back to the DOS shell. Then, you start the next program you want from the program list.

262   Chapter 15

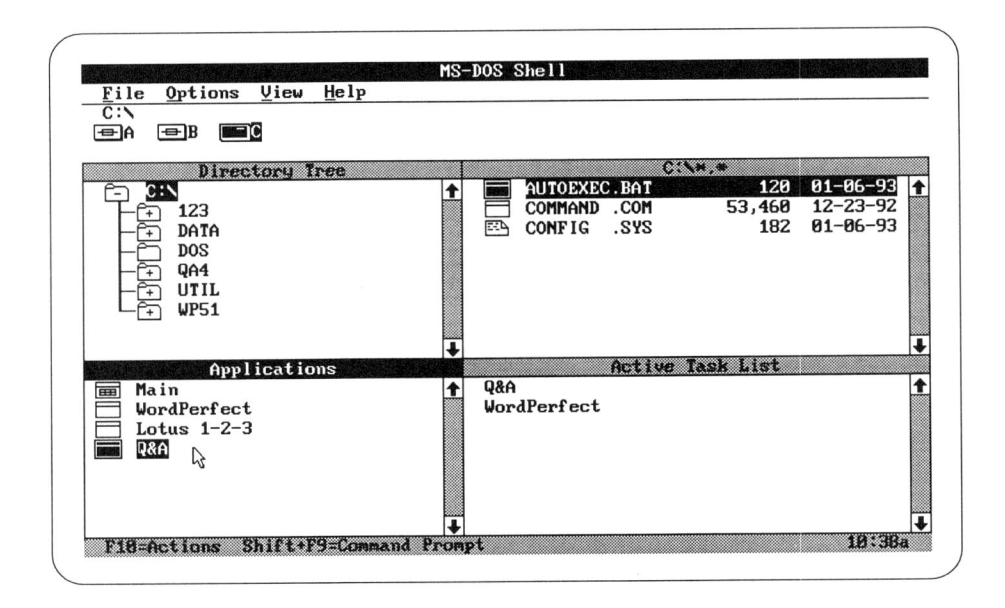

Figure 15-3   Two application programs that have been loaded in the active task list

After you've loaded your programs, you can switch between them using the active task list instead of the program list. To switch to the *WordPerfect* task in figure 15-3, for example, you just double-click on the *WordPerfect* entry in the active task list. Then, when you want to switch to the next task, you use the Ctrl+Esc key combination to return to the DOS shell. Now, you can switch to *Q&A* by double clicking on the *Q&A* task entry.

How to switch between programs more efficiently

The Task Swapper also lets you switch between active tasks without using the DOS shell as an intermediate step. To do that, you use special keystroke combinations that DOS 5.0 and 6.0 provide. Or you can assign your own keystroke combinations to each program.

Special keystroke combinations   Figure 15-4 presents the keystroke combinations you can use to switch between programs. You'll probably use the first two most often. The Ctrl+Esc combination always switches you back to the DOS shell. The Alt+Tab key combination switches you back to the most recent task. If you just used the DOS shell, for example, this key combination will return you to the shell. But if you switched from another application program, it will return you to that program. With the Alt+Tab key combination, you can also cycle through the

Keystrokes	Functions
Ctrl+Esc	Switches from the current application program to the DOS 5.0/6.0 shell.
Alt+Tab	As you hold down the Alt key and repeatedly press the Tab key, you cycle through the active task list. As the list cycles, the title of each program is displayed at the top of the screen. When you release the Alt key, the Task Swapper switches you to the program you selected.
Alt+Esc	Switches to the next application program on the active task list.
Shift+Alt+Esc	Switches to the previous application program on the active task list.

Figure 15-4 The special keystrokes you can use to switch between programs

programs on the active task list by holding down the Alt key as you repeatedly press the Tab key. Each time you press the Tab key, it shows the title of the next active task at the top of the screen. When you release the Alt key, you're switched to the task that's displayed.

The last two key combinations are Alt+Esc and Shift+Alt+Esc. You can use these to switch to the next program on the active task list or to the previous program on the active task list. Most of the time, though, it's easier to switch tasks using the Alt+Tab key combination than using either of these two.

How to assign a keystroke combination to a program In addition to the keystrokes you've learned so far, you can assign a unique keystroke combination to a program. You can, for example, assign the keystroke combination Alt+W to *WordPerfect*. Then, whenever *WordPerfect* is in the active task list, you can switch directly to it by pressing the Alt+W key combination. Note that if you assign a keystroke combination to a program while the program is in the active task list, you can't use the keystroke combination until you unload the program and load it again.

Figure 15-5 shows the dialog box you use to assign a keystroke combination to a program. To get to this box, you first activate the program-list area and select the appropriate program from the list. Then, after you pull down the File menu, you select the Properties function. In the dialog box, you use the Application-shortcut-key entry to assign a keystroke combination to the program. To do this, you press the actual keystroke combination you want to use. You can use the Alt, Ctrl, or Shift key in combination with another key.

Since you learned how to use the first three entries of this box in chapter 13 to create an option for a program list, most of this procedure should be familiar. In fact, now that you know about assigning key combinations, you'll probably make the assignment when you create the option.

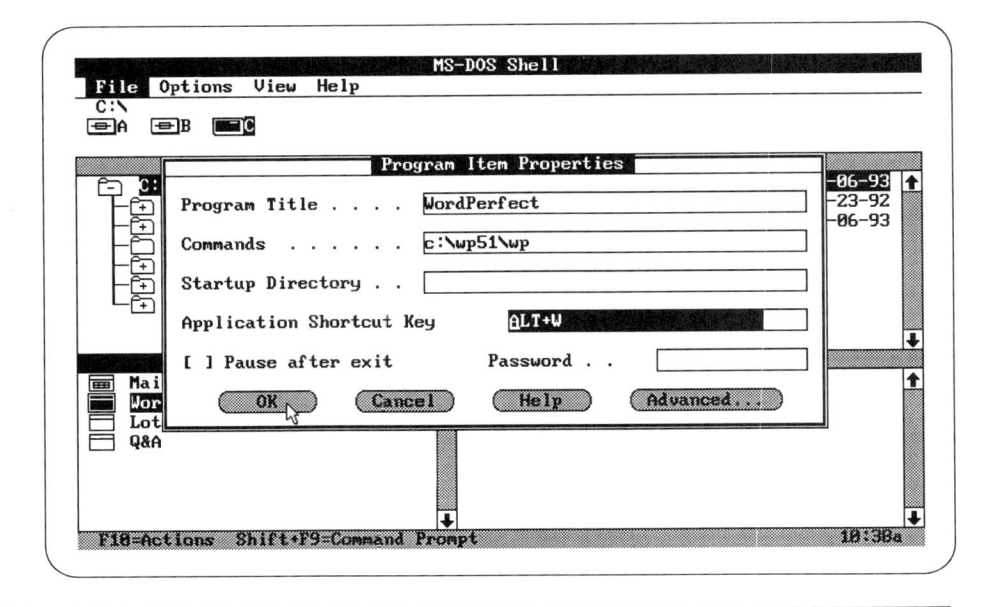

Figure 15-5 The dialog box that you use to assign a keystroke combination to a program

Figure 15-6 shows how programs are displayed on the active task list after you've assigned a keystroke combination to them. This list shows that *WordPerfect* is started by the Alt+W key combination, and that *Q&A* is started by the Alt+A key combination.

Some perspective on the Task Swapper

Without much trouble, you should be able to use the task swapping capabilities of the DOS shell. If you occasionally need to switch between two or more programs, the Task Swapper can help you work more efficiently. However, on some PCs the Task Swapper is just too slow to be practical. In addition, the Task Swapper may not work correctly with some older versions of application programs. As a result, you may find that you're better off running only one program at a time.

If you have a 386 or 486 PC with at least 2MB of memory, you may want to consider a utility that provides true *multi-tasking* capabilities. These utilities actually let two or more application programs run concurrently on your PC. Consequently, you can view and run two or more programs in small windows, each of which is displayed on a portion of the screen. This makes it possible to transfer data between two programs, and it makes it easier to switch between programs quickly. Also, these utilities often let your application programs run more efficiently. Today, the most popular multi-tasking utility is Microsoft *Windows*.

How to use the DOS shell to switch between programs quickly **265**

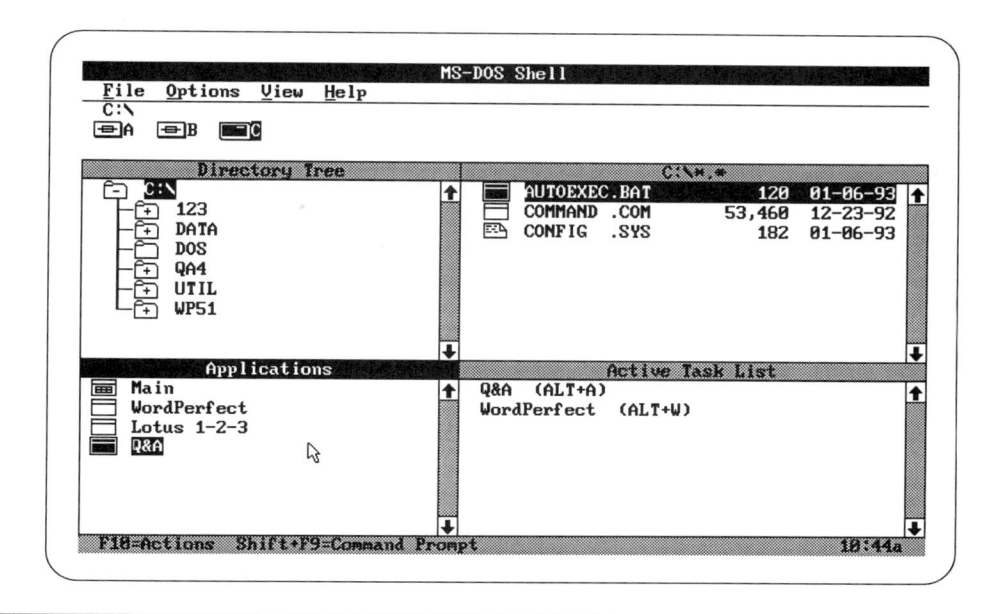

```
┌─────────────────────── MS-DOS Shell ───────────────────────┐
│ File  Options  View  Help                                  │
│ C:\                                                        │
│ [=]A  [=]B  [=]C                                           │
│ ┌───── Directory Tree ─────┐ ┌───────── C:\*.* ──────────┐ │
│ │ ┌─ C:\                   │ │ AUTOEXEC.BAT   120 01-06-93│ │
│ │ ├[+] 123                 │ │ COMMAND .COM 53,460 12-23-92│ │
│ │ ├[+] DATA                │ │ CONFIG  .SYS   182 01-06-93│ │
│ │ ├[+] DOS                 │ │                           │ │
│ │ ├[+] QA4                 │ │                           │ │
│ │ ├[+] UTIL                │ │                           │ │
│ │ └[+] WP51                │ │                           │ │
│ └──────────────────────────┘ └───────────────────────────┘ │
│ ┌────── Applications ──────┐ ┌────── Active Task List ───┐ │
│ │ [=] Main                 │ │ Q&A         (ALT+A)       │ │
│ │ [ ] WordPerfect          │ │ WordPerfect (ALT+W)       │ │
│ │ [ ] Lotus 1-2-3          │ │                           │ │
│ │ [=] Q&A                  │ │                           │ │
│ └──────────────────────────┘ └───────────────────────────┘ │
│ F10=Actions  Shift+F9=Command Prompt              10:44a   │
└────────────────────────────────────────────────────────────┘
```

Figure 15-6 Two programs that have had keystroke combinations assigned to them

Terms

task switching
task swapping
active task
active task list
multi-tasking

Objectives

1. Describe how the task swapper uses internal memory and disk storage to switch between tasks.

2. After enabling the task swapper, load two or more programs from the program-list area and switch between them.

3. If you frequently have two or more programs in the active task list at the same time, assign keystroke combinations to these programs.

Section 5

Some additional perspective

Many DOS users will never need the DOS commands and features that aren't presented in the first four sections of this book. But some users will. So the one chapter in this section introduces you to the DOS commands and features that aren't a part of "the least you need to know about DOS."

If you need one or more of these commands and features, you can probably learn them from your DOS manual. A more efficient way to learn them, though, is to use *The Only DOS Book You'll Ever Need*. That book covers all of the features described here in detail. And it focuses on the practical application of these features so that you can make more effective use of your PC. If you're interested in *The Only DOS Book You'll Ever Need*, you'll find information on it at the back of this book.

Chapter 16

Other DOS features that you ought to be aware of

When you master the DOS commands and features I've presented in the first four sections of this book, you'll be able to use DOS effectively. You'll be able to manage the files and directories on your hard disk, start your application programs, back up the data on your hard disk, and perform many other daily chores associated with using a PC. In short, you'll be a competent, self-sufficient PC user.

However, this book has focused only on the most essential DOS skills, skills that require you to learn only a small subset of DOS commands and features. If you page through the DOS manual or the on-line help available with DOS 5.0 and 6.0, you'll notice that DOS provides many commands and features that aren't covered in this book. In fact, this book has presented only about one-third of the commands that are available under DOS. I omitted most of those commands and features because they're obsolete or so specialized that they're useful only in unusual situations. But I omitted others not because they aren't useful, but because they aren't essential. They aren't a part of "the least you need to know about DOS." But that doesn't mean you might not need to use one or more of them on occasion.

If you're interested in learning about the other useful features DOS provides beyond what I've presented so far in this book, read through this chapter. It won't teach you how to use these features. But it will let you know what features are available so you can decide if you should invest time in learning them. If so, you can then consult a more advanced DOS book, such as *The Only DOS Book You'll Ever Need*.

The DOS 6.0 utilities

DOS has never been everything people have wanted it to be, so utility programs have become one of the best-selling categories of software for DOS systems. Many utility programs duplicate functions that are already provided by DOS, but improve upon them. For example, backup utilities duplicate the function of the DOS Backup command, but are faster, easier to use, and more flexible. Other utilities provide functions that DOS doesn't, such as checking your hard disk for potential problems or

DOS 6.0 utility	Function
DoubleSpace	Increases the capacity of your hard drive by compressing data.
Microsoft Anti-Virus	Detects and removes computer viruses from your system.
Microsoft Defrag	Eliminates file fragmentation so that the allocation units for a single file aren't spread out all over the disk.
Interlnk	Lets you connect a portable computer to your desktop computer.
Power	Shuts down certain system functions on a portable computer when the system is idle to save battery power.
Microsoft Diagnostics	Displays information about your computer system's configuration.

Figure 16-1 The DOS 6.0 utilities for advanced functions

compressing data to increase the amount of information you can store on your hard disk.

The two best known makers of utility programs are Symantec, maker of *The Norton Utilities*, and Central Point Software, maker of *PC Tools*. Both *The Norton Utilities* and *PC Tools* are comprehensive utility collections, bundling a variety of useful utility programs into a single package. With DOS 6.0, Microsoft has included scaled-down versions of some of the utility programs made by Symantec and Central Point Software. You've already been introduced to one of these utility programs: Microsoft Backup, a scaled-down version of *Norton Backup* by Symantec.

In addition, DOS 6.0 includes a handful of new utility programs developed by Microsoft. Together, the utilities licensed by Microsoft from Symantec and Central Point Software and the new Microsoft utility programs are sometimes called *the DOS 6.0 utilities*. Besides Microsoft Backup, these include the utilities listed in figure 16-1: DoubleSpace, Microsoft Anti-Virus, Microsoft Defrag, Interlnk, Power, and Microsoft Diagnostics. I'll briefly describe each of these utilities here. Then, if you want to know more about how to use them, you'll find an entire chapter on each one in *The Only DOS Book You'll Ever Need*.

DoubleSpace Figure 16-2 shows the opening screen of DoubleSpace, a DOS 6.0 utility that significantly increases the capacity of a disk drive by compressing the data that's stored on it. Although the degree of compression depends on the contents of your files, DoubleSpace can typically double the capacity of your disk drive. As a result, if you're running out of space on your hard disk, DoubleSpace is an excellent alternative to purchasing a larger hard drive.

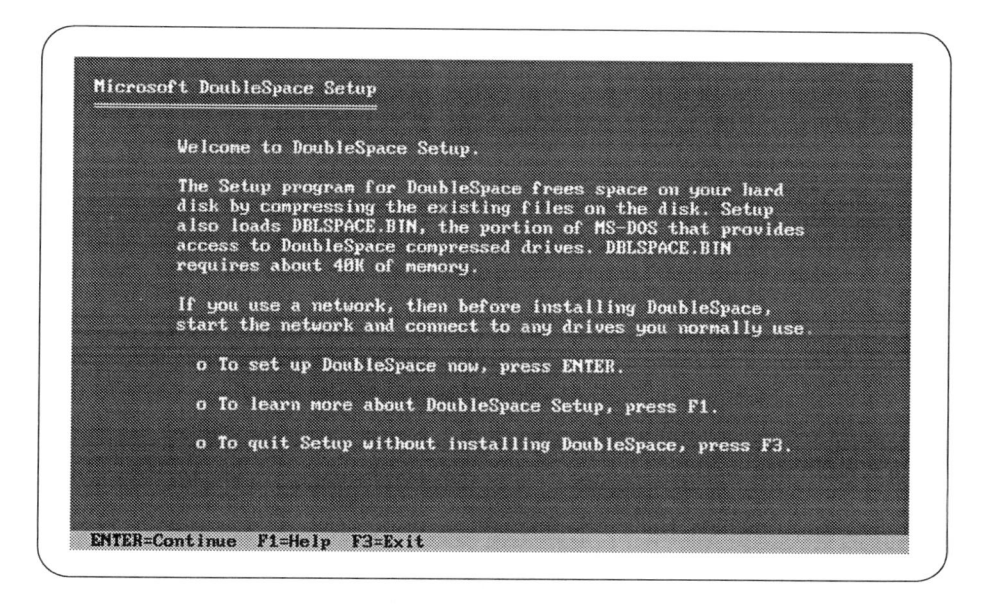

Figure 16-2   DoubleSpace increases the capacity of your hard drive (DOS 6.0)

DoubleSpace compression is entirely transparent to your application programs. When you use DoubleSpace, DOS automatically compresses data as it writes it to the disk and automatically decompresses data as it reads it from the disk. That way, your application programs are unaware that the data is stored on disk in a compressed format.

Contrary to what you might expect, DoubleSpace probably won't slow down your computer, either. Although it does take a small amount of time to compress and decompress data as it's written to and read from the disk, this overhead is offset by the fact that fewer read and write operations are required. To illustrate, suppose a 20KB word processing document is compressed so that it requires only 10KB of disk storage. When you open this document, DOS must access the disk to read the file. In uncompressed form, DOS would have to read 20KB from the disk. In compressed form, DOS only has to read 10KB from the disk. In most cases, the amount of time saved by having to read less data from the disk is more than the extra time needed to decompress the data. The net result is that DoubleSpace not only increases your disk capacity, but often speeds up disk access as well.

If you purchased a new computer with DOS 6.0 installed, odds are that DoubleSpace has already been set up for you. If not, you can install it yourself by typing DBLSPACE at the command prompt and following the instructions on the screen.

Microsoft Anti-Virus Computer viruses have received a lot of publicity in recent years. Unfortunately, much of the information spread about computer viruses in the press has been confusing or misleading. As a result, many computer users don't have a clear idea of what a computer virus is, how computer viruses spread, and what computer viruses can and cannot do. And they aren't certain whether or not they should be concerned about protecting their systems from computer viruses.

Simply put, a *computer virus* is a special type of computer program that's designed so that it can reproduce itself. This self-replicating capability is what makes computer viruses potentially harmful. Once a virus is present on a computer system, it will attempt to infect other computer systems, often by copying itself to every diskette accessed by the computer. Then, if any of those diskettes are used in another computer system, that computer becomes infected, and the virus spreads. Alternatively, if the infected computer is attached to a local area network, the virus may try to spread to other computers via the network.

Most computer viruses do more than just secretly replicate themselves. After a certain time period, on a particular date, or when a certain event occurs, most viruses reveal their presence. Some simply display a message, such as "Gotcha!" Others do obvious damage to your system by reformatting your hard disk or scrambling your hard disk so it is completely inaccessible. Still others do more subtle damage, such as randomly linking the same allocation units to two or more files (this is called *cross-linking* files). You won't notice this problem until you try to access the corrupted files.

Figure 16-3 shows the opening screen of Microsoft Anti-Virus, which comes with DOS 6.0. You can use Microsoft Anti-Virus periodically to detect and remove any computer viruses that have found their way onto your system. And Microsoft Anti-Virus comes with a program you can start from your AUTOEXEC.BAT file to constantly monitor your computer for signs of computer viruses.

Microsoft Anti-Virus is a scaled-back version of Central Point Software's *Central Point Antivirus*. It's important to realize, though, that it's not scaled back in terms of the number of viruses it can detect or the type of virus protection it provides. The main difference is that Microsoft Anti-Virus is designed for individual computers, while *Central Point Antivirus* has advanced features that make it more useful on computer networks.

Microsoft Defrag As you use your PC to create and delete files, a condition known as *fragmentation* is likely to occur. Fragmentation occurs when the allocation units for a particular file aren't adjacent to one another. This happens because when DOS creates a new file, it uses the first available disk space it finds. If this space isn't large enough for the entire file, DOS stores as much of the file as it can and looks for the next available space. DOS continues in this way until the entire file is stored on disk.

Fragmentation is not a problem in itself, but it can contribute to other disk problems. Every disk contains a special area called the *File Allocation Table (FAT)* that keeps tracks of all the allocation units on the disk. Now, suppose your disk's FAT

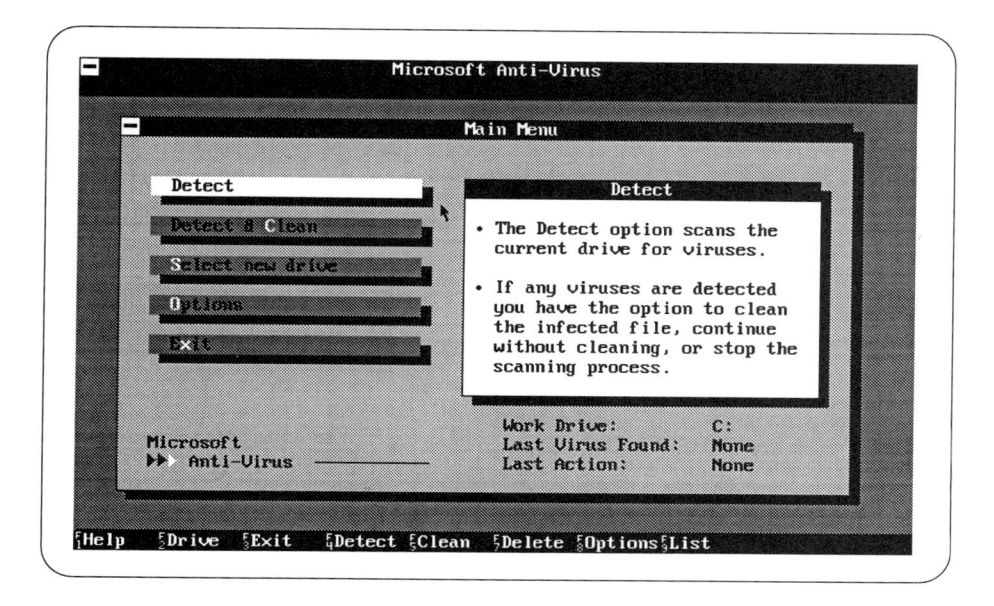

Figure 16-3 Microsoft Anti-Virus detects and removes computer viruses from your system (DOS 6.0)

becomes scrambled, resulting in cross-linked files or *lost clusters* (allocation units that contain data but aren't part of any file). The problem will be more difficult to correct if the disk has a lot of fragmentation. Fragmentation also reduces the chances of successfully undeleting a file (I'll tell you about the Undelete command in a few minutes).

Fragmentation can also slow down the performance of a hard disk. If, for example, a file is divided into three fragments, the read/write mechanism of the disk drive has to move to three different disk locations in order to read the file. If the file isn't fragmented, the read/write mechanism has to move only once. When many of the files on a disk are heavily fragmented, the decrease in speed can be noticeable.

Before DOS 6.0, there were only two ways to restore a hard disk to an unfragmented condition: (1) do a complete backup of your hard disk, reformat the hard disk, then do a complete restore; or (2) purchase a commercial disk utility such as *PC Tools* or *The Norton Utilities*. Both of these utility packages include programs that can *defragment* a disk in place. Now, you can defragment a disk using Microsoft Defrag, as shown in figure 16-4.

Microsoft Defrag is actually a subset of the *SpeedDisk* program that comes with *The Norton Utilities*. Microsoft licensed the program from Symantec. Although the full-blown *SpeedDisk* program is much more powerful, Microsoft Defrag does its basic task of defragmenting your hard disk well.

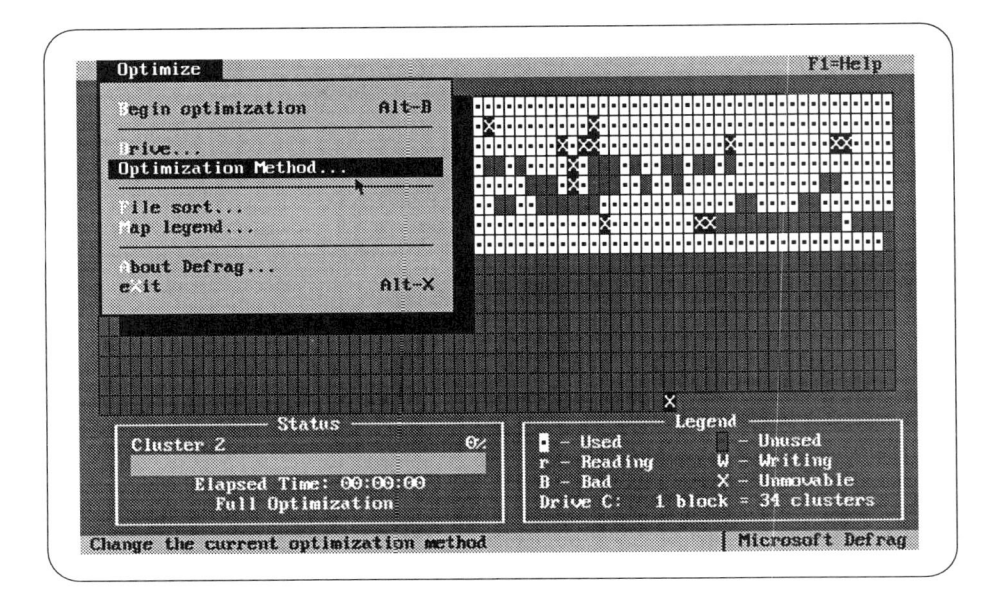

Figure 16-4   Microsoft Defrag improves the operation of your hard disk by eliminating fragmentation (DOS 6.0)

Interlnk and Power   DOS 6.0 includes two new utility programs that are designed for users of portable computers. The first, called Interlnk (pronounced "Interlink"), lets you connect two computers together as shown in figure 16-5. Then, you can copy files between the two computers or access one of the computer's printers from the other computer. For example, you might take a portable computer with you on a sales trip, using it to record orders, take notes, and keep track of trip expenses. When you return to the office, you can use Interlnk to copy the files from your portable to your desktop computer.

You can also use Interlnk to copy files from the desktop computer to the portable. For example, you might copy a report document from your desktop computer to your portable computer so you can work on it during your trip. Once you invest the time to get Interlnk set up properly, I think you'll find it's actually easier to share even small files using Interlnk than it is to copy them from one computer to the other using diskettes.

Interlnk is similar to commercial file transfer utilities such as Traveling Software's *Laplink Pro*. Because *Laplink Pro* is both faster and more flexible than Interlnk, you should consider using it instead of Interlnk if you frequently need to exchange data between a portable and a desktop computer.

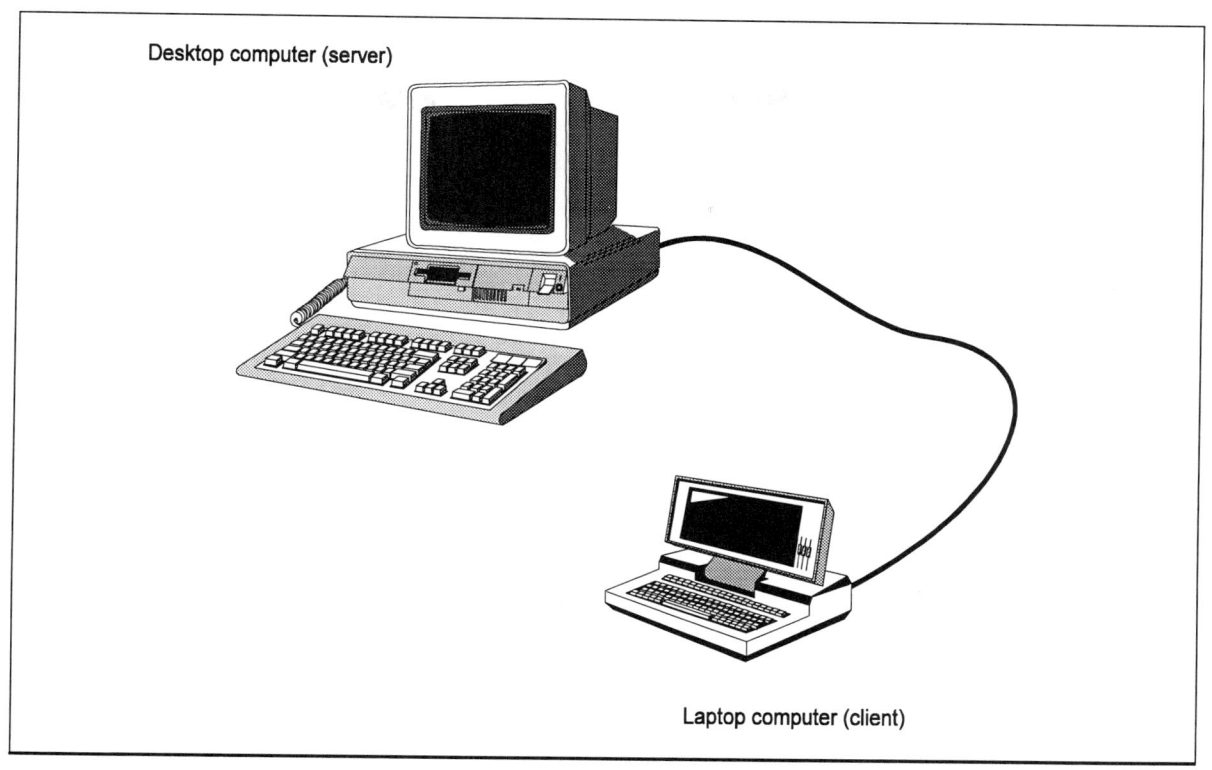

Figure 16-5 Interlnk lets you connect a portable computer to your desktop computer (DOS 6.0)

The second program for portable computers, called Power, extends the life of your portable's battery by shutting down certain system functions when the system is idle. If your portable computer conforms to a standard recently developed by Intel and Microsoft called Advanced Power Management, or APM, Power can extend the useful life of your battery by as much as 25 percent.

Microsoft Diagnostics   Microsoft Diagnostics, or *MSD*, is a utility program that displays useful information about your computer system's configuration. Figure 16-6 shows the opening MSD screen. Here, you can see the kind of information displayed by MSD. Each of the selection items on this screen (Computer, Memory, Video, and so on) leads to a detailed display of information about the indicated feature. For example, you can select Disk Drives to see detailed information about your disk drives.

MSD is useful when you're installing new hardware and need to resolve conflicts with existing hardware components, when you're trying to optimize the way your computer uses its memory, or when you just want to learn more about how your

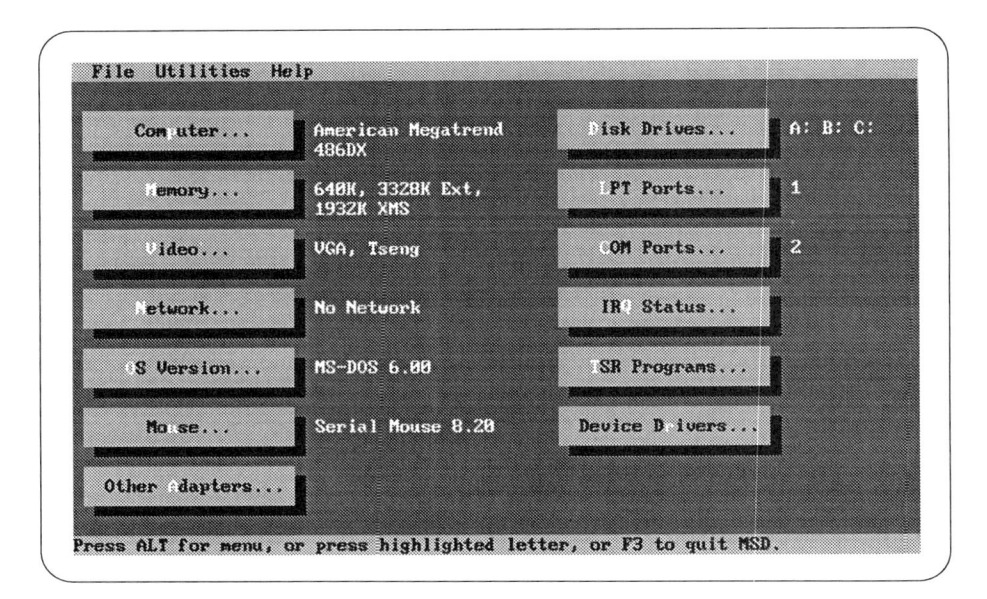

Figure 16-6 Microsoft Diagnostics displays information about your computer system (DOS 6.0)

computer works. Although both *PC Tools* and *The Norton Utilities* have similar features, Microsoft developed MSD on its own.

Advanced DOS commands and techniques

As I said earlier, DOS provides many additional commands besides the ones I've presented so far in this book. Here, I'll introduce you to the most useful of these commands. Although it's not easy to categorize these commands, I've classified them as commands you use to manipulate files, commands you use to recover files that have been lost or damaged, commands you use in batch files, and miscellaneous DOS commands. I'll also briefly describe three command-processing techniques that you can use with most DOS commands: redirection, filters, and piping.

Commands you use to manipulate files   You already know how to use basic DOS commands to manipulate files: Copy, Rename, Delete, and so on. Figure 16-7 lists seven advanced DOS commands you can use to manipulate files. The one I use most often is the Attrib command. It lets you change the *attributes* associated with a file. For example, you can make a file read-only by issuing an Attrib command, and then no one can change or delete the file. The Attrib command can

Command	Function
Append	Creates a directory search path used to locate data files (similar to the search path established by the Path command to locate program files).
Attrib	Changes the attributes of one or more files, such as whether the files are read-only files.
Comp	Compares files byte-by-byte.
Diskcomp	Compares the contents of two diskettes.
FC	An enhanced file-compare command; lets you control whether the compare operation treats upper- and lower-case letters as if they were the same and whether it ignores extraneous tabs and spaces.
Replace	Replaces or adds files in one directory from another directory.
Subst	Substitutes a drive letter for a path. Then, you can use the drive letter instead of the complete path specification.

Figure 16-7   Advanced DOS commands for manipulating files

change other file attributes as well, but the read-only attribute is the one you're most likely to use.

The remaining commands may save you some time for certain functions. The Append command works much like the Path command. It establishes a list of directories that DOS searches to find data files, just as the Path command establishes a search list for program files. The Comp, Diskcomp, and FC commands let you compare files and disks to see if their contents are identical.

The Replace command is an advanced command for copying files. It works much like Xcopy, but it has additional switches that give you extra control. For example, you can specify that a file should be copied only if an older file with the same name already exists in the target directory. That way, you can update older versions of files with newer versions. Alternatively, you can specify that a file should be copied only if there is no file with the same name in the target directory. Then, you can copy new files into a directory without worrying about copying over existing files.

The Subst command lets you substitute a drive letter for a complete DOS path. For example, if you keep your *WordPerfect* files in a directory named C:\WP51\DOCS, you can add a Subst command to your AUTOEXEC.BAT file equating drive F with the DOCS directory. Then, whenever you refer to a file on drive F, DOS will replace the F drive letter with the C:\WP51\DOCS path.

Command	Function
Undelete	Undeletes a deleted file.
Unformat	Unformats the specified drive. The unformat operation will be more reliable if an image file recently created by the Mirror command exists.
Mirror	Creates an image file used to unformat a drive.

Figure 16-8 Advanced DOS commands for file recovery

Commands you use to recover files   The three commands shown in figure 16-8, all introduced in DOS 5.0, help you to recover files you've lost because of user errors. The Undelete command lets you recover files that you deleted accidentally. The Unformat command lets you recover data from a disk you've formatted accidentally. And the Mirror command improves the success of the Undelete and Unformat commands.

The Mirror command is *not* included with DOS 6.0, but is available on the supplemental program disk that you can obtain from Microsoft for a nominal fee. In DOS 6.0, the part of the Mirror command that improved Undelete's success has been incorporated into the Undelete command. To improve the Unformat command's success, however, you still need the Mirror command.

Commands you use in batch files   In chapters 6 and 7, you learned how to set up your AUTOEXEC.BAT file and how to create simple batch files to start your application programs. You should be aware that DOS provides additional commands that let you create more sophisticated batch files that can accept multiple parameters, execute different DOS commands in different situations, and even prompt the user for input. Figure 16-9 shows those commands.

Of the commands in figure 16-9, the one you'll probably use the most is the Call command. This command simply lets you invoke another batch file. When the second batch file is finished, the first one picks up with the command immediately following the Call command. This technique is useful because it lets you isolate functions into separate batch files. For example, if your PC is a part of a network, you could place all of the commands needed to attach your PC to the network in a file called STARTNET.BAT. Then, you could include this command in your AUTOEXEC.BAT file:

```
call startnet
```

That way, if you're having trouble with the network, you can remove this one line from the AUTOEXEC.BAT file and reboot your PC without accessing the network.

Command	Function
Rem	Includes a remark in a batch file that is displayed if the Echo command is on. A remark helps document what the batch file does and how it does it.
Pause	Stops the execution of the batch file and displays this message: "Strike a key when ready . . .". You can include a message in this command to be displayed before the "Strike a key" message.
If	Determines whether a specified condition is true. If it is, a command given within the If command is executed. Otherwise, the next command in the batch file is executed.
Goto	Skips from this command to the label given.
:label	Used anywhere within a batch file to set up a label that can be specified in a Goto command.
Shift	Moves the parameters given in the command that starts the batch file so that they're one parameter to the left of their original position. The leftmost parameter is lost.
For/Do	Allows you to execute (do) a given command for each member of a set. For example, if the members are the files within a directory, the command is executed once for each file. When there are no more members, the next command in the batch file is executed.
Call	Executes the commands in a second batch file and returns to the first batch file when finished.
Choice	Displays a message to the user and allows the user to respond by pressing one of several keys. New in DOS 6.0.

Figure 16-9　DOS commands for advanced batch files

The Choice command, introduced in DOS 6.0, is useful if you ever want to prompt a user for input from a batch file. It lets you specify both the prompt and the acceptable keyboard responses, if there are any besides *y* and *n*. When it's executed, it sets the value of a field called ERRORLEVEL based on the user's response. Figure 16-10 shows how you might use this command along with an If command, a Goto command, and a label in an AUTOEXEC.BAT file. (Although you won't understand all the command details, this example will give you an idea of how the batch file commands work together.) When the Choice command is executed, it displays this prompt:

```
Start the DOS shell?
```

```
echo off
prompt $p$g
path=c:\dos;c:\util
choice /T:y,10 Start the DOS shell?
if errorlevel==2 goto END
dosshell
:END
```

Figure 16-10   An AUTOEXEC.BAT file that uses some of the batch file commands in figure 16-9

Command	Function
Doskey	Improves the usefulness of the DOS command line by providing editing keys, command recall, and keyboard macros.
Fdisk	Sets up partitions and logical drives on a hard disk.
Mem	Displays information about how internal memory is being used.
Setver	Lets you use software that requires a specific DOS version.

Figure 16-11   Other advanced DOS commands

If the user enters *y*, the batch file runs the Dosshell command. If the user enters *n*, the batch file executes the Goto command and bypasses the Dosshell command by branching to the :End label.

Miscellaneous commands   Figure 16-11 lists four other DOS commands that I describe in detail in *The Only DOS Book You'll Ever Need*. These commands provide a hodgepodge of unrelated functions that may come in handy from time to time.

The Doskey command, introduced with DOS 5.0, is the one I think you'll use most often. It makes DOS easier to work with by improving the way you enter commands. To activate the Doskey function, just enter the command name, DOSKEY, at the command prompt or add it to your AUTOEXEC.BAT file. Then, you can use the Left and Right arrow keys along with the Insert and Delete keys to edit DOS commands as you enter them. You can also use the Up and Down arrow keys to redisplay commands you've previously entered. This can be a real time-saver

Example 1:	Uses redirection to print the results of the Tree command.
	`C:\>tree > prn`
Example 2:	Uses the More filter and redirection to display the contents of the file A:READ.ME one screen at a time.
	`C:\>more < a:read.me`
Example 3:	Uses piping and the More filter to display the results of the Tree command one screen at a time.
	`C:\>tree	more`

Figure 16-12 Redirection, filters, and piping

when you're entering a long sequence of similar commands. Doskey also lets you create simple *macros* that are similar to batch files but that aren't saved from one PC session to another.

The other three commands in figure 16-11 are for specialized functions. The Fdisk command lets you set up partitions on a new hard disk or change the partition structure of your hard disk. You shouldn't use this command unless you know what you're doing, though, because it can quickly erase all of the data on your hard disk. The Mem command displays information about the internal memory on your PC. This is useful if you're trying to increase the amount of memory available to your application programs. And the Setver command lets you use software that requires a DOS version other than the one you're using.

Redirection, filters, and piping   Among the most confusing features of DOS are redirection, filters, and piping. These techniques appear baffling at first, but if you use DOS commands frequently, you'll soon come to appreciate their usefulness.

Redirection is a technique that lets you send a command's output to a file or to some device other than the monitor. It also allows you to receive command input from a file or from some device other than the keyboard. To redirect a command's output, you follow the command with a greater-than sign and the name of the device you want the command's output redirected to; to redirect input, you use a less-than sign. For instance, example 1 in figure 16-12 shows how to redirect the output of the Tree command to your printer. When you use this command, the directory tree will be printed instead of displayed on your screen.

A *filter* is a special type of DOS command that accepts input from the keyboard, manipulates it in some way, and displays it on the screen. Filters are most useful when you redirect their input, output, or both. DOS comes with three filters: More, Sort,

```
files=100
buffers=3
device=c:\dos\himem.sys
device=c:\dos\emm386.exe ram
dos=high,umb
devicehigh=c:\mouse\mouse.sys
loadhigh=c:\dos\smartdrv.exe 3084
```

Figure 16-13   A CONFIG.SYS file

and Find. The More filter simply copies lines from input to output one screenful at a time. Example 2 in figure 16-12 shows how you can use the More filter to display the contents of a file.

Piping is a special DOS technique that lets you chain commands together, using the output from one command as the input to the next command. To use piping, you separate the commands with a vertical bar, as example 3 in figure 16-12 shows. Here, I've piped the output from the Tree command into the More filter. The result is that the directory tree will be displayed on the monitor one screenful at a time.

Configuring your system for optimum performance

One of the most useful DOS skills not presented in this book is the ability to configure DOS so that it makes the best use of your system's internal memory and disk memory. You do that by placing specialized configuration commands in your computer's CONFIG.SYS file. For example, figure 16-13 shows a CONFIG.SYS file that includes the most commonly used configuration commands. These commands work together to free up as much memory as possible for your application programs.

The last command in figure 16-13 runs a program called Smartdrv. This program sets up a *disk cache* that substantially improves your computer's disk speed by setting aside a large block of internal memory to store disk data. When an application program reads data from disk, Smartdrv keeps a copy of the data in its cache. Then, if the program needs to read the same data again, Smartdrv reads it from the cache rather than from the disk. Because internal memory can be accessed much faster than disk storage, Smartdrv can often make a noticeable improvement in your computer's performance.

Unfortunately, the commands that are best for your CONFIG.SYS file depend on many factors, such as the type of processor your computer has, the amount of memory that is available, and the types of application programs you use. So you can't just copy the CONFIG.SYS file from figure 16-13 onto your system and expect it to work properly. Instead, you have to invest some time to learn what each command does.

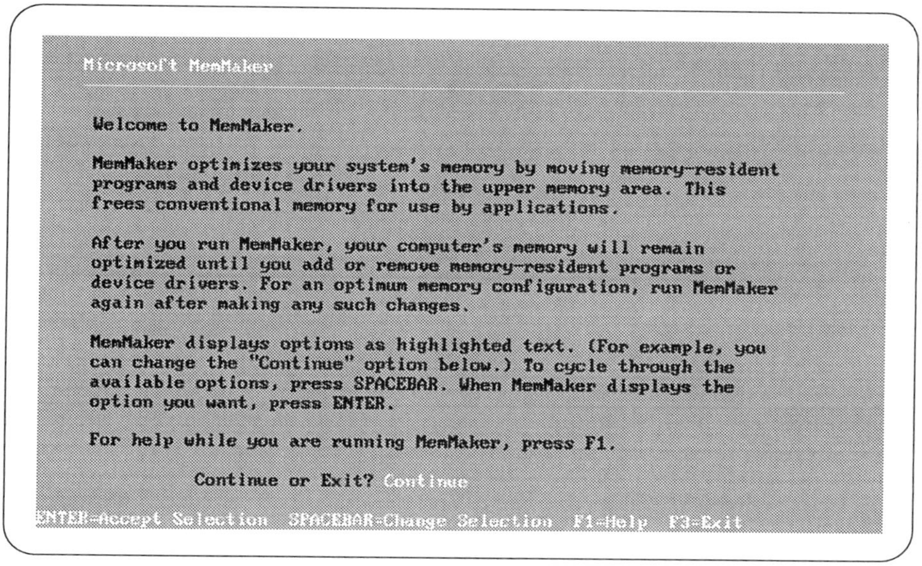

Figure 16-14   MemMaker automatically sets up your CONFIG.SYS file to optimize memory (DOS 6.0)

Then, you have to experiment with various CONFIG.SYS settings until you find the ones that are optimum for your system.

With DOS 6.0, Microsoft includes a program called MemMaker that's designed to automate this process. Figure 16-14 shows MemMaker's opening display. When you use MemMaker, it asks you several questions about your computer's configuration and your needs. Then, it automatically updates your CONFIG.SYS file with commands that should provide optimum performance. Although it's not foolproof, MemMaker usually works well.

DOS 6.0 also provides a new configuration feature called Multi-config. Most users won't need to use Multi-config. However, you might find that your ideal CONFIG.SYS settings vary depending on the type of work you're doing. For example, if you use Interlnk once in a while, you might not want it to take up valuable memory space when you don't need it. With Multi-config, you can create two configurations in CONFIG.SYS—one with Interlnk, the other without—along with a menu that lists these two choices. When you start your computer, DOS 6.0 displays the CONFIG.SYS menu and prompts you to pick one of the menu selections. Then, DOS processes only the CONFIG.SYS commands that are associated with the menu selection you pick.

284   Chapter 16

Discussion   If you want to use any of the commands or features I've just introduced, you may be able to figure out how to use them on your own by using the DOS manual and the on-line help feature. Unfortunately, though, this is likely to be both a frustrating and inefficient experience.

A better alternative is to get the companion book to this one called *The Only DOS Book You'll Ever Need*. This book presents a thorough explanation of the DOS 6.0 utilities. And it describes in detail how to use each of the DOS commands and features I've mentioned in this chapter. In short, if you intend to use any of the DOS features I've presented here, *The Only DOS Book* should quickly pay for itself by reducing your research and reference time.

Terms

DOS 6.0 utilities
data compression
computer virus
cross-linked files
fragmentation
File Allocation Table (FAT)
lost clusters
defragment

MSD
file attribute
macro
redirection
filter
piping
disk cache

Appendix

A quick summary of the DOS commands presented in this book

This appendix summarizes the formats and functions of all the DOS commands presented in this book. For each command, this appendix gives the MS-DOS version in which the command or switch first became available. If you're not using MS-DOS, you may have to check your PC or your DOS manual to see whether a command is available to you. In case you need more information about a command, this appendix also gives you the figure numbers that present each command.

Functional commands

Command format	MS-DOS	Figures	Function
BACKUP source-spec target-spec [/S] [/M]	2.0	10-3, 10-4, 10-6, 10-8	Back up a hard disk.
BACKUP source-spec target-spec [/S] [/M] [/A]	3.3	10-3, 10-4, 10-6, 10-8	Back up a hard disk.
CD [directory]	2.0	4-3, 4-7	Change the current directory.
CHKDSK [drive]	All	5-1, 5-5	Check a logical drive.
CLS	2.0	5-1, 6-1	Clear the screen.
command-name /?	5.0	4-10	Display help information for the specified command.
COPY source-spec [target-spec]	All	8-6, 8-7, 8-14, 8-19, 9-6	Copy one or more files.
DATE	All	5-1, 5-3	Set the system date.
DEL file-spec	All	8-6, 8-9, 8-15	Delete one or more files.
DEL file-spec [/P]	4.0	8-6, 8-9, 8-18, 8-19, 8-20	Confirm before each file is deleted.
DELTREE directory	6.0	8-1, 8-18, 8-20	Delete a directory with all its subdirectories and files.
DIR [file-spec] [/P] [/W]	All	4-3, 4-5, 4-6, 8-13	Display a directory.
DIR [file-spec] [/P] [/W] [/O] [/S]	5.0	4-3, 4-5, 4-6, 8-1, 8-2, 8-3, 8-13	Display a directory.
DISKCOPY source-drive target-drive	2.0	9-2, 9-5	Copy a diskette.
DOSSHELL	4.0	Chapters 12 through 15	Start the DOS shell (this book covers the DOS 5.0/6.0 shell only).
Drive-spec	All	4-3, 4-4	Change the current drive.
EDIT file-spec	5.0	6-4, 6-5, 6-6	Create or edit a text file.
EDLIN file-spec	All	6-7, 6-8	Create or edit a text file.
FORMAT drive [/4] [/N:sectors] [/T:tracks] [/S]	All	9-2, 9-3, 9-4	Format a diskette.
FORMAT drive [/F:capacity] [/S]	4.0	9-2, 9-3, 9-4	Format a diskette.
FORMAT drive [/F:capacity] [/S] [/Q] [/U]	5.0	9-2, 9-3, 9-4	Format a diskette.

A quick summary of the DOS commands presented in this book **287**

Command format	MS-DOS	Figures	Function
HELP [command-name]	5.0	4-10, 4-11, 4-12, 4-13	Provide help information (in DOS 6.0, this invokes the full-screen help feature).
MD directory	2.0	8-1, 8-17, 8-19	Make a directory.
MOVE source-spec-1 [source-spec-2] target-spec	6.0	8-6, 8-11, 8-16	1. Move one or more files.
		8-1, 8-19	2. Rename a directory (when the source and target specifications are directory names).
MSBACKUP	6.0	Chapter 11	Start the Microsoft Backup utility.
PATH=directory-list	2.0	5-1, 5-4, 6-1, 7-3	Set up a directory search sequence for commands or programs.
PRINT file-spec	2.0	5-1, 5-6	Print a text file.
PROMPT pg	2.0	4-3, 4-4, 6-1	Set up the format of the command prompt.
RD directory	2.0	8-1, 8-18, 8-19, 8-20	Delete a directory.
REN source-spec target-spec	All	8-6, 8-10, 8-14	Rename a file.
RESTORE source-spec target-spec [/S]	2.0	10-3, 10-5	Restore a hard disk.
TIME	All	5-1, 5-3	Set the system time.
TREE [drive] [/F]	3.2	8-1, 8-4, 8-5	Display a directory structure.
TYPE file-spec	All	5-1, 5-6	Display a text file.
VER	2.0	5-1, 5-2	Display the version of DOS being used.
XCOPY source-spec [target-spec] [/S]	3.2	8-6, 8-8, 8-14, 8-20	Copy one or more files.

Batch file commands

ECHO [ON] [OFF] [message]	2.0	6-2, 6-3	Display or don't display the commands of a batch file; display a message.
%number	All	7-4	Allow entry of a parameter when executing the batch file (replaceable parameter).

Index

A

A drive, 35, 45
Active task, 259
Active task list, 261
Advanced Power Management (APM), 275
Allocation unit, 75
Alt (Alternate) key, 5
Anti-virus utility, 272
APM, 275
Append command, 277
Appended incremental backup, 156, 158, 173
    and restore operation, 160-161
Application program, 17-18
    directory for, 131
    file specifications within, 39, 41-42, 43
    loading for Task Swapper, 261-262
    and operating system, 20, 24
    saving work from, 12, 63
    starting from AUTOEXEC.BAT, 86
    starting from command prompt, 54-57
    starting from DOS shell, 227-232
Archive bit, 154
Arrow key, 5, 7
ASCII, 77
Asterisk wildcard, 42-43, 119-122
AT, 3
Attrib command, 276
Attribute, 276
AUTOEXEC.BAT file, 52, 83-93, 105, 272

B

B drive, 35
Backslash, 37-38, 40, 47, 48, 54
Backup, 153-168
    guidelines for, 162-165
    using Microsoft Backup, 171-200

Backup (continued)
    selecting files for, 187-189
    types of, 154-156, 173-175
Backup catalog, 193-196
Backup command, 153, 156-159
    compared to Microsoft Backup, 171-172, 197
Backup configuration, 190-191
Backup cycle, 193
Backup file, 159
    created by Edlin, 93
Backup log, 165
Backup option, 181
Backup set, 193
Backup utility, 30, 167-168, 200
Bad sector, 74-75
BAT extension, 83, 99
Batch file, 83, 99-105
    for backup, 164
    changing, 87-93
    commands for, 278-280
    compared to program item in DOS shell, 233
    creating, 87-93
    directory for, 85, 131
    executing from the DOS shell, 232
Booting the system, 46
Brackets
    in command format, 49
    for directories, 52
Break (Pause) key, 48
Button, 175, 211
Byte, 8

C

C drive, 35, 36
Call command, 278
Cancelling a DOS command, 48
Catalog, 193-196

Cathode ray tube (CRT), 4-5
Central processing unit (CPU), 12-13
CGA, 5
Change-directory (CD) command, 52, 54, 109
Change-drive command, 50-51
Check-disk (CHKDSK) command, 74-77
Choice command, 279
Clear-screen (CLS) command, 72
Click a mouse, 7, 175, 209
Click-and-drag a mouse, 7, 238
Clock speed, 13
Clone, 3
Color Graphics Adapter (CGA), 5
Color monitor, 4
COM extension, 71
Command file, 55, 71-72
Command name, 47
Command processor, 20-24
Command prompt, 20, 46, 49-50, 52, 54
COMMAND.COM file, 52
Comp command, 277
Compare function, 199
Compatibility test, 180, 201-202
Compatible PC, 3
Compressing data, 30, 172, 270-271
Computer virus, 272
CONFIG.SYS file, 52, 83, 282-283
Configuration, 179-180, 275-276, 282-283
Configure function, 179-180
Context-sensitive help, 177, 211
Conventional memory, 12
Copy command, 113-115, 147
    compared to Backup command, 158-159
    wildcards in, 120
Copying data from one PC to another, 147-148
Copying a directory with subdirectories, 115
Copying a diskette, 145-147
Copying files, 113-115, 147
    using DOS shell, 240, 250
Correcting a DOS command, 48
CPU, 12-13
Creating a batch file, 87-93
Creating a directory, 110, 124
    using DOS shell, 249
Cross-linked files, 272, 273
CRT, 4-5
Ctrl (Control) key, 5
Current directory, 39, 40-41
    specified by period, 52, 119
Cursor, 5
    mouse, 7
Cursor control key, 5, 7

D

Data compression, 30, 172, 270-271
Database, 17
Database program, 17, 18
Date command, 72, 83
Default drive, 39, 50
Defragmentation utility, 272-273
Delete (DEL) command, 116
    wildcards in, 120
Delete-tree (DELTREE) command, 112, 124-126
Deleting a directory, 110, 112, 124-126
    using DOS shell, 246
Deleting files, 116, 120
    using DOS shell, 240, 250
Desktop publishing program, 18
Dialog box, 180, 213
Differential backup, 173-175, 183
Direct Memory Access (DMA), 172
Directory, 26, 37
    current, 39, 40-41
Directory (DIR) command, 51-52, 108-109
    wildcards in, 120
Directory listing, 51-52
Directory management, 107-112, 124-135
    using DOS shell, 217, 219, 237-258
Directory name, 110, 111-112, 130
Directory search list, 102
Directory structure, 110-111, 129-130, 131-133, 216
Directory tree, 216
Disk cache, 282
Disk capacity, 8-11, 36, 74, 139-140
Disk drive, 8, 10-11, 35-36
Disk error, 75
Disk Operating System (DOS), 19
Disk storage information, 74-77
Disk-utilities program list, 214
Diskcomp command, 277
Diskcopy command, 145
Diskette, 8-10, 11, 139-150
    and backup, 156, 164-165, 167
Diskette drive, 8-10. See also *Drive*

Index

Display, 4-5
Display adapter, 4-5
Displaying file contents, 77
    using DOS shell, 242, 244
Displaying file listing, 51-52, 108-109
    using DOS shell, 251
DMA, 172
Document, 17
DOS, 19, 20
    evolution of, 26-30
DOS 5.0, 27-28
    help feature, 59-60
DOS 6.0, 27-30
    help feature, 59, 60-62
    utilities, 30, 171-200, 269-276
DOS command, 26
    cancelling, 48
    correcting, 48
    and DOS directory, 131
    entering, 46
    format of, 47
    repeating, 48
DOS commands
    Append, 277
    Attrib, 276
    Backup, 153, 156-159, 171-172
    Call, 278
    Change-Directory (CD), 52, 54, 109
    Change-drive, 50-51
    Check-disk (CHKDSK), 74-77
    Choice, 279
    Clear-screen (CLS), 72
    Comp, 277
    Copy, 113-115, 120, 147
    Date, 72, 83
    Delete (DEL), 116, 120
    Delete-tree (DELTREE), 112, 124-126
    Directory (DIR), 51-52, 108-109, 120
    Diskcomp, 277
    Diskcopy, 145
    Doskey, 280-281
    Dosshell, 86, 207
    Echo, 84
    Edit, 87-90
    Edlin, 90-93
    Exit, 212
    FC, 277

DOS commands (continued)
    Fdisk, 281
    For/Do, 279
    Format, 141-145, 148-149
    Goto, 279
    Help, 59, 60
    If, 279
    Make-directory (MD), 110, 124
    Mem, 281
    Mirror, 278
    Move, 111-112, 117-119, 120, 126-127
    Path, 72-74, 84-85, 100, 102-104
    Pause, 279
    Print, 77
    Prompt, 49-50, 84
    Rem, 279
    Remove-directory (RD), 110, 126
    Rename (REN), 116-117
    Replace, 277
    Restore, 154, 159-161
    Setver, 281
    Shift, 279
    Smartdrv, 282
    Subst, 277
    Time, 72, 83
    Tree, 110-111
    Type, 77
    Undelete, 278
    Unformat, 278
    Version (VER), 26, 72
    Xcopy, 115-116, 120, 147
DOS services, 24-26
DOS shell, 27-28, 134-135, 205-265
    active area, 209
    active task list, 261
    collapsing a directory, 219
    Confirmation function, 250-251
    Copy function, 240, 250
    Create-directory function, 249
    current directory, changing, 217
    customizing a dialog box, 232
    default drive, changing, 217
    Delete function, 240, 246, 250
    Deselect-all function, 244
    dialog box, 213
    directory, collapsing a, 219
    directory, expanding a, 219

DOS shell (continued)
    directory tree, 216, 219
    directory-tree area, 208, 216, 237
    Disk-utilities program list, 214
    displaying file contents, 242-244
    Display function, 253-254
    drive icon, 208
    drive-icon bar, 208
    Dual-file-lists view, 255
    executing Edit command from, 213
    exiting from, 211
    expanding a directory, 219
    file icon, 217
    file list, 217
    file management, 216-221
    File menu (directory-tree area), 246-249
    File menu (file-list area), 238-245
    File menu (program-list area), 210, 230
    file selection, 219-221, 237, 244, 253
    File-display-options function, 251
    file-list area, 208, 223, 237
    file-list display, 251
    graphics mode, 209, 253
    H drive, 208
    help information, 210-211
    Main program list, 212-213, 226-227
    menu, 209-210, 221
    menu bar, 208
    menu system, 225-235
    Move function, 238, 250
    Options menu, 249-254
    path bar, 216
    Program/File-lists view, 210, 255
    program group, 226
    program item, 226-235
    program list, 212, 225-235
    program-list area, 208, 225-226
    program-list functions, 212-215, 225-235
    program-list title bar, 212
    Program-list view, 255
    pull-down menu, 209-210, 221
    Refresh function, 255, 257
    Rename function, 242, 246, 249
    Repaint function, 255, 257
    scroll bar, 217
    scroll box, 217
    scrolling a directory tree, 219
    scrolling a file list, 217

DOS shell (continued)
    Search function, 242
    Select-across-directories function, 253
    Select-all function, 244
    selecting files, 219-221, 237, 244, 253
    selection cursor, 217
    shortcut key, 210
    Single-file-list view, 254
    starting (from DOS), 207, 211, 212
    starting commands and programs, 223
    status bar, 208
    Task Swapper, 259-265
    Task Swapper keystrokes, 262, 263
    text mode, 209, 253
    View menu, 210, 254-257
    View-file-contents function, 242-244
Doskey command, 280-281
Dosshell command, 207
    in AUTOEXEC.BAT, 86
Dot-matrix printer, 7
Double-click a mouse, 7, 181, 213
Double-density diskette, 8, 139-140
DoubleSpace, 30, 51, 208, 270-271
Draft mode, 7
Drag a mouse, 7, 238
Drawing program, 18
Drive, 8-11, 35-36, 277
Drive icon, 208
Drive-icon bar, 208

E

Echo command, 84
Edit command, 87-90
    executing from DOS shell, 213
Editor, text, 87-90, 90-93
Edlin, 90-93
EGA, 5
Electronics unit, 4
Enhanced Graphics Adapter (EGA), 5
Enter key, 46
Entering a DOS command, 46
Error message, 57-58
Esc (Escape) key, 5
EXE extension, 71
Exit command, 212
Exiting from DOS shell, 211
Expansion slot, 12
Extended memory, 12

Index

Extended-density diskette, 8, 140
Extension, 39
    for backup file, 159
        BAT, 83, 99
        COM, 71
        EXE, 71
External command, 71-72, 84

F

FAT, 272
FC command, 277
Fdisk command, 281
File, 26
    command, 55, 71-72
File Allocation Table (FAT), 272
File compression, 172
File icon, 217
File list, 217
File management, 112-119, 124-135
    and backup, 164
    using DOS shell, 216-221, 237-258
File name, 39, 134
File specification, 35-39
    in application program, 39, 41-42, 43
Filter, 281-282
Finding a file, 109
    using DOS shell, 242
Fixed disk, 10-11
Floppy disk, 8-10. See also *Diskette*
Font, 7
For/Do command, 279
Format command, 141-145, 148-149
Formatting a diskette, 141-145, 156
Fragmentation, 272-273
Full backup, 154, 157, 173
    using Microsoft Backup, 181-183
    and restore operation, 160, 194
Function key, 5

G

General-purpose program, 18
Goto command, 279
Graphical user interface (GUI), 19
Graphics mode, 209, 213
GUI, 19

H

H drive, 51, 208
Hard disk, 10-11

Hard disk drive, 10-11. See also *Drive*
Hardware, 3
    for backups, 167
Help command, 59, 60
Help feature, 59-62
Help information, 59-62
    in DOS shell, 210-211
    in Microsoft Backup, 177-179
Hercules adapter, 4
Hex code, 244
Hidden file, 74
High-density diskette, 8, 139-140
High-Resolution VGA (HRVGA), 5
Host drive, 208
Host volume, 51
HRVGA, 5

I

I/O service, 24
IBM clone, 3
IBM compatible, 3
If command, 279
Incremental backup, 154, 156, 158, 173
    and Microsoft Backup, 173, 183
    and restore operation, 160-161, 193
Input device, 5, 7
Input/output service, 24
Interlnk, 274
Internal command, 71
Internal memory, 11-12, 20, 282-283
Internal storage. See *Internal memory*.

K

KB, 9
Keyboard, 5-7
Keyword, 47, 49
Kilobyte (KB), 9

L

Label (in batch file), 279
Laser printer, 8
Letter quality mode, 7
Logical drive, 35
Lost cluster, 273
Lowercase letters (in DOS commands), 47, 49

M

Macro, 281
Main program list, 212-213

Make-directory (MD) command, 110, 124
Managing directories, 107-112, 124-135
    using DOS shell, 246-249
Managing files, 112-119, 124-135
    using DOS shell, 238-245
Master catalog, 193
MB, 9
MDA, 4
Megabyte (MB), 9
Megahertz (Mhz), 13
Mem command, 281
MemMaker, 283
Memory. See *Internal memory*.
Memory expansion card, 12
Menu bar, 177, 208
Menu
    DOS shell, 209-210
    Edit command, 88-90
    Microsoft Backup, 177
    MS-DOS Help, 61
Menu system, 225-235
Mhz, 13
Microprocessor, 12-13
Microprocessor chip, 12, 13
Microsoft Anti-Virus, 272
Microsoft Backup, 30, 153, 171-200
Microsoft Defrag, 272-273
Microsoft Diagnostics (MSD), 275-276
Microsoft *Windows*, 19, 20
Mirror command, 278
Monitor, 4-5
Monochrome Display Adapter (MDA), 4
Monochrome monitor, 4
Motherboard, 12
Mouse, 7
    and DOS shell, 209, 213, 217, 219, 238, 240
    and Microsoft Backup, 175, 177-179
Mouse cursor, 7
Mouse pad, 7
Move command
    for files, 117-119
    to rename a directory, 111-112, 126-127
    wildcards in, 120
Moving data from one PC to another, 147-148
Moving a directory, 128-129
Moving a file, 117-119
    using DOS shell, 238, 250
MS-DOS, 20

MS-DOS Help, 60-62
MSBACKUP command, 175
MSD, 275-276
Multi-config, 283
Multi-tasking, 264

N
Name (portion of file name), 39
Naming a directory, 110, 111-112, 126-127, 130
Naming a file, 39, 116, 134
Num-lock key, 5, 7

O
Operating system, 18-20
Operating System/2 (OS/2), 19, 20
OS/2, 19, 20
Output device, 4, 7

P
Page-down key, 5
Page-up key, 5
Parameter, 47, 49
    how to use with batch file, 104
Parent directory, 52
    specified by two periods, 109
Path, 37-39, 40-41
    finding for a file, 109, 242
Path bar, 216
Path command, 72-74, 84-85
    in AUTOEXEC.BAT file, 100
    and search for COM, EXE, and BAT files, 102-104
Path list, 72-74, 84-85
Pause (Break) key, 48
Pause command, 279
PC, 3
PC-DOS, 20
Personal computer, 3
Piping, 282
Portable computer, 274-275
POST, 46
Power, 275
Power-On-Self-Test, 46
Presentation graphics program, 18
Print command, 77
Printer, 7-8
Processor, 12-13
Processor speed, 13
Program, 17

Index   295

Prompt command, 49-50, 84
PS/2, 3
Pull-down menu, 88, 177, 209-210

Q

Question mark wildcard, 120

R

RAM. See *Internal memory*
Random Access Memory (RAM). See *Internal memory*
README file, 77
Redirection, 281
Reformatting a diskette, 142-143
Rem command, 279
Remove-directory (RD) command, 110, 126
Rename (REN) command, 116-117
    wildcards in, 120
Renaming a directory, 111-112, 126-127
    using DOS shell, 246, 249
Renaming a file, 116-117
    using DOS shell, 242
Repeating a DOS command, 48
Replace command, 277
Replaceable parameter, 104
Resolution
    monitor, 4
    printer, 8
Restarting a PC, 63, 93
Restore command, 154, 159-161
Restoring files, 159-161
    using Microsoft Backup, 192-197
Return key, 46
Root directory, 37, 40, 54, 129

S

Safe format, 141, 144
Saving a backup configuration, 190-191
Saving to disk, 12, 24, 63
Screen, 4-5
Scroll bar, 179, 217
Scroll box, 179, 217
Search list, 72-74, 84-85, 102
Searching for a file, 109
    using DOS shell, 242
Sector, 139
Selection cursor, 217
Self-test, PC, 46

Separate incremental backup, 156, 158, 173
    and restore operation, 160, 193
Setup file, 190-191
Setver command, 281
Shell, 27-28, 30, 134-135, 205. See also *DOS shell*
Shift command, 279
Shortcut key, 175, 210
Shutting down PC, 63
Slash, 47, 48
Smartdrv command, 282
Software, 17
Sorting a directory listing, 108
Source diskette, 145
Source file, 114
Speed
    clock, 13
    processor, 13
Spreadsheet, 17
Spreadsheet program, 17, 18
Star wildcard, 119-122
Starting a PC, 45, 63, 83, 93
Starting an application program, 54-57
    from batch file, 99-102
    from DOS shell, 223, 225, 232
Subdirectory, 37
Subst command, 277
Super VGA (SVGA), 5
SVGA, 5
Switch, 47, 49
System configuration, 275-276, 282-283
System disk. See *System diskette*.
System diskette, 143, 148-149
Systems chassis. See *Systems unit*
Systems unit, 4, 8-13

T

Tape drive, 167
Target diskette, 145
Target file, 114
Task Swapper, 259-265
Task swapping, 259-265
Task switching. See *Task swapping*.
Testing an AUTOEXEC.BAT file, 93
Text editor, 87-90, 90-93
Text file, 77, 244
Text mode, 209, 213
Time command, 72, 83

Track, 139
Transferring data between PCs, 10, 147-148
Tree command, 110-111
Turning PC off, 63
Type command, 77

U

Undelete command, 278
Unformat command, 278
Uppercase letters (in DOS commands), 47
Utility, 30, 269-270
    backup, 30, 167-168, 200
    configuration, 275-276
    data compression, 30, 51, 208, 270-271
    directory for, 131
    DOS 6.0, 30, 269-276
    multi-tasking, 264
    for portable computer, 274-275
    shell, 205
    task swapping, 264
Utility program. See *Utility*.

V

Verifying a backup, 199
Version (VER) command, 26, 72
Version of DOS, 26
VGA, 5
Video Graphics Array (VGA), 5
Virus, 272
Volume label, 145

W

Wildcard, 42-43, 119-122
Window, 177, 210
Windows, 19, 20
    and Microsoft Backup, 199
    as multi-tasking utility, 264
Word processing program, 17, 18
    to create or change a batch file, 90
Write-protect a diskette, 148

X

Xcopy command, 115-116, 147
    wildcards in, 120
XT, 3

Other

? wildcard, 120
* wildcard, 42-43, 119-122
3-1/2 inch diskette, 8-10, 140
5-1/4 inch diskette, 8-10, 139-140

Now includes in-depth coverage of DOS 6.0 commands and features, along with a comprehensive command reference

The Only DOS Book You'll Ever Need

Second Edition

Doug Lowe

This book is for anyone who wants...or needs...to know more about DOS than what's covered in *The Least You Need to Know about DOS*. So if you don't have anyone to set your PC up for you or to help you solve more technical problems, this book is for you. It's also the ideal book for people who provide support to less technical PC users. As a result, we recommend it for every corporate help desk, for every PC support person, and for the lead technical person in every user department.

Everything in the *Least* book is also in this book, though much of it is in expanded form. So there are chapters on hardware and software concepts and terms, managing files and directories, backing up your hard disk, working with diskettes, using the DOS 5.0/6.0 shell, and making changes to the AUTOEXEC.BAT file. In addition, though, this book covers:

- all the DOS 6.0 utilities—for jobs like data compression, virus detection and removal, and file defragmentation—with a complete chapter on each one (that includes a 40-page chapter on all the details of DoubleSpace)

- how to upgrade to DOS 6.0
- how to make the most efficient use of your PC's memory
- how to improve the performance of your PC without buying new hardware
- how to prevent, detect, and recover from disk problems and user errors
- how to partition and format a hard disk
- how to set up your CONFIG.SYS file
- how to write and use advanced batch files
- and more!

What's more, this book includes a comprehensive command reference that will come in especially handy if you have DOS 6.0, since DOS 6.0 doesn't include a printed command reference.

So if you want to expand your DOS knowledge still further...or if you're looking for a resource for PC support...get your copy of *The Only DOS Book You'll Ever Need* TODAY!

Covers all DOS versions from 2.0 through 6.0.

27 chapters, 596 pages, $27.50
ISBN 0-911625-71-2

Everything you need to know
to be a competent, independent user of *WordPerfect* 5.0 or 5.1

The Least You Need to Know about *WordPerfect*

Joel Murach

WordPerfect has a tough learning curve...whether you're learning it for the first time or whether you're an experienced user who wants to know the features and shortcuts that will let you work more efficiently.

But this book cuts through the *WordPerfect* complications and quickly teaches you the skills you need to be a capable, confident user. You'll learn:

- the interrelationships between *WordPerfect*, your PC, and DOS that affect your work every day
- the basics of *WordPerfect*, presented in a tutorial manner that will have you creating, editing, and printing simple one- and two-page documents in just a couple of hours
- variations for editing, formatting, and printing your documents, and when to use them
- how to set up *WordPerfect* so it works the way you want it to
- how to develop and use a practical set of macros
- how to troubleshoot *WordPerfect* problems
- what other features *WordPerfect* has to offer that might help you out with special applications

To help you learn more easily, the 3 chapters in the tutorial section of this book all end with step-by-step, practice exercises. These let you try out all the commands and features you've just learned in the chapter, so you can see how they work for yourself. You'll find this practice gives you confidence in using *WordPerfect* on your own.

So don't let the *WordPerfect* learning curve get you down. Let *The Least You Need to Know about WordPerfect* be your guide to becoming a confident, self-sufficient *WordPerfect* user.

14 chapters, 380 pages, $20.00
ISBN 0-911625-66-6

To order by phone, call toll-free 1-**800**-221-5528 (Weekdays, 8 to 5, Pacific Standard Time)

The basics of *WordPerfect* 5.0 and 5.1

The *WordPerfect* Tutorial

Joel Murach

If you're looking for a very short course in *WordPerfect*, this may be the book for you. It consists of just the tutorial section from our *Least/WordPerfect* book, along with about 30 pages of resource material for people who don't have much PC experience.

We've tested this tutorial on students with several levels of PC experience...including no experience at all...and we believe it's the most effective *WordPerfect* tutorial currently available. Although some tutorials take less time, they don't teach you what you need to know to be a competent *WordPerfect* user. Worse, many tutorials take more time and *still* don't teach you enough to be competent.

But in just 3 to 6 hours (depending on how much PC experience you have), this tutorial will teach you how to use *WordPerfect* with professional style and efficiency. In fact, you may be surprised to discover that you're more competent than people who have been using *WordPerfect* for years.

3 units plus 4 resource modules for people with limited PC experience, 132 pages, $10.00
ISBN 0-911625-77-1

Contents

Unit 1: How to create, print, and save a one-page letter • **Unit 2**: How to retrieve and edit the letter • **Unit 3**: How to create and edit a two-page report

Module A: How to give a file specification when you're using *WordPerfect* • **Module B**: Hardware concepts and terms for every *WordPerfect* user • **Module C**: When and how to use the *WordPerfect 5.1* pull-down menus • **Module D**: A brief summary of the *WordPerfect* keystrokes and commands presented in this book

Note: If you use *WordPerfect* extensively, the *Least/WordPerfect* is the right book for you because of all the additional information it gives you. But if you just need a short course in the *WordPerfect* basics...or if you know someone else who does...give *The WordPerfect Tutorial* a try.

To order by phone, call toll-free 1-**800**-221-5528 (Weekdays, 8 to 5, Pacific Standard Time)

Covers all releases through 2.4 and 3.1

The Least You Need to Know about *Lotus 1-2-3*

Patrick Bultema

Lotus 1-2-3 isn't a difficult program to use for basic spreadsheets. Like all software products, though, it's evolved far beyond its original design. So its menu structure isn't particularly logical. And it offers far more functions than any one PC user is ever likely to use. And some of its functions are hidden behind function keys. And the notation used in its formulas is probably confusing to people without a strong algebraic background. And ...

Well, maybe it *is* difficult to learn how to use *Lotus 1-2-3*! That's where this book comes in. It zeroes in on the essential skills you need, so you'll be creating and using your own spreadsheets in less time than you thought possible...even if you're not a math major. Then, it expands on those skills, teaching you the features and shortcuts that will help you get more out of *Lotus* each day.

Section 1 presents the hardware and software background you need to understand if you're new to *Lotus* or to PCs.

Section 2 presents a *Lotus* tutorial that will have you creating and using your own spreadsheets in just 3-6 hours, depending on how much PC experience you have.

Section 3 covers the additional skills that will let you use *Lotus* proficiently and professionally every day (the chapters in this section are designed for quick reference, and can be read at any time, in any order).

Section 4 gives you some perspective by telling you about other *Lotus* features you might want to use, depending on the type of work you do.

Each section is filled with spreadsheet and screen examples that help you learn faster...even if you're not in front of a PC. And later on, these examples make quick and easy references for functions that you don't use often enough to have memorized.

So whether you need to learn *Lotus 1-2-3* from scratch or you want to hone your *Lotus* skills so you can work more productively, this book is for YOU.

12 chapters, 261 pages, $20.00
ISBN 0-911625-65-8

To order by phone, call toll-free 1-**800**-221-5528 (Weekdays, 8 to 5, Pacific Standard Time)

Covers all releases from 2.0 through 2.4 and 3.0 through 3.4

The Practical Guide to *Lotus 1-2-3*

Patrick Bultema

The upgrades to *Lotus 1-2-3* since release 2.0 have added dozens of enhancements and layers of menus to what was already a complex spreadsheet program. That makes it tough to get the most out of *Lotus*. It's hard to find the options you're looking for. It's hard to know which features are essential to you. And it's hard to figure out which advanced features will help you and which ones you should avoid using.

But *The Practical Guide to Lotus 1-2-3* is arranged by function, not by menu choices, so that you can learn a new, timesaving *Lotus* feature whenever you have 10 or 15 minutes. And it's loaded with practical advice, so you'll find out right away if a particular feature will help you with the type of spreadsheets you're doing.

This book covers subjects like:

- how to use range names to organize a spreadsheet
- how to protect areas of spreadsheet
- how to sort the data in a spreadsheet
- how to share data and link cells between spreadsheets
- how to import data from or export data to another program
- how to manage *Lotus* files
- how to use the *WYSIWYG* add-in program
- how to use other add-in programs to enhance *Lotus 1-2-3*
- setup, printing, networking, and range commands for occasional use
- how to graph the data in a spreadsheet (that includes coverage of the enhanced graphing features of releases 2.3 through 3.4)
- and more!

Although it doesn't teach *Lotus* from scratch, this book does cover most of the material in *The Least You Need to Know about Lotus 1-2-3*. And it includes an introduction to *Lotus* for spreadsheet users that will give you the background you need for the rest of the book, even if you've been using a spreadsheet program other than *Lotus*. So unless you're completely new to spreadsheet software or you use *Lotus* only for simple spreadsheets, we recommend you get this book rather than the *Least/Lotus*. It covers much more material, so we think you'll get far more use out of it.

22 chapters, 400 pages, $25.00
ISBN 0-911625-70-4

A 3-in-1 guide for the occasional PC user

DOS, *WordPerfect*, and *Lotus* Essentials

Patrick Bultema and Joel Murach

If you use *WordPerfect* and *Lotus 1-2-3* mostly for short, simple documents—or if you work with people who do—this may be the book you're looking for. It quickly teaches the essential features you need to get started using these programs (and DOS, too, if you want to understand more about how your PC works). At the same time, it gives you the background you need to use your software effectively. It's *not* a mindless keystroke-by-keystroke guide that will leave you stranded whenever you run into problems.

After an introduction to PC hardware and software, this book is divided into 3 "mini-books"—one each on DOS, *WordPerfect*, and *Lotus 1-2-3*.

Each mini-book begins with a tutorial, complete with practice exercises, that teaches you to use the software from scratch (these tutorials are basically the same as the ones in our *Least* books). Even if you don't have any PC background at all, you'll be able to learn this material in just 3-6 hours. And the step-by-step exercises are detailed enough to give you plenty of practice, yet foolproof enough to keep you from running into problems. After you've gone through them, you'll have a good grasp of how you can use the software for your own projects.

Then, the second section in each mini-book teaches you additional skills that will save you time and frustration every time you use the software. In contrast to the tutorial chapters in the first section, the chapters in the second section are designed to stand alone, so you don't have to read them in sequence. That means you can learn what you want to learn, whenever you want to learn it. That also means you can refer back to the chapters whenever you need to quickly refresh your memory about how to use a function or feature.

If you use your PC only for limited projects, this book will quickly train you in the essentials of DOS, *WordPerfect*, and *Lotus 1-2-3*...and yet give you the perspective that's missing in other "quick-start" books.

Covers DOS versions 2.0 through 5.0; *WordPerfect* 5.0 and 5.1; *Lotus 1-2-3* releases through 2.4 and 3.1.

**3 books in one plus an introduction,
526 pages, $25.00
ISBN 0-911625-69-0**

To order by phone, call toll-free 1-**800**-221-5528 (Weekdays, 8 to 5, Pacific Standard Time)

You'll never again dread a writing project of any size with this guide to business writing at your PC

Write Better with a PC

A publisher's guide to business and technical writing   Mike Murach

No matter what you write at work—memos, letters, proposals, feasibility studies, procedure manuals, training materials—our writing book will help you break the project down into manageable parts that are easy for you to write.

The book is called *Write Better with a PC: A Publisher's Guide to Business and Technical Writing*. In it, you'll learn a step-by-step method for writing any business or technical document. You'll learn how easy it is to write convincing, readable paragraphs and sentences (in contrast to the way you were taught in school, these skills are taught starting with paragraphs, and then moving down to sentences, grammar, and punctuation; by focusing on the biggest units first, you can make the most dramatic improvements in your writing right away). At the same time, you'll learn how to use 12 types of PC software to make writing easier and faster for you than ever before.

To be specific, you'll learn:

- how to write the documents that people will read...and act upon
- why word processing alone won't make you a better writer
- how to avoid endless rewrites by planning what you're going to write *before* you start writing
- how to get started on any writing project...no matter how big...and how to keep going without getting frustrated
- how to edit your work to make it stronger...and how to know when to *stop* editing
- when and how to create visual aids that help you get your message across
- how to use spelling checkers, writing analyzers, and outline processors to improve your writing
- when and how to make your documents look better using desktop publishing and other graphics programs
- and much, much more!

So don't wait any longer to improve your business writing skills. Get your copy of *Write Better with a PC* TODAY!

15 chapters, 406 pages, $19.95
ISBN 0-911625-51-8

Order Form

Our Ironclad Guarantee

To our customers who order directly from us: You must be satisfied. Our books must work for you, or you can send them back for a full refund...no questions asked.

Name (& Title, if any) _____
Company (if company address)_____
Street address _____
City, State, Zip _____
Phone number (including area code) _____
Fax number (if you fax your order to us) _____

Qty	Product code and title	*Price
DOS		
____	LDSR The Least You Need to Know about DOS (2nd. Ed.)	$20.00
____	DOSR The Only DOS Book You'll Ever Need (2nd Ed.)	27.50
Lotus 1-2-3		
____	GLOT The Practical Guide to *Lotus 1-2-3*	$25.00
____	LLOT The Least You Need to Know about *Lotus 1-2-3*	20.00

Qty	Product code and title	*Price
WordPerfect		
____	LWP The Least You Need to Know about *WordPerfect*	$20.00
____	WPTU The *WordPerfect* Tutorial	10.00
Multiple Programs		
____	DWPL DOS, *WordPerfect*, and *Lotus* Essentials	$25.00
Business Writing		
____	WBPC Write Better with a PC	$19.95

☐ Bill the appropriate book prices plus UPS shipping and handling (and sales tax in California) to my
____VISA ____MasterCard:

Card number _____
Valid thru (month/year) _____
Cardowner's signature _____

☐ Bill me.

☐ Bill my company. P.O.#_____

☐ I want to **save** UPS shipping and handling charges. Here's my check or money order for $_____. Calif. residents, please add sales tax to your total. (Offer valid in the U.S.)

To order more quickly,

Call **toll-free** 1-800-221-5528

(Weekdays, 8 to 5 Pacific Standard Time)

Fax: 1-209-275-9035

Mike Murach & Associates, Inc.

4697 West Jacquelyn Avenue
Fresno, California 93722-6427
(209) 275-3335

* Prices are subject to change. Please call for current prices.

BUSINESS REPLY MAIL

FIRST-CLASS MAIL PERMIT NO. 3063 FRESNO, CA

POSTAGE WILL BE PAID BY ADDRESSEE

Mike Murach & Associates, Inc.

4697 W JACQUELYN AVE
FRESNO CA 93722-9888

NO POSTAGE
NECESSARY
IF MAILED
IN THE
UNITED STATES

Order Form

Our Ironclad Guarantee

To our customers who order directly from us: You must be satisfied. Our books must work for you, or you can send them back for a full refund...no questions asked.

Name (& Title, if any) _____

Company (if company address) _____

Street address _____

City, State, Zip _____

Phone number (including area code) _____

Fax number (if you fax your order to us) _____

Qty	Product code and title	*Price
DOS		
____	LDSR The Least You Need to Know about DOS (2nd. Ed.)	$20.00
____	DOSR The Only DOS Book You'll Ever Need (2nd Ed.)	27.50
Lotus 1-2-3		
____	GLOT The Practical Guide to *Lotus 1-2-3*	$25.00
____	LLOT The Least You Need to Know about *Lotus 1-2-3*	20.00

Qty	Product code and title	*Price
WordPerfect		
____	LWP The Least You Need to Know about *WordPerfect*	$20.00
____	WPTU The *WordPerfect* Tutorial	10.00
Multiple Programs		
____	DWPL DOS, *WordPerfect*, and *Lotus* Essentials	$25.00
Business Writing		
____	WBPC Write Better with a PC	$19.95

☐ Bill the appropriate book prices plus UPS shipping and handling (and sales tax in California) to my
   ____ VISA   ____ MasterCard:

   Card number _____

   Valid thru (month/year) _____

   Cardowner's signature _____

☐ Bill me.

☐ Bill my company. P.O.# _____

☐ I want to **save** UPS shipping and handling charges. Here's my check or money order for $_____. Calif. residents, please add sales tax to your total. (Offer valid in the U.S.)

To order more quickly,

Call **toll-free** 1-800-221-5528

(Weekdays, 8 to 5 Pacific Standard Time)

Fax: 1-209-275-9035

Mike Murach & Associates, Inc.

4697 West Jacquelyn Avenue
Fresno, California 93722-6427
(209) 275-3335

* Prices are subject to change. Please call for current prices.

BUSINESS REPLY MAIL

FIRST-CLASS MAIL   PERMIT NO. 3063   FRESNO, CA

POSTAGE WILL BE PAID BY ADDRESSEE

Mike Murach & Associates, Inc.

4697 W JACQUELYN AVE
FRESNO CA 93722-9888

NO POSTAGE
NECESSARY
IF MAILED
IN THE
UNITED STATES

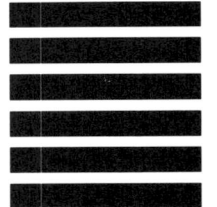

Comment Form

Your opinions count

If you have any comments, criticisms, or suggestions for us, I'm eager to get them. Your opinions today will affect our products of tomorrow. And if you find any errors in this book, typographical or otherwise, please point them out so we can correct them in the next printing.

Thanks for your help.

Mike Murach

Book title: The Least You Need to Know about DOS (Second Edition)

Dear Mike: _____

_____
_____
_____
_____
_____
_____
_____
_____
_____
_____
_____
_____
_____
_____
_____
_____

Name _____
Company (if company address) _____
Address _____
City, State, Zip _____

Fold where indicated and tape closed.
No postage necessary if mailed in the U.S.

BUSINESS REPLY MAIL

FIRST-CLASS MAIL   PERMIT NO. 3063   FRESNO, CA

POSTAGE WILL BE PAID BY ADDRESSEE

Mike Murach & Associates, Inc.

4697 W JACQUELYN AVE
FRESNO CA 93722-9888

NO POSTAGE
NECESSARY
IF MAILED
IN THE
UNITED STATES

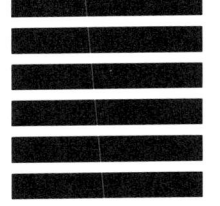

5093